PEACEKEEPING AND CONFLICT RESOLUTION

THE CASS SERIES ON PEACEKEEPING

ISSN 1367-9880

General Editor: Michael Pugh

This series examines all aspects of peacekeeping, from the political, operational and legal dimensions to the developmental and humanitarian issues that must be dealt with by all those involved with peacekeeping in the world today.

1. *Beyond the Emergency: Development within UN Missions*
   edited by Jeremy Ginifer

2. *The UN, Peace and Force*
   edited by Michael Pugh

3. *Mediating in Cyprus: The Cypriot Communities and the United Nations*
   by Oliver P. Richmond

4. *Peacekeeping and the UN Agencies*
   edited by Jim Whitman

5. *Peacekeeping and Public Information: Caught in the Crossfire*
   by Ingrid A. Lehman

6. *US Peacekeeping Policy under Clinton: A Fairweather Friend?*
   by Michael G. MacKinnon

7. *Peacebuilding and Police Reform*
   edited by Tor Tanke Holm and Espen Barth Eide

8. *Peacekeeping and Conflict Resolution*
   edited by Tom Woodhouse and Oliver Ramsbotham

Peacekeeping and Conflict Resolution

Editors
TOM WOODHOUSE
OLIVER RAMSBOTHAM

FRANK CASS
LONDON • PORTLAND, OR

First published in 2000 in Great Britain by
FRANK CASS PUBLISHERS
2 Park Square, Milton Park, Abingdon, Oxon, OX14 4RN

and in the United States of America by
FRANK CASS PUBLISHERS
270 Madison Ave, New York NY 10016

Transferred to Digital Printing 2006

Website www.frankcass.com

British Library Cataloguing in Publication Data

Peacekeeping and conflict resolution. – (The Cass series on
peacekeeping; no.8)
1. Conflict management 2.Pacific settlement of international
disputes 3. Arbitration, International
I. Woodhouse, Tom II. Ramsbotham, Oliver
327.1'7

ISBN 0 7146 4976 7 (cloth)
ISBN 0 7146 8039 7 (paper)
ISSN 1367 9880

Library of Congress Cataloging-in-Publication Data

Peacekeeping and conflict resolution / editors, Tom Woodhouse,
Oliver Ramsbotham
p. cm. – (Cass series on peacekeeping; 8)
Includes bibliographical references and index.
ISBN 0-7146-4976-7 – ISBN 0-7146-8039-7 (pbk.)
1. Peacekeeping forces. 2. Conflict management.
I. Ramsbotham, Oliver. II. Woodhouse, Tom. III. Series.
JZ6374.P42 2000
341.5'84–dc21 00-043000

This group of studies first appeared in a special issue of *International Peacekeeping*, [ISSN 1353-3312] Vol.7, No.1 (Spring 2000) published by Frank Cass and Co. Ltd.

Publisher's Note

The publisher has gone to great lengths to ensure the quality of this reprint but points out that some imperfections in the original may be apparent

Printed and bound by CPI Antony Rowe, Eastbourne

Contents

Acronyms and Abbreviations

CIVPOL	United Nations Civilian Police
CMOC	Civil-Military Operations Centre
DPA	UN Department of Political Affairs
DPKO	UN Department of Peacekeeping Operations
ECOMOG	Economic Community Military Observer Group, Liberia
ECOWAS	Economic Community of West African States
ECPS	Executive Committee on Peace and Security
FORD	Friends of Rapid Deployment
HUMPROFOR	Humanitarian Protection Force
IFOR	Implementation Force, Bosnia and Herzegovina
INTERFET	International Force for East Timor
KFOR	Kosovo Security Force
KLA	Kosovo Liberation Army
KVM	Kosovo Verification Mission
MINURSO	United Nations Mission for the Referendum in Western Sahara
MONUA	United Nations Observer Mission in Angola
NPFL	National Patriotic Front of Liberia
OAU	Organisation of African Unity
OAS	Organisation of American States
ONUC	Operation des Nations Unies au Congo / United Nations Operation in the Congo
ONUCA	UN Observer Group in Central America
ONUMOZ	United Nations Operation in Mozambique
ONUSAL	UN Observer Mission in El Salvador
OOTW	Operations Other Than War
OSCE	Organization for Security and Cooperation in Europe
OSU	Operations Support Unit (in UNDP)
OUNHAC	Office of the UN Humanitarian Assistance Coordinator
OUNS	United Nations System Support and Services

PAT	Auxilliary Transitory Police, El Salvador
RDMHQ	Rapidly Deployable Mission Headquarters
RPF	Rwandese Patriotic Front
SOP	Standard Operating Procedures
SWAPO	South West African People's Organisation (Namibia)
SWAPOL	South West Africa Police
SHIRBRIG	Multinational Standby Forces High Readiness Brigade
UNAMIR	UN Assistance Mission for Rwanda
UNAMSIL	UN Mission in Sierra Leone
UNAVEM II/III	UN Angola Verification Mission
UNDP	UN Development Programme
UNEF	United Nations Emergency Force I and II, 1956–1967, 1973–1979
UNFICYP	United Nations Peacekeeping Force in Cyprus
UNHCR	UN High Commissioner for Refugees
UNIFIL	United Nations Interim Force in Lebanon
UNITA	National Union for the Total Independence of Angola
UNITAF	Unified Task Force, Somalia
UNMIH	United Nations Mission in Haiti
UNMIK	UN Interim Administration in Kosovo
UNOMIG	UN Observer Mission in Georgia
UNOMIL	United Nations Observer Mission in Liberia
UNOSOM II	UN Operation in Somalia
UNPREDEP	UN Preventive Deployment Force
UNPROFOR	UN Protection Force, Bosnia
UNSAS	UN Standby Arrangement System
UNTAC	UN Transitional Authority in Cambodia
UNTAET	UN Transitional Administration in East Timor
UNTAG	UN Transition Assistance Group Namibia

Introduction

OLIVER RAMSBOTHAM and TOM WOODHOUSE

> Sadly, in the fiftieth year of UN peacekeeping operations, the perceived failures and costs of the UN mission in former Yugoslavia, and recent experiences in Somalia, have led to widespread disillusionment. Yet if the world loses faith in peacekeeping, and responses to the new world disorder are limited to the extremes of total war or total peace, the world will become a more dangerous place. Rather than lose faith in the whole peace process, we need to analyse the changed operational circumstances and try to determine new doctrines for the future.
>
> *General Sir Michael Rose, Commander*
> UN Protection Force in Bosnia, 1994–95

Since the formation of the United Nations the Nobel Peace Prize has been awarded to the two individuals credited with the launching of the first peacekeeping operations (to Lester Pearson in 1957 and posthumously to Dag Hammarskjold in 1961). In 1988 UN peacekeeping forces collectively were presented with the Award. However the image of the world organization and particularly its peacekeeping arm has not been so positively perceived during the 1990s. Conflicts in the post-Cold War period have tested its capabilities to the limits, and failures in Somalia, Rwanda, and Bosnia have produced damning assessments in the academic literature.

At the end of the decade the UN system itself published the reports of inquiries into two events which marked the nadir of its experience of efforts to resolve conflicts.[2] Approximately 800,000 people were killed during the 1994 genocide in Rwanda during April and July of 1994, described as 'one of the most abhorrent events of the twentieth century'. A year later, in one of the worst war crimes committed in Europe since the end of the Second World War, the Bosnian Muslim town of Srebrenica fell to a siege by Serb militias, during which 8,000 Muslims were killed under the eyes of the UN peacekeeping contingent deployed when Srebenica had become the world's first ever civilian safe area in 1993 (under Security Council Resolution 819 of 16 April). Both reports concluded that faced with attempts to murder, expel or terrorize entire populations, the neutral, impartial and mediating role of the United Nations was inadequate. Both reports also called for a process of reflection to clarify and to improve the capacity of the United Nations to respond to various forms of conflict and especially to 'address the mistakes of peacekeeping at the end of this century and to meet the challenges of the next one'.[3]

The future of UN peacekeeping will depend on the capability and willingness to reform and strengthen peacekeeping mechanisms, and to clarify its role in conflict resolution. The purpose of this volume is to consider the contribution which conflict resolution can make in the development of the new concepts and practices of peacekeeping called for by Michael Rose in the quotation at the head of this introduction. The collection begins with a contribution by Tom Woodhouse, who confronts recent criticisms of conflict resolution, and presents an account of the converging interests and perspectives of peacekeepers and academics in the conflict resolution field. He suggests that closer cooperation between these groups will provide a productive coalition in the effort to discern effective conflict management mechanisms suitable for use in future conflicts.

We might begin to discern the framework of an emerging 'post-1990s' international conflict management system in the response of the international community to events in Kosovo. In October 1998 NATO authorized the use of air strikes against Serbia, to back up diplomatic efforts to force President Milošević to withdraw military forces from Kosovo and to facilitate the return of refugees. President Milosevic agreed to this and it was also agreed that the OSCE would establish a Kosovo Verification Mission (KVM) and that NATO would establish an aerial surveillance mission (UNSCR 1203). Additionally, a special military task force under NATO command was established in Macedonia to assist with the emergency evacuation of KVM staff should the situation deteriorate.

By January 1999 a number of acts of provocation and fears of further escalation led to renewed efforts to find a political solution. The six-nation Contact Group (originally established by the 1992 London conference on former Yugoslavia) agreed to convene negotiations between the parties. Negotiations were held at Rambouillet near Paris, 6–23 February; and a second round was held in Paris, 15–18 March. The Kosovo Albanians signed a peace agreement but the Serb delegation walked out without signing. Serb military forces then intensified their operations against Kosovo Albanians, breaking their compliance with the October agreement.

On 23 March the order was given to commence air strikes against Serbia (Operation *Allied Force*). After an air campaign of 77 days NATO called off its air strikes following an agreement between it and the Yugoslav army, and an agreement with Yugoslavia brokered by the EU and Russian special envoys in early June. On 10 June UNSCR 1244 announced the decision to deploy an international civil and security presence in Kosovo under UN auspices. The resolution to the conflict was to be based on principles adopted on 6 May by the foreign ministers of the G8 (including the Russian Federation); and by paper accepted by the government of the Federal Republic of Yugoslavia (FRY) and presented by the EU and the Russian Federation on June 3. These principles were: an immediate and verifiable end of violence and repression; the withdrawal of military, police and paramilitary forces of the FRY; the deployment of effective international and security presence, with substantial NATO participation and a unified command in the security presence; the safe return of all refugees; a political process providing for self-government and the demilitarization of the KLA; and a comprehensive approach to the economic development of the crisis region.

General Michael Jackson took command of the security presence, under Chapter 7 of the UN charter, and under the command of NATO's North Atlantic Council. The security force was called KFOR. Under Operation *Joint Guardian*, KFOR entered Kosovo on 12 June. By 20 June the Serb withdrawal was complete. On 10 June the Security Council authorized the Secretary General to establish an interim civilian administration to develop substantial autonomy for the people of Kosovo. By 12 June Kofi Annan presented an operational concept for what became known as UNMIK (the UN Interim Administration in Kosovo). By mid-July 1999 the SG presented a comprehensive framework for the work of UNMIK.

UNMIK was given authority in Kosovo over all legislative and executive powers, and the administration of the judiciary. Its work was to be integrated into five phases, covering support for returning refugees; the restoration of public services (including health, education and social services); the deployment of CIVPOL; the development of an economic recovery plan; and the development of institutions for democratic and autonomous self-government.

UNMIK was under the leadership of the SRSG, Dr Bernard Kouchner, who took up office on 15 July. Kouchner presided over four sectors, each of which is involved in the civilian aspects of restoring peace. These sectors are known as the four pillars. Pillar One is the civilian administration, under UN direction; Pillar Two is concerned with humanitarian assistance, led by UNHCR; Pillar Three is concerned with democratization and institution building, led by OSCE; Pillar Four is concerned with economic reconstruction, led by the European Union.

It is too early to comment on how well this project in Kosovo will work. The OSCE has reported that the situation for the Serbian and other minority groups in Kosovo is precarious and that there is a climate of violence and impunity, as well as widespread discrimination, harassment and intimidation directed against non-Albanians.[4] It is also not possible to say whether peace enforcement operations, 'sub-contracted' by the UN to security organizations such as NATO, will replace the classical and second-generation peacekeeping which prevailed until the mid 1990s.

A previous volume in the Cass Peacekeeping Series focused on the use of force in peacekeeping missions.[5] This collection continues that exploration by attempting to draw on perspectives from the academic field of conflict resolution. What is clear is that we need to understand better the links between the effective control and containment of violence in war-torn regions and the processes by which trust and cooperation can be restored. As David Last has expressed the problem in this volume, societies which have experienced the brutalizing experience of civil war come under the physical and psychological control of thugs and warlords. They become convinced that only hawks survive. In these situations, he suggests, 'There are actually two gaps in our ability to help war-torn societies rebuild peace and cooperation. The first is a gap in our ability to control violence between the parties. This is required to put the hawks in a box. The second is a gap in our ability to rebuild the trust that permits cooperation between the parties. This lets the doves out of their boxes.' The attempts to construct a more robust doctrine and practice of peacekeeping which is nevertheless integrally connected to the long-term goals of conflict resolution and sustainable peacebuilding are dealt with in this volume by John Mackinlay, who considers the problem of dealing with warlords and examines the history of warlordism; by Philip Wilkinson, who looks at the emergence of new doctrine in the form of peace support operations; by David Last who presents the idea of the need for a holistic approach to peacebuilding, in which military and civilian assets are combined; and by Peter Langille, who identifies efforts to strengthen UN capability for conflict prevention through proposals for rapid deployment and standby forces.

However it is only very recently that peacekeeping has been treated within the literature of conflict resolution, which has its own distinctive concepts and assumptions about conflict processes and which has emerged from a tradition of research over the last 30 years or so. Inspired by earlier conflict theorists, including Quincy Wright and Lewis Richardson in the 1920s and 1930s, Kenneth Boulding coined the term 'conflict resolution' in the 1950s and described the new discipline as one which combined the analytic-descriptive science of 'polemologie' (conflict study) with the 'minimum normativeness' of positive conflict management (the theory and practice of peaceful resolution).[6] UN peacekeeping and conflict resolution as a distinct discipline are not only closely related conceptually, but originate in the same historical period. The Hammarskjold-Pearson principles for the UN Emergency Force I (UNEF I, 1956–67) were seminal for the former, and the founding of the *Journal of Conflict Resolution* in

1957 may be seen as the formal initiation of the latter.

Stephen Ryan suggests that there has not been a very fruitful relationship between the academic peace and conflict research community and the practitioners and doctrine writers of peacekeeping. With only a few exceptions there has been little analysis of peacekeeping in the literature of conflict analysis and conflict resolution.[7] Conversely the literature on peacekeeping rarely refers to peace and conflict theory.[8] This is now changing, partly in response to the call, also made by Ryan, and in an earlier study by Betts Fetherston, of the need to go beyond the pragmatic approach which has been typical of the history of peacekeeping operations. Ryan in his contribution to this volume has also pointed to ways in which the academic community can assist in the definition of a stronger conceptual framework for peacekeeping which responds to the ways in which it has performed in conflicts in the past decade. Fetherston has argued that because of the historical origins of peacekeeping as an *ad hoc* adaptation to specific international crises, writing about peacekeeping has tended to be functional and descriptive rather than theoretically informed.[9] Traditional definitions of peacekeeping have tended to be narrow and have failed in particular to address the question of how peacekeeping can be related to the processes of peacemaking and peacebuilding. They have also, correspondingly, neglected to relate the techniques of peacekeeping to broader models of third-party peacemaking linked in turn to the concept of positive peace rather than to negative peace (the containment of hostilities). For this reason, Betts Fetherston argues in this volume that a continued openness to critical theory may benefit peacekeeping, especially if it is to engage in the demanding agendas of conflict resolution rather than neutral interposition and containment. Indeed she provocatively suggests that conflict resolution itself is bounded by limitations and that genuine liberation will come from insights drawn from the work of theorists such as Gramsci, Foucault and Habermas.

Where peacekeeping has been touched upon in the conflict resolution literature, it has been seen as a device of an older form of conflict management, conflict containment or conflict suppression, dealing within symptoms and not concerned with fundamental resolution. In general in the work of new conflict theorists, certainly in the 1970s and 1980s, the stress was placed on discovering new processes of resolution, especially developed from the theory of problem solving in international relations, or from theories of mediation, and peacekeeping was not seen to have a part to play in this. Signs of changes in this way of thinking came when Bercovitch *et al.* and Fisher and Keashly began to define conflict resolution as a process involving the use of different forms of intervention at different stages of conflict escalation and de-escalation. Within this broader process, (based on ideas of contingency and complementarity), peacekeeping was seen to have a part to play, in that it was claimed as one of the peaceful intervention strategies whose long-term goal was not conflict containment but resolution.[10] It can be seen that this has much in common with the work of Mackinlay, Wilkinson and Last, each of them experienced military peacekeepers seeking to enrich peacekeeping by uses of conflict theory. In all of this work a broad spectrum or multi-modal and multi-level approach is indicated. In this volume Sean Byrne and Loraleligh Keashly develop the original work of Fisher and Keashly by examining the wide range of social forces and social actors which need to be considered when peacekeeping is shifted from a conflict containment orientation to a conflict resolution one. Given the developing partnership between civilian and military actors in contemporary peacekeeping, Pamela Aall looks at the roles of the increasing number of NGOs and suggests that while mutual understanding between the military and civilian/NGO wings will develop more coherence between the activities of these groups, coordination will not be an easy process. The practice of a multi-modal and multi-level process of peacekeeping, identified in the contributions of Wilkinson, Last, Byrne and Keashly, and Aall, is examined further in the concluding contributions in this volume. Tamara Duffey, drawing on conflict resolution theory, argues for a better awareness of the cultural dimensions and implications of contemporary peacekeeping and, based on an analysis of events in Somalia, highlights the importance of understanding the cultural dynamics of intervention. Finally, Oliver Ramsbotham reflects on a decade of experimentation in UN-directed peacebuilding operations. He identifies a UN 'standard operating procedure' for peacebuilding and offers a critique from a conflict resolution perspective of the experiences in a variety of areas, suggesting that, with some cause for optimism, the experiment has not been shown to have failed.

NOTES

1. Substantial critiques were presented by, for example; Richard Betts, 'The Delusion of Impartial Intervention', *Foreign Affairs*, Vol.73, No.6, 1994, pp.20–33; David Rieff, 'The Illusions of Peacekeeping', *World Policy Journal*, Vol.11, No.3, 1994, pp.1–18; and Edward Luttwak, 'Give War a Chance', *Foreign Affairs*, Vol.78, No.4, 1999.
2. Report on the Fall of Srebrenica, United Nations, New York, A54/549, November 1999; Report of the Independent Inquiry into the Actions of the United Nations during the 1994 Genocide in Rwanda, United Nations, New York, December 1999.
3. Rwanda report (n.3 above). p.81.
4. See the report of the OSCE Mission in Kosovo (UNHCR/OSCE Overview of the Situation of Ethnic Minorities in Kosovo), 3 November 1999
5. M. Pugh (ed.), 'The UN, Peace and Force', *International Peacekeeping*, Special issue, Vol.3, No.4, Winter 1996.
6. K. Boulding, 'Future Directions in Conflict and Peace Studies', *Journal of Conflict Resolution*, Vol.22, No.2, 1978, p.343.

7. The editors of this volume have attempted to address this in the following jointly authored publications: 'UNPROFOR: Some Observations from a Conflict Resolution Perspective,' *International Peacekeeping*, Vol.1, No.2, 1994, pp.179–203; 'Terra Incognita: Here be Dragons; Peacekeeping and Conflict Resolution in Contemporary Conflict', University of Ulster/INCORE/United Nations University, Derry, 1996; and in *Encyclopedia of International Peacekeeping Operations*, Denver and Oxford: ABC/CLIO, 1999.
8. Johan Galtung attempted an early synthesis in his 'Three Approaches to Peace: Peacekeeping, Peacemaking and Peacebuilding', *Peace, War and Defence: Essays in Peace Research*, Vol.II, Copenhagen: Christian Ejlers, pp.282–304.
9. A.B. Fetherston, *Towards a Theory of United Nations Peacekeeping*, Macmillan, London, 1994, especially the discussion in Chapter 5.
10. See J. Bercovitch *et al.*, 'Some conceptual issues and empirical trends in the study of successful mediation in international relations', *Journal of Peace Research*, Vol.28, No.1, 1991, pp.7–17; and R.J. Fisher and L. Keashly, 'The potential complementarity of mediation and consultation within a contingency model of third party intervention', *Journal of Peace Research*, Vol.28, No.1, 1991, pp.29–42.

Conflict Resolution and Peacekeeping: Critiques and Responses

TOM WOODHOUSE

Three critiques, presented recently in separate pieces by David Shearer, Christopher Clapham and Mark Duffield, raise serious issues about the nature of conflict resolution and its usefulness and relevance for the international community.[1] It is important that they be responded to for a number of reasons. First, the implications of the critiques tend to imply that armed conflict becomes the primary arbiter of change in the international system. Second, they may also encourage inactivity and paralysis in the face of what are perceived to be overwhelmingly powerful forces of global structural change, on which we can have no influence. Third, they make very little reference to the literature on conflict resolution and, therefore, dismiss or are unaware of perspectives coming from this literature. These perspectives do not provide such a negative view of the ability of the international community to intervene effectively in conflicts, guided by an impartial humanitarian concern for the victims of conflict. Fourth, there has been a proliferation of 'non-official' conflict resolution organizations in the last ten years or so whose work in areas of conflict throughout the world has been built upon principles of non-violent peacemaking. This practice of non-violent conflict resolution provides the basis for a global 'peace praxis', that is, the development of skills, processes and resources necessary to sustain and develop cultures of peace. This dimension of practice is also largely ignored by our critics.

The first section considers three critics of conflict resolution. It is argued that while the criticisms made are constructive, they tend to be inaccurate or superficial in their representation of the significance of conflict resolution theory and practice. This is so first in relation to lessons learned about the use of force and the relationship between UN peacekeeping and conflict resolution, and second in relation to the nature of third-party roles and the dynamics of peacebuilding from below.[2]

Three Critics

David Shearer

The first critic to consider is David Shearer.[3] He argues that attempts to resolve conflicts in the 1990s are based on different assumptions than those that dominated the Cold War era. Now the stress is on promoting multi-track efforts to reach agreements in civil wars by negotiation, consensus and compromise, whereas conventionally, Western policy was targeted at promoting victory by one side or another in civil wars. Shearer, reflecting on events in Sierra Leone, questions whether the consensus promoting strategy, based on impartial mediation and negotiation by the international community, is appropriate in all cases. In particular, he suggests that what have been typified as 'war lord insurgencies' may be especially resistant to resolution by consent and negotiation. In these situations, the role of military force in the resolution of conflict may need to be better understood. The implications of these and similar arguments can be seen as a direct challenge to some of the core assumptions and approaches of conflict resolution, which in this analytical perspective are perceived to be ineffective, lacking in prescriptive guidelines for policy-makers, and even positively harmful. This is so because the pursuit of mediated settlements can have the unintended effect of prolonging the conflict, with civilian populations suffering most, while military action might have the effect of foreshortening the conflict by persuading those losing ground to accept a settlement. Citing Stedman and Licklider, Shearer observes that in civil wars, in general, most settlements followed a military victory rather than political negotiations or mediated interventions. Shearer is not advocating military action rather than consent-based conflict resolution, but rather pointing to the need to examine carefully and to understand more about the limits (and possibilities) of consent-based strategies. This is given further urgency at a time when there may be an implicit move by states in the direction of preferring conflict settlement by force (even to the extent of contracting the services of specialized mercenary forces).

Christopher Clapham

Christopher Clapham,[4] based on an examination of the conflict in Rwanda, adds further words of warning about Western conflict resolution assumptions. Like Shearer, he suggests that in recent years the international community has been actively involved in intervening in civil wars and has, in the process of this intervention, articulated a standardized conflict resolution mechanism that has been universally applied. Clapham argues that following the collapse of the Soviet Union, the victors of the Cold War (that is, Western capitalist liberal democratic states led by the United States, as well as NGOs and international agencies often funded by those states) set about a programme of international conflict resolution. These programmes followed processes and rules made in the image of these victorious institutions. The processes and rules of the post-Cold War approach are quite different from those that guided Cold War policy which gave a privileged place in conflict resolution to sovereign states, and to the territorial integrity and the non-intervention norms that are associated with them. State structures were to be kept intact, and the only movements that challenged existing state structures with some legitimacy were those involved in liberation struggles against colonial regimes.

Post-Cold War, the special status of states was diluted. All parties to a conflict were accorded a 'standing', and the break-up of the Soviet Union meant that secession and independence from existing states became a recognized form of conflict resolution. The inviolability of state sovereignty was challenged, as democratic values and respect for human rights became part of the international humanitarian value system, and opposition groups, claiming to be victims of state repression, could be admitted to peacemaking processes on terms broadly equal to state authorities. Following this change in standing of conflict parties, a new model of conflict resolution was indicated. Ceasefires were negotiated to provide space and time for an agreed peace settlement; the peace agreement was in turn tied to a process of third party mediation, which itself carried the values of Western liberal democracy.

The basic model of conflict resolution to emerge from this had two variants or mechanisms through which a peace agreement was to be fashioned. In one variant of the model the parties negotiated an agreed constitution (based on multi-party democracy and respect for human rights) followed by elections under international supervision (Angola and Mozambique in the early 1990s). In the second variant a provisional coalition government is formed to introduce a series of confidence-building measures (disarmament under international supervision), which would make it possible to agree a new constitution, and then to have multi-party elections (attempted in Somalia and Liberia). In most cases, where variants one and two of the model have been used, international peacekeeping forces were used to supervise the peace process. In Rwanda, variant two of the model was applied, with disastrous consequences. Extremist parties, who were committed to an ideology of Hutu exclusivism, used the Arusha peace process, which was being managed by the international community, as a cover and during a phase when they effectively organized the genocide that occurred in April 1994.

In advancing this argument, Christopher Clapham does not claim that he is offering a general critique of conflict resolution, nor does he offer guidelines for policy in general. He does suggest that, based on what happened in Rwanda, we might be wise to exercise much more caution in our use of intervention strategies in civil wars. His fundamental point is that the conflict resolution model may be inherently flawed, its rules and prescriptions taken for granted. Reflecting on the Rwanda experience, what were the flaws in the peacemaking strategy? The approach did not recognize the need for the resolution of the deep-seated differences that caused the conflict. The timescale for effecting the peace process was short. The approach was mechanistic, and ignored the need to fashion a basic political agreement that rested on the support of key actors who shared at least some commitment to ideological norms, necessary to underpin the peace process. In relation to the latter point, Clapham raises a profound question about the 'Western' assumptions built into the model, principally in the idea that the viability of negotiated solutions to civil wars rests on the assumption that conflict parties share a common value framework, within which differences can be negotiated. In Rwanda, says Clapham, this idea was 'fundamentally misconceived', and even in Western culture it is a relatively new assumption historically, with most major conflicts from the sixteenth century onwards fought to a conclusion, either with a victor emerging or with mutual exhaustion resulting in a compromise settlement. A second assumption in the model that was not challenged was the idea that mediation is inherently a good thing, being a neutral action and intended to fulfil humanitarian concerns. In reality mediators are not neutral bystanders, and in Rwanda they may have created conditions which allowed extremists groups to organize genocide, while they (the mediators) were pursuing a negotiated settlement to which the Hutu extremists would not have subscribed. Eventually, the war in Rwanda was ended, not by the three and a half years of international mediation, but by the military victory of the Rwandese Patriotic Front (RPF).

In the aftermath of the war, as the new RPF regime attempted to establish control over the country, large numbers of NGOs arrived as part of a major international response to provide humanitarian assistance. Clapham raises significant questions about their role and impact. He raises three areas of concern. First, that they adopted a victim complex, seeing all the refugees in the camps in Zaire and Tanzania as victims of the conflict, when many of the camps were controlled by the extremists responsible for the genocide. Second, they developed a juridical complex, following Western legal norms about trial and punishment, when these norms could not be implemented in Rwandan conditions. Third, they carried a reconciliation complex, where some NGOs promoted rehabilitation of individuals implicated in genocide, again, according to Clapham, of limited applicability to the situation in Rwanda. At this level also, therefore, the application to African conflicts of Western values gave rise to problems, adding further force to the idea that the appropriateness of the Western conflict resolution model needs to be more extensively examined.

Mark Duffield

Another influential critic of the assumptions of methods of conflict resolution is Mark Duffield. Duffield has argued that rather than being an aberrant, irrational and non-productive phenomenon, contemporary internal wars may represent 'the emergence of entirely new types of social formation adapted for survival on the margins of the global economy'.[5] Actors like the international drug cartels in Central and South America, and rebel groups in West Africa, have effectively set up parallel economies, trading in precious resources such as hardwoods, diamonds, drugs and so on. Although this does not apply to all internal conflicts, there are war zone economies where civilians are seen as 'a resource base to be either corralled, plundered, or cleansed'.[6] Humanitarian and development aid is captured, and humanitarian workers kidnapped, held hostage and killed. These wars can be seen to be both lucrative and rational for those who can take advantage and are prepared to act violently to gain power.

Conflict resolution projects in this critique can be seen as part of a 'delegitimizing discourse' which has enabled Western regulation of third world politics.[7] Duffield and Clapham's critiques overlap at this point. With the collapse of 'Third Worldism' and of 'international socialism', the liberal-democratic model of capitalist development has emerged unchallenged in the 1990s. The implications of this for the political settlement of conflicts has already been pointed to by Clapham. For Duffield, in the field of development, it means that inequality, economic growth and resource distribution are issues that have been sidelined in favour of the 'human development' paradigm in the 1990s.[8] This largely involves securing 'behavioural and attitudinal change', so that people can 'cope with their situation' and be supported in 'mitigating the risks and stresses involved'.[9] Thus underdevelopment, and more recently transitions to democracy, have been 'internalized', that is, seen as issues of the internal, domestic relations of the countries concerned. The process of change then becomes one of supporting behavioural change in civil society in conflict-afflicted countries. In pursuit of this goal, aid has been privatized, NGOs have become the main agents of change, and conflict resolution 'represents an extreme form of this paradigm'.[10]

For Duffield, the whole approach of conflict resolution is questionable because of the assumptions on which it is grounded. Conflict resolution, he claims, is based on a socio-psychological model. This model assumes that functional harmony is the natural state, and conflict is an aberrant and irrational condition which is dysfunctional. The model also assumes that the origins of conflict lie in localized misunderstandings, ignorance and disagreements that may then lead to war. Conflict resolving interventions are intended to remove misunderstandings and restore functional harmony through a number of strategies: first, the use of multi-track diplomacy to energize a peace process through the efforts of international, regional, national and local actors, where the end goal of the peace process is 'a strong, plural civil society';[11] second, plural institutions are encouraged by small-scale resource distribution to encourage cooperation on joint projects, by the promotion of multicultural projects, and so on; and third, the use of 'psychological interventions' directed towards re-establishing confidence and trust between groups. These interventions occur through conferences, workshops and programmes of training in conflict resolution skills designed to provide 'psychological and inter-personal tools for defusing potentially tense situations'.[12]

Duffield has a number of specific criticisms and problems with the model, which may be summarized as follows. First, the way in which conflict resolution training provides 'concentrated immersion within the socio-psychological model of conflict', can look more like indoctrination than training. Second, the concentration on communication breakdowns and individual failings means that all people in conflict situations are as bad as each other. All are victims. This means that, in effect, the perpetrators of political violence are absolved from blame (peace is placed above justice in the model), and that in any case they rarely participate in the conferences and training prescribed by the model. Conflict resolution training does not impress Mark Duffield, presenting 'little threat to those in power'; providing Western donors with a cheap means of 'doing something' in conflict situations; and even because it may be conducted by 'people who are without professional qualifications'.[13] Finally, he has linked conflict resolution, together with aid and human development programmes, with a critique which sees Western intervention generally as a new form of imperialism, where 'Western humanitarian and liberal democratic discourse has the effect of disqualifying local political projects as inadequate or lacking'. In Africa, NGOs have undermined local capabilities and have 'made matters worse'.[14]

It is not the intention here to take on the task of replying to all of these criticisms, point by point. To a large extent, they amount to a concern about three core areas: first, on the use of force (raised by Shearer and Clapham); second, on the nature of the Western and interventionist motivations behind the conflict resolution model (in Clapham and Duffield); and third, on the prescriptions for action which come from the model, which are based, it is alleged, on a misunderstanding of conflict especially by Western NGOs (in Clapham and Duffield). These questions are considered in turn below.

Core Areas of Criticism

On the use of force and the development of peacekeeping

Shearer pointed out that intervention might prolong the misery and suffering of civil wars by unintentionally prolonging the conflict. However, as he recognizes, the costs of military enforcement or victory by one side over another may be as high, or higher, than political intervention. In some cases (Somalia), it did not work.[15] In others where it did work, the winning side has gone on to commit genocide against the defeated. There is, in short, no such thing as a military 'quick fix'. In answer to Shearer's question, the humanitarian imperative (the need to apply internationally agreed humanitarian standards) compels that serious and sustained attention be given to understanding the processes and circumstances by which the conclusions of conflict resolution approaches can be operationalized. The point is not to encourage victory by one side, in cases where civilian populations on both sides have become the targets of combatants, but to link forceful intervention, which is internationally legitimized, with consent-based strategies, to develop a politically sustainable solution. Thus robust peacekeeping (with a capacity to enforce international agreements, and to apply human rights standards, especially for non-combatants), linked to conflict resolution mechanisms, is a clear policy option for the international community, and it is one which is emerging from assessments made post-1994 Rwanda and post-1993 Somalia and Bosnia.[16]

Among the most comprehensive assessments of the 1994 catastrophe has been the Joint Evaluation conducted at the instigation of the Danish Ministry of Foreign Affairs and its development wing, Danida.[17] Oxfam has also produced a concise and carefully focused analysis of the response of the international community to the Rwanda crisis. For example, Vassall-Adams concludes that, while primary responsibility for the genocide lay with extremist groups inside Rwanda, the international community (specifically the major powers) was culpable by failing to respond effectively.[18] These and other evaluations suggested that a major reform of the UN, both in its peacekeeping role and in its humanitarian capacity, was needed.[19] For the future, Vassall-Adams suggests that the UN form an Office of Preventive Diplomacy in order to be better able to respond to emerging conflicts; that UN peacekeeping be reformed including better preparation for early and rapid deployment of forces; that the efforts of civilian/humanitarian agencies be better co-ordinated both among themselves and with the military; and that arms flows to conflict areas should be much more strictly controlled and regulated through the UN's Register of Conventional Arms (and should cover small arms and land mines, in particular to governments or groups which violate the basic human rights of their citizens). The Joint Evaluation study found that the NGO response to the crisis was mixed, with criticisms directed at the duplication and waste of resources and at some examples of unprofessional and irresponsible conduct.[20]

The decision by the Security Council to reduce its peacekeeping force in Rwanda to a minimum once the Belgian contingent was withdrawn is seen to be precisely the reverse of what should have been done. The ability of the small rump force left behind in Kigali to protect thousands of civilians during the period of the genocide indicates that the caution about peacekeeping, which resulted from experience in Somalia, should be reviewed and a renewed commitment to peacekeeping made. UN peacekeeping forces, mandated to protect civilians and to provide the security necessary for the delivery of humanitarian aid, are an important part of the conflict resolution process in war zones, providing the platform from which political and humanitarian spaces can be maintained even under the most extreme pressures. This means, in the short term, much more positive support by those UN member states with the greatest military capacity to provide expertise, training, logistical support and finance for deploying UN peacekeepers under existing stand-by arrangements. For the longer term, both the Oxfam study and the Joint Evaluation recommended that UN peacekeeping capability should be strengthened by the creation of a rapid deployment force, either directly under UN control, or, with UN support, under the control of regional organizations such as the OAU and the OAS. Both reports also called for a 'harder' concept of peacekeeping which nevertheless belongs within the category of non-coercive forms of conflict management, through the definition of standard operating procedures for UN peacekeeping missions, enabling and resourcing them to protect civilians threatened by political violence.[21]

On the nature of the Western and interventionist motivations behind the conflict resolution model

In recent years we can observe a tendency by experienced peacekeepers to call for the integration of conflict resolution mechanisms in their policy-making and operational practices. The same approach is taken in American doctrine covering peace support operations.[22] Here, the managing of consent (based on the principles of impartiality, legitimacy, mutual respect, minimum force, credibility, and transparency) is related to the techniques of promoting good communication, of negotiation and mediation, and of positive approaches to community relations through an active civil affairs programme which is amply resourced to win 'hearts and minds'. The development of such an approach to conflict resolution provides some prospect for developing intervention strategies which do attempt to address the deeper causes of conflicts. This is a clear and preferable alternative for the international community than the role of passive observer in the face of the violation of humanitarian standards, which may be implied by aspects of Clapham's and Duffield's critique. Over the past few years there have been innovative efforts to combine military peacekeeping with conflict resolution strategies. These efforts are briefly reviewed below.

John Mackinlay was among the first to argue that the concepts and doctrine which defined classical peacekeeping were no longer adequate to cope with the demands placed on peacekeepers in the civil wars into which they were drawn in the 1990s. Nevertheless, while he argued for broadened and strengthened forms of peacekeeping, he still maintained that consent is the major precondition for the success of peace support operations.[23] In a redefinition of British peacekeeping doctrine beyond *Wider Peacekeeping*, Philip Wilkinson also expands the range of action to include a possible greater use of force, citing impartiality rather than consent as the key determinant in distinguishing forcible peacekeeping from war. But he, too, continues to see the nurturing and building of consent within the wider peace constituency as an essential aim. In particular, he identifies six different sets of techniques designed to maintain consent in conflict areas where peacekeepers are deployed and which are particularly important because 'the military element's presence in the operational area does not always inspire local support for them. For this reason, land forces will have to spend more time and effort, down to the individual level, in consent promoting activity.'[24] The six techniques are related to: (a) negotiation and mediation; (b) liaison; (c) civilian affairs; (d) community information; (e) public information; and (f) community relations. The objective of this kind of activity is to provide good information in order to reduce rumour, uncertainty and prejudice on the one hand, and to foster trust and stability in the area of conflict and positive perceptions of the role of peacekeepers and the nature of the peace process, on the other. A further example of the use of conflict resolution theory in relation to peacekeeping is in the work of David Last, a Canadian officer with experience in the UNFICYP (Cyprus) and UNPROFOR operations. Last set out to review the contribution of peacekeeping to conflict resolution as practised in the past; he also wished to identify 'what new techniques may be used to help peacekeepers work more actively with civilians to eliminate violent conflict':

> To argue by analogy, I believe the situation of peacekeepers today is much like the situation of commanders on the Western Front in 1916, who were bogged down in defensive operations. To push the analogy somewhat, new tools of war were becoming available to commanders

> in 1916 that would permit them to take the offensive if they could only adjust their thinking about how to use their forces. In the same way, new techniques of peacekeeping, taken from conflict resolution theory and civilian experience, now permit peacekeepers to take the offensive to restore peace.[25]

The integration of the operational and practical aspects of approaches from conflict resolution, and at this level of detail, into the processes of peacekeeping in the field is still at a somewhat unsystematic and rudimentary stage, but the requirement is now quite widely recognized. David Last provides a refinement of this approach in his contribution to this volume.

On the prescriptions for action coming from the model

Finally, the UN Secretary-General Kofi Annan has pointed to the need for peacekeeping forces to find new capabilities for what he refers to as positive inducements to gain support for peacekeeping mandates among populations in conflict zones. Reliance on coercion alone is insufficient, he argued, because, while peacekeeping forces in the future will need to have a greater coercive capacity, the effect of coercion will erode over time. It is better, therefore, to attempt to influence the behaviour of people in conflict situations by the use of the carrot rather than the stick. Thus while coercion can restrain violence at least temporarily, it cannot promote lasting peace. A durable peace and a lasting solution require not only stopping the violence but, crucially, 'taking the next step'. For Annan, taking the next step means offering positive incentives or inducements. Peacekeeping forces, in other words, need to be able to make available rewards in the mission area. Annan defines two broad categories of reward:

> The first is what some military establishments have called 'civic action'. Its purpose is limited, namely to gain the good will and consequent cooperation of the population. The second, which might be termed 'peace incentives', is more ambitious. It is intended as leverage to further the reconciliation process. It provides incentives – a structure of rewards – for erstwhile antagonists to cooperate with each other on some endeavour, usually a limited one at first, which has the potential for expansion if all goes well.[26]

This concept, which Annan sees as absolutely essential for the future effectiveness of peacekeeping operations brings peacekeeping squarely into the realm of conflict resolution. Working in conflict zones thus becomes a complex process of balancing coercive with positive inducements; of supplementing military containment and humanitarian relief roles; and of promoting civic action to rebuild communities economically, politically and socially. A wide range of actors and agencies, military and civilian, governmental and non-governmental, indigenous and external, therefore constitute the conflict resolution capability in war zones. Simultaneous activities are targeted on broadening the security, humanitarian, political, and development spaces in which peace processes can take root. In this complicated arena the issue of the co-ordination of multi-agency activity becomes paramount.

At the field level, post-conflict evaluations are also yielding consistent recommendations. For Dallaire, the UNAMIR force commander in Rwanda, it is vital that co-ordination mechanisms be improved by the creation of a UN multi-disciplinary team of senior crisis managers, and that there should be regular meetings between the UN and NGOs through civil-military operations centres (CMOCs). From this should emerge a culture of understanding between the various agencies, leading in turn to better-defined standard operating procedures. In Dallaire's view, too, an interdisciplinary UN-led crisis management and humanitarian assistance centre is needed.[27] Speaking of the various agencies of the international community, whether they are primarily concerned with opening up security, humanitarian, or political spaces, Dallaire said: 'We are intertwined by the very nature of the crisis... Clearly, peacekeeping cannot be an end in itself – it only buys time. In its goals and its design, it must always be a part of the larger continuum of peacemaking, that is to say conflict avoidance, resolution, rehabilitation and development.'[28]

Similar conclusions were made from Somalia. Drawing on his experience as the UN Secretary General's Special Representative in Somalia, and as Deputy Secretary-General of the OAU, Mohamed Sahnoun proposed a new international institution for conflict management. Its role would be to 'mobilise all approaches to conflict resolution and...increase communications and networks among different communities in local conflict areas through the integrated efforts of NGOs and the United Nations'.[29] The main challenge for such an institution would be to overcome well-founded objections to 'interventionary humanitarianism' from countries of the South on the one hand, and reluctance to be drawn into conflict zones unless clear national interests were involved on the part of powerful, mainly Western, governments on the other. In sum, the effort of conflict resolution research is focused on the challenge of strengthening the institutions of the international community to resolve civil wars non-violently. Of course there are many areas of concern related to new concepts and practices of peacekeeping, not least the question of how effectively military forces can be re-oriented to peacemaking roles, and how they relate to civilian agencies in areas of conflict.[30] Yet it is by no means the case that the only lesson learned from Rwanda is for the international community to be uninvolved in such conflicts.

Peacekeeping, Conflict Resolution and Sustainability

In the past few years the field of conflict resolution has come under scrutiny from ideas generated by the literature of critical social theory, and from more pragmatic policy based concerns coming from field workers in both the UN system and in humanitarian agencies of various kinds. In particular, exponents working within the tradition of conflict resolution wished, as practitioner-scholars, to strengthen its concepts and practices, and learned from experiences and perspectives coming from diverse fields such as participatory community development, non-violent peace advocacy groups and grassroots peace action campaigns. There has also been an enriching discourse with academic fields such as anthropology and development analysis.

The revision of thinking resulting from this has led to clearer understanding in three areas: First, in the recognition that embedded cultures and economies of violence provide more formidable barriers to constructive intervention than originally assumed by the earlier research of conflict theory. In these conflicts 'simple' one dimensional interventions, whether by traditional mediators aiming at formal peace agreements, or by peacekeepers placed to supervise ceasefires or oversee elections, are unlikely to produce comprehensive or lasting resolution. Second, in the specification of the significance of post-conflict peacebuilding and of the idea that formal agreements need to be underpinned by understandings, structures and long-term development frameworks that will erode cultures of violence and sustain peace processes on the ground. Third, in the related idea of the significance of local actors and of the importance of local knowledge and wisdom.

These shifts in thinking, which have given greater recognition to peacebuilding from below, can be illustrated in the work of two scholar-practitioners, Adam Curle and John Paul Lederach. Curle, a Quaker, has been deeply involved in the practice of peacemaking throughout his academic career (which ended formally in 1978 when he retired from the Chair of Peace Studies at the University of Bradford), and also through the period of his 'retirement'. In the 1990s much of this involvement took the form of supporting the activity of the Osijek Centre for Peace, Nonviolence and Human Rights. Osijek, a city in Eastern Slavonia, was, with the adjacent town of Vukovar, the site of the most violent fighting of the Serb Croat War. This involvement with the people of Osijek, who were trying to rebuild a tolerant society while surrounded by the enraged and embittered feelings caused by the war, caused a considerable amount of reflection by Curle about the problems of practical peacemaking. It was apparent, for example, that the model of mediation specified in his earlier book (*In the Middle*) and distilled from his experiences in the conflicts of the 1970s and

1980s, was very difficult to apply on the ground in the confusion and chaos of the type of conflict epitomized by the wars in former Yugoslavia. He realized, through his involvement with the Osijek project, that the range of conflict traumas and problems was so vast that the model of mediation based on the intervention of outsider-neutrals was simply not powerful or relevant enough to promote peace. He made two important revisions to his peace praxis: First,

> Since conflict resolution by outside bodies and individuals has so far proved ineffective [in the chaotic conditions of contemporary ethnic conflict – particularly, but not exclusively, in Somalia, Eastern Europe and the former USSR], it is essential to consider the peacemaking potential within the conflicting communities themselves.[31]

Curle now sees the role of conflict resolution in post-Cold War conflicts as providing a variety of support to local peacemakers through an advisory, consultative-facilitative role which offers workshops, training and support in a wide variety of potential fields which the local groups might identify as necessary. The task is to empower people of goodwill in conflict-affected communities to rebuild democratic institutions, and the starting point for this to help in 'the development of the local peacemakers inner resources of wisdom, courage and compassionate non-violence'.[32]

Second, Curle recognized an important role for the UN in this process of empowerment and in this sense recognizes the need to make connections between the official mandates of the UN agencies, including peacekeeping, and the unofficial roles of the NGOs in conflict zones. The approach of Curle has been to transform his original idea of active mediation as an outsider intervention into an empowering approach which is much more context sensitive. Curle's approach may still be an example of the socio-psychological model which Duffield has identified. However Curle sees the model as a starting point for a conflict resolution process, not the totality of that process, or its end point. The project is concerned with the objectives of transforming behaviours, attitudes, and structures. This may be illustrated in the work of two other peace researchers/conflict resolvers, Caroline Nordstrom and John Paul Lederach.

Following field research in Mozambique and Sri Lanka, Nordstrom explained the many accounts of absurd destruction and the use of terror in warfare as deliberate efforts to destroy the normal meanings that define and guide daily life.[33] This is the process whereby dirty war becomes the means through which economies of violence merge with what Nordstrom calls 'cultures of violence'. As she puts it, 'violence parallels power' and people come to have no alternative but to accept 'fundamental knowledge constructs that are based on force'.[34] Nordstrom argues that there is a 'need to create a counter-life-world construct to challenge the politico-military one'. Obviously, it is very difficult for civilians wishing to seek an alternative to 'the dirty war paradigm as a survival mechanism' to find one in the vicious and dangerous environment of an active war zone.[35] Nevertheless, there are innumerable examples of resistance to the 'rationality' and 'culture' of the war zone to set beside the otherwise overwhelming catalogue of brutalization and atrocity. These are the usually unsung heroes of conflict resolution and peacemaking in the midst of violence, often at great personal risk. In Burundi's capital, Bujumbura, for example, residents in two neighbourhoods, one Hutu and one Tutsi, formed a mixed committee of 55 men and women to try to protect each other from attack. In Colombia there has been the growth of 'communities of peace', many of them developed by Colombia's indigenous Indians, declaring themselves neutral in the fighting between the military and guerrillas. Many have been killed for taking this position, but they persist with the help of an organization, the Antioquia Indigenous Organisation, supported by Oxfam, to help provide food, shelter and medicine, and to publicize their situation. In Liberia some communities have formed community watch teams to protect themselves against armed groups which threaten their communities.[36]

In many of these community responses women are often the main creators of new modes of survival and conflict resolution, usually at local level and nearly always unrecorded. This is, for obvious reasons, much more difficult to chronicle – as also in the case of male victims and unsung peacemakers. Attempts have been made to compare the effectiveness of men and women as mediators, with mixed results.[37] A number of social anthropological studies of peacemaking practices in different parts of the world have emphasized the key role played by women.[38]

The question has also been asked as to whether the discourses and institutions that reproduce militarism and violence are themselves gendered so that successful long-term conflict resolution requires a radical transformation here as well.[39] Duffey[40] has pointed out that the involvement of women in formal peace processes and negotiations has been very limited, and that they are largely excluded from high-level negotiations despite their active participation in local peace movements and peacemaking initiatives. The exclusion of women from the discourse about new political structures defined in peace agreements, and the political process of negotiations determined at international level, may well be factors which perpetuate the exclusionist and violent discourses and institutions which contribute to the conflict in the first place. Byrne has noted that, despite the many local organizations which represented women's interests in former Yugoslavia, there were no women representatives involved in the Dayton peace talks in 1995.[41] Similarly, Duffey has demonstrated that the exclusion of women from the UN-sponsored peace conferences in Somalia served to increase the legitimacy and power of the warlords, who were frequently unaccountable to the local community. When women are excluded from contributing to peace negotiations, the realities of a conflict in terms of its impact on communities may not be fully comprehended. For this reason, Berhane-Selassie[42] argues that the international community should consult and involve women in order to understand more about the root causes of conflict, to understand how obstacles to peace processes can be removed, and to gain insight about how traditional practices can offer alternative ways of ending conflicts. In its recently published Code of Conduct, the NGO *International Alert* identified ten principles which guided its work in conflict resolution, one of which recognized and supported 'the distinctive peacemaking role of women in societies affected by violent conflict'.[43]

John Paul Lederach, working as a scholar-practitioner and within a Mennonite tradition which shares many of the values and ideas of the Quakers, and with practical experience in Central America, has also stressed the importance of this approach, which he calls indigenous empowerment. Thus:

> The principle of indigenous empowerment suggests that conflict transformation must actively envision, include, respect, and promote the human and cultural resources from within a given setting. This involves a new set of lenses through which we do not primarily 'see' the setting and the people in it as the 'problem' and the outsider as the 'answer'. Rather, we understand the long-term goal of transformation as validating and building on people and resources within the setting.[44]

The approach also suggests that it is important to identify the 'cultural modalities and resources' within the setting of the conflict in order to evolve a comprehensive framework which embodies both short-term and long-term perspectives for conflict transformation. The importance of cultural relevance and sensitivity within conflict resolution theory has emerged partly in response to learning from case experience, and partly as an explicit critique of earlier forms of conflict resolution theory where local culture was given marginal significance. In the former case, both Lederach and Wehr, reflecting on their work in Central America found that the 'Western' model of outsider neutral mediators was not understood or trusted in many Central American settings, while the idea of insider partial peacemaking was.[45] In the case of critiques of John Burton's universal theory, Kevin Avruch and Peter Black, drawing on perspectives from anthropology, have argued for greater recognition of the issue of culture in the theory and practice of conflict resolution. They suggest that ethnoconflict theories (derived from locally constructed common sense views of conflict) and ethnopraxis (techniques and customs for dealing with conflict derived from these understandings) need to be developed and incorporated into the construction of general theory.[46] What has emerged, then, is the recognition of a need for what Lederach has called a comprehensive approach to conflict resolution which is attentive to how short-term intervention which aims to halt violence is integrated with long-term resolution processes. This long-term strategy will be sustainable if outsiders/experts support and nurture rather than displace resources which can form part of a peace constituency and if the strategy addresses all levels of an affected population.

Lederach's comprehensive approach entails building what he refers to as an infrastructure for peace involving all of the affected population. He describes the affected population as a triangle, with the key military and political leaders at the apex, at level one. In the middle, at level two, are the national leaders who have significance as leaders in sectors such as health, education and within the military hierarchies. Finally, at the grassroots level, level three, are the vast majority of the affected population: the common people, displaced and refugee populations, local leaders, elders, church groups and locally based NGOs. At this level also, the armed combatants are represented as guerrillas and soldiers in militias. Most peacemaking at the level of international diplomacy operates at level one of this triangle, but for conflict resolution to be successful and sustainable then the co-ordination of peacemaking strategies across all three levels must be undertaken. In this new thinking, peacebuilding from below is of decisive importance for it is the means by which, according to Lederach, a peace constituency can be built within the setting of the conflict itself. Once again this is a departure from conventional practice where peacemaking resources from outside the conflict (diplomats, third party interveners etc) are valued more highly than peacemaking assets which may exist within the community.

Conclusion

In this response to critiques I do not wish to claim that conflict resolution is a problem-free area of enquiry and practice. The challenges posed by our three critics are valid, helpful and challenging. My argument is that none of the critics have seriously engaged with the literature on the theory and practice of conflict resolution. While it does not claim to be universally effective, the field is more robust and self-questioning than many of its critics recognize. Further, there is a literature and a practice of conflict resolution and its cognate field of peace research spanning over 40 years which is hardly touched upon by any of our three critics. The emerging policies on the doctrinal and operational links between peacekeeping conflict resolution indicates a potential to deal with the issues of the security of people in conflict zones. Finally, in applying a 'peacebuilding from below' approach, the way in which a conflict is viewed is transformed, thus engaging with concerns about inappropriate intervention raised by our critics. Whereas normally people within the conflict are seen as the problem, with outsiders providing the solution to the conflict, in the perspective of peacebuilding from below solutions are derived and built from local resources. Commenting on the many examples of local level cross-community peacebuilding work in Eastern Croatia as a complement to the 1995 political-constitutional level settlement, Judith Large concludes that, although it is easy for outside critics to be dismissive of these small-scale and usually unpublicized initiatives, this is not how things look from the inside. Here it is the practical transformative work of all those who oppose the 'discourses of violence' – peacekeepers, humanitarian agencies, conflict resolvers, human rights activists, development workers and others – that is cumulatively crucial.

NOTES

1. Broader critiques are considered in Norbert Ropers, 'Towards a Hippocratic Oath of Conflict Management?' in *Prevention and Management of Violent Conflict: An International Directory*, European Platform for Conflict Prevention and Transformation: Utrecht, 1998, pp.27–33.
2. There are also criticisms of the theory base of conflict resolution which are not dealt with here for reasons of space. On this see Tom Woodhouse, 'International Conflict Resolution: Some Critiques and a Response' *Centre for Conflict Resolution Working Paper 1*, University of Bradford, June 1999.
3. David Shearer, 'Exploring the Limits of Consent: Conflict resolution in Sierra Leonne', *Millennium: Journal of International Studies*, Vol.26, No.3, 1997, pp.845–60
4. Christopher Clapham, 'Rwanda: The perils of Peacemaking', *Journal of Peace Research*, Vol.25, No.2, March 1998, pp.103–210.
5. Mark Duffield, 'Evaluating conflict resolution-contexts, models and methodology', in Gunnar M. Sorbo, Joanna Macrae and Lennart Wohlegemuth (eds.), *NGOs in Conflict – An Evaluation of International Alert*, Chr. Michelsen Institute, CMI Report Series, Bergen, Norway: 79–112. Quote at p.100
6. Ibid. p.103.
7. Ibid. p.98.
8. Ibid. p.80
9. Ibid.
10. Ibid.
11. Ibid. p.95
12. Ibid. p.97
13. Ibid.
14. Ibid. p.98.
15. See the article of Duffey in this volume.
16. See the recommendations in the reports on Rwanda and Bosnia (Srebrenica), cited in note 2 of the introduction to this volume (p.6).
17. Eriksson, *The International Response to Conflict and Genocide: Lessons from the Rwanda*

Experience. Copenhagen: DANIDA/Steering Committee of Joint Evaluation of Emergency Assistance to Rwanda, 1996 (three volumes)
18. Guy Vassall-Adams, *Rwanda: An Agenda for International Action*. Oxford: Oxfam, 1994.
19. Jim Whitman and David Pocock (eds.), *After Rwanda: The Coordination of United Nations Humanitarian Assistance*. London: Macmillan, 1996.
20. Eriksson (n.17 above), Vol.3, pp.152–3, and pp.59–60.
21. David Last and Philip Wilkinson deal with the development of these 'harder' forms of peacekeeping. The British doctrine is described in Philip Wilkinson's article. The connections between peace support operations and conflict resolution is explored in Tom Woodhouse, 'The Gentle Hand of Peace? British Peacekeeping and Conflict Resolution in Complex Political Emergencies', *International Peacekeeping*, Vol.6, No.2, Summer 1999, pp.24–37
22. A. Chayes, and G. Raach, *Peace Operations: Developing the American Strategy*. Washington DC: National Defense University Press, Institute for National Strategic Studies, 1995.
23. John Mackinlay and J. Chopra, 'Second Generation Multinational Operations, *The Washington Quarterly*, Summer, 1992, pp.113–31.
24. Philip Wilkinson, *Peace Support Operations*. London: Ministry of Defence/Joint Warfare Publications 3.05, 1998.
25. David Last, *Theory, Doctrine and Practice of Conflict De-escalation in Peacekeeping Operations*. Nova Scotia: Lester B. Pearson Canadian International Peacekeeping Training Centre, 1997, p.129.
26. Kofi Annan, K. *Peace Operations and the UN*. Conflict Resolution Monitor, 1, Bradford: Centre for Conflict Resolution, Department of Peace Studies, 25–32, 1997. Quote at p.27–8.
27. Romeo Dallaire, 'The Changing Role of UN Peacekeeping Forces: The Relationship between UN Peacekeepers and NGOs in Rwanda', in Whitman and Pocock (n.27 above), pp.205–18, quote at p.216.
28. Dallaire (n.35 above), p.217.
29. Sahnoun, quoted in Pamela Aall, 'Nongovernmental Organisations and Peacemaking'. In C. Crocker and F. Hampson (eds.), *Managing Global Chaos: Sources of and International Conflict*, Washington DC: United States Institute for Peace, 1996, pp.433–42.
30. Civil military roles and relations form the theme of many of the contributions to this volume. See also Hugo Slim, 'The Stretcher and the Drum: Civil–Military Relations in Peace Support Operations', *International Peacekeeping*, Vol.3, No.2, 1996, pp.123–40.
31. Adam Curle, 'New Challenges For Citizen Peacemaking', *Medicine and War*, Vol.10, No.20, 1994, pp.96–105, quote at p.96.
32. Curle (n.31 above), p.104.
33. Carolyn Nordstrom, 'The Backyard Front'. In Nordstrom and J. Martin (eds.), *The Paths to Domination, Resistance and Terror*, Berkeley: University of California Press, 1992, pp.260–74, quote at p.269
34. Nordstrom (n.33 above), p.269.
35. Nordstrom (n.33 above), p.270.
36. See Ed Cairns, *A Safer Future: Reducing the Human Costs of War*. Oxford: Oxfam Publications, 1997, pp.85–6.
37. Linda Stamato, 'Voice, place and process: Research on gender, negotiation and conflict resolution'. *Mediation Quarterly*, Vol.9, No.4, 1992, pp.375–86
38. Tamara Duffey, *Culture, Conflict Resolution and Peacekeeping*, PhD Thesis, University of Bradford, Department of Peace Studies, Bradford, 1998.
39. Taylor, A. and J. Miller (eds.), *Conflict and Gender*. Cresskill, NJ: Hampton Press, 1994.
40. Duffey (n.38 above).
41. Byrne, B 'Towards a Gendered Understanding of Conflict', *IDS Bulletin*, Vol.27, No.3, 1996, pp.31–40.
42. Berhane-Selassie, T., 1994, 'African Women in Conflict Resolution,' *Counter Focus*, Issue 120, pp.1–3.
43. International Alert, *Code of Conduct, Conflict Transformation Work*, International Alert, London, 1999.

44. John Paul Lederach, 'Conflict Transformation in Protracted Conflicts: The Case for a Comprehensive Framework', in Kumar Rupesinghe (ed) *Conflict Transformation*, Basingstoke: Macmillan, 1995, pp.201–22, quote at p.212.
45. John Paul Lederach, J.P. and Paul Wehr, 'Mediating Conflict in Central America', *Journal of Peace Research*, Vol.28, No.1, 1991, pp.85–98
46. Kevin Avruch, Peter Black, and Joseph Scimecca, *Conflict Resolution: Cross-Cultural Perspectives*, Westport CT: Greenwood Press, 1991.

United Nations Peacekeeping: A Matter of Principles?

STEPHEN RYAN

A citizen is influenced by principle in direct proportion to his distance from the political situation. (*Rakove's Second Law of Principle and Politics*)

Peacekeeping began as an unplanned UN response to a particular set of problems at a particular time. During the Cold War, although the mandates of missions varied from case to case, its geo-political task was to ensure that local conflicts did not escalate to drag in larger regional neighbours or the two superpowers. It was, in some situations, an effective tool of crisis management which did reduce the chances of a Greek-Turkish war in Cyprus or an Israeli-Syrian war in Lebanon. It is, perhaps, no accident that the majority of peacekeeping forces were deployed in the Middle East, which was outside the sphere of influence of either superpower and where the US and the USSR backed different sides. The danger of a slide into chaos was always a possibility there, and the superpowers could see the advantages in using the UN in a 'shock absorber' role as a component of their own crisis management efforts.

Indeed, international peacekeeping was 'invented' in the Middle East and then evolved into a flexible mechanism to respond to certain other crises. During this era peacekeeping, which was never officially defined by the UN, seemed to value a certain *ad hoc*, pragmatic approach. Urquhart has warned that 'care should be taken in attempting to generalise excessively about peacekeeping and to improve upon what has been part of the recipe of success, namely improvisation'.[1] While Tharoor has noted how the Special Committee on Peacekeeping regularly declined to issue a declaration on principles because it feared that it would introduce an inflexible element into the 'most pragmatic instrument at the disposal of the world community'.[2]

However, this flexibility was not as unlimited as it may seem, for at least two reasons. First, UN peacekeeping operated within the tight constraints of Cold War confrontation where the limits on UN action were well understood. Second, although peacekeeping remained undefined, the ground rules for such operations were not. They were devised for the UN Emergency Force (UNEF), the first large-scale peacekeeping mission. Analysts will differ slightly on what these were, but most would agree with Boutros-Ghali that the basic principles were:

> the consent of the parties; troops provided by member states serving under the command of the secretary general; minimum use of force; collective financing. It was also learned, often the hard way, that peacekeeping success requires the cooperation of the parties, a clear and practicable mandate, the continuing support of the Security Council and adequate financial arrangements.[3]

Of course, the history of peacekeeping reveals that these principles were not always followed in practice. Mandates were sometimes not practicable and financing has been a perpetual problem. Nonetheless the Hammarskjöld-Pearson principles did establish a set of basic guidelines that were thought to be valuable and did offer direction of sorts. In retrospect it is remarkable how similar most UN peacekeeping missions were during the Cold War.

Rethinking Peacekeeping

This was so as long as superpower conflict persisted. Its ending, however, created a new set of circumstances where pragmatism was left floundering and the accepted wisdom about peacekeeping was called into question. We should not confuse pragmatism, an attitude which emphasizes the facts of a particular case and which is suspicious of general theory, with Pragmatism, a theory that equates truth with usefulness.[4] One can espouse the former without being the latter. Nonetheless, an interesting parallel can be drawn between them because the anti-foundationalism of both makes it hard for either to respond effectively to serious upheavals. This is a point made by Gellner, who condemns Pragmatism because of its failure 'to consider crisis and radical discontinuity'.[5] It is an optimistic, evolutionary approach to knowledge that finds it hard to cope when self-maintaining systems collapse. For during such cataclysmic periods a 'happy reliance on the existing stock of tools and ideas without any effort at a prior philosophy...is not a workable strategy'.[6] During a time of fundamental change Gellner believes that there is a need to go back to fundamental principles. Yet this is difficult for a Pragmatist because of their suspicion that other forms of empiricism contain 'Cartesian residues, logical axioms and cognitive bedrock'.[7] This provides an important insight into peacekeeping. For as the general context within which the *ad hoc* approach operated started to transform at bewildering speed and as peacekeeping practice moved into new areas, so some commentators felt the need to go back to first principles in order to place peacekeeping on a surer conceptual footing. If Gellner is correct than this could not happen within the Pragmatic approach, which denies that intuitions have to be 'checked and corrected by some philosophically established independent criterion'.[8]

Even if we restrict ourselves to the UN and ignore recent developments at NATO, the OSCE, regional organizations and sub-regional organizations (ECOWAS in Liberia) we are now faced with a bewildering range of peacekeeping or quasi-peacekeeping operations. Mission tasks now involve a 'multiplicity of functions'.[9] As a result there is now much more to peacekeeping than military patrols along a ceasefire line and observation of the parties to ensure their separation and compliance with agreements – what has been called 'cooking and looking'.[10] The 'second generation' peacekeeping operations that began in Namibia have been more diverse and more complex than this, involving tasks such as the administration and conduct of elections and referendums, human rights monitoring (in El Salvador and Guatemala), police training and monitoring, the temporary administration of 'failed states', the supervision of the quartering and demobilization of armed groups, overseeing the security arrangements of leaders (MONUA), monitoring the repatriation of refugees and the resettlement of displaced persons, monitoring and verifying the withdrawal of foreign forces (ONUMOZ), ensuring the release of political prisoners or detainees (MINURSO), monitoring prisons (UNAMIR) and the provision of humanitarian assistance and coordination with international relief agencies. So Hammarskjöld's famous dictum that peacekeeping is not a job for a soldier but only a soldier can do it no longer seems as apposite as it once did. For as one of his successors has pointed out, peacekeeping operations 'still invariably include military personnel', but 'now the civilian elements often have an even more important role'.[11]

Some commentators now felt that a more conceptual approach was needed, that an *ad hoc* approach in a fluid and uncertain environment where the rules of the game were unclear was not quite the same as an *ad hoc* approach within the more predictable Cold War context. Weiss points out how the 'dramatic increase in UN operations in the post-Cold War period has catalysed analysis'.[12] He also claims that one problem has been that 'the UN has relied too heavily on the experience of past operations when coping with post-Cold War crises instead of delineating distinct new characteristics'. The Organization was, he claims, 'conceptually bereft'.[13] Tharoor seems to agree and states that 'classical, consensual peacekeeping does not respond fully to the nature of the world we live in and the challenges the new world disorder poses to the international community'.[14] De Cuellar has stated that one reason why the UN was unprepared for the post-Cold War challenges is that it lacked 'guidelines (or precedents) for ending societal disruptions and conflict within states'.[15] Fetherston claims it is clear that the *ad hoc* system of peacekeeping 'does not meet the demands posed by the post-Cold War world'.[16]

It also became more clear how an *ad hoc* approach, which makes advanced planning difficult, could undermine the funding, coordination and even the reliability of peacekeeping missions. One result was that the early 1990s witnessed the emergence of a number of national peacekeeping centres in countries like Canada (The Pearson Peacekeeping Center, established in 1994), Australia (RAAF Williamstown, established in 1993) and Ireland (The United Nations Training School Ireland, established in 1994). Courses for the training of civilian peacekeepers have been established at Stadtschlaining in Austria and at Pisa, Italy.

The *ad hoc* approach also meant that UN peacekeeping was always reactive rather than proactive, carried along by developments it seemed ill-prepared for. This certainly seemed to be the case with 'third generation' missions such as UNPROFOR and UNOSOM. Furthermore, although the absence of a peacekeeping 'doctrine', 'strategy' or 'theory' may have helped promote freedom of action and flexibility, it was becoming clear that in a more complex global environment an *ad hoc* approach also could result in drift and uncertainty. In discussing the UN and human rights interventions Hoffmann notes that even if a case-by-case approach is the wise one, it leaves the normative scene poorer.[17] Perhaps it is not surprising, therefore, that both analysts and practitioners started to search around for some conceptual underpinning to guide future UN action. Examples include the 1992 *An Agenda for Peace*, and the 1994 US re-assessment of peacekeeping in Presidential Decision Directive 25.

Much has been said about *An Agenda for Peace*, which was written at a time of growing optimism about the role of the UN. Roberts thought it a flawed document which overlooked the problem of overload, overestimated the ability of the UN to organize and control Chapter VII missions, seemed oblivious to the shortcomings of the Security Council, was unrealistic about funding, and lacked a proper appreciation of the changing character of conflict.[18] Boutros-Ghali also displayed a very traditionalist and unimaginative idea of peacemaking and a rather superficial and technical conceptualization of conflict prevention.[19] The role of NGOs in peacebuilding is also underestimated.[20] However, the criticism most often made is that the *Agenda* blurred the boundary between peacekeeping and peace enforcement – paragraph 20 states that peacekeeping 'is the deployment of a United Nations presence in the field, *hitherto* with the consent of all the parties' (emphasis added). Interestingly, in a March 1994 UN report of the Secretary-General on *Improving the Capacity of the United Nations for Peacekeeping* the definition of peacekeeping now read 'a United Nations presence in the field (normally including military and civilian personnel), with the consent of the parties'.[21] This demonstrates the turning away from peace enforcement that is most clear in the 1995 *Supplement to An Agenda for Peace*. Traditional peacekeeping did indeed always operate according to the principle of consent, usually expressed in a ceasefire agreement. In peace enforcement, however, the violence was ongoing and there was no peace to keep. This meant that missions were deployed into much more dangerous and complex situations where it was harder for the UN to preserve its neutrality.

Released on 5 May 1994, PDD-25 *Reforming Multilateral Peace Operations* set new, tighter conditions for US participation in peacekeeping missions. This contrasted with a more positive attitude to peacekeeping displayed at the start of the Clinton presidency. However, as Berdal points out, this favourable policy was based on a number of misperceptions about the nature of the new world order, the UN, and the consequences of military interventions in ethnic conflicts.[22] It is no surprise, therefore, that the reassessment of US policy came quite quickly after the problems encountered in Bosnia and Somalia. Now US involvement with UN peacekeeping had to meet a number of preconditions. There had to be a clear threat to international peace and security, and involvement would have to advance the interest of the US at an acceptable risk. Adequate command, control and communication procedures had to be available and there had to be clear objectives and a clear exit strategy. The document heralded the start of what Hill and Malik have termed a 'new frugality' on the part of the US administration to peacekeeping, which now imposed 17 preconditions for US involvement with UN missions.[23] As if this was not enough the National Security Revitalization Act of the following year allowed Congress to add even more preconditions.

Both *An Agenda for Peace* and PDD-25 were flawed, the former because it was too broad and led the UN to attempt too much, the latter because it was too restrictive and inhibited an effective international response to a number of crises, including Rwanda, where the world watched as the Hutu killers murdered at a rate five times greater than the Nazi death camps.[24] UN Ambassador Madelaine Allbright informed Congress in May 1994 that PDD-25 had already been employed to refuse operations in Burundi, Sudan, Nagorno-Karabakh, Tajikistan, Afghanistan and Sierra Leone. She also stated that clauses had been introduced into resolutions authorizing or extending missions that meant that the burden of proof now rested with those who wanted these missions extended rather than terminated.[25] The aim of the US government seemed to be to limit UN missions, not just US participation in them, because of a fear at the Pentagon that the US would be required to bail out failed deployments.[26]

The Neglect of Peacekeeping in Conflict Research

What is especially striking is the lack of interest in the academic fields of peace and conflict research in these debates about peacekeeping. Of course there are individual writers who have a strong interest in peacekeeping operations and there is an extensive literature on specific missions or on peacekeeping in general. But within conflict research there is a reluctance to make contributions at a theoretical level.[27] This seems remarkable, given that both peacekeeping and peace and conflict research were 'invented' about the same time in the mid 1950s and share a common interest in the dynamics and resolution of conflict.[28]

Impediments to dialogue are not just found on the academic side. The practical men of action who form the backbone of many operations often express little interest in how their work can be theorized about. Or, even when sympathetic to academic interrogation, their experiences may be inaccessible because of the unwillingness of governments or the UN to grant access to the experiences of the ordinary soldier on peacekeeping duty. This blocks analysis of questions such as why certain contingents in certain locations seem better at peacekeeping than others. Berdal makes an interesting comparison between the Italian contingent based in Kismayo and the US troops based in Mogadishu.[29] The former managed to avoid most of the problems encountered by the latter. Why was this? Such information could provide important information about how to win the support of local groups in war zones. Yet, as Boulding and Oberg have noted, peace research has failed to document the experiences of peacekeepers and should engage in a systematic recording of such information.[30]

We may be able understand the lack of interest better if we examine the writings of one of the most influential conflict theorists of the past generation. John Burton can be described as the founder of a distinct school of thought, created in the 1960s at the Centre for the Analysis of Conflict based in University College London. Members included John Groom, Chris Mitchell, Tony de Reuck, Ed Azar and Michael Banks.[31] These 'scholar-practitioners' share certain common characteristics: a rejection of the realist, state-centric view of international politics in favour of a 'world society' approach; participation in conflict resolution interventions through problem-solving workshops; and an acceptance that an important part of real conflict resolution involves the fulfilment of basic human needs.[32]

Burton's writings hardly mention peacekeeping at all, but what he does say challenges the view that peacekeeping has played positive roles in responding to violent conflict. If we take Burton's most recent study we encounter several negative comments. It is described as a way of dealing with conflict through 'enforcement and suppression'.[33] It is claimed that a peacekeeping operation 'merely perpetuates the conflict',[34] and it is a form of intervention 'which probably does more harm than good in the longer term'.[35] Burton also argues that 'the empirical evidence has been that peace-keeping and like attempts to prevent conflict are self-defeating', though he does not offer any evidence to back up this claim.[36]

One feature of Burton's analysis is the sharp distinction made between management and resolution. The former is to be avoided because it does not address the underlying causes of conflict and sustains an unjust status quo. However, this dichotomy seems to be too polarizing since it ignores the possibility that what we require in promoting conflict resolution is both conflict management and conflict resolution.[37] The aim should be to relate peacekeeping more to other strategies. As Groom has noted, peacekeeping would have greater relevance if it could be related more directly to conflict resolution and peacemaking.[38]

This is why the writings of Galtung on this topic are more subtle, dynamic and interesting. In his famous categorization of conflict resolution strategies into peacekeeping, peacemaking and peacebuilding, Galtung explicitly recognizes the importance of interventions that lower the level of destructiveness by stopping or reducing violent behaviour.[39] His groundbreaking article points out the problems with conventional peacekeeping: it may reduce direct violence, but not structural violence; it is a device intended for relatively weak states and is ignored by powerful states; and its sphere of applicability is low because of the norm of non-intervention. Nonetheless, he also argues that military training is 'indispensable' if violence is to be contained.[40]

Yet his idea of peacekeeping is a little dated. In 1976 it may have been correct to think of peacekeeping as a negative and 'dissociative strategy that merely tried to return the parties to the *status quo ante*' and did not address the causes of violence. But since the end of the Cold War we have witnessed 'second generation' peacekeeping in Namibia and Cambodia where the *status quo ante* has been rejected and where the aim is to construct a more peaceful and just society less prone to violence. Such attempts may not have been entirely successful, but they deserve recognition as a new type of mission. This Galtung does not seem to do. His recent major work on peace studies still refers to peacekeeping as a strategy to 'control the actors so that they at least stop destroying things, others, and themselves'.[41]

Another attempt to integrate peacekeeping into a more general theory of conflict resolution, which also seems to be based on outdated definitions, can be found in the work of Fisher. Along with Keashley he has developed a 'contingency model' of conflict.[42] Here 'third party interventions are coordinated and sequenced to deal effectively with the complex interplay of objective and subjective factors' that are found in all protracted conflicts.[43] Peacekeeping is included in this model, though in a rather restricted manner. There seem to be two weaknesses in his approach. First, Fisher thinks peacekeeping exists when 'an outside third party (typically the UN) provides military personnel to supervise and monitor a cease-fire between antagonists'.[44] This ignores non-military aspects of peacekeeping and the wide variety of tasks that recent peacekeepers have been asked to perform. Second, he believes that peacekeeping is limited to one particular part of his taxonomy of the intervention sequence: the destructive phase, where violence has to be controlled and the protagonists think in lose–lose terms. So, Fisher claims that the challenge 'with highly escalated and protracted conflicts is to institute peacekeeping as soon as possible to control the violence and to follow that initial intervention with other ones to facilitate de-escalation before intractability sets in'.[45] This leads on to a discussion of the interface of peacekeeping and peacebuilding, where three key peacebuilding strategies are identified once peacekeeping has the violence under control: dialogue, training and reconciliation.

Two points can be made about Fisher's approach. The first is that his sequence of intervention strategies may be too rigid. His belief that peacekeeping is the first strategy that creates the conditions for successful peacemaking and peacebuilding ignores the fact that traditional peacekeepers are usually deployed only after a ceasefire agreement – which usually requires some form of peacemaking work. Second, by restricting peacekeeping to one stage of the conflict cycle Fisher may be underestimating the role that this technique could play at other stages of conflict. Indeed, instead of attempting to restrict peacekeeping to one stage of conflict we should be assessing how peacekeeping can be made more appropriate for all stages.

One of the most interesting developments in recent thinking is the recognition that conflict seems to progress through several stages.[46] The exact terminology will differ from writer to writer, but the main stages of conflict can be characterized as follows:

Stage	*Strategy*
1. Pre-violence	Conflict prevention
2. Escalation	Crisis/humanitarian intervention
3. Endurance	Peacemaking and relief work
4. De-escalation	Peacemaking and 'traditional' peacekeeping
5. Post-violence	Peacebuilding/transformation

Different conflicts will move through all stages, though it is important to remember that some conflicts can stagnate at stage three for a considerable time, or a conflict could even move back to stage three from stage four or five. During the Cold War peacekeeping was restricted mainly to stage four, especially after the parties had agreed a ceasefire which might not be self-sustaining. However, there does seem to be scope for greater peacekeeping involvement at all stages of the conflict cycle, and there has been special interest in recent years in the pre-violence (prevention), the escalation (humanitarian intervention) and post-violence (peacebuilding) stages. It is this question that will be examined in the remainder of this article. As it is not possible to do full justice to all the issues and debates that have arisen in these three areas, we shall concentrate on just a few key issues under each heading.

The Pre-violence Stage: Conflict Prevention

The record in the first category is mixed. In the Republic of Macedonia we have witnessed the first, and only, deployment of a UN preventive peacekeeping force. This was established by Security Council Resolution 795, which authorized the Secretary-General to extend the deployment of UNPROFOR in order to stop the spread of the wars of Yugoslavian succession into Macedonia, a new state with a large Albanian minority and covetous neighbours. The military component monitors the borders with both Albania and the Republic of Yugoslavia. A civilian police contingent works with the local police to maintain order and protect human rights. Civilian members of the United Nations Preventive Deployment Force (UNPREDEP) monitor elections and advise the government. In June 1993 the US offered approximately 300 troops to join UNPROFOR in Macedonia. One of the principles of traditional peacekeeping was that the superpowers would not contribute contingents to deployments because this would threaten their neutrality. However, it is probably true that a preventive deployment benefits from the presence of such military contingents because it adds to its deterrence capabilities. Dedring claims that the presence of US troops on the ground with UNPROFOR/ UNPREDEP 'must have removed the last remaining doubts about the sincerity of the members of the Security Council with regard to the purpose of UN presence in Macedonia and to the expectation of its full success'.[47] This seems to endorse the views of analysts who suggest that prevention work requires leverage over the actors.[48] This, in turn, depends on resources, credibility, capability and a willingness to act – characteristics not always associated with the UN.

However, in Rwanda a chance to take effective action against an impending genocide was squandered. This was despite the fact that 'foreign observers, humanitarian workers, politicians and even the UN peacekeeping forces in Rwanda were aware of the potential for genocide some time in advance'.[49] Indeed, Kofi Annan recognized this when he told an audience on a visit to Rwanda in May 1998 that a failure of political will meant that 'no one can deny that the world failed the people of Rwanda...in their greatest hour of need'.[50] Clapham agrees that the reinforcement of UNAMIR at a crucial point could have saved the lives of Rwandan citizens, but he does not believe that it was possible to construct a long-term peace on the basis of the Arusha Agreement.[51] Clapham claims that this was because of the incompatible expectations of the Hutu factions and the Tutsi RPF. Indeed, he is critical of the Arusha Agreement for stopping the RPF offensive that could have defeated the Hutu forces in 1993 and so have prevented the genocide a year later. This is an interesting argument, and one that questions a basic assumption that conflict prevention is based on resolution not victory. However, Clapham does leave out of the analysis any attempt at a long-term prognosis of what a Hutu defeat would have meant for future intercommunal relations in Rwanda.

The sad fact is that the UN and regional organizations are poorly equipped to deal quickly with emerging crises. Part of the problem is a technical one. It takes time to assemble forces and to prepare them for deployment. Accounts of many peacekeeping deployments bemoan their tardy arrival in the mission area. In the case of Namibia Security Council Resolution 435 created UNTAG in 1978, ten years before its deployment. Thus the Organization should have had plenty of time to prepare for the mission. Yet one of the few criticisms of this landmark operation was that units were too slow getting to the mission area. This enabled fighters belonging to the South West African People's Organization (SWAPO) to infiltrate back into the country against the terms of the ceasefire agreement, and this provoked a brutal response by South African forces. For a brief period there was a danger that the whole peace process there would collapse.

In neighbouring Angola Security Council Resolution 975 authorized the deployment of the third United Nations Angolan Verification Mission (UNAVEM III) on February 8 1995, but an advance party did not arrive until 20 April and full deployment did not take place until the end of November.[52] Angola is an interesting example of how the UN and its member states seem to be unable to learn the lessons of previous missions. UNAVEM II was clearly a failure because it was under-resourced, yet UNAVEM III was still not provided with the numbers needed to ensure a successful mission. In the Cambodian case Doyle has complained about the late appointment of the police commissioner, which compounded the problems faced by UNTAC's civilian police.[53]

A quicker and more efficient response from the UN would undoubtedly save lives. Supporters of a quick reaction volunteer force or their civilian equivalents such as a UN Peace Corps, a 'rapid response team' or 'peace team units' tend to focus on the technical aspects of this problem.[54] Yet there is a deeper constraint that is inherent in all inter-governmental organizations. This is that states still have to agree on what needs to be done. A rapid response capability may help peacekeeping when there is agreement on this, but it cannot itself create such consensus. In fact many members of the UN would not want to see it developing an independent capacity for peacekeeping. The most that the UN can hope for is to negotiate stand-by arrangements with its members. In 1993 the UN created a Stand-by Forces Planning Team to facilitate this.

However, if even small steps are to be taken towards conflict prevention there will be a need for a stronger early warning system. This is where academics have been playing an important role developing models that will allow the international community to recognize impending crises.[55] It is now theoretically possible to create a new early warning centre linked to an effective global monitoring system.[56]

The Escalation Phase: Humanitarian Intervention

Most of the UN missions created in the late 1980s and early 1990s had a significant humanitarian component. However, humanitarian work undertaken by UN peacekeeping is not a new phenomenon. Liu has examined the humanitarian activities of first generation missions and notes 'extensive involvement in humanitarian activities' in Cyprus (UNFICYP), Lebanon (UNIFIL) and the Congo (ONUC).[57] Indeed, missions in 'internal conflicts' nearly always involved work that could be labelled as humanitarian. ONUC (1960–64) initiated relief programmes and delivered emergency supplies and was instructed to place an area threatened by armed bands under UN protection. UNFICYP was mandated to re-create normal conditions and has delivered supplies to the small Greek-Cypriot community in the Turkish Cypriot part of the island and facilitates family meetings between them and Greek Cypriots living in the south of the island. UNIFIL has helped to organize vaccination campaigns for children.[58] Most UN missions help to restore essential services and basic infrastructure, mark or remove mines, and offer an emergency medical service to locals.

What is different about some more recent humanitarian actions is that they have been the main purpose of peacekeeping/enforcement and they have taken place when violent conflicts are still escalating. In the face of public pressure energized by media coverage of awful human tragedy, the international community has felt the need to resort to what has been termed 'military humanitarianism'.

One manifestation of this has been the creation of safe havens and/or no-fly zones to protect civilians from attack. A relatively successful example of the two approaches working together can be found in Kurdish and Shiite areas of Iraq. After the end of the Gulf War Security Council Resolution 688 in April 1991 triggered, but did not directly authorize, Operation *Provide Comfort* by a coalition of western states. This created six safe havens protected by 8,000 US, British and French troops and a no-fly zone north of the thirty-sixth parallel. This was without the permission of Baghdad, who did agree however, to allow in a humanitarian programme under the control of the UNHCR and protected by 500 UN guards. A second no-fly zone was established in Iraq south of the thirty-second parallel in August 1991.

The no-fly zone in Bosnia was established by Security Council Resolution 781 in October 1992 The following April the UN began to implement a 'safe areas' policy, beginning with the town of Srebrenica. This was then extended to Bihac, Gorazde, Tuzla, Zepa and Sarajevo. Unfortunately, member states were not willing to provide enough troops to make this policy effective, and there was also a reluctance to call on NATO air strikes against Serbs who violated the policy. The credibility of the safe areas policy collapsed at Srebrenica in July 1995 when the Dutch UN contingent based there was withdrawn after UN officials stopped an air strike against their attackers and the town fell to Serb forces. This was followed by the massacre of thousands of Bosnian Moslem men. The safe area of Zepa fell to Bosnian Serbs three days later.

Another problem with humanitarian assistance by the international community during a period of violent conflict is that supplies can be appropriated by the warring factions, increasing their ability to prosecute the conflict. This has been examined by Prendergast.[59] He demonstrates how international aid can enhance the status and effectiveness of warlords through direct theft, corruption, setting exorbitant exchange rates for the supply of materials, and charging for the supply of fuel and bodyguards. He also claims that warring factions can set up their own NGOs to obtain funds and supplies. In response Prendergast calls for a 'tough love' approach that could allow for the delivery of assistance without sustaining the conflict. The key principles he recommends are transparency, independence, accountability, codes of conduct and proper coordination. He also points to the need for deeper analysis in planning, which is another area where academics and practitioners could engage in some fruitful discussions.

Some interesting suggestions have emerged as to how to improve humanitarian work during violent conflict. Ramsbotham and Woodhouse have developed a set of 12 framework principles for humanitarian intervention.[60] Weiss has proposed the creation of a specialized cadre, answerable to the Security Council, to deliver emergency aid in war zones – something he calls a Humanitarian Protection Force (HUMPROFOR) – and the use of the UN Trusteeship Council to administer collapsed states for a temporary period.[61] Also of significance are the writings of Garcia on zones of peace.[62]

There is still a dispute over the extent to which peacekeeping should be integrated with humanitarian relief work. James, for example, wants to separate them, arguing that each of them 'is far too important to be put in needless jeopardy through an unnecessarily close association with the other'.[63] Chopra, on the other hand, seems to want to integrate them more fully under the more unified concept of peace maintenance that integrates diplomatic, military and humanitarian activities as part of a general political strategy.[64]

The Post-violence Stage: Conflict Transformation

Separating peacekeeping and peacebuilding has become difficult because 'second generation' missions perform peacebuilding tasks but under the title of peacekeeping. There is very little in the literature on the peacekeeping dimensions of peacebuilding, yet there is a clear overlap between the two approaches. Indeed, there is a need to examine this relationship more systematically. This has been recognized by Woodhouse and Ramsbotham, who claim that 'the future of peacekeeping as a middle ground between abstention and enforcement will depend on the capability and willingness to reform and strengthen peacekeeping, and to *reconceptualize its role in conflict transformation*' (emphasis added).[65]

Peacebuilding, or conflict transformation, work should address issues such as long term security, economic justice, and the culture of violence. The ill-fated UN Confidence Restoration Operation in Croatia, for example, was mandated to 'support local confidence-building measures, including socio-economic and reconstruction activities, people-to-people contacts and information exchanges of mutual benefit'.[66] In other words 'successful peacebuilding addresses root causes of violent conflict' and attempts to build a sustainable peace.[67] This may not appear to be a task for peacekeeping, which, as we have seen, has usually been directed at conflict management. Yet peacekeeping may be essential in the early states of this work. Relief supplies may need military escorts. Refugees may only return to their homes if their security is guaranteed by a strong military force (the Kosovars). Cross-community contacts in situations like Cyprus may only take place under UN supervision and protection. Elections have to be monitored, and the monitors may require protection. A new justice system may have to be created, and this involves the training and monitoring of police officers. A culture of respect for human rights may have to be created, which means that the activities of governments and other groups have to be monitored. This has also been a significant component of missions in Cambodia, El Salvador and Guatemala.

Demilitarization is also an important part of peacebuilding, and peacekeeping forces may be required to do this. In Somalia this issue led to conflict between the UN Secretary-General, who believed that the disarmament of the factions was implicit in the mandate of UNITAF to create a secure environment, and the US government, which adopted a narrower interpretation in order to avoid anything that could prolong or complicate UNITAF's mission. In Haiti the failure of the peacekeepers to disarm certain factions has left the fragile democracy there 'seriously exposed'.[69] Given this range of peacekeeping tasks it is not surprising that Kumar argues that peacekeepers are critical 'for promoting peace accords, maintaining cease fires, and resolving thorny political and military issues during transition'.[69] Here we see peacekeepers acting less like a conflict manager and more like a midwife at the birth of a new society.[70] It is important, however, that this metaphor does not blind us to the deep-rooted problems that have to be overcome in promoting a culture of peace. One recurring criticism of the UN's peacekeeping/peacebuilding is the incomplete nature of the work done because of a shallow conceptualization of what peacebuilding requires. There is often a short-termism to the actions of the UN, individual governments and even NGOs. Prendergast points out that many groups involved in conflict areas are more interested in high profile relief rather than reconciliation.[71] In his study of the UN's role in Cambodia Doyle talks about 'incomplete reconciliation' and the 'excessive good faith' assumed by UNTAC.[72] As a result there is little evidence to suggest that Cambodia has moved on to a new phase of pluralist democracy that has been accepted by all the main parties. Indeed, Doyle claims that in the area of human rights 'UNTAC met little success in its corrective role'.[73] This warns us to avoid too much easy optimism. One of the factors to ponder here is that the UN may be placing too much emphasis on a high profile 'fair and free' election as convincing evidence of the good that peacebuilding can do. However, democratic elections, especially those based on simple majoritarianism, may do no more than re-channel conflicts rather than transform them, leaving the hostile win/lose orientation unaffected.[74]

Not all groups will want transformation. Some analysts feel that the UN is often too cautious in the way it responds to what Stedman has called 'spoilers'.[75] These are groups who may be opposed to a peace process, or may even sign up to a peace agreement they have no intention of keeping, perhaps because they are unable to resist pressure from patrons. In Rwanda, for example, some Hutu factions clearly used the time given to them by the 1993 Arusha Accords to prepare for the 1994 genocide. In Angola UNITA turned against the peace process when it lost the elections. If we return again to Doyle's analysis of UNTAC, we find some criticisms of the unwillingness to enforce mandates when challenged by the Khmer Rouge, who refused to cooperate with the UN. In one notable incident Special Representative Yasushi Akashi and force commander Sanderson refused to take a tough line with the Khmer Rouge in May 1992, when they were stopped by bamboo pole from crossing a Khmer Rouge area near Pailin. Akashi also drew criticisms for his role in the former Yugoslavia when, again as Special Representative, he refused to call on NATO airstrikes to protect the safe areas.

Stedman points out that spoilers only exist where there is a peace process to undermine and they come in many forms.[76] He then examines three strategies for spoiler management (inducement, socialization into a set of norms, and coercion) and relates these to spoiler types. Inducements may work with a 'limited spoiler', and socialization is a long-term strategy to adopt with 'greedy spoilers'. However neither will work with a 'total spoiler' because he views the war in all-or-nothing terms. Here the use of force to defeat the spoiler may be necessary.

Another, neglected, aspect of post-conflict peacebuilding should be the improved status of women. Here, unfortunately, UN peacekeeping may actually exacerbate the problem. One criticism of UNTAC, for example, was the way its members contributed to the problem of prostitution. Recent research has helped illuminated this problem. Both Fetherston (1998) and Whitworth (1998) point to the use of child prostitutes by UN personnel in Cambodia (less likelihood of contracting AIDS), the huge increase in sexually transmitted diseases, and accusations of sexual assault and sexual harassment.[77] When the head of mission, Akashi, appeared unwilling to take a strong stand against this action more than 160 women, including UN personnel, NGO workers and local Cambodians sent him a letter of protest. Problems with prostitution have also arisen on UN missions in the former Yugoslavia and Mozambique. Both Fetherston and Whitaker ask what sort of peace is being created here? This raises some important questions about 'militarized masculinity' and how this is affected by peacekeeping duties.[78]

The Future

The current trend may be away from UN peacekeeping, yet this may not always be so. New areas may open up for peacekeeping under a general heading of good global governance. As the world moves beyond the Westphalian system where the primary principle is respect for state sovereignty to a world that is more interdependent and 'globalized', so we may see a greater willingness to take action against international problems that prick the conscience of world society where individual states may be unable or unwilling to take what is deemed to be appropriate action. Specialists are already identifying areas where some form of international intervention may be required. These are what Hoffmann, in his search for a *jus ad interventionem*, has termed 'community causes'.[80] He has produced an interesting analysis which recognizes a need to define the circumstances that would justify humanitarian intervention, but also calls for norms in the following areas: nuclear proliferation; other weapons of mass destruction; and the protection of minorities. Brauch, Mesjasz and Moller have also focused on arms control and have proposed that the UN could create an International Monitoring Agency to oversee arms agreements and 'discourage' illegal shipments of technology or arms.[80] A precedent may have been set in the arms control area by Security Council Resolution 687 of 3 April 1991 which has attempted to destroy Saddam Hussein's weapons of mass destruction. The UN authorized the use of 'all necessary means' to ensure compliance with Resolution 687, and this has been used to legitimize a number of Western air raids against Iraq.

Other areas linked to what Giddens has termed the 'globalization of risk' could also become significant. Drug interdiction has been mentioned by some analysts.[83] So has the suppression of piracy.[82] Other studies have suggested that violent conflicts over water resources may increase in the next century, either because states will struggle between themselves to ensure an adequate supply, or because governments that cannot stop water shortages may face internal conflicts from disaffected groups. Several stress points have already been identified in the Middle East and Africa. In the former region water issues have caused strains in relations between Turkey and Syria and Turkey and Iraq over the Tigris and the Euphrates. It has also complicated relations between Israel and the Palestinians. In Africa there a large number of flash points. Egypt is worried about threats to the flow of the Nile from upstream states. South Africa's plan to obtain water supplies from the Zambezi could lead it into conflict with neighbouring states and Namibia's plan to drain water from the Okavango river has increased tensions with Botswana. These two states are already involved in an International Court of Justice case over Sedudu island in the Chobe river. Mozambique also finds that its water supplies are being threatened by the actions of upstream states. Other major rivers that could form the focus of interstate conflict are the Danube and the Mekong.

A 1995 World Bank report estimates that 40 per cent of the world's population live in river basins that are shared by two or more states and 28 countries are already regarded as 'water stressed'.[83] In such circumstances it may be that a protracted water-based conflict may arise which requires some form of international response. So we may see in the future some form of international supervision of transboundary water supplies to ensure a fair distribution of this most vital of resources. Nor is water likely to be the only source of environmental conflict. Problems requiring some form of international response are likely to arise over climate (global warming), air quality, fisheries, food, forests and mining.[84] Such environmental problems have led to speculation that there could be a UN force established to protect vital resources – the Green Helmets.

Conclusions

It has been argued that there has been a lack of up-to-date and insightful theoretical analysis of peacekeeping. It is necessary, however, to warn against too much theorizing. To move from neglect to over-theorizing is not likely to help us in the search for constructive interventions in destructive conflicts. For it is important to recognize the positive side of an *ad hoc* policy. It creates space for 'creative improvisation' and 'creative and spontaneous adaptations'.[85] This should not be stifled.

However, there is a need to produce a stronger conceptual framework for peacekeeping which recognizes the new ways it has involved itself in conflict over the last decade. Here we have offered some very sketchy suggestions about how the academic community can help this rethinking in three areas of the conflict cycle where 'first generation' peacekeeping have rarely been used: conflict prevention, conflict escalation and conflict transformation. We also have to realize that in all of these areas UN involvement could add to the complexity of the situation and may even create new conflicts.[86]

Several key events appear to sum up the sorry state of UN peacekeeping since the early 1990s. The abandonment of Srebrenica, UN peacekeepers chained to Bosnian Serb positions to deter air strikes by NATO, the fire fights in Mogadishu between UN personnel and the supporters of General Aideed, and the withdrawal of most of UNAMIR after the murder of ten Belgian peacekeepers by the Interahamwe. In the light of such problems we can better understand the current mood to return to a 'traditional' approach to peacekeeping. Yet it should not be forgotten how out of favour this form of conflict intervention had become by last decade of the Cold War. After the UNIFIL deployment in 1978 there was no new UN peacekeeping mission created until UNTAG in Namibia took the Organization into 'multidimensional' peacekeeping.

The UN has already moved beyond 'traditional' peacekeeping. To try to return to the 'brave old world' of 'buffer zones and policing cease-fires' could be a retrograde step.[87] To ignore the rich experiences of military and civilian peacekeepers over the past decade would itself be a betrayal of the flexible and pragmatic attitudes that enabled peacekeeping to develop in the first place. Anyway, in an age of global media it is unlikely that the UN can turn its back on human suffering on a massive scale when this is being reported by journalists with satellite up-links. What is needed is some serious thinking about how peacekeeping and conflict theory can engage in a dialogue that may encourage and nurture this process. As Tharoor has stated, the aim should not be to go back to basics but to redefine basics.[88]

NOTES

1. Brian Urquhart, 'Reflections by the Chairman', in I.J. Rikhye and Kjell Skjelsbaek (eds.), *The United Nations and Peacekeeping: Results, Limitations and Prospects*, Basingstoke: Macmillan, 1990, p.18.
2. Shashi Tharoor, 'Should United Nations Peacekeeping Go "Back to Basics"?', *Survival*, Vol.37, No.2, 1995, p.56.
3. Boutros Boutros-Ghali, *An Agenda for Peace*, New York: United Nations, 1992.
4. See, for example, Richard Rorty, *Contingency, Irony and Solidarity*, Cambridge: Cambridge University Press, 1989.
5. Ernest Gellner, 'Pragmatism and the Importance of Being Earnest', in Ernest Gellner, *Spectacles and Predicaments*, Cambridge: Cambridge University Press, 1979, p.249.
6. Ibid. p.259.
7. Ernest Gellner, 'The Rubber Cage: Disenchantment with Disenchantment', in Ernest Gellner, *Culture, Identity and Politics*, Cambridge: Cambridge University Press, 1987, p.156.
8. Ibid.
9. Henry Wiseman, 'Peacekeeping in the International Political Context: Historical Analysis and Future Direction', in Rikhye and Skjelsbaek (n.1 above), p.35
10. James H. Allen, *Peacekeeping: Outspoken Observations by a Field Officer*, Westport: Praeger, 1996, p.45.
11. Boutros-Ghali (n.3 above), p.91.
12. Thomas G. Weiss, Conflict and Cooperation: Humanitarian Action in a Changing World', in Eric A. Belgrad and Nitza Nachmias (eds.), *The Politics of International Humanitarian Operations* Westport: Praeger, 1997, p.174.
13. Thomas G. Weiss, 'Overcoming the Somalia Syndrome "Operation Rekindle Hope"?' *Global Governance*, Vol.1, No.2, 1995, p.174.
14. Tharoor (n.2 above), p.53.
15. Javier Perez de Cuellar, 'Reflecting the Past, Contemplating the Future', *Global Governance*, Vol.1, No.2. 1995, p.167. The other factors he mentions are: a lack of adequate funding; managerial staff and command and control procedures; appropriately trained troops; and an effective system of coordination and integration.
16. A. Betts Fetherston, *Towards a Theory of United Nations Peacekeeping*, Basingstoke: Macmillan, 1994, p.xvi.
17. Stanley Hoffmann, *The Ethics and Politics and Humanitarian Intervention* Notre Dame: University of Notre Dame Press, 1996, p.29.
18. Adam Roberts, 'The United Nations and International Security', *Survival*, Vol.35, No.2 1993, pp.3–30.
19. Stephen Ryan, 'Preventive Diplomacy, Conflict Prevention, and Ethnic Conflict', in David Carment and Patrick James (eds), *Peace in the Midst of Wars: Preventing and Managing International Ethnic Conflicts* Columbia: University of South Carolina Press, 1998, pp.63–92.
20. Kumar Rupesinghe, 'Coping with Internal Conflicts: Teaching the Elephant to Dance', in Chadwick F. Alger (ed.), *The Future of the United Nations System: Potential for the Twenty-First Century*, Tokyo: United Nations University Press, 1998, pp.155–82.
21. UN Doc. S/26450, par.4.
22. Mats R. Berdal, 'Fateful Encounter: The United States and UN Peacekeeping', *Survival*, Vol.36, No.1, 1994, pp.30–50.
23. S.M. Hill and S.P. Malik, *Peacekeeping and the United Nations*, Aldershot: Dartmouth, 1996, p.156–7.
24. Girard Prunier, *The Rwandan Crisis, 1959–1994*, London: Hurst, 1995, p.261.
25. Hill and Malik (n.23 above), p.156–7.

26. Holly J. Burkhalter, 'The Question of Genocide: The Clinton Administration and Rwanda', *World Policy Journal*, Vol.11, No.4, 1994–95, pp.44–54.
27. Enrico Augelli and Craig N.Murphy, 'Lessons of Somalia for Future Multilateral Humanitarian Assistance Operations', *Global Governance*, Vol.1, No.3, 1995, pp.339–65.
28. Stephen Ryan, 'The Theory of Conflict Resolution and the Practice of Peacekeeping', in Edward Moxon-Browne (ed.), *A Future for Peacekeeping?* Basingstoke: Macmillan, 1998, pp.26–39.
29. Berdal (n.22 above), p.43.
30. Elise Boulding and Jan Oberg, 'United Nations Peacekeeping and NGO Peace-building: Towards Partnership', in Alger (n.20 above), pp.127–54.
31. R.J. Fisher, *Interactive Conflict Resolution*, Syracuse:Syracuse University Press, 1997, p.205.
32. Michael Banks, *Conflict in World Society*, Brighton: Harvester Wheatsheaf, 1984.
33. John W. Burton, *Violence Explained* Manchester: Manchester University, 1997, p.44
34. Ibid., p.75.
35. Ibid., p.109.
36. Ibid., p.150.
37. Stephen Ryan, 'Conflict Management and Conflict Resolution', *Terrorism and Political Violence*, Vol.2, No.1, 1990, pp.54–71.
38. John Groom, 'The Quest for Peace and Security', in Paul Taylor and A.J.R. Groom (eds.), *International Institutions at Work*, London: Pinter, 1988, p.95.
39. Johan Galtung, 'Three Approaches to Peace: Peacekeeping, Peacemaking, and Peacebuilding', in *Peace, War and Defence: Essays in Peace Research Volume II*, Copenhagen: Christian Eljers, 1976, pp.282–304.
40. Johan Galtung, *Peace By Peaceful Means*, London: Sage, 1996, p.270.
41. Ibid. p.103.
42. Loraleigh Keashly and R.J. Fisher, 'Towards a Contingency Approach to Third Party Intervention in Regional Conflict: Cyprus in Illustration', *International Journal*, Vol.45, Spring 1990, pp.424–53.
43. Fisher, p.164.
44. Ibid., p.165.
45. Ibid., p.168.
46. See especially: Keashley and Fisher (n.43 above); Louis Kriesberg, *Constructive Conflicts*, Lanham: Rowman, and Littlefield, 1998; Christopher R. Mitchell, *The Structure of International Conflict*, Basingstoke: Macmillan, 1981; Kumar Rupesinghe, *Civil Wars, Civil Peace*, London: Pluto Press, 1998; and Tom Woodhouse and Oliver Ramsbotham, 1996. *Terra Incognita: Here be Dragons. Peacekeeping and Conflict Resolution in Contemporary Conflict: Some Relationships Considered*, Derry: INCORE, 1996.
47. Jürgen Dedring, 'The Security Council in Preventive Action', in Peter Wallensteen (ed.), *Preventing Violent Conflicts: Past Record and Future Challenges*, Uppsala: Department of Peace and Conflict Research, 1998, p.55.
48. See, for example, David Carment and Patrick James, 'The United Nations at 50: Managing Ethnic Crises Past and Present', *Journal of Peace Research*, Vol.35, No.1, 1998, pp.61–82.
49. Rupesinghe (n.46 above), p.21.
50. In Ladislas Bizimana, *Conflict in the African Great Lakes Region*, Bilbao: University of Deusto, 1999, p.95.
51. Christopher Clapham, 1998, 'Rwanda: The Perils of Peacemaking', *Journal of Peace Research*, Vol.35, No.2, 1998, pp.193–210.
52. Paul Hare, *Angola's Last Best Chance for Peace. An Insider's Account of the Peace Process*, Washington D.C: United States Institute of Peace, 1998, Ch.3.
53. Michael W. Doyle, *UN Peacekeeping in Cambodia: UNTAC's Civil Mandate*, Boulder: Lynne Rienner for International Peace Academy, 1995, p.48.
54. Commission on Global Governance, *Our Global Neighbourhood*, Oxford: Oxford University Press, 1995; Independent Working Group on the Future of the United Nations, *The Report of the Independent Working Group on the Future of the United Nations*, New York: Ford Foundation, 1995.

55. Ted R. Gurr and Barbara Harff, 'Systematic Early Warning of Humanitarian Emergencies', *Journal of Peace Research*, Vol.3, No.5, 1998, pp.557–80.
56. International Alert, *Preventive Diplomacy: Recommendations of a Round Table on Preventive Diplomacy and the UN's Agenda for Peace*, London: International Alert, 1993
57. F.T. Liu, 'Peacekeeping and Humanitarian Assistance', in Leon Gordenker and Thomas G. Weiss (eds.), *Soldiers, Peacekeepers and Disasters*, Basingstoke: Macmillan, 1991, pp.33–51.
58. Ibid.
59. John Prendergast, *Frontline Diplomacy: Humanitarian Aid and Conflict in Africa* Boulder: Lynne Rienner, 1996.
60. Oliver Ramsbotham and Tom Woodhouse, *Humanitarian Intervention in Contemporary Conflict*, Cambridge: Polity Press, 1996.
61. Weiss (n.12 and 13 above).
62. Ed Garcia, *A Distant Peace*, Quezon: University of Philippines Press, 1991.
63. Alan James, 'Humanitarian Aid Operations and Peacekeeping', in Belgrad and Nachmias (n.12 above), p.64.
64. Jarat Chopra (ed.), *The Politics of Peace Maintenance*, Boulder: Lynne Rienner, 1998.
65. Tom Woodhouse and Oliver Ramsbotham, 'Peacekeeping and Humanitarian Intervention in Post-Cold War Conflict', in Tom Woodhouse, Robert Bruce and Malcolm Dando (eds.), *Peacekeeping and Peacemaking: Towards Effective Intervention in Post-Cold War Conflicts*, Basingstoke: Macmillan, 1998, p.63.
66. UN Doc. S/1995/320 par.19.
67. John G. Cockell, 'Peacebuilding and Human Security: Framework for International Responses to Internal Conflict', in Wallensteen (n.47 above), p.212.
68. Andrew Reding, 'Exorcising Haiti's Ghosts', *World Policy Journal*, Vol.13, No.1, 1996, pp.15–26.
69. Krishna Kumar, 'The Nature and of International Assistance for Rebuilding War-Torn Societies', in Krishna Kumar (ed.), *Rebuilding Societies After Civil War*, Boulder: Lynne Rienner, 1997, pp.1–2.
70. David S. Whittaker, *The United Nations in Action*, London: University College London Press, 1995, p.204.
71. Prendergast (n.59 above), p.121.
72. Doyle (n.53 above), p.69.
73. Ibid., p.46.
74. See, for example, Hizkias Assefa, *Peace and Reconciliation as a Paradigm*, Nairobi: Nairobi Peace Initiative, 1993; Chetan Kumar, *Building Peace in Haiti*, Boulder: International Peace Academy. 1998.
75. Stephen John Stedman, 1998. 'Conflict Prevention as Strategic Interaction: The Spoiler Problem and the Case of Rwanda', in Wallensteen (n.47 above), pp.67–86.
76. Ibid.
77. See A. Betts Fetherston, 'Voices from Warzones: Implications for Training UN Peacekeepers', in Moxon-Browne (n.28 above), pp.158–75; Sandra Whitworth, 'Gender, Race and the Politics of Peacekeeping', in Moxon-Browne (n.28 above), pp.176–91.
78. Cynthia Enloe, 'Are UN Peacekeepers Real Men? And Other Post-Cold War Puzzles', in Cynthia Enloe, *The Morning After: Sexual Politics at the End of the Cold War*, Berkeley: University of California Press, 1993, pp.10–37.
79. Hoffmann (n.17 above).
80. Hans Gunter Brauch, Czeslaw Mesjasz and Bjorn Moller, 'Controlling Weapons in the Quest for Peace', in Alger (n.20 above), pp.15–53.
81. Indar Jit Rikhye, 1990. 'The Future of Peacekeeping', in Rikhye and Skjelsbaek (n.1 above), p.184.
82. Michael Pugh (ed.), *Maritime Security and Peacekeeping*, Manchester University Press, 1995.
83. International Committee of the Red Cross, *Forum: War and Water*, Geneva: International Committee of the Red Cross, 1999, p.110.
84. Mohamed Suliman, *Ecology, Politics and Violent Conflict*, London: Zed Press, 1999.

85. Augustus Richard Norton and Thomas G. Weiss, 'Rethinking Peacekeeping', in Rikhye and Skjelsbaek (n.1 above), p.31
86. Carment and James (n.48 above), p.77.
87. Tharoor (n.2 above), p.54.
88. Ibid.

Defining Warlords

JOHN MACKINLAY

Warlordism is an ugly, pejorative expression, evoking brutality, racketeering and the suffering of civil communities. In this study the term 'warlord' refers to the leader of an armed band, possibly numbering up to several thousand fighters, who can hold territory locally and at the same time act financially and politically in the international system without interference from the state in which he is based.[1] In crisis zones around the world where civil war and humanitarian disasters accompany the struggles of societies in transition, the warlord is the key actor. He confronts national governments, plunders their resources, moves and exterminates uncooperative populations, interdicts international relief and development and derails peace processes. With only a few exceptions the modern warlord lives successfully beyond the reach and jurisdiction of civil society. His ability to seek refuge in the crisis zone and the lack of international commitment to take effective action together ensure his survival.

Although the warlord is a principle factor in today's war zones, the international military forces, humanitarian relief and development agencies and the international civil administration units involved in stabilization and restoration spend little effort in defining and isolating this shadowy figure who will, in some form, be certain to impact negatively on their agenda. There is certainly a flourishing genre of writing under the banner of the 'economy of civil war' which explains many aspects of the warlord's economic survival and exploitation of the resources of a failing state and is an important step towards understanding the warlord syndrome. However warlordism implies a diversity of activities and cultural structures; a definitive picture must also involve other disciplines including anthropologists and military experts in addition to the humanitarians who are at the epicentre of the 'economy of civil war' approach. This study sets out to show the warlord in more general terms, suggesting that warlordism is derived from a culture that predates its manifestations in the twentieth century, explaining his predatory status in the conflict zone, his military capabilities and the sociology of his personal controlling devices. The study also suggests that besides spending more effort on defining warlords, the international community should take a more targeted and determined approach towards dealing with them.

Warlords and Civil Society

Before the tribes of Europe achieved statehood they were subdivided among local rulers or barons and their tenants. A baron was more than a landlord. He might pay homage to a king but on his own territory he was autonomous, collecting revenues, raising armies and enforcing his version of the law. In return for paying taxes, his tenants and kinsmen expected his protection while they remained within his territory. The itinerant chieftains whose clans lived in poorer areas as herdsmen were less able to enjoy the settled lifestyle of a cultivator. They extorted money from traders whose caravans passed below their fortified keeps in the mountain passes. The relationship between the baron with his rich agricultural territory and the clan chieftain with his herds on the mountain pass was that their autonomy and power to act freely in their own territory rested on their ability to protect it by force of arms. Despite their abuse of power and at times unattractive behaviour, local rulers also performed important social functions, supporting religion, culture and encouraging some aspects of a primitive form of civil society. The warlord by contrast was a negative phenomenon. Although, like the baron and the chieftain, his power rested on the possession of military forces, he occupied territory in a strictly predatory manner and his social activities seldom enriched the lives of civilian families in his grasp. Warlordism involved the use of military force in a narrower, more selfish way than the baron or the chieftain. It implied protectionism, racketeering and the interception of revenues, without any mitigating cultural or religious commitments and was not a concept that became intellectually developed in our culture.

John Keegan's analysis of the Mongols, Huns and Buminid Turks sets them apart from the agricultural European races as the 'horse peoples', a nomadic culture that lived by war alone. Their failure to survive as a society was linked to their inability to translate conquest into permanent power. Their presence was 'extractive not stabilising, designed to support the nomad way of life, not to change it'.[2] The horse people of Genghis Khan were ultimately defeated. Very little of their culture and life style survived in civil society today. Their pursuit of warfare as a way of life also fell beyond the comprehension of Clausewitzian writers and communicators whose only concept of violence was as an instrument of policy. In this manner warlordism and the nomad raiders arouse similarly negative responses, existing at the dark edges of our history, mercifully failing to make much cultural impact on our social development, but also failing to attract intellectual attention or any exploratory effort to understand them as a phenomenon. Even if barons and chieftains were in a sense warlords, it was not in that role that they survive in the fabric of our lives today and it is possible to speculate that the longstanding dissonance between warlordism and civil society is such that is almost impossible for the one to deal intuitively with the other.

The Significance of the Chinese Warlords

Warlordism became more relevant after the collapse of the Qing dynasty in 1911 when China was devastated by a series of civil wars between competing provincial rulers. The term achieved a sensational connotation when foreign correspondents used it to describe the violent and rapine behaviour of the provincial rulers. The warlord period in China from 1911 until the outbreak of the Anti-Japanese war in 1937 was a time of chaos and rapid change. According to Diana Lary the violence was pervasive, soldiers fought each other constantly in an average of eight full-scale wars a year in addition to the innumerable small-scale clashes and in 1923 there were 16 separate campaigns.[3] To a society which for centuries had followed the Confucian ethic of brush over sword, the rude invasion of rampaging militarism was a calamity. The Chinese upper classes were in a sense paying the full price of their failure to acknowledge the importance of military power. For centuries they had disdained the attributes of the warrior and all that went with it, including physical entertainments, prize fighting and team sports. The military were not only despised by the Chinese elite but also by society at large.[4]

By the time China's effetist society woke up to the realities of military power, it was too late. The conditions that were to encourage the rise of the local warlords already prevailed. During the declining Qing dynasty in the mid-nineteenth century, there had been a devolution of power to provincial level. According to Franz Michael, China's twentieth-century warlords began life as provincial military commanders. The weakness of the Qing rulers and their reluctance to concentrate military power into a central command structure encouraged fragmentation. They believed a dispersal of interests would protect them from the possibility of a widespread military uprising. However as the provincial force commanders' power increased they expected a greater freedom to administer their own territory and began to organize their own revenues. While the reach of the Qing court diminished, provincial commanders grew more assertive, so that when the dynasty finally collapsed in 1911, the autonomous military commanders were already poised to fill the political vacuum that had enlarged in the final years of the dynasty. An environment which encouraged warlordism had begun to emerge in the preceding 30 years of gradual collapse as the state-wide military structure devolved to a more personalized regional system.[5] There were also qualitative differences in the military forces that developed during in this period. Some provincial armies, such as Yunnan, were organized on the lines of modern military formations based on the prevailing European doctrines, whereas many of the provincial forces were individually organized around the personality of the new local commander.

The violent struggle that followed is well documented both by Chinese biographers of the warlords and by foreign analysts.[6] The characteristics of the violence and the behaviour of the armed bands involved are relevant to our understanding of modern civil conflict. Despite the longstanding contempt of the literati and upper classes for the military profession, Chinese society became pervasively militarized at a surprising speed. In the chaotic circumstances of the civil wars, volunteering for the military offered a chance for the downtrodden peasant to escape from the drudgery of rural serfdom. For them the military offered the possibility of wealth and unaccustomed power. Belonging to a military band and possessing a gun appealed to a barely suppressed instinct that was older and possibly stronger than the effete cultures of the outgoing regime. In many cases it was enough to carry a weapon, there was no need for ammunition or a proficiency in its use; the breech-loading rifle itself was the symbol of new power. Armed in this manner a force in occupation could requisition buildings, seize war materials, conscript labour and levy taxes. At a much lower level, beyond the restrictions of army discipline, small groups of soldiers could use the threat of their weapons to loot personal property, to rape, to steal harvests and commit casual acts of terrible violence without fear of reprisal. In this way the warlords destroyed much of China's social and cultural heritage. The marauding bands which detached themselves from warlord armies were 'more dangerous as groups than as individuals, because the group gave its members the courage to behave badly. The real horror was the unpredictability'.[7]

On the whole Chinese analysts rationalized the brutality of the warring militias by explaining that the men involved were from the lowest order of society, poor blank creatures, so stupid as to lack any sense of self-preservation who were simply acting in accordance with the expectations of society. Lary however shows that some Guomintang leaders took the more sophisticated view that the raw material of the militia was not cruel and violent by nature.[8] They had been brutalized by the army where they were routinely beaten, abused and physically endangered by careless leadership. This constant assault by their immediate superiors removed their normal sensitivities and reasoning faculties. Lary's conclusions about this newly emerging, fragile military regime have much relevance to the power structures of the modern warlord. With some accuracy she observed how a personalized gang culture replaced, or emerged in place of, the formal military command structure and how that acted as a spur and a licence to the gratuitous violence of the sub-groups within the faction. 'The Chinese military world of the warlord was too new and too fragmented to have established formal standards of behaviour. Soldiers learned how to behave in an ad hoc fashion. They became predatory towards the civilian world, not as a matter of policy, but in imitation of the way their commanders treated them.'[9]

An unrelated but important issue to emerge from the later period of the Chinese civil wars was the fundamental distinction between the modus operandi of the warlord and the insurgent. Mao's approach to this same chaotic period reveals a military force with radically different objectives and survival ethics. The Chinese warlord on the one hand had established himself from the power base of a former provincial leader and thus endowed could in the short term afford to take a rapine attitude towards the local population. In stark contrast, Mao's forces, if they were to survive tactical defeat, had to *rely* on widespread popular support. Mao had to woo his constituency; they must want to feed him, to hide him and to act as his eyes and ears. The population were unlikely to do this if his soldiers acted violently towards them. Mao's army was therefore sternly disciplined in its relationship to the local population. As a result, in contrast to the warlord, Red Army fighters were welcomed because they were regarded as part of the local constituency. It is also interesting that unlike his Mandarin masters, Mao also had no illusions about the importance of military power. In particular, during his later efforts to stabilize China he entertained no soft options for a negotiated settlement. The party, he insisted, must possess the gun: 'War can only be abolished through war, in order to get rid of the gun we must first grasp it in our hand.'.[10]

The Chinese experience of warlords is important and provides a reliable perspective. The obvious lessons are perhaps now less interesting. The conditions which encouraged the growing power and opportunities for the warlord are widely understood and have been exhaustively analysed.[11] It is Lary's minutiae on the sociology of the warlord gang and the dislocation of its individual members which may need to be re-discovered and hopefully progressed into a new chapter of understanding. Lary seemed to be on the threshold of explaining some of the behavioural logic of the faction fighters, collectively and individually. Her version of the abandoned military code of conduct and the adoption of ad hoc rules based on personal controlling devices of a much more primitive kind seem to explain some of the cruelty and passion of the Chinese civil wars and today's modern violence. The violence and destruction of the Chinese experience reinforces the pejorative sense of the earlier definition of warlords; it distinguishes the warlord as a negative phenomenon, a scourge on the population that seemed to offer no mitigating benefits.

A New Strategic Era

The Chinese warlord phenomenon was a response to a pattern of decline within the state. The warlords were reactive, they did not try to seize power from the hands of a thriving government as an insurgent might, and with a few exceptions they acted only when the state had become terminally weak. If the determining factor of their existence was the environment, why should the warlords of the 1990s resemble the early Chinese version? Are there not likely to be important differences dictated by the circumstances of Qing dynasty China that were far removed from the 1990s world? In her effort to define the new strategic era, Mary Kaldor compares the 'new wars' of this decade to the 'old wars' of the Clausewitzian paradigm.[12] 'Old wars' were conducted between states and in her model the state was strong, it had achieved a monopoly of violence within its territory, it had eliminated private wars, private armies and civilian militias. There was a separation of war from peace, military from civil and public from private. The armies were professionally officered and raised under the provisions of the state. The armed soldier was distinguished from the civilian by his uniform. There were rules for combat which governed the relationship of the officer to the soldier, the treatment of wounded, the custody of prisoners and the protection of non-combatants. The violence was impersonal, the soldier pressing the trigger did not recognize his target as an individual. After the passion of physical contact in battle was over there was seldom an overriding desire to continue in a cycle of revenge killing. The conflict was contained in time and space.

However the 'new wars' of this decade are an antithesis in every respect. The state has become terminally weakened, its monopoly of violence has disintegrated, state power has declined, its reach has shrunk back to the enclaves around the capital. The professional armies have broken apart and are replaced by private security forces, civilian militias and bandit gangs that recruit child soldiers. The rules and distinctions have disappeared. The vast majority of the casualties are civilians. The armed man no longer wears a uniform, there are no frontlines, no separations of civil from military, state from private and war from peace. To some extent the civil wars in China reflected these conditions. Many of the characteristics of 'new war' flowed from the weakness of the state, and in the case of China the failing Qing dynasty had also collapsed with plenty of evidence of the same pervasive violence that overwhelmed the separations of war from peace and civil from military. The difference between the 1911 warlord and the 1990 warlord was dictated by the environment beyond the local conflict zone, it was the difference between the 1911 world and the 1990 world.

For the commander of a warring band who had to move and operate freely beyond the reach of the government of the host state in which he was based, the most significant change was that the world had become increasingly harnessed to the purposes of organized society. It was impossible for the new warlord to be in isolation, there was no longer a space or a wilderness which could also be a refuge. In a physical sense there were fewer wild and unreachable areas within a state and in an intangible sense there was less cultural space, less separation between states. Another dimension of global compression in the last 30 years has been the intensive developments in electronics, transport technology and the use of space. There are more than 200 communications satellites in the sky today.[13] The warlord in the war zone in Zaire is only a phone call away from the broker in Wall Street. The voters in Islington can see on a daily basis what is happening in the streets of Pristina. A surge of communications of every kind seemed to be dragging individuality away from the state, away from the distinct communities and ethnic groups towards a global culture – at its worst an American culture, personified by the Marlboro cowboy in his jeans. Some saw particularism and identity politics as a local reaction to these stresses.[14] The physical nature of the land and the dynamics of urban development were also changing. In conflict areas of sub-Saharan Africa there has been a general migration of the displaced population towards the township areas.[15] Densely populated cities expanded to become conurbations which continued to grow, crossing borders and spanning waterways as they have in the Niger delta, in the Hong Kong–Shenzen–Canton economic zones and in the convergence of European populations in urban areas from Southampton to Essen.

During the 1970s many newly emerged nations fell into debt. In some cases their already fragile economies were disrupted by civil conflict, others were weakened by the collapse of the price of their exports. Debts attracted huge loans which had to be repaid on a regular basis. It is impossible to explain in a complete sense the enormous importance of these developments in this essay except to emphasize the most significant results as they relate to the understanding of warlords. The combination of loan repayment obligations and the diminishing value of the state assets removed executive power from the governments of the nation-states. National institutions such as trade unions, parliaments and the media were supplanted by international influences exercised by transnational corporations, international broadcasting agencies, the global currency market and international development agencies. Even the most intimate responsibilities of the state for law and order, welfare, education and health were now subjected to international scrutiny. Another consequence of this crisis was to widen the gap between the rich and the poor. In sub-Saharan African nations, GDP decreased from an average of 14 per cent of that enjoyed by most industrialized states to 5–8 per cent.[16] It was now possible for a more globalized society to see with great clarity the scale of inequality, the enormous wealth of the rich nations and the wretchedness of the poor. The concept of a global market place touched the warlord and his immediate environment. The speed and volume of capital flows from one country to another had no antecedent in the old strategic paradigm. Electronic money at the rate of more than a trillion dollars each day now passed from one side of the world to another at the click of a mouse, destabilizing the solid economies of one state in favour of a market trend in another.[17] Some felt that a global community which condoned the inequality that resulted from free markets, which exposed the weakest to the mercies of volatile economies, must also expect that the most deprived elements of that society would in due course find a way of striking back.[18]

The New War Zone

The new manifestation of the warlord emerged gradually before the end of the Cold War as local faction leaders adapted their role in longstanding conflict areas such as Burma, Colombia, Cambodia, Afghanistan and parts of Sub-Saharan Africa to meet the changing environment. The dramatic end of the bi-polar strategic era and the swift collapse of the Soviet empire accelerated these changes. New states such as Georgia, Tajikistan and Moldova were from their debut sickly bodies weakened by identity politics and collapsing infrastructures. Yugoslavia, already growing weaker and weaker in the late 1980s, now fell apart under the stress of Milosovic's messages of violence and sectarianism. In sub-Saharan Africa extreme poverty and the removal of superpower interest accelerated the collapse of terminally weakened states. Each of these conflict zones had its individual characteristics, its own versions of humanitarian disasters and the collapse of power. But in most cases there were also the common factors of extreme poverty, massive civil displacement, huge civilian casualty figures and a state government whose writ had gradually shrunk back to the capital city. It was in the spaces created by this withdrawal of power, in the no-go areas, that the new warlords appeared. The 1990s warlord was responding to a new field of global pressures, opportunities and stresses. Broadly speaking his traditionally negative role in society remained largely unchanged, he was still the hyena of conflict zone, lacking the courage or the long-term commitment to confront the strong and instead, preying off the weak and sickly, ensuring his survival by living within a territory that he could secure in a military sense. But in his new environment he could no longer ignore the attractions of global compression and its tendency to reach into the sanctuary of his territory.

A characteristic of the post-Cold War era was the greatly increased civilian presence and involvement of every kind. Statistics since the 1914–18 War showed a steady inversion from a vast majority of military rather than civilian casualties, to the present era, when civil casualties are proportionally enormous in comparison to the military[19] (except in the isolated statistic of the Iran–Iraq war). To a much greater extent than before the control of the civilian population was a primary objective for the warlord. He would remove the element of the population that might succour his opponents and surround himself with friendly communities. The forcible removal or extermination of the opposing elements of the civil population institutionalized the casual violence which in the Chinese context had been so destructive. There was also a greatly increased international presence. On the whole the new warlords (as opposed to their rank and file) were remarkably astute in their relations with international military organizations. They were usually smart enough to sense the possibility of retribution even if they molested apparently unarmed but uniformed observers. Apart from the fairly well known and highly attributable cases where international observers were taken and beaten or executed, there were few incidents of physical conflict between warlords and international military observers.[20]

Another dimension of the new conflict zone was the hugely increased involvement of international emergency relief and long-term development programmes. The warlords had less respect for international agencies that had to operate in territory they controlled. Not only were they extremely adept at seizing the cargoes that were useful, but in many cases they did it in a way that encouraged the flow of relief to continue. In the Horn of Africa warlords even organized sub-units of their factions to interface with the aid communities which were 'versed in the aid-speak of empowerment, capacity building and civil society.'[21] This rapacious approach towards the international relief and development agencies included sacrosanct organizations like the Red Cross and the UN. The humanitarian community, which had to some extent emerged from the Cold War traditions of a regulated battlefield in which armies respected non-combatants, was initially shocked and caught off-guard by this development. It confronted their neutral status and moral position which had previously elevated them from the military imbroglios and protected their activities. The warlord had involved them, their options for neutrality were reduced; not only were they a key element of the solution but now also part of the problem.

Another distinction of the new warlords was the nature of their military activities . In China, where there was a great deal of intensive war-fighting between armed factions and government forces, the threat of combat meant that if a warlord wished to survive he had to organize his faction as an effective military unit. The more successful warlords had understood this and adopted the benefits of the European military reforms and technology. As a result, in the documentation and photography that survived them they had the appearance and structure of military forces that could engage effectively in combat. However post-Cold War irregular forces do not have uniformly developed war-fighting capabilities. At the 'exceptionally professional' end of a spectrum could be the rebel forces of the Eritrean civil war whose military organization was legendary. However they barely fit the definition of a warlord's faction. The majority of the warlord forces of sub-Saharan Africa lie at the opposing end of the spectrum and do not have the attitude or structure of effective military units. They rely instead on their frightening behaviour and appearance, and their combat effectiveness is largely symbolic. They are organized around the magnetism of their leaders which implies they do not have to rely on a rigorously maintained war-fighting capability for their survival. Why not? Perhaps because the forces at the lower end of the spectrum spent little time in a posture of military deployment or on force-on-force engagements at the intensity of ammunition and logistic expenditure that would approach the definition of war-fighting. To trained military observers that were involved locally, they did not have the organization or demeanour of units determined to take part in serious fighting. Their appearance and aggression were in the style of a force that did not expect to be contested.[22] Certainly they were menacing and killed many people but very seldom in the heat of a conflict with another armed force. In many cases a warlord conceded to the presence of a challenging warlord by withdrawing out of harm's way rather than becoming engaged in the mutual destruction of combat. Observers have suggested that this careful avoidance of a mutual engagement was dictated by a mutual recognition of each other's territory and resource exploitation interests.[23]

Western politicians and communicators however often failed to see that the warlord could nevertheless be very dangerous in other ways and was unlikely to expose himself to intervention forces in a war-fighting confrontation. The warlord has many other options for the use of force. Firm military action by international forces against warlord bands has had mixed results. A well-organized warlord was capable of absorbing a defeat in one district and executing his revenge at another venue. General Rose explained the problem in the Bosnia context. He maintained that unless there was a uniformity of purpose right across all the elements of the international presence it was dangerous for the military to go on the offensive against a particular faction while other agencies in the same area were still operating under fragile neutrality arrangements. Furthermore Aideed's offensive in Mogadishu[24] and Taylor's campaign against ECOMOG troops in Liberia proved that in some cases warlords were capable of concerted military action against intervention forces.

At the lowest level of the warlord gang, in a group of 10–20 faction fighters, the gang culture of the post-Cold War era was not vastly different from the Chinese antecedents. The faction fighters had the same predatory life style, preying on the weak so long as there could be no threat of reprisal. There was also the same brutality in their relationships to each other and to civilians. In 1993 Professor Delvin Walker, an agriculturist, found himself trapped in the National Patriotic Front of Liberia (NPFL)-held town of Gbarnger in Liberia. Here he watched the new recruits being indoctrinated and brutalized at the NPFL training centre. His observations provided the basis for UNOMIL's rehabilitation strategy.[25] The effects of this treatment were similar to those observed by Lary in China – the brutality of their superiors licensed the young recruits' own brutality towards civilians. Recruits in some West African factions were also forced to reject the influence of their traditional family and village hierarchy. In some cases indoctrination required them to commit atrocities against their own communities. In many instances recruits had to be renamed as if to throw off the ties of family tradition and adopt warrior names.[26] This detachment from their social context probably made them more effective as fighters but less responsible for their terrible conduct. The new warlords also committed the same atrocities – rape, vandalism and serial looting – as the China warlords before them.

Assessment of the Motives of the New Warlord

So far there have been two phases of assessment of the 1990s version of warlordism. In the first phase, the world media using a similarly sensational approach as the correspondents in China 80 years before them, reacted with outrage to the activities of warring factions around the world. 'Must It Go On?' demanded Time Magazine in red letters on its front cover across a photograph of semi-naked Muslims behind the wires of a Serbian detention camp.[27] The initial response was that the warlords were mostly mindless barbarians bent on dragging the population that lived in the areas they controlled back to a dark age of tribalism. West Africa was reverting to the Africa of the Victorian atlas, its government withering away, replaced by the rise of tribal and regional domains, the unchecked spread of disease and the growing pervasiveness of war.[28] This first phase of assessment was, not surprisingly, fairly superficial. It was largely an emotive response to the horrible images of warlordism that were being widely used, not only by the media but also by the relief agencies, as a funding expedient on the media.

The second phase of assessment, which continues to unfold, is led by the group, mainly of humanitarians, writing under the banner of the 'economy of civil war'[29] In some cases individuals had a direct experience of the subject, having had to work with, survive and try to reconcile their humanitarian agenda with the activities of the warlord operating in his own environment where he could disregard almost all the pressures and negotiating ploys of the international community. It is hard to do justice to the 'economies of civil war' writers in the space of this essay, which addresses a wider canvas. Perhaps, because of the comparative homogeneity of their experience, they largely agreed on several key issues. Firstly the warlord was not a mindless barbarian returning an ungoverned population back to a tribal phase in their evolution. The warlord might be a negative phenomenon, perhaps an evil phenomenon, but there was nothing mindless or irrational about his behaviour. He followed a ruthless logic in his activities. He was a product of his time and of his environment, intensely modern, not regressive or backward looking.[30] Second, the warlord was above all exploiting the same global market place and universal culture that increasingly dominated organized society in the world at large. It was this overwhelming commercial motive, this international dimension of his operations that distinguished the new warlord from his Chinese antecedents. The proposition that warlords were not (using Keegan's definition)[31] *true* warriors who would stand and fight in a disciplined, Clausewitzian manner, but *real* warriors who followed a Cossack fighting tradition and saw war as an opportunity for profit and as a way of life, was not new. What was new about the new warlords, and was exhaustively reported by the second phase of writers, was that their commercial agenda had become extremely sophisticated, in some cases involving huge international trading accounts. The warlord was still an extractive presence within his territory, his fighters continued to loot in a physical sense for personal and logistic purposes. However in many cases an additional dimension of a warlord's wealth was derived from much larger deals in which the state's natural resources – gold, diamonds, gemstones, hardwood timber, fisheries, latex, even bananas and coffee – were traded out onto the international markets. The new warlord was now able to gain wealth far in excess of the day-to-day spoils that were the expectations of a traditional plunderer. Warlords were not alone in exploiting these resources – private security companies, elements of international forces and even rulers of weak states were also involved. The value of these unseen trading accounts and the relative ease with which most of these commodities could be removed and transacted, influenced the size and configuration of a warlord's war-fighting needs and dictated his priorities for survival.

Conclusions

The warlord is a virus of the new strategic era. In the same way that the political and social conditions of the 1950s and 1960s encouraged a wide variety of insurgent movements, so the warlord is the logical consequence of the post-Cold War developments. The combinations of failing states, societies in transition, globalized markets, easy communications, improved transport technology and unprotected national resources have propagated new plunderers. The warlord faction in the definition of this study is not the same as the Mafia gang: although the latter increasingly takes advantage of the same global market place, the Mafia in most cases live as citizens of a free society and their freedom to move and communicate is not guaranteed by their own military strength but by the institutions of their host state.[32] Nor is the warlord to be confused with the insurgent: the former deals with the local population in a rapine and predatory manner, the latter has to use the population as its resource. The insurgent may use some of the trading techniques of the warlord but if he really is an insurgent with a long-term political agenda, he will return to a political end game in which he will have to submit himself to the electorate. The warlord as defined above is a wholly negative phenomenon. There is, so far, no mitigating Robin Hood tendency which might show him to be a redresser of global inequality. It is therefore, inconsistent to uphold the values of civil society and at the same time define the warlord in the anodyne circumlocutions of the politically correct as a 'non-state actor'. The warlord is a warlord, until there is evidence to the contrary; it is a way of life that confronts every aspiration of civil society. If we are for civil society we cannot condone the warlord by using soft focus expressions to describe his status in the war zone.

The international community has not yet developed a language and an approach to tackle the warlord; its political leaders are influenced by a deeply rooted statist culture which cannot see the crises of the new strategic era in their elemental terms. Instead of addressing the realities of the war zone, they create an alternative version of the crisis which is politically more comfortable in which warlords are disarmed, faction fighters return to their factories, elections are freely and fairly held and soon after the troops return home. This version of reality fails above all to understand the significance of the warlord, his urge to survive, his network of vested interests and his imperative to resist a peace process at all costs. The international community must take a more robust and inquisitive approach towards warlords, its response should be graduated and targeted. It is still the case that heads of state and the barons of the humanitarian world can afford to take an absolute and condemnatory view of warlords, whereas at the lowest level of their organizations the soldier and the aid worker at the hostile road block have to be much more accommodating. However this does not excuse the international community from making a greater effort to cut off the warlord's access to the global market place, proscribing his trading accounts and blacklisting his exports. To some extent this has been done successfully in the case of illicit diamond traders in Angola. A much more systemic approach is needed that would drive the warlord out of the lucrative markets into a more competitive area of the grey economy where returns are lower, competition is more dangerous, life is harsher and peace settlements seem more attractive.

NOTES

1. This provisional definition is derived from Duffield, 'Post –Modern Conflict, Aid Policy and Humanitarian Conditionality', a discussion paper prepared for DFID, July 1997, p.18.
2. John Keegan, *A History of Warfare,* London: Hutchison, 1993, p.207.
3. Diana Lary, *Warlord Soldiers,* Cambridge University Press 1985, p.5.
4. Edward Mccord, *The Power of the Gun,* University of California Press, London, 1993, p.3.
5. Franz Michael, 'Military Organisation and Power Structure of China during the Taiping Rebellion', *Pacific Historical Journal,* Vol.18, November 1949, in Mccord (n.2 above), p.7.
6. Lary (n.3 above), p.7.
7. Lary (n.3 above), p.80.
8. Zhu Zhixin, *Zhu Zhixin Ji,* in Lary (n.3 above) p.80.
9. Lary (n.3 above), p.88.
10. Mao Tse-tung, Vol.2, *Selected Works,* International Publishers. New York 1954, p.273.
11. Steven Ratner and Gerald Helman, 'Saving Failed States' *Foreign Policy,* No.89, Winter 1992–93, introduced this tidal wave of papers.
12. Mary Kaldor, *New and Old Wars,* Polity Press, Cambridge, 1999.
13. Anthony Giddens, BBC Reith lectures 1999, Lecture I: 'Globalisation'.
14. Kaldor, (n.12 above), p.11.
15. Alao, Mackinlay and Olonosakin, *Peacekeepers, Politicians and Warlords,* United Nations University Press Tokyo, 1999, p.48.
16. Eric Hobsbawn, *Age of Extremes,* London: Abacus, 1997, pp.422–6.
17. Giddens (n.13 above), p.2.
18. *The Observer,* Editorial, 2 Jan 2000, p.24.
19. Raimo Vayrynen, 'The Age of Humanitarian Emergencies' UNU WIDER, Series No.25, Helsinki 1996, p.21.
20. In Rwanda, Liberia Cambodia and less attributably in Tajikistan, UNMOs, and in the case of Liberia, ECOMOG soldiers, were executed, murdered, beaten and humiliated. These are well documented exceptions to the tendency that warlords did not as a rule attack international military observers.
21. Mark Duffield, 'Post-Modern Conflict, Warlords, Post Adjustment States and Private Protection', *Journal of Civil Wars,* April 1998.
22. Alao *et al.* (n.15 above), p.46.
23. David Keen, The Economic Functions of Violence in Civil Wars, IISS Adelphi Paper 320, 1998, pp.18–21.
24. For a concise account of both campaigns see Oliver Ramsbotham and Tom Woodhouse, *Encyclopaedia of International Peacekeeping Operations,* ABC-CLIO, Oxford, 1999, pp.226 and 139.
25. Alao *et al.* (n.15 above) p.74. See note 9.
26. Sam Gbaydee Doe, 'Former Child Soldiers In Liberia', *Relief and Rehabilitation Network,* No.12, November 1998, pp.1–3.
27. *Time,* 17 August 1992.
28. Robert Kaplan, 'The Coming Anarchy', *The Atlantic Monthly,* Vol.272, No.2, February 1994, p.48.

29. For the most recent collection of these authors see: M. Berdal and D. Malone (eds.), 'Greed and Grievance: Economic Agendas in Civil Wars', Colorado: Lynne Rienner, 2000. Authors of chapters include: D. Keen, W. Reno, M. Duffield, S. Porteous, D. Shearer and T. Farer.
30. Duffield (n.21 above), p.16.
31. Keegan (n.2 above), pp.9 and 16.
32. J. Lloyd, 'The Godfathers Go Global', *New Statesman*, 20 December 1999.

Sharpening the Weapons of Peace: Peace Support Operations and Complex Emergencies

PHILIP WILKINSON

In 1997 Kofi Annan, the Secretary General of the United Nations, wrote a paper called 'Peace Operations and the United Nations: Preparing for the Next Century'. In it, he stated: 'To stand still while the world moves forward is to slide helplessly backward. The United Nations must face challenges which do not fit into a neat peacekeeping package: the volatile, so called "grey area" operations;' and 'If consent carries with it certain rewards, and the failure to consent carries certain costs, this obviously affects the decision as to whether or not consent will be granted.' He then went on to describe a multidisciplinary approach requiring 'the right force structure to be able to carry out the mandate and to protect the operation'. Such an approach would use a combination of 'inducing consent' and 'coercive inducement'.[1]

The aim of this analysis is to discuss how the international response community, in particular the military, has developed a doctrine in response to the challenge posed by the Secretary General. It will first address the challenge of coordinating civil and military activities before discussing the specifics of the new military doctrine.

Establishing the Conceptual Context: Historical Background

The formulation of military doctrine for operations involving troops, directly or indirectly on behalf of the United Nations has been through several significant stages of development since the late 1980s. In the Cold War era, with the exception of the Korean War, UN forces were principally involved in what has become known as traditional peacekeeping operations. While not specifically mentioned in the UN Charter peacekeeping operations, involving both unarmed military observers and peacekeeping forces, were deployed in the aftermath of an inter-state conflict to monitor and facilitate a peace agreement. The parties to the conflict were relatively responsible and judgements concerning their commitment to the peace process could be made with some certainty. In such circumstances, the requirement to use force was limited to self-defence, in expectation that the parties would maintain the peace process without the exercise of military power. While generally benign, with the exceptions of the Lebanon and Congo, such operations were relatively straightforward to manage and could be delegated from UN HQ often directly to a military Force Commander in theatre. For more complex operations UN HQ might deploy a Special Representative of the Secretary General (SRSG) as the Head of Mission. At that, stage, the permanent members of the UN Security Council did not become directly involved in UN activities, the 1950–53 war in Korea being the one major exception. Apart from reasons of scale, this was also due to concerns for both politically perceived partiality in the ongoing ideological struggle and because countering Warsaw Pact aggression in Europe dominated the military thinking and doctrine of the NATO powers. In addition, many of the European colonial powers (up until the 1960s) were also engaged in countering insurgencies in their various dependencies.

Changing Strategic Environment – Complex Emergencies

The end of the Cold War and the removal of regional superpower interests and the associated ideological pressures allowed new local and regional conflicts to emerge, often characterized by the fragmentation of sovereign states. The academic community, humanitarian workers, UN policy staff and military planners have come to refer to these kinds of conflicts as 'complex emergencies' or 'complex political emergencies'. John Mackinlay has defined them as follows:

> A complex emergency is a humanitarian disaster that occurs in a conflict zone and is complicated by, or results from, the conflicting interests of warring parties. Its causes are seldom exclusively natural or military: in many cases a marginally subsistent population is precipitated towards disaster by the consequences of militia action… The presence of militias and their interests in controlling and extorting the local population will impede and in some cases seriously threaten relief efforts. In addition to violence against the civilian populations, civilian installations such as hospitals, schools, refugee centers, and cultural sites will become war objectives and may be looted frequently or destroyed.[2]

No longer were ethnic groups within the superpowers' areas limited in their ambitions to gain nation status nor were nations reluctant to challenge the arbitrary lines drawn on colonial maps. As a consequence the number of ethnic and intra-state rather than inter-state conflicts increased and it is estimated that of the 82 conflicts between 1992 and 1995 which involved the loss of over 1,000 lives, all but three were intra-state conflicts or civil wars.

Such conflicts are frequently based on latent disputes between intermingled ethnic groups which are then cynically resurrected and exploited by sub-state actors, warlords and bandits as a means to gain aggrandisement and power. Fuelled by the availability of large quantities of modern weaponry, such conflicts are usually conducted by irregular and undisciplined troops who are often indistinguishable from the people at large. In such circumstances, it is all too often the ordinary people of the opposing ethnic group who become the targets of the militia gangs and human rights abuses, including incidents of genocide may become wide spread. These largely intra-state conflicts all too often result in the collapse of social cohesion and the state infrastructures necessary to sustain life.[3]

When such circumstances are either the cause or consequence of a natural disaster such as a famine, the result may be catastrophic in terms of human suffering. As a consequence it became evident to even the most conservative military analysts that intervention into such high risk and uncertain environments as Cambodia, Somalia, Bosnia, Rwanda and Kosovo would pose challenges more complex than the more conventional military operations or traditional peacekeeping. As Kofi Annan stated, 'the prerequisites of traditional peacekeeping will not exist in the majority of cases. If the UN has no other method at its disposal, it will become largely irrelevant.'[4] It is perhaps because the UN still has no other more robust method of operations at its disposal than traditional PEACEKEEPING, that regional organizations and military alliances have felt it necessary to become engaged in such as Bosnia (NATO, I/SFOR) and Liberia and Sierra Leone (ECOMOG).

A New Response Paradigm: Peace Support Operations in Complex Emergencies

When conflict occurs between states with sovereign control over their populations and armies, the problems of conflict resolution are relatively clear cut and rest largely at the political level. A functioning state can generally be treated as a responsible and unitary actor. However, this is rarely the case in intra-state conflicts and complex emergencies where there may be no apparent national control or coordinating infrastructure above the local level. On the other hand, what might appear as random atrocities by militia gangs may be in reality part of a deliberate and orchestrated national campaign against another ethnic group. Whatever the circumstances, it is likely that crime will be endemic and indistinguishable from the other various and diverse sources of social tensions and violence. Identification of a counter strategy may therefore prove highly problematic. That this counter-strategy or doctrine will need to be multidimensional and multifunctional, may also challenge the conception that there can ever be a military solution to what is essentially a political problem, and this in itself may prove highly contentious for certain national military forces.

In a war fighting operation, political issues could generally be dealt with at the strategic level, allowing the Military Force Commander to be the principal in theatre operational commander and to focus on military matters – the military campaign plan being the major functional activity. However, in a Peace Support Operation (PSO) a wide range of political, diplomatic, economic, humanitarian and other considerations are drawn down to the operational level and will need to be coordinated and harmonized at that level into some form of strategic framework or mission plan, if scarce resources are not to be frittered away needlessly. In such profoundly political circumstances in which military activities will be but one functional line or area of operations, it would be entirely inappropriate for the Military Force Commander to be the in-theatre Head of Mission. In a complex PSO in which the military will be but one of many actors and the one, who if the mission is to be successful, will spend the least amount of time in theatre, the Head of Mission should be a political representative of the authorizing political body. He has to manage the interactions between external political activities and the in theatre tactical actions of all military and civilian agencies. The Head of Mission will also have to manage the reality that just as political decisions may impact directly at the tactical level so may tactical actions, viewed instantaneously in national capitals, directly influence political policy decisions.

Complex emergencies have their origins in a myriad of economic, cultural or ethical factors but most prevalent of all are hunger and poverty. However, such crises do not spring up overnight but will inevitably occur where local problems and scarcities are beyond the ability of the local authorities to resolve, and a lack of funds and resources have limited the effectiveness of donor funded development programmes. Should development and assistance programmes not be successful and the humanitarian and political situation deteriorate it will be necessary to deploy a diplomatic conflict prevention strategy to try to resolve and de-escalate the situation before attitudes harden and ethnic disputes become rife. Such a strategy may require the military to posture as a political demonstration of resolve or to be engaged in such activities as security sector reform projects. Early investment in a conflict prevention strategy will generally prove more cost effective in the longer term. Should conflict prevention fail, and there is the political will to intervene with emergency aid or military forces, the symptoms to be addressed are generally defined in terms of human rights abuses or breaches of International Humanitarian Law. To address the symptoms and redress the underlying causes of such a

FIGURE 1
HYPOTHETICAL MISSION PLAN FOR PEACE SUPPORT OPERATIONS

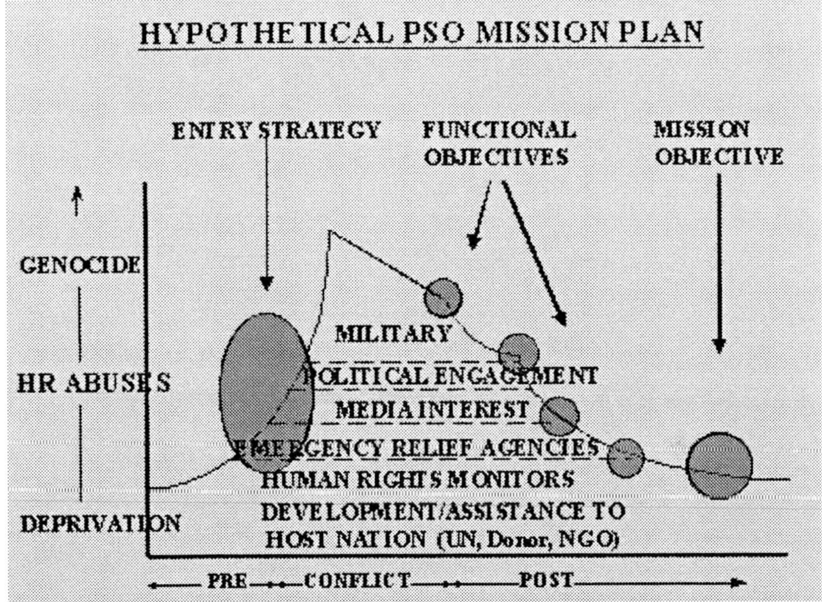

complex emergency involves the development of a composite response strategy and doctrine, which embraces the many different development, emergency aid, diplomatic and military agencies which may become engaged in an *ad hoc* and incremental manner.

This *ad hoc* and incremental engagement is illustrated in Figure 1. The vertical axis represents the symptoms of the crises and the horizontal axis time in terms of pre-conflict, conflict and post-conflict, although these will overlap and in reality the whole process may be cyclical. The overlay of functional activities and agencies is indicative of a typical incremental and *ad hoc* engagement. These should not be viewed as separate activities because as each engagement occurs it will influence, and in turn be influenced by those agencies already engaged. In many ways, Figure 1 can also be viewed as a portrayal of the strategic structure necessary to formulate a mission plan. The dotted lines represent functional lines of operation which need to be focused on the mission objective and the functional objectives as stepping stones to achieving that mission objective.

From Complex Emergencies to Complex Intervention

Having been involved in the definition of the political parameters, functional objectives and desired political end-state in the development of the mandate, it is the responsibility of the Head of Mission to develop the detail of the mission plan. To do so requires not only the assistance of the military force commander but also representation from all functional lines of operation and the major involved agencies in the field. Unlike purely military campaigns, PSOs do not have a clearly defined start or culmination, respectively predicated on entry and military victory. PSO mission plans require an entry strategy that coordinates the *ad hoc* and incremental engagement of a plethora of agencies from the international community. Without an entry strategy, indicated in Figure 1, to coordinate the activities of those entering theatre with those already engaged, the operation is likely to be unbalanced from the outset. Such coordination, which may have to transcend national and international barriers, should ideally synchronize and synergize activities but at the least should attempt to minimize any potential negative effects that might occur if no coordination was to take place. Without positive and robust political leadership and a clear and unambiguous operational directive, operational activities may run counter to higher political intent.

Military activities in PSOs are designed to conclude conflict by conciliation among the competing parties or ethnic groups, rather than a short-term and superficial termination of the conflict by force. A stable settlement, not military victory, is the ultimate measure of success. Military activities will generally focus on alleviating the symptoms of the crisis while creating the conditions in which other diplomatic and humanitarian agencies can more ably redress the underlying causes of the conflict. This may involve reconciling the competing groups, the achievement of conditions conducive to civil development and assisting the indigenous population to create a self-sustaining peace. The achievement of the conditions for an effective transfer of responsibilities to the civilian agencies and the indigenous population will require close coordination among the principle staff and functional commanders of the mission. Success and the achievement of the exit criteria for the military force will require that commanders at all levels seek to grasp and maintain the initiative and create operational tempo. In purely military terms, success may be measured by a reduction of the military profile and the handover of the security function, possibly to an international police force or the indigenous authorities. In the context of a complex, multinational operation empowered to use enforcement measures, carried out by NATO or a coalition of willing states, military success may be determined by the creation of conditions for the handover of the operation to a UN peacekeeping force. A lowering of the military operational profile or the cessation of military activities, however, is unlikely to signal the end of the operation, simply a switch in main effort to a civilian peacebuilding activities. The definition of those conditions that constitute military success must be specified in the mandate and operational directive, and refined in the Head of Mission's estimate and mission plan.

At the operational level, the mission plan should be developed from the estimate of the situation produced by the Head of Mission's planning staff and principal advisors, both military and civilian. This mission plan should coordinate and direct the actions of all involved agencies, including the military force, towards the desired end-state. This plan should also specify those mechanisms required for detailed coordination, such as the establishment of communication networks and exchanges of liaison officers. The plan should allocate agencies and resources to lines of operation and specify the coordination mechanisms that would allow the main effort to switch from one line of operation, or agency, to another as the mission develops. Tactical coordination can best be effected by the establishment of committees or centres for dialogue, called civil military operation centres, and trying to ensure, as far as possible, that the operational areas of responsibility of engaged military formations and units coincide with implementing partners and overlap those of the indigenous authorities. It is by the facilitation of dialogue rather than attempts to establish military command style relationships that coordination is best effected.

Humanitarian agencies, including human rights groups and diplomatic offices, will have identified the early symptoms of a complex emergency and using a variety of conflict prevention and peace maintenance strategies, will have attempted resolution some time before the situation attracts the attention of the international media and some form of wider political, emergency and military response. However, should the situation degenerate and human rights violations increase beyond the immediate capacity of the deployed agencies and NGOs to resolve, and the situation escalate into a full-scale and conflict-related disaster, a wider composite response may be required. Having redressed the most obvious symptoms that is by no means the end of the operation. All too frequently insufficient effort and resources are allocated to the reconciliation and peacebuilding processes that are necessary to create those conditions which are self-sustaining and acceptable to the indigenous population. It is this failure to allocate resources to the post conflict peacebuilding phase, to oversee the return of refugees, to reform the security sector and to assist in the establishment of a workable form of government that causes the majority of operations to end in stalemate from which the engaged military and civilian agencies can not disengage. Described in this way there are therefore three broad and overlapping phases to any PSO:

Phase 1: A conflict-prevention phase designed to maintain the peace.

Phase 2: An emergency response phase which overlays emergency relief and military operations on those development and preventative strategies already in operation.

Phase 3: A post-conflict reconciliation and peacebuilding phase designed to create a self-sustaining peace such that outside assistance is no longer necessary.

A doctrine which embraces the actions of so many diverse players and acknowledges the necessity to reconcile the often competing agendas of development programmes, emergency aid, military and political objectives, and the objectives of long-term conflict resolution, can only respond effectively to the intimate control of an in-theatre political Head of Mission. Such a doctrine provides a useful means of examining the incremental engagement of agencies in time, set against the various political and tactical requirements of the civilian agencies and military forces in theatre. From a military perspective this involves a hierarchical examination of the linkages and necessary conduits between the military and involved civilian agencies in the transitions between Phases 1 and 2 and Phases 2 and 3. However, before military doctrine can be designed for such requirements there are some fundamental issues of policy which need to be addressed.

Before doctrine can be defined for any transition between phases there needs to be a common definition of tasks and agreement as to which agency should lead and finance what task. Within the one-mission plan, agreement as to which agency should be responsible for what task is essential even before discussions concerning the management of transition and a transfer of responsibility can be negotiated between agencies. Unfortunately, within the international military community there is no common understanding of which roles and tasks the military can and should perform in a complex multi-agency operation. At one end of the spectrum, there are those who would take on military governorship or control of specific areas of governance. At the other end are those who consider that the direct provision of functions and resources leads to dependency and who therefore restrict themselves to a supportive role only, or at most a partnership. Those who favour a facilitative role tend to regard the promotion of good civil–military relations as core military business rather than an extraordinary military activity to be conducted by specialists. The allocation of tasks and division of labour and other resources should be addressed at the outset of the planning process. Unfortunately, the tendency is that when the military has deployed and created the secure conditions in which civilian agencies can commence the reconciliation and reconstruction programmes, international interest and funding for the essential elements of peacebuilding tend to diminish. Consequently, the military find themselves drawn into areas for which they are not appropriately equipped and which other civilian agencies could perhaps perform more cost-effectively.

The Conduct of Peace Support Operations

Peace Support Operation (PSO) was a term first used by the military to cover both peacekeeping and peace enforcement operations, but is now used more widely to embrace in addition those other peace-related operations which include conflict prevention, peacemaking, peacebuilding and humanitarian assistance.[5] The military doctrine in which the concept is defined was issued in 1998 as *Joint Warfare Publication 3.05*, and replaced the earlier concept of *Wider Peacekeeping* (issued in 1994).[6]

All military operations are conducted with a degree of restraint, be that only an adherence to the Law of Armed Conflict or Geneva Conventions. What makes PSOs distinct is their impartial nature. PSOs are neither in support of nor against a particular party, but are conducted in an impartial and even-handed manner. Rather than achieve a short-term military victory, PSOs are designed to enforce compliance with the operation's mandate and to create a secure environment in which civilian agencies can rebuild the infrastructure necessary to create a self-sustaining peace. PSO Force actions are based upon judgements of the degree of compliance and/or non-compliance of the parties with the operation's mandate and not against any bias or predetermined designation. The conduct of a PSO force should be analogous to that of a third-party referee and should remain that way even if only one party consistently fails to comply with the mandate and suffers the consequences. In peacekeeping (PK) mode, the level of consent is such that the referee requires relatively few resources. In peace enforcement (PE), however, the referee requires enough resources to enforce compliance with the mandate, no matter how much the parties may object. But the referee must not become a party to the conflict. Referee status requires a very different approach from that of a player whose ambition is to defeat the other team or teams. The operational plans for I/SFOR and KFOR all directed military operations to enforce compliance in an impartial and even-handed manner.

The distinction between PSOs, including PE, on the one hand and other enforcement actions or war with a designated enemy, on the other, will be determined in an examination of the mandate and desired political end-state. A PSO mandate, including one for PE, should not designate an enemy, neither should it relate to military victory. However, a military enforcement operation with a designated enemy, rather than a peace enforcement operation, may attempt to change the correlation of local forces and impose a solution by force alone. Such a partial enforcement operation may need to be the precursor to a PSO. A PSO mandate will generally refer to such issues as the restoration and maintenance of peace and security, and support for the principles of the UN and international humanitarian law. Mixing and muddling humanitarian and incompatible warlike objectives in the same mandate, as was the case in the Kosovo air campaign, will generally result in an incoherent and unattainable political end-state. In PSOs, the active participation of the parties in the formulation and achievement of the political end-state will be essential. As military operations move towards war, the need to engage the parties in dialogue will diminish until ultimately the strategic objectives specified in the mandate and political end-state could be imposed on the parties without consultation.

When consent and compliance for a PSO is high, PE and PK forces will adopt similar approaches. Both PK and PE are designed to achieve the same end-state, that is, a secure environment and a self-sustaining peace. However, in the first instance a PK force bases its operations on the consent of the parties and is not capable of exercising force beyond that required for self-defence. Such a force would find its freedom of action considerably more constrained than a combat capable PE force, should consent be uncertain or withdrawn. A lightly armed PK force, therefore, should not be given, or attempt to conduct, enforcement tasks which may provoke hostile reactions that are beyond its ability to manage and that may escalate to war. Only a PE force prepared for combat and capable of effective coercion should be deployed into a potentially hostile environment.

Force Posture

It is generally agreed in most military doctrines for PSOs that there are essentially two different profiles and approaches that a military force can adopt and these will be determined by the higher political authority in the development of the operational directive. Should diplomatic, economic and other preventative measures fail, and a military response be considered necessary, there are a number of vital issues to be considered which will decide the nature of the military intervention. All involved implementing partners and agencies should make a thorough estimate of the operational environment. Major factors to be considered will be the likely level of consent of the belligerent parties to any intervening military force, their attitudes to each other, the incidence of human rights abuses and the resource requirements of peacebuilding. If a peace process is in place and it is considered that there is a genuine will and intention to abide by agreements, a PK posture may be appropriate, based on the full and clearly demonstrated consent of the parties. Should consent be uncertain and it be considered that certain parties may renege on, or ignore the agreements, a combat capable enforcement posture will be more appropriate. I/SFOR in Bosnia and KFOR in Kosovo are examples. If the decision is to deploy a PE capable force, the object to which force is to be applied and the consequent effects of the use of force will need to be balanced with the requirements of the other involved civilian agencies and the achievement of the political end-state. This was particularly pertinent in Kosovo where coordination had to be affected between NATO, the UN, the OSCE and the EU – the four pillars of Kosovo. Should it be considered necessary to conduct operations against a particular party and to change the correlation of forces and impose a solution by force, that operation will be conducted as war, albeit under

FIGURE 2
THE CONCEPTUAL MODEL OF PSO AND WAR

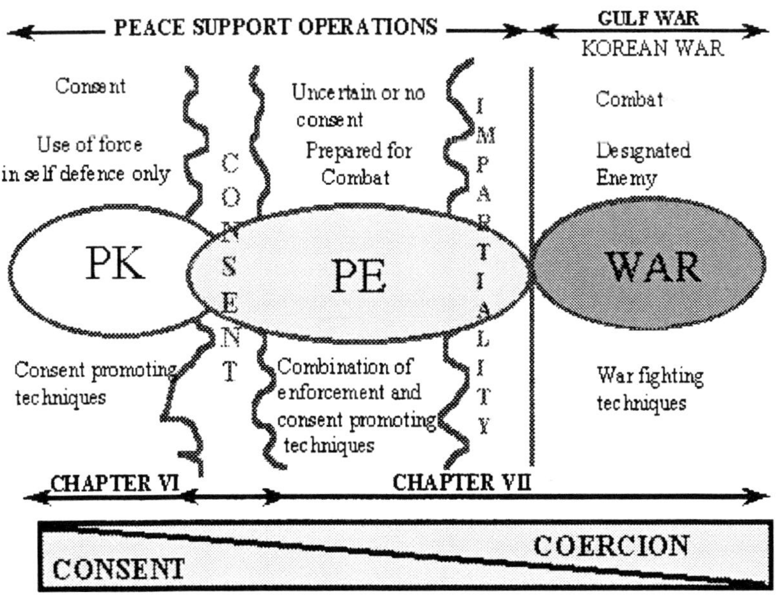

Chapter VII and not as a PSO. The distinction between PSO and war and PK and PE are shown diagrammatically in Figure 2. The air campaign in Kosovo and Serbia can only be described as a war to set the operational conditions for a subsequent PSO. The air campaign has been described as a humanitarian war; however, when concerns over casualties to one's own military forces render innocent civilians as casualties, such actions can hardly be described as war without a declared violation of the Geneva Conventions and certainly cannot be described as humanitarian. If it is considered possible to use force or the threat of force in an impartial manner to create peace, a PSO under Chapter VII will be more appropriate. Should peace rather than military victory be the desired end-state the commitment of resources of various military and non-military natures may be required over a protracted period of time. Paradoxically, however, the timely deployment of a combat capable military force may deter potential opposition and may allow the military force to use other means to enhance compliance and thus to conduct operations on a consensual peacekeeping basis from the outset, while remaining poised to escalate if necessary.

For a PE force, such as IFOR (Bosnia 95/96), which finds on deployment that it is able to lower its operational profile to one more akin to PK, the consent divide is of little immediate significance. For a PE force with robust Rules of Engagement (ROE), such as KFOR, the transition to a PK profile or the exercise of coercion can be left to the judgement of the Head of Mission and Force Commander.

Spectrum of Military Tasks in Peace Support Operations

Multifunctional military PSOs encompass both elements of traditional peacekeeping and new tasks, which may involve both coercion and the application of military force, and the means of persuasive inducement. In broad terms the most effective strategy will be one which builds on, and expands areas in which consent for the PSO and some form of sustainable infrastructure already exists, at the expense of areas where there is little compliance, a breakdown of law and order and no sustainable infrastructure. Military tasks should all be viewed as either supporting or assisting civilian agencies or the local authorities or as aiming to create the security conditions in which they can more ably redress the underlying causes of the complex emergency. The delineation between military tasks and activities and those of civilian agencies may not always be clear; however, the spectrum of likely military tasks is as follows:

- The control and verification of compliance with peace agreements, ceasefire agreements or armistices. The exercise of control and the enforcement of compliance may require combat actions.

- Negotiation and mediation efforts to assist other diplomatic initiatives to persuade the parties to fulfil agreements on peaceful settlements of a conflict.

- Contribution to diplomatic conflict prevention strategies through security sector reform programmes or the deployment of military assets, generally air and maritime, as a form of political signalling.

- Guarantee, or denial of, freedom of movement (FOM). Such operations at the operational level may involve the engagement of military assets in sanctions and embargo operations, and at the tactical level operations to ensure the delivery of aid.

- Conduct, supervise or support mine-clearing and Explosive Ordnance Disposal (EOD). Legally the responsibility to clear mines and other ordnance rests with those who lay them. In the first instance military mine-clearing assets will concentrate on clearing locations and lines of communications to support military operations. Subsequently the military may be tasked with operations in support of the wider operation.

- Demilitarization or demobilization operations, including those involving foreign military personnel. While the PSO force may focus on disarmament, the control of weapons and the training of the rump of the indigenous forces, demilitarization and demobilization will only be durable if it is part of a wider peacebuilding strategy, that is, if there is an infrastructure to sustain those who are demobilized.

- Supporting humanitarian relief and assistance operations to civilian populations, including refugees. The military should only become directly involved in the provision of major humanitarian relief operations when there are no civilian agencies available or when conditions make their employment impractical and as a last resort. Military activities in this area should focus on providing support and assistance to those civilian agencies for which humanitarian activities are their main and principal function.

- Providing support to human rights agencies and organizations such as the CIRCA or Amnesty International, eliminating human rights abuses and supporting the restoration of human rights may be an important role for the military.

- Assisting in planning and monitoring elections.

- The military may be tasked with supporting the restoration of civil order and the rule of law, including the apprehension of war criminals and the provision of evidence to the International Criminal Court. Not all military forces, however, are trained directly for such roles and may only be able to provide a support function to other law enforcement agencies.

- Assisting in the coordination of activities supporting economic rehabilitation and reconstruction. There is always a danger that when resources for peacebuilding are limited and the military directly involve themselves in peacebuilding projects, they inadvertently create a 'dependency culture' that limits other efforts to create conditions that are self-sustaining. However, the military may do a great deal to harmonize their activities with the humanitarian community and indigenous people so as to foster good community relations and to better coordinate activities.

The Timing of Peace Support Operations

Peacekeeping is only likely to be viable in the absence of human rights abuses and when the parties to the conflict are disciplined, responsible and committed to peace. In such circumstances, the deployment of a peace enforcement force might indicate a lack of trust that could prove counter-productive to the achievement of the mission. However, in the unpredictable and uncertain circumstances of a complex emergency an assessment of likely tasks will generally indicate that only a force deployed in a peace enforcement posture will be able to maintain its freedom of action and operate effectively. As military interventions are increasingly in response to complex emergencies, it would appear that the incidence of peace enforcement is set to increase. While early diplomatic and economic engagement in a complex emergency may prove most economic and effective, to quote Kofi Annan, 'The CNN factor tends to mobilize pressure at the peak of the problem – which is to say, at the very moment when effective intervention is most costly, most dangerous and least likely to succeed.'[7] In such circumstances, early engagement designed to create a self-sustaining peace will inevitably require a very considerable and protracted commitment of resources. The commitment of a high level of resources to an early conflict prevention strategy, while it may prove more cost effective in the longer term is unlikely to be politically attractive.

Moral and Legal Dilemmas Posed by Human Rights Abuses

Moral and media driven pressure and legal imperatives to intervene to prevent human suffering are often the political triggers for a PSO. Leaving aside the legal arguments for the intervention into Kosovo, the declared rationale for intervention was of overwhelming humanitarian necessity. However, military personnel deploying in support of a humanitarian relief operation can often find their actions constrained by their mandate and ROE. A tightly drawn peacekeeping mandate under Chapter VI and ROE, for example limited to supporting the delivery of aid, may render forces powerless to intervene when in the course of its mission it is confronted by human rights abuses. A military force mandated to deliver aid, and authorized only to use force in its own defence, could find itself unable to stop, for example, ethnic cleansing despite the immediate horrors of the situation. Apart from being morally wrong and contrary to International Humanitarian Law, such a situation, may attract adverse media coverage which itself may have a negative effect upon the public perception of the credibility of the force and thus their support for the mission. In addition, troops faced with such a dilemma may suffer a loss of morale and self-esteem. Such a situation can be avoided by a thorough understanding of the inherent mandate of any UN operation to protect life and a detailed estimate of the operational environment. The consequences of a limited mandate and restrictive Rules of Engagement when faced with human rights abuses should be robustly represented to those responsible for the formulation of the operational mandate and the allocation of resources to the mission. Nevertheless, just as ROE may place unsustainable restraints upon a military force so there will be occasions when the legitimate use of force may prove counterproductive in the wider sense and may even destabilize the operation politically. It is for this reason that military commanders at all levels are cautioned to consider the long-term consequences of the use of force and to balance that against the wider attainment of mission success.

Key Concepts of Peace Support Operations

Military activities in PSOs are based on an understanding of the three principal concepts of consent, impartiality and the minimum necessary force. The concepts of consent and the minimum use of force and how they determine the conduct of military actions are relatively well understood; however, the concept of a military force acting impartially is not so well understood. The reality is that, even if all military force actions are in support of an impartial mandate and conducted impartially, they will not be perceived that way. Notions of impartiality as providing some form of protection appear increasingly spurious in the face of warlords who seem to perceive all actions which do not favour them as against them and behave accordingly. Even such symbols as the Red Cross and Crescent no longer provide the protection that they did and ought under international law. From a military perspective impartiality is not neutrality, which suggests observation and passivity. Impartiality requires a set of principles, generally enshrined in international humanitarian law and/or the mandate, against which the actions of the belligerent parties can be judged and acted upon. Actions will be taken against or in support of any party, depending on its compliance or non-compliance with the mandate and not because of whom it represents. Inevitably positive actions, whether the delivery of aid or the use of force, whether conducted impartially or not, will have consequences which penalize or favour one party more than another. However, the parties will inevitably see peace support activities as partial at some stage of the operation, and the force will be accused of being so. So long as activities are driven purely by principled and clearly defined impartiality, such accusations can be refuted by a proactive information campaign, and the subsequent damage to the consent of the indigenous peoples can eventually be rebuilt.

Conclusion

In PSOs, success will generally be related to the achievement of a number of pre-determined strategic objectives that form elements of the overall political end-state and should be stated in the operation's mandate. The nature of PSOs is such that these objectives will generally relate to the establishment of a secure, stable and self-sustaining environment for the local population. The achievement of the political end-state will be the defining criteria for the success of the entire operation, including the military mission. The achievement of security-related military objectives will usually be a precursor, or stepping stone on the way to attaining the political end-state specified in the operation's mandate.

The achievement of military goals is relatively easy to state. However, the real or actual success of the operation is related to the daily circumstances of the local populace in the former conflict area and the realization of a situation in which conflicts are no longer solved using force. Unfortunately, such circumstances are difficult to quantify and translate into measurable political objectives. The achievement of milestones and the other strategic objectives related to the political end-state requires perseverance and the efforts of a wide range of civilian organizations and local agencies.[8] The actual success of an operation will therefore be measured against the overall result and not just on the achievement of the military objectives. Clearly, the achievement of military objectives and the creation of a secure environment do not guarantee the establishment of a self-sustaining peace. Nevertheless, without security (and justice), the reconciliation and other development programmes necessary to create a self-sustaining peace are unlikely to be effective. However, once the security-related military objectives have been achieved, the attainment of the political end-state will require the mission's main effort to be switched from the PSO Force to the peacebuilding activities of the civilian components of the mission. Without such a switch of main effort and a commensurate switch of funding and resources, the operation is unlikely to progress beyond that of a military stalemate – as in Bosnia. There is a need, therefore, to develop a close dialogue between military peacekeepers and those engaged in the theory and practice of conflict resolution and post-conflict peacebuilding.[9]

NOTES

1. Kofi Annan, 'Peace Operations and the United Nations: Preparing for the Next Century', *Conflict Resolution Monitor*, Centre for Conflict Resolution, Department of Peace Studies, University of Bradford, Issue 1, Summer 1997, pp.27–8.
2. John Mackinlay (ed.), *A Guide to Peace Support Operations*, Providence, RI: Brown University, Thomas J. Watson Jr. Institute for International Studies, 1996, pp.14–15.
3. See Peter Wallensteen and M. Sollenberg, 'After the Cold War: Emerging Patterns of Armed Conflicts', *Journal of Peace Research*, Vol.32, No.3, 1996, pp.345–60.
4. Kofi Annan (n.1 above), p.27.
5. For a good account of the nature of peace support operations see Mackinlay, note 2.
6. See *Joint Warfare Publication Publication 3.50: Peace Support Operations*, Northwood, UK: Ministry of Defence, 1998.
7. Kofi Annan (n.1 above), p.27.
8. This introduces the concepts of 'peacebuilding from below' and of 'indigenous empowerment', on which a strong literature is developing. See, for example, John Paul Lederach, *Building Peace: Sustainable Reconciliation in Divided Societies*, Washington DC, United States Institute for Peace, 1997.
9. For a discussion of the links between peace support operations and conflict resolution, see Tom Woodhouse, 'The Gentle Hand of Peace? British Peacekeeping and Conflict Resolution in Complex Emergencies', *International Peacekeeping*, Vol.6, No.2, Summer 1999, pp.24–37. For other perspectives on this see David Last, *Theory, Doctrine, and Practice of Conflict De-Escalation in Peacekeeping Operations*, Nova Scotia: Lester B. Pearson Canadian International Peacekeeping Training Center, 1997.

Organizing for Effective Peacebuilding

DAVID LAST

> Peacebuilding is the effort to promote human security in societies marked by conflict. The overarching goal of peacebuilding is to strengthen the capacity of societies to manage conflict without violence, as a means to achieve sustainable human security.
>
> *Canadian Peacebuilding Coordinating Committee*[1]

After General Raul Cédras fled Haiti, his thugs melted into the Port au Prince slums and waged a campaign of terror for profit, retaining their positions of power and privilege until forcibly removed. Many of them are still there. After NATO's Implementation Force deployed in Bosnia, Radavan Karadzi 's special police continued to run their extortion and intimidation rackets, extracting the funds that paid their salaries to keep the hard-liners in control. In Namibia, during the UN-supervised interregnum leading to elections and self-determination, the South-African controlled 'Kuhfut' special police continued to beat up and intimidate enemies of the state. In each case, these sources of violence were defectors or spoilers in the peace process. In each case, their activities delayed or derailed the difficult work of rebuilding wartorn societies and restoring trust between neighbours.

A lot of people and organizations pursue the elusive goal of building a stable peace in wartorn regions. We have not yet found a way of organizing these energies to be as effective as they might be. The first requirement – if we are to manage conflict without violence – is to stop violent behaviour. Peacekeeping missions have only begun to organize themselves to do this, because we are only beginning to understand the nature of the violence inherent in protracted social conflicts. The way we control violence needs to be intimately linked to rebuilding relationships. Those relationships are the means for managing conflict without violence. We need good relationships at community level to manage conflict without violence, but we cannot build relationships in an atmosphere of violence and intimidation.

My argument is in three parts. First, game theory and simulation work on the evolution of cooperation give us a model for controlling defectors. Peacekeeping experience and peacebuilding initiatives can show us what this means in practice. The second part of the argument is to look at the organizations that support these activities. I conclude that we have a gap in the way we combine available assets. The third part of the argument is to propose a pair of organizational solutions that include the coercive tools necessary to stop violence and the relationship-building skills necessary to rebuild functional communities from the ground up.

Game Theory and Practical Peacebuilding

John Maynard Smith, an engineer and geneticist, set up a game called Hawk and Dove. Hawk beats dove, but both lose when hawk meets hawk. Dove gains from any interaction with another dove, but loses to hawk. In short games hawk wins. But with more repetitions, dove has more opportunity to gain points, and wins out over hawk. The most successful player in Maynard Smith's game was 'retaliator', which was a dove that turned into a hawk when it met another hawk.[2] This was a version of a classic prisoner's dilemma game.

In a prisoner's dilemma, there is a modest reward to each player for cooperating, but a larger reward for the player who defects at the expense of the other. If both defect, both are punished. To understand how cooperative regimes evolve, Robert Axelrod set up a computer tournament between programmes representing different strategies. Each programme was pitted against itself, a random programme, and each of the other 14 programmes entered, in a series of moves. All the relatively high-scoring entries were 'nice'. They decided not to be the first to defect. The programme with the highest score was Anatol Rapoport's tit-for-tat strategy, which began by cooperating, and then did whatever its opponent did last. A second round of the tournament included 63 entries and more than a million moves. Tit-for-tat still came first.

What accounts for Tit-for-tat's robust success is its combination of being nice, retaliatory, forgiving and clear. Its niceness prevents it from getting into unnecessary trouble. Its retaliation discourages the other side from persisting whenever defection is tried. Its forgiveness helps restore mutual cooperation. And its clarity makes it intelligible to the other player, thereby eliciting long-term cooperation.[3] Could this be the key to successful peacebuilding? We are looking for interventions designed to encourage long-term cooperation between hostile parties, in the way that Tit-for-tat seems to work in a computer tournament.

Consider the more complex realities of a society at peace and a society recovering from war. In a peaceful community, people can expect to cooperate with their neighbours. Relationships are stable, and word about cheaters quickly gets around. Serious transgressions can lead to serious socially approved sanctions. This is a society of 'doves' with community policemen on the beat to act as 'retaliators'. Beyond the police there is the muscle of riot squads and the army, all under civilian control for the maintenance of peace, order and good government.

Contrast this to the situation in wartorn societies. Government may have broken down. Regions are under the control of thugs and warlords. There is a cycle of violence and reprisals without consequence to the perpetrators. Serbs drove Albanians out of Kosovo and looted their houses. Albanians returned to expel Serbs and loot their houses in turn. Neither community will live with the other. Fear and hatred is built on immediate past experience, and on the stories each side tells of the past. Albanians cite lost autonomy and ten years of repression under Milo evi . Serbs cite Albanian collaboration with the fascists in the Second World War and the tyranny of the Albanian majority in the 1980s. We have seen the pattern before in Croatia and Bosnia.[4] These are societies convinced that only hawks survive, although every encounter leaves both parties bloody.

This is where third parties enter the game. Unable to win decisively, both parties accept a third party as 'retaliator' with sufficient power to prevent defection from a peace agreement. Of course, both parties think that the 'retaliator' should be on *their* side, because they know the other side initiates the violence. NATO's Implementation Force (IFOR) and Stabilization Force (SFOR) and now the Kosovo Force (KFOR) are all soldiers in 'retaliator' mode. They patrol as 'doves', sometimes supporting humanitarian work, until they encounter a source of violence – illegal weapons, armed mobs, or soldiers in places they should not be. When they find such transgressions, they turn into 'hawks'. The impact of this retaliation is to reassure ordinary citizens that soldiers of the opposing party will not attack them. But the protection of a peacekeeping force (or occupying army) cannot extend to the violent acts of disgruntled individuals. Nor does it go as far as encouraging active cooperation with neighbours.

The Peacebuilding Capability Gap

There are actually two gaps in our ability to help wartorn societies rebuild peace and cooperation. The first is a gap in our ability to control violence between the parties. This is required to put the hawks in a box. The second is a gap in our ability to rebuild the trust that permits cooperation *between* the parties and lets the doves out of their boxes. This has to go beyond letting communities live in hostile isolation, if cooperation is to take hold.

Assets to Control Violence

A holistic approach to peacebuilding cannot focus just on controlling violence by organized military forces. Nor can soldiers perform most of the necessary peacebuilding functions. When organized military formations have been brought under control, police and community security must be addressed. This is tied inextricably to rebuilding the legal and social institutions that permit civilian policing to be effective. Thus, when military peacekeeping forces become involved by default in the civilian tasks of humanitarian relief, development, democratization, and so on, their objective should be to unload those tasks as quickly as possible. The torch is passed both from military to international civilian missions, and from international missions to local authorities, appropriately prepared for the task.

This transfer of control from military to civilian can be seen in the process by which violence was brought under control in Bosnia. Figure 1 is adapted from Michael Dziedzic's work on policing the new world disorder.[5] The vertical axis represents the potential for organized violence, and the horizontal axis shows time. There was initially a large military presence. With time, civilian police monitors of the International Police Task Force (IPTF) came with a mandate to monitor, train and assist the local police, working towards internationally acceptable standards of community policing. The overlapping ovals illustrate the declining importance of a military, paramilitary and police presence as organized violence is brought under control. In fact, excessive security presence or the wrong type of presence can be provocative and dangerous.[6] After violence has been contained the visibility of armed security forces indicates problems and dysfunction.

When the international community first intervenes in a protracted social conflict, it must do so with sufficient force to guarantee all the parties to the conflict that they will not be attacked *and* that they cannot achieve their objectives by force. The size and capability of the force necessary depends

FIGURE 1
BUILDING SECURITY

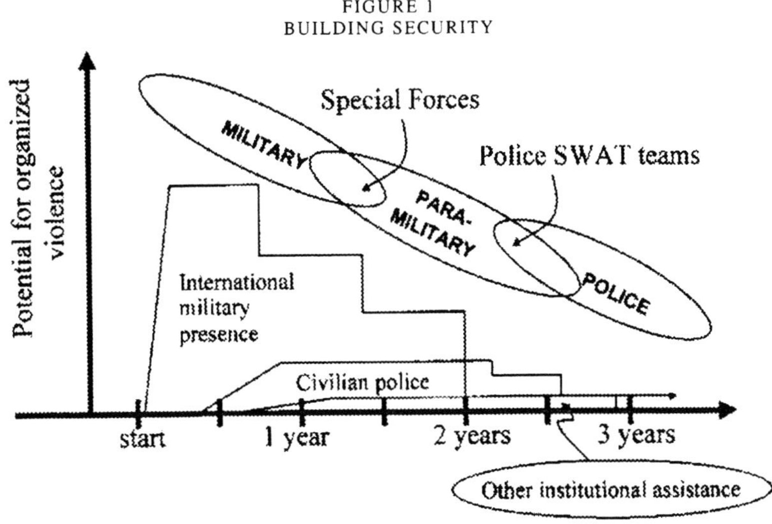

on the degree to which the parties are prepared to cooperate with it.[7]

Military forces are effective at guaranteeing security against military opposition. They are much less effective against riots and civilian disturbances like the ones experienced in Bosnia as the refugees tried to go home, or those seen more recently in Kosovo. They are impotent in the face of bricks through windows or threatening calls in the night. So we need a spectrum of forces to bring violence under control.

Figure 1 shows the place of paramilitary forces or *gendarmeries*. Organized in platoons and companies along military lines, paramilitary forces deal with large-scale civil disturbances and with armed and organized criminal elements. To avoid embroiling heavily armed troops in crowd control, the UN Transitional Authority in Eastern Slavonia (UNTAES) included a Polish riot-control company. In Bosnia, SFOR developed the Multinational Specialized Unit (MSU) including police and paramilitary Italian *Carabinieri*.[8]

International civilian police missions do not usually have jurisdiction to arrest or detain. They monitor and assist the local police, and provide training on human rights and community policing.[9] When the local police obstruct the process or violate agreements, as the Serb Republic police did in Banja Luka in 1998, the international police monitors may call upon the military force to shut down a police station, seize illegal weapons, or take action to ensure public safety. The international military force is the backup that helps to force violence down to levels where effective civilian police can handle it.

Building Relationships

The problem with simply controlling violence is that soldiers and police do not operate in isolation. To restore order they need honest courts, uncorrupted judges and fair laws. Fair laws and an effective justice system depend on functioning government. Government that attempts to do everything is likely to be either inefficient or oppressive or both. And so, in countries like Bosnia, Somalia, Sierra Leone, and other places where human security has utterly broken down, the international community is faced with a challenge that goes far beyond controlling violence. It must help to rebuild government and civil society to balance it. It must support the public space in which issues are debated, and help replace the infrastructure of governance – media, meeting places, and community leaders free from fear. When communities have been at each other's throats, as they were in Bosnia, international assistance must help communities to become reconciled to living and working together again. Throughout this process the international community will probably have to provide emergency relief to uprooted populations, while trying to help reconstruct essential infrastructure and develop an equitable market economy.

Controlling violence is a small part of personal security, and security is only one of at least four components of peacebuilding suggested above. Balancing the powers of government and civil society to achieve effective governance is another.[10] Relief and development to alleviate human suffering is a third.[11] The pursuit of truth, mercy and justice that make up reconciliation is a fourth essential component of peacebuilding.[12] There are definable tasks and skills associated with each of these. Table 1 illustrates core peacebuilding tasks identified by the Canadian Peacebuilding Coordinating Committee (CPCC). A field experiment conducted by the Pearson Peacekeeping Center (PPC) identified skills necessary to carry out these tasks.[13] The table also lists examples of some of the member organizations of the CPCC involved in peacebuilding.

Two sorts of skills are evident in Table 1. Facilitating meetings, developing leaders, teaching entrepreneurial skills and building businesses might be thought of as organizational skills. It is comparatively simple to apply them in peaceful and orderly communities, where trust and confidence in the future are commonplace. In wartorn societies, they must be accompanied by 'therapeutic' skills if they are to be effective. These skills include rebuilding relationships across boundaries, managing the psychosocial dynamics of residual conflict, and supporting individuals and communities who lack confidence in their future. Both skill-sets are essential for peacebuilding.

In practice, we find a gap between the range of skills needed to support peacebuilding, and the skills embodied in typical international missions. Major international agencies tend to embody organizational skills, while therapeutic and psychosocial skills often reside in smaller NGOs that have difficulty deploying and sustaining themselves in mission areas. The membership of the CPCC and the practical difficulties the United Nations High Commission for Refugees (UNHCR) has experienced in Bosnia illustrate this problem.

The CPCC represents a cross-section of organizations and individuals active in peacebuilding, broadly defined. The chart of peacebuilding activities on their web site lists 44 activities in 14 categories. Most of these fall within the four categories listed above. Relief and development functions are well served by major international NGOs (CARE, OXFAM, and the like), which have a record of cooperation with international organizations like the World Food Programme (WFP) and the UNHCR.

Handing out food and rebuilding schools and hospitals are good for fund-raising and require less sophistication and long-term commitment than psychosocial repairs and conflict resolution. These functions are often met by smaller NGOs with a domestic focus, where their real expertise lies.

TABLE 1
SOME PEACEBUILDING REQUIREMENTS

	Tasks (from CPCC)	**Skills** (from PPC)	**Sample Organizations** (from CPCC)
Security	• Demobilization • Disarmament • Demining • Protecting civilian populations • Police and security force reform • Personal security issues (e.g. Racial-cultural or gender specific violence) • Human rights	• Non-violent civil defence techniques • Witnessing • Accompaniment • Neighbourhood watch • *Support and networking*	• Canadian International Demining Centre • Centre de ressources sur la nonviolence • Peace Brigades International • Ploughshares
Governance	• Institutional capacity-building • Transparency and accountability • Electoral assistance • Civic education and training • Judicial reform • Media development and training • Policy development and advocacy	• Facilitating meetings • Developing group leaders • Group decision-making techniques • *Encouraging and supporting action*	• CANADEM • Canadian Bar Association • Institute for Media Policy and Civil Society • International Centre for Human Rights and Democratic Development
Relief and Development	• Infrastructure development • Market reform • Economic and financial institutions • Small business • Meeting basic needs • Social services	• Engineering and technical competence • Business acumen • Business development • Entrepreneurial skills • Leadership and teaching • *Rebuilding relationships across boundaries*	• Adventist Development and Relief Agency (ADRA) • CARE • CUSO • Oxfam • Save the Children • UNICEF • WUSC
Reconciliation	• Psycho-social trauma • Reintegration of refugees and displaced people • Peace education • Community-based initiatives	• *Interpersonal communications* • *Group facilitation* • *Managing psycho-social dynamics of conflict*	• Canadian Centres for Teaching Peace • Canadian Institute for Conflict Resolution • Canadian International Institute of Applied Negotiation • Centre for Negotiation and Dispute Resolution • Education for Peace

Organizations like the Canadian International Institute for Applied Negotiation (CIIAN) and the Canadian Institute for Conflict Resolution (CICR) are repositories of considerable expertise, but they are neither large nor internationally connected. In comparison to the big international NGOs like CARE, ADRA, and World Vision they are not well positioned to launch or sustain involvement in foreign missions.

The disappointing progress of refugee return in Northwest Bosnia caused the UNHCR to look for implementing partners to support the crucial 'social component' of refugee return. Although more than 70 NGOs were operating out of Bihac and Banja Luka by 1998, few were positioned to offer the psychological, social and institutional assistance that UNHCR officers felt was needed. The shortfall existed partly because most NGOs were still focused on reconstruction and development – bricks and mortar that could be photographed for the donors at home. Even when NGOs like Norwegian Refugee Council shifted focus, they found that local employees were reluctant to take personal risks, and international employees lacked the language skills and local knowledge necessary.

Peacebuilding Capability Gaps

The UN, NATO, and OSCE missions in Bosnia have made slow progress towards reconstruction and reconciliation. The biggest problem has been organizing for the two sides of peacebuilding – stopping violence and building relationships. International military intervention has been an incomplete solution to physical security shortfalls, because it does not incorporate effective paramilitary and police elements. We have also been reticent in the use of precise tools like Special Forces and SWAT teams to deal with spoilers. Part of our reluctance stems from the lack of a legal framework for arresting and detaining malefactors, if their crimes are not egregious enough to warrant indictment under international law for war crimes. Relying on domestic law and courts in broken societies like Bosnia or Haiti is not satisfactory, yet we seem to lack the means to help institutions become functional. The international community is therefore less than effective in controlling the hawks that disrupt peacebuilding.

We have not been completely successful in deploying the skills necessary for each of the four major peacebuilding components identified. International organizations like UNHCR and UNDP enter from the top with a presence in the capital city. They do not immediately penetrate down to community level. Military peacekeeping deployments quickly reach small communities, but lack key peacebuilding skills, particularly those involving language, culture and relationship building. NGOs that have the core skills, on the other hand, often lack the means to deploy or sustain themselves in the small communities where they are most needed. They also lack the resources to support recruitment and training of locals to develop peacebuilding capacity at community level. The result has sometimes been lopsided missions with a heavy military presence unable to implement peace agreements, or even deal with the violence that continues to affect ordinary people.

An Organizational Solution for Peacebuilding

An organizational solution to these peacebuilding problems must take existing constraints into account. NGOs will continue to be largely autonomous. Military forces will continue to report to a UN or regional multinational headquarters. Civil missions may report to a separate headquarters sponsored by the UN or a regional organization. We are looking for a combination of structures that can be nice, retaliatory, forgiving and clear.

Joulwan and Shoemaker, two former Generals with peacekeeping experience, have advocated a unified Civil-Military Implementation Staff. A military component (with military, police and private sector support) and a civil component (with international organizations and NGOs) would report to a single Chairman at the operational level in a peacekeeping theatre.[14] Their solution is not unlike the structure of the UN Transition Assistance Group (UNTAG) in Namibia.[15] Thomas Weiss, reviewing an extensive study of humanitarian interventions, argues that, 'Rather than extant feudal arrangements, a single body is necessary to set priorities, to raise and distribute resources, and to coordinate emergency inputs.'[16] But he goes on to explain that national calls for central coordination are disingenuous in light of their desire to wave national flags over assistance rendered. Everyone wants coordination, but no-one wants to be coordinated by others. The unified solution is well argued and logical, but has not been put into practice. Even in Namibia, UN agencies often acted outside the unified structure, and NGOs are always unwilling to relinquish autonomy, even when acting as implementing partners. We should continue to seek closer civil-military collaboration and central coordination at the highest levels, with the understanding that it is unlikely to be achieved. Is there an alternative?

The good news is that we can compensate for imperfect coordination at higher levels by focusing on building peaceful communities *from the bottom up*, where structures have the most impact on people's lives. This approach demands that we improve organization for peacebuilding within 'extant feudal arrangements'. We need a focus. We could choose the UNHCR and its network of implementing partnerships, but they lack the mechanisms for controlling violence, and operate in parallel with deployed forces. We could choose national bilateral arrangements like the US Agency for International Development (USAID) and its Office of Transition Initiatives (OTI) but the same applies. Even the military structure of a mission is fragmented into national areas of responsibility. This fragmentation presents an opportunity.

From the earliest days of peacekeeping to the present, national units or contingents have been assigned areas of operational responsibility. Typically, a 'unit' is a battalion or battle group, usually consisting of about 1000 soldiers. In the 1990s the UN tried to standardize the size and capabilities of deployed units, largely for accounting and planning purposes. Areas of responsibility vary in size according to the forces available, level of threat, geography and so on. Within an area, there are usually a number of communities (towns, villages and rural areas) with diverse characteristics. Drawing a line around a manageable area, within which there is third party responsibility for controlling violence and building relationships, is the beginning of organizing for peacebuilding. It can be a focus for bilateral assistance, combining an opportunity to wave the national flag with the assistance available from other international agencies and the UN system. National leadership within an area will not preclude the deployment of multinational assets.

Within each area, the third party must have the capacity for controlling the full spectrum of violence and building relationships in each of the four main components described above – security, development, governance and reconciliation.

Full Spectrum Control of Violence

In a functioning society, the decision to escalate from police to paramilitary to military involvement in civil disorder is usually taken at the highest level of state or national government. In an international intervention, we see the reverse. International military forces are deployed to preserve order, and civilian police are gradually reintroduced (Figure 1). It may take months or years to legitimize local police through certification by international police monitors, but the need for civil order is immediate. Part of the solution is to deploy the full range of security forces including police and paramilitary forces with the initial military deployment. This is only part of the solution, because police cannot be effective unless they are linked to the communities they are protecting. They must be able to talk to people and understand the local situation if they are to investigate incidents, respond to complaints and enforce laws to which the community assents. This is why UN Civil Police are usually confined to monitoring, training and assistance.

One model for the transition to an effective local police is the Auxiliary Transitory Police (PAT) developed in El Salvador under the United Nations Observer Mission in El Salvador (ONUSAL). Units were made up of cadets selected for the new civilian police academy, and commanded by ONUSAL Civil Police officers. Without the power to investigate crimes or arrest people (except when caught in the act), their role was mainly crime prevention and maintenance of public order. By providing on-job training by experienced foreign police, the PAT helped bridge the gap to the establishment of a national police force meeting international standards.[17] While the framework for an interim police force would have to be negotiated as part of a comprehensive settlement, it could be implemented regionally, as it was in El Salvador (in the zones of conflict).

A transitional police force under international supervision presents an opportunity for oversight by intercommunal committees. Where there are hostile groups in a community, each might nominate members to an oversight committee under international chairmanship to supervise policing and security issues. Thus a civil affairs officer or UN Police Chief in Mostar might chair a mixed committee of Muslim and Croat community leaders to monitor policing problems. In consultation with the local commander of the international military force (SFOR) he should have access to paramilitary or military forces. He might also need to call on SWAT teams or Special Forces to deal with violent obstruction to the peace process, when this can be pinpointed. By starting to work for civilian control and community policing early in a mission, the mechanisms for control of violence do not become permanently vested in international military forces.

Although it is difficult to get former enemies to the same table, this is an essential step towards rebuilding functioning communities. By taking the step early and linking it to the core issue of personal security at community level, the third party lays the foundation for the other components of peacebuilding. The basic model of international facilitation of intergroup contact is at the heart of third-party peacebuilding. It is necessary both for controlling violence and rebuilding relationships, and works best at the lowest possible level – between people, within communities.

Community Based Civilian Peacebuilding

International forces can impose military stability, but all the rest depends ultimately on the locals. They must help in the restoration of peace, order, good government and a sustainable economy. A mind-boggling array of international organizations and NGOs has tried to support this process in Bosnia. I would like to suggest an alternative, which would help deployed military forces to build human security from the bottom up, fostering local cooperation at grass-roots level. Soldiers cannot achieve these objectives, but they can help to establish a framework that will let civilians – both local and international – do what is needed. Soldiers are well suited for this enabling role for three reasons. They arrive in organized groups with vehicles, communications and their own security. They can cover an area like a blanket with a systematic command, control and intelligence network. And they have the capacity to stifle violence, permitting cooperation to take root. However they are not effective at cultivating cooperation, because they lack the core therapeutic peacebuilding skills that will help relationships grow again between hostile communities.

Figure 2 shows the boundaries of a military unit or formation deployed on a peacekeeping mission. It might be a NATO Battle Group deployed in Northwest Bosnia or Kosovo. Towns are lettered and routes are numbered.

FIGURE 2
AREA DEPLOYMENT OF A PEACEKEEPING FORCE

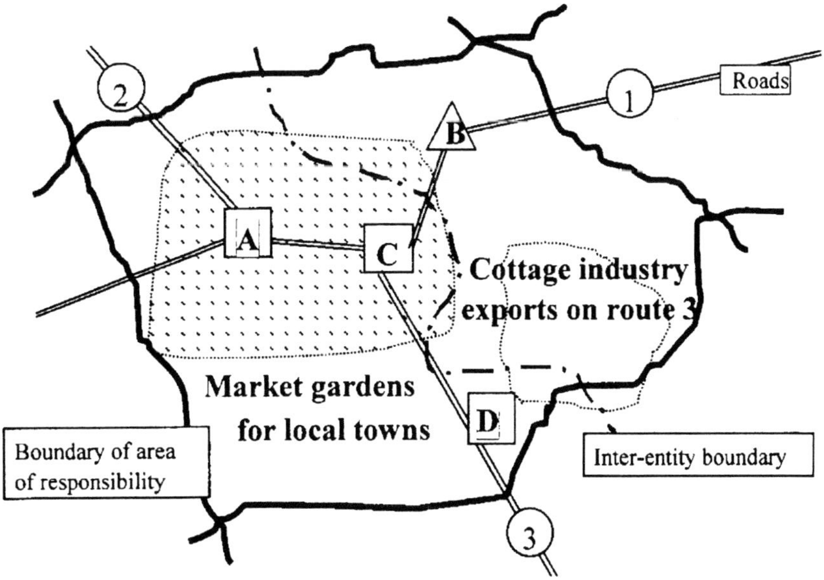

Each town has an economic and social zone around it, market gardens, resource extraction or cottage industry, for example. The dashed line represents a boundary between factions or formerly hostile entities. The hostility does not disappear overnight. The boundary, and the difficulty of moving across it, creates barriers to economic and political recovery. The cottage industry is cut off from the town (D) that supplies its labour, and from Route 3 on which its exports must move. That is precisely the situation faced by towns all over the former Yugoslavia.

The peacebuilding challenges fall in all four areas – security, relief and development, government and civil society, and reconciliation. As a civil affairs officer in Bosnia in the first six months of NATO's deployment I lacked sufficient knowledge of the language, culture and local history. I could not find the moderate allies that I needed. I was not knowledgeable enough in any of the peacebuilding areas, and I did not have civilian NGOs or international agencies to work with, until they began to trickle in 6–12 months after the beginning of the mandate.

The Pearson Peacekeeping Center experimented with a solution to these problems. The Neighbourhood Facilitators Project trained 20 local Bosnian Muslims, Serbs and Croats in Banja Luka in a variety of interpersonal and conflict resolution skills. It then trained international facilitators and selected five for deployment to Bosnia. The locals and internationals were brought together in mixed teams, and given further training that reflected the circumstances in Banja Luka, including the difficulties associated with minority return. A community centre with a mobile team was established, and from March to July 1998, the facilitators helped local people develop solutions to their own problems.[18] Crucial to the success of the Neighbourhood Facilitators was the combination of local facilitators with diverse backgrounds, and internationals who provided expertise and a link to the supporting international community. The most important limiting factors were lack of money for salaries and rent, and lack of reach into the surrounding areas because of the security problems experienced by the mobile teams.

The Neighbourhood Facilitators Project developed the concept of a community centre as a home base for teams, each of which included local and international facilitators. Some of the teams were mobile, equipped to work away from the centre. Others worked in or from the centre itself. Within the centre, there was a small local support staff, to provide translation and administrative services. Each of the four towns in the area of operations depicted in Figure 2 might have a different mix of mobile and static teams, embodying a variety of skills depending on the evolution of its needs. Early on, the focus might be on refugee return, immediate aid and reconstruction, with most teams being mobile. Development, reconciliation and governance might be more important later.

The core of each team, at least initially, is an international facilitator. As the teams and mission evolve, local facilitators should be increasingly central. Ideally, the local–international partnership should be an equal one from the outset, but the balance of skills may leave a leading role to international facilitators by default.

What do these teams do? A community centre and its teams can be the glue for all the other services and organizations that come to its area to help repair the damage of violent conflict. Because the teams are fundamentally *local* as well as international, they help to rebuild the country from the ground up, developing people who will stay there for the long haul. Because they are part of a formal and well-supported structure, they are a reliable interface between a multinational military force or observer mission, international organizations, NGOs and the local population. Because they are party to a larger campaign plan, they can facilitate local and international effort at the community level.

Local and international facilitators must possess a variety of skills to be selected. Self-awareness and ability to work with people across cultural and linguistic barriers is a basic prerequisite. This includes the ability to transcend the barriers that separate locals and internationals, soldiers and civilians. Beyond this, necessary skills fall into four categories: economic, security, governance, and reconciliation. Table 1 illustrates some of the skills required in each category. Facilitators need expertise so they have to specialize.

The teams embody a mixture of individual skills – a broad understanding of all the issues, plus deeper expertise in specific areas. A team operating across boundaries or in an area with vulnerable minorities, for example, might need to include someone with detailed knowledge of non-violent security techniques, of the sort developed by Peace Brigades International. The expertise must be sufficient to teach others and lead them in action. (When the threat is very high, teams may travel with military units.) A team dealing with minority return will need economic and reconciliation expertise. Governance expertise may become increasingly important later in a mission to teach democracy and develop civil society, or to help prepare for elections.

Working in small teams at community level, local and international facilitators can use access to international resources to reward cooperation and help rebuild the relationships that were destroyed by violent conflict. They are the nucleus of a new, cooperative way of doing business. Many small interactions at local level multiply the chance that cooperation will take hold and spread, as long as violence is controlled.

The balance of skills and resources needed for a successful international intervention should change as a mission evolves. At the outset, catalytic and leadership skills will be most important. As the confidence and cooperation of local allies grows, training and education skills will become increasingly important. In Bosnia, it was probably about two years before this occurred. Training and education are used to develop local capacity to perform the key community-building functions. Locals must take over these functions before the process can become self-sustaining. Sustaining progress, developing new programmes to meet evolving need, and making the transition to full local ownership requires nurturing and mentoring skills. Figure 3 illustrates this sequence in the evolution of a mission, in parallel with a transition in the mechanisms for controlling violent behaviour.

FIGURE 3
SEQUENCE OF A MISSION

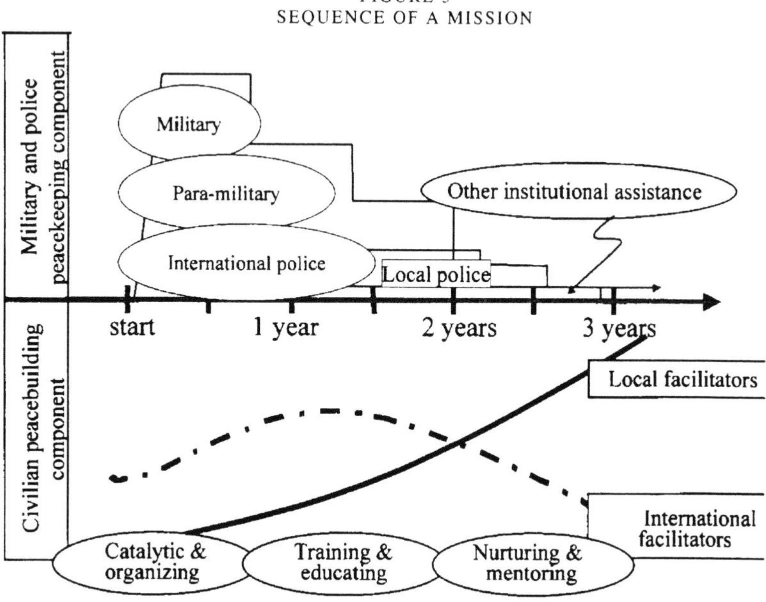

This sequence implies a deliberate but gradual reduction in the international presence. Violence is brought under control early on by a concerted effort from police, paramilitary and military forces. As local institutions develop, local civilian police can take over the control of violence through community policing. Locals gradually take over the process of building relationships between formerly hostile communities.

Conclusion

There is no such thing as a guaranteed solution to protracted social conflict. All operations are experimental, and the foregoing argument is no more than a template for another experiment. If we are to improve peace operations, we need to structure and learn from our experiments more systematically. That means studying the factors that influence success, modelling them, changing variables, and evaluating progress over time.

Here I have suggested that game theory offers a model for the control of defectors and the evolution of cooperation. Military, paramilitary and police organizations and sometimes Special Forces and SWAT teams can play a role in controlling violence. Transitional police forces at local level, with civilian oversight, help bridge the gap between military security and public order. Mixed teams of local and international facilitators, with increasing reliance on locals, can help to build up confidence and cooperation by drawing on international resources to enhance security, development, governance and reconciliation at grass roots level.

It might be unrealistic to expect this level of synergy in a UN mission or in the alphabet soup of international organizations we see today in Sarajevo. But launching this experiment is within the scope of any country that deploys a national contingent and international aid resources. It can be started at community level within any area of operations. We could see competing experimental models in British, French and American sectors. Eventually, the beneficiaries can tell us which models work.

NOTES

1. Canadian Peacebuilding Co-ordinating Committee, 'Peacebuilding Activities Chart,' . CPCC is an umbrella for non-governmental organizations involved in peacebuilding. It is sponsored in part by the Peacebuilding Branch of the Canadian Department of Foreign Affairs and International Trade (DFAIT).
2. Matt Ridley, *The Origins of Virtue: Human Instincts and the Evolution of Cooperation*, New York: Penguin, 1996, pp.58–60.
3. Robert Axelrod, *The Evolution of Cooperation*, New York: Basic Books, 1984, p.54.
4. David M. Last, 'Defeating Fear and Hatred: Multiplying the Impact of a Military Contribution', *Canadian Foreign Policy*, Vol.5, No.2, Winter 1998, pp.149–67.
5. Michael Dziedzic, 'Introduction', in Robert B. Oakley, Michael J. Dziedzic, and Eliot M. Goldberg (eds.), *Policing the New World Disorder: Peace Operations and Public Security*, Washington DC: National Defence University Press, 1998, p.16. The spectrum of forces is described in David Last, 'Winning the Savage Wars of Peace', in John T. Fishel (ed.), *The Savage Wars of Peace: Toward a New Paradigm of Peace Operations*, Boulder CO: Westview Press, 1998, pp.224–26.
6. Anthony Deane-Drummond, *Riot Control*, London: Royal United Services Institute, 1975, pp.67–85.
7. Charles Dobbie, 'A Concept for Post-Cold War Peacekeeping', *Survival*, Vol.36, No.3, Autumn 1994.
8. Private communication to author.
9. Robert C. Johansen, University of Notre Dame, 'Strengthening International Enforcement without Military Combat: Towards a United Nations Civilian Police and Peacebuilding Force', paper presented at the International Studies Association 40th Annual Convention, Washington DC, 20 February 1999. Johansen argues that enforcement by UN Civil Police is an option for peacekeeping missions. I believe this is plausible only where a society gives its full cooperation to the international community. Even then, there are problems of language, culture and law that must be overcome before community policing can be effective.
10. A forthcoming monograph by the Pearson Peacekeeping Centre reports on the results of an international conference on peacekeeping and governance held in Montreal, 30–31 March 1999.
11. Jean H. Guilmette illustrates the problems that arise when development is postponed in favour of emergency relief in 'Beyond Emergency Assistance: Early Warning, Conflict Prevention and Decision-Making', a discussion paper, July 1995 (CIDA/ACDI), pp.18–19. Jeremy Ginifer argues that development should be recast with a central role in peacekeeping and conflict resolution. 'Development and the UN Peace Mission: A New Interface Required?' *International Peacekeeping*, Vol.3, No.2, Summer 1996, pp.3–13.
12. Cynthia Sampson addresses the religious aspects in 'Religion and Peacebuilding,' in I. William Zartman and J. Lewis Rasmussen (eds.), *Peacemaking in International Conflict: Methods and Techniques*, Washington, DC: United States Institute of Peace, 1997,

pp.273–316. John Paul Lederach takes a more secular and structural approach, informed by the same values. *Building Peace: Sustainable Reconciliation in Divided Societies* , Washington, DC: United States Institute of Peace, 1997.

13. Major D.M. Last, *From Peacekeeping to Peacebuilding: Theory, Cases, Experiments and Solutions* (Kingston, ON: Royal Military College of Canada Working Paper, May 1999) p.53.
14. George A. Joulwan and Christopher C. Shoemaker, *Civilian–Military Cooperation in the Prevention of Deadly Conflict: Implementing Agreements in Bosnia and Beyond.* A Report to the Carnegie Commission on Preventing Deadly Conflict, New York: Carnegie Corporation, December 1998, p.42.
15. *The Blue Helmets: A Review of United Nations Peacekeeping*, New York: UN Department of Public Information, 1996, pp.209–14.
16. Thomas G. Weiss, *Military–Civilian Interactions: Intervening in Humanitarian Crises*, Lanham: Rowman and Littlefield, 1999, p.201.
17. William Stanley and Robert Loosle, 'El Salvador: The Civilian Police Component of Peace Operations', in Robert B. Oakley *et al.* (n.5 above), p.124.
18. The experiment is reported in detail in Last, 1999 (n.13 above). The Neighbourhood Facilitators Project consisted of one community centre in Banja Luka with five mixed local–international teams, three of which worked outside the Centre at various times.

Working with Ethno-political Conflict: A Multi-modal Approach

SEAN BYRNE and LORALEIGH KEASHLY

This analysis is the result of conversations between the two of us in which we tried to bring together our respective writing and thinking on dealing with international ethno-political conflict. Sean's work with Neal Carter on the six forces in ethno-territorial conflicts identified the social factors – objective and subjective – that need to be addressed in building a constructive peace. Loraleigh's work with Ronald J. Fisher on a contingency model of third-party intervention in such conflicts is also premised on the notion of objective and subjective elements in conflicts as cues to stages of escalation and, thus, the selection and coordination of appropriate and varied interventions.[2] In essence, Byrne and Carter draw our attention to the need to address a broad range of forces and thus, increase the range of what we consider 'intervention' while Fisher and Keashly highlight the value and necessity of coordinated and complementary 'intervention' efforts required to deal with these factors in a comprehensive manner. Merging these two perspectives focuses attention on recognizing that protracted inter-communal conflicts develop and are sustained through the complex and continuous interaction of a number of factors, ranging from economic to historical to sociological to psychocultural to political. Consequently, a multiplicity of intervention efforts must run simultaneously and sometimes sequentially at all levels to de-escalate the conflict through all of the stages of escalation and to transform the underlying nature of conflict over time.

In our conversations, we realized that the acknowledgement and articulation of these social forces are critical to selecting and coordinating efforts at different levels to address these various sources. Thus, there is something to be learned both conceptually and practically in developing a multi-modal, multilevel approach to resolving inter-communal conflict. It is also clear from our conversations that this is no minor undertaking and could best be approached by working on the 'multi-modal' part first and the 'multilevel' piece in subsequent work. In terms of multi-modal, our intent in this analysis is to argue for an increase in the range of what the scholarly literature considers 'intervention' and to illustrate the different forces on which they can and do have an impact. Thus, this study will attempt to identify some of these activities and explore coordination/complementarity issues.

We realize that we are not alone in our belief of a multi-modal approach. For example, Diamond and McDonald in their work on multi-track diplomacy highlight the variety of individuals, activities, institutions and communities that are necessary for building a sustainable constructive peace.[3] They identify at least nine tracks to such diplomacy: government; non-government/professional; business; private citizens; research, training and education; activism; religion; funding; and communications and the media. We will incorporate some of these types of actors and activities in our discussion of intervention possibilities. Diamond and McDonald also note that the manner in which these interconnected parts operate together is sometimes graceful, often awkward. We would argue that frequently they do not operate together at all but rather in parallel, with little if any contact.

Similarly, Lederach advocates an integrated holistic peacebuilding framework with coordinated points of contact that can make peace possible instead of the traditional diplomatic processes.[4] Such an approach would coordinate process, resources, structure, training, and external third-party intervention to effect reconciliation to transform the conflict, and create a sustainable peace over the long term

More specific ideas about how particular interventions should be sequenced have also been proposed. Lund suggests a strategic intervention of peacemaking/peace enforcement to create a ceasefire after the outbreak of fighting; peacekeeping/crisis management to settle or terminate a conflict; and, post-conflict peacebuilding/peacetime diplomacy to build a stable and just peace.[5] Indeed, some activities such as military intervention for peacekeeping and peace-pushing efforts such as mediated peace agreements in extremely violent conflicts, like Bosnia-Herzegovina, may of necessity precede full-scale coordinated activities such as physical reconstruction, economic development and rejuvenation, and inter-communal activities.[6] However, with regard to the Northern Ireland conflict, many of these latter activities are occurring in the midst of violent confrontation.[7] The premise of our conversations and of this study is that the effectiveness of all of these efforts would be greatly enhanced by a multi-modal coordinated effort that recognizes the multiplicity and interactive nature of the social forces involved, any one of which, if left unaddressed, can refuel the flame of destructive conflict.

In recognition of the diversity of factors that fuel ethno-territorial conflicts, we are broadening the definition of intervention to include any efforts involving external and/or internal parties that focus on amelioration of social, economic, political, physical and psychocultural conditions in the conflict region. Thus, in addition to the more political forms of arbitration, mediation, negotiation, conciliation and reconciliation, as well as the more recently acknowledged informal forms of interactive conflict resolution, we also include: structural change, short-term developmental aid efforts, long-term economic investment plans – both public and private, public education, community-building efforts, physical and mental health care, religious reconciliation work, activism for political rights, community empowerment, healing and storytelling, trust-building, forgiveness, problem-solving workshops, integrated education and media development and education.[8]

Focusing on the 'multi-modal' nature of intervention in ethno-political conflict, we will discuss these different interventions in two ways. First, we will briefly discuss each of the six forces outlined by Byrne and Carter and illustrate the specific activities and parties that address each of them using examples from past and current ethnic conflicts where possible. Second, we will switch perspectives from forces to the intervention activities and parties themselves and illustrate how they address more than one of these factors, that is, cross-level activity. In a third section, we will consider some ways to facilitate the explicit coordination that our approach suggests.

Six Social Forces of Ethnic Conflict

Byrne and Carter identify and illustrate the operation of six social forces – historical, religious, demographic, political, economic, and psychocultural – that combine to produce patterns of intergroup behaviour in the ethno-territorial politics of Northern Ireland and Quebec. In this section, we will describe each set of factors and identify activities designed to address the concerns reflected therein.

Historical Factors

Historical factors focus on how stories of past events, as viewed from different perspectives, influence current political institutions and hence, perceptions of political possibilities.[9] The invocations of these interpretations of past events serve to support each party's subsequent actions.

The inter-communal dispute in Cyprus between Greek Cypriots and Turkish Cypriots while relatively 'recent' in modern times is based in a thousand-year history of a continually conquered island. The 1974 war brought about the current physical separation arrangements which essentially isolated the two communities to separate parts of the island. To illustrate the power of different perspectives on the same event, the Greek Cypriots refer to the 1974 war as the Turkish invasion while Turkish Cypriots refer to it as the Turkish peace mission to prevent Greece from taking over the island.[10] In these few words, it is easy to see how these different perspectives support the current separation.

While one cannot 'rewrite' history, it may be possible to reframe and refocus that history, using perhaps a more expansive and interpretive approach to history. The activities necessary to do this require overcoming long time 'collective memories' that have been shared across generations as well as those memories of such recent conflicts as Bosnia.[11] One possibility is the juxtaposition of the historical interpretations and then joint efforts to write a more complete and comprehensive history. For example, integrated schools in Northern Ireland have been instrumental in teaching Protestant and Catholic children about their joint history and cultural experience.[12] This process would clearly involve the activities of public education aimed at children as well as continuing education effort for adults. Providers of such activities would include formal Ministries of Education, teacher unions and parent groups, peace education groups as well as the media.

Recent work by Ron Fisher and colleagues using a problem-solving peacebuilding workshop generated ideas among Greek Cypriot and Turkish Cypriot educators as to how to facilitate the production of joint textbooks of the history of the region. Currently, historical texts for schools typically come from Greece or Turkey to their respective communities. For dealing with more recent memories, there is greater opportunity for change as minds are more open to interpretation although clearly strong feelings of pain, anger and loss must be dealt with initially and in tandem with more substantive interpretive activities. Clearly such efforts would also require some appreciation of and teaching about social psychological processes of perception formation, stereotyping, discrimination, and group identity which we will discuss in more detail regarding psychocultural factors.[13]

Religious Factors

The political presence and influence of religious institutions in ethnic conflicts can certainly serve to fuel or to reconcile war-torn communities.[14] The conflict in Bosnia was often described as one between Christians (Roman Catholic, Eastern Orthodox) and Muslims. Activities and groups relevant to dealing with religious influence include not only the religious organizations indigenous to the regions but also other religious groups or organizations. For example, the World Council of Churches, the Friends Service Community, and Mennonite Central Committee are examples of 'external' organizations that direct their efforts in war-torn regions to focus on recognition and reconciliation. They also attempt to refocus attention on building the element of cooperation and compassion and reducing reliance on the holy war aspects, both elements which are part of most world religions. An example of the role of 'internal' religious organizations in inter-ethnic conflict is illustrated in Byrne and Carter's discussion of Northern Ireland and Quebec. Briefly, they argue that religious differences in Northern Ireland 'tend to create a moral rejection of compromise' while in Quebec, religious differences have helped maintain relatively peaceful coexistence.[15] Thus, religious organizations as sources of activities focused on amelioration of ethno-political conflict have a vital role to play.

Demographic Factors

Demographic factors refer to issues of majority or minority status within a particular geographic region and how those relate to control over economic, territorial and political resources. Byrne and Carter nicely illustrate the effect of Federal political policies of multiculturalism that define Anglophones and Francophones as both minorities within a diverse multicultural country of Canada. Regarding Northern Ireland, each ethnic group (Unionists and Nationalists) feel insecure regarding control over critical resources.[16] Thus activities and groups focused on the development of political equity as seen in South Africa have much to offer in addressing these issues of minority status.[17] The move by Serb leader Slobodan Milošević to use nationalism to expand the Serbian territory altered relations between Bosnian Serbs, Croats, and Muslims from one of equal status to one in which Croats and Muslims in particular became disenfranchised minorities.[18] The Dayton peace agreement focuses on providing each of the three groups with relative power bases in terms of territorial influence. Relevant activities then include political policies of multiculturalism and inter-ethnic cooperation that are tied to actual power resources as well as peace education efforts focused on understanding similarities and the appreciation of differences.

Political Factors

Related to discussions of demographic factors, political factors refer to the territorial delineation of political institutions in which ethnic groups can participate. The current situation in Cyprus is that the Greek Cypriots live primarily in the southern part of the island known as the Republic of Cyprus which is an internationally recognized political state. Turkish Cypriots live in the northern part of the Island in territory named the Turkish Republic of North Cyprus. This 'fragility' and lack of legitimacy of this territorial division have certainly not ended ethnic tensions and, indeed, may keep historical memories and tensions alive.[19] Political agreements that have the support of both parties are required to establish legitimate and solid territory for each group, particularly if separation is deemed the appropriate means to handle inter-communal tensions.[20] Byrne and Carter point out, however, the role of intergroup conflict between both moderates and extremists in exacerbating tensions within and between ethnic communities. A holistic model of peacebuilding must take this important factor into consideration.

Economic Factors

Economic factors refer to the extent that there are sufficient economic resources which are distributed equitably to the main parties. In Cyprus and in Northern Ireland, for example, Greek Cypriots and Unionists, respectively have greater access to economic resources.[21] In Northern Cyprus, unemployment is high and economic development is limited by the international sanction regarding legitimacy of the state. Reliance is heavy on Turkey for support. The economy in the Republic of Cyprus is booming with a heavy influence from tourism and petrol dollars from the Middle East as banking and investment switched from war-torn Lebanon to the Southern part of the island. Indeed, the Republic's economy is heavily reliant on cheap Turkish Cypriot labour to meet these demands. The partition of the island delivered some of the prime tourist locations to Northern Cyprus (like Kyrenia) which significantly affects the Republic's revenue.[22] While the current economic disparity may heighten the inter-communal tensions, the current existence of economic reliance on the Northern Cyprus work force as well as the tremendous potential for further tourism presents an opportunity for further economic development directed at more equitable distributions of resources. Relevant economic activities are not only internal to the island (such as bi-communal efforts in running and maintaining Nicosia) but also come from outside in the form of public and more private forms of investment. This is hindered considerably by the international refusal to acknowledge the legitimacy of Northern Cyprus – an example of where political solutions and economic activities need to go hand-in-hand.

The more recent war-torn areas of Bosnia, Rwanda, and Kosovo suffer from the most basic problem of rebuilding an economy and putting people back to work, that is, social-economic sustainable development. For example, the current peace agreement in Northern Ireland does include efforts/activities focusing on rebuilding the economy and re-employment.

Psychocultural Factors

Psychocultural factors concern the more social psychological or subjective aspects of inter-ethnic conflict.[23] They refer to the intergroup perceptions and ethnocentrism that often characterizes escalated disputes. Fisher and Keashly's stages of escalation succinctly describe the perceptual shifts that occur to facilitate conflict escalation.[24] Briefly, each group moves from mutual recognition and valuing of each other to valuing their own group as more of everything in comparison to the other group. The other group or groups now become the enemy and the survival of one group may become connected to the demise of the other. 'Ethnic cleansing' in Bosnia and Kosovo is an example of the extremity of these perceptual shifts.

A variety of activities and events can be used by each group to support the developing image of the enemy. The earlier discussion of historical factors illustrates how interpretations of past events can be made to support the superiority of one group and the need for the destruction of the other. A 1994 movie on Canadian–United States relations – *Canadian Bacon* – humorously illustrates the process of developing stereotyping and prejudice to create the enemy. In this case, Canada was portrayed as an enemy of the United States by interpretation of innocuous past events as examples of evil intention. For example, demographically more than 90 per cent of Canada's population lives along the border with the United States. This was reinterpreted in the media as a 'massing' on the border in order to facilitate an attack. As humorous as this started out to be, the movie quickly illustrates how tensions can be fuelled where none existed before by the manipulation of information by invested parties.

Several groups and activities can be instrumental in reconstructing these perceptions and images – just as they may have been in constructing them.[25] We have already mentioned the role of the media when we discussed historical reeducation. The media can be critical here in the portrayal of the main parties and what activities and events they choose to focus on.[26] Since 1994, efforts between Canadian journalists and *The Network: Interaction for Conflict Resolution*, a non-profit public education network, have focused on developing media awareness and skill in the tools of conflict analysis which have included the social psychological factors influencing perceptions and stereotyping and their connection to conflict escalation. In a more punitive way, the media can focus on 'outrageous' examples of a party's behaviour in an effort to bring unwanted public attention to bear. A Colonel with the Canadian unit of United Nations Protection Force (UNPROFOR) in Bosnia-Herzegovina in 1995 talked in an interview about how 'threats' to have the media focus on Serb violation of United Nations passage through checkpoints facilitated the end to a blockade. This latter use of the media is suggested in moderation if only to get parties to the table.

Continuing with the intergroup level, efforts and activities at bringing together members of the communities in joint cooperative and mutually beneficial efforts would also be useful. The notion of superordinate goal comes in to play here. Briefly, a superordinate goal is a goal that all parties want to achieve but cannot be achieved without the participation of all parties.[27] Intergroup contact can facilitate enhanced positive attitudes under particular conditions: (1) high acquaintance potential situations which permit parties to come to know each other as individuals; (2) equal status contact in which parties interact on a coequal basis; (3) support of key institutional authorities; (4) joint cooperative task and reward structure; and (5) the characteristics of the individual participants who are moderate-to-highly competent and mild-to-moderately prejudiced.[28] In Nicosia, the divided city, water, sewage, and building maintenance are carried out by a bi-communal group of Greek and Turkish Cypriots representing the two communities. Informal sessions to bring together influential Greek and Turkish Cypriots to involve them in interactive problem-solving discussions and the development of bi-communal projects in education have been facilitated by Canadian and American academics.

Concerted reeducation efforts and policies around inter-cultural contact and perhaps multiculturalism – assuming the political will – would also be critical in challenging these stereotypes and replacing them with more realistic and flexible ones. The process of community-building is critical here as well. This can come in the direct form of reconciliation work often facilitated by various religious groups, and storytellers, or more indirectly through the physical, economic, and social redevelopment efforts of a number of Non-Governmental Organizations (NGOs).[29]

On a more individual level, mental and physical health aid would be critical in dealing with the nightmares, terrors, and fears generated by a violent conflict and that continue to fuel the stereotypes, prejudice, and discrimination long after the violence is ended.[30] These experiences at the hands of one another form one of the major stumbling blocks to peace in Bosnia and Rwanda.

A multi-modal model of conflict resolution and termination must recognize that these six forces are interrelated and operate simultaneously at different levels along different time lines. A holistic systems approach, therefore, must consider cross-level efforts that are both sensitive and flexible in our efforts at building sustainable peace in protracted ethno-political conflicts.

The Impact of Cross-Level Efforts

A multi-track and multi-disciplinary evolutionary systems approach to socio-economic, political, psychocultural and structural peacebuilding brings together an intricate web of individuals, groups, organizations, interventions and processes with their own approaches, perspectives, resources, and other systems to make the time ripe to successfully enable a conflict-habituated system to become a peace system.[31] This approach includes a variety of subjective and objective conflict resolution intervention and peacebuilding strategies working together simultaneously to de-escalate and transform conflict and to address different concerns using different activities to initiate constitutional agreements and develop relationships. As noted earlier, Diamond and McDonald's articulation of multiple tracks involved in peacebuilding work describe the broadest range of possible intervention actors and activities. From this range, we will focus on the following configuration of players and mechanisms: (1) a functional governmental system, (2) middle-tier elites, (3) public opinion and communication, (4) research, training and education, (5) religious, (6) funding and business, (7) professional conflict resolution, (8) private citizen activism, and (9) exogenous actors and factors.[32]

Functional Governmental System

Functionalism is based on the idea that cooperation between parties on non-political specific issues would build trust and mutual understanding, and would de-escalate tensions, changing expectations about interaction. This process of enthused collaboration would ensure the development of interlocking functional units as the route to international order. In order to prevent regional conflict in the future between Germany and France, Robert Schuman and Jean Monnet, therefore, believed in 1945 that it was necessary to bypass state sovereignty and the rivalry of states by establishing habits of cooperation in non-political matters free of the conflict of national interests. The idea was to develop a supranational authority that was independent of the member states, moving to political unity by integrating one sector at a time – social and economic. Cooperation in socio-economic areas would build habits of interaction and common values that would spill over into the political system and develop a working-peace system where the emphasis would be on transactions not constitutions.[33] For example, interdependent relationships in the European Union are more or less asymmetrical depending on the characteristics of issue areas, the interests of elites and the aggregate levels of power of the states involved.

The transfer of sovereignty through non-political activities would focus on common needs and let people think in non-national terms. Apolitical technical cooperation would whittle away the independent sovereign nation and allow this process of ramification to sneak-up on the authority of the state.[34] Incremental integration would attract public affinity away from the nation-state to increase the web of regional authority.[35] A functional type of community is stable, would keep the peace, limit nationalism, allow collective bargaining and creative conflict management, and is as effective as a federated type.[36] Federalism assumes strong nationalism while functionalism or integration tries to limit it.

As an example, a European Economic Community (EEC) could be set up between economic elites in Israel, Jordan and the Palestinian Authority that would address economic interests and in the process establish a working peace system in the region. The three states could set up regional institutions to provide rules and procedures to manage conflict and their interdependent relations.[37] Thus, neo-functionalism or elite power-sharing refines and facilitates the goals of the functionalist model by getting economic and political elites to buy into interdependent activities and arrangements.

Middle Tier Elites

Lederach makes the most important point, that middle-range approaches to peacebuilding 'contains a set of leaders with a determinant location in the conflict who, if integrated properly, might provide the key to creating an infrastructure for achieving and sustaining peace.'[38] Consequently, middle-range economic, political and bureaucratic elites working together in an interdependent and integrative way are a critical track in any peacebuilding system.

Within the context of the EEC, for example, Haas replaced non-empirical community interest with empirical plurality interest.[39] It is within the elites' rational self-interest to collaborate for mutual gain and increase their welfare. Self-interest and welfare would lead to cooperation that would result in the peaceful transformation of regional conflicts.

Spillover may not be an automatic or a necessary consequence of technical cooperation, as Mitrany had hoped, because the integrated community may not separate technical tasks from politics or welfare from power. Power is the means and welfare an end, but power is not the end for the state. The elites or mandarins must see that integration is in their economic and political interests. They are important linkages in assessing what the state will realistically concede and what it will expect. Opposing perceptions of conflict can escalate among organizational actors who find themselves thrust into a confused and turbulent milieu by the regional integration process.

The number of (organizational) actors is very large. Each pursues a variety of objectives which are mutually incompatible, but each is also unsure of the trade-offs between the objectives. Each actor is tied into a network of interdependencies with other actors that are as confused as the first. Yet some of the objectives sought by each cannot be obtained without cooperation from others.[40]

There are some criticisms that one can make of the neo-functionalist approach to ethno-political conflict transformation. First, Haas does not illustrate how to inject emotional idealism into the European movement against nationalism.[41] Economic improvements may in fact exacerbate conflict based on ethnic cleavages. Hence, the international community must move from a wholly statist analysis to one which is communally centred. Second, just because there is cooperation in some areas does not mean loyalties will be transferred to the regional level or that state authority will be surrendered to regional supranational institutions. For example, the strikes by Eurocrats in Euratom in 1972 illustrate a breakdown in the neo-functionalist thesis of integration by bureaucratic inducement. On the other hand, the relative political stability of the Benelux countries is through the collegial cooperation of political elites.[42] Finally, in the past, De Gaulle and Thatcher's realist focus on the *grandeur* of the nation-state ensured that France and Britain did not initially accept the *engrenage* of the European community's institutions or the erosion of national sovereignty. However, actors' motives, perceptions, and objectives have changed. Britain and France now realize that they can only influence world affairs as part of the European Union (EU) than on their own. Also, the enlargement of the EU has increased benefits of transactions for all members.

Dialogue groups, problem-solving workshops and storytelling that deals with the psychocultural factors of superordinate goals, stereotypes and attitude change, may be a useful intervention approach here. The media is also a critical component in shaping public opinion and communication.

Public Opinion and Communication

The media is a critical track in a holistic peacebuilding system because it can assist in reconstructing a common history, preventing enemy imaging, focusing public attention on violations of individual, political and human rights, and by getting protagonists to the table. The present electronic age is shaping civilization in an image of the 'Tribal Village'.[43] In fact, the global communications network has been used for crisis management by the military in the past.[44] The mass media, therefore, shapes a dual climate of opinion because issues it focuses on are what people have opinions about and the facts that the media presents are what people base their opinions on.[45]

The media can act as facilitators of negotiations in protracted conflict situations. Journalists can influence ethno-political conflicts and their resolution because they tell the public what is happening. After the Tet Offensive during the Vietnam War, the evening 'body counts' of the media turned the United States public against the war. Similarly, the Muslims of Bosnia wanted the Pope to come and say mass in the Olympic stadium in Sarajevo after the siege lifted in the summer of 1996 because the media would cover the event. People had begun to forget the Muslims, but having the Pope in Bosnia would renew media interest in the plight of the Muslim people.[46]

Also, the British government was having secret talks with the Provisional IRA (PIRA) nine months prior to the eventual ceasefire called in November 1995. Gerry Adams was banned from travelling to Britain and Sinn Fein was prevented from appearing on television or on radio. An observer leaked to the press that the PIRA was having secret negotiations with the British government. A member of the Reverend Paisley's

Democratic Unionists Party (DUP) stole the documents and passed them to Eamonn O'Malley, a journalist in the Republic of Ireland. Two weeks previously the British Prime Minister, John Major, who stated in a questions-and-answers period in the House of Commons that it would 'turn his stomach' to talk to the PIRA, had to act quickly to gain credibility. Three weeks later, on 15 December 1993, the Downing Street Declaration was announced in a public relations coup by John Major and his Irish counterpart, Albert Reynolds. The peace process would be in a different place today if the media had not broken the story and propelled the British government into action. The Joint Declaration, with its emphasis on the mutual consent of both communities to find an acceptable agreement, was instrumental in getting the PIRA to announce a 'complete cessation of military operations' on 31 August 1994.[47]

Unlike some of the other interventions, the possibilities for the media to be constructive are still just possibilities with little concrete evidence so far as to whether it can be truly constructive.[48] Yet, most people who receive their information from broadcasting sources may not get the whole story or the full picture of a particular conflict. For example, the middle classes in Bosnia and Kosovo speak English, tend to be more conciliatory, and are more accessible to reporters and know that if they tell a good story that it will get on the news; and the Kuwaiti ambassador's daughter during the Gulf War talked of the rapes of Kuwaiti women by Iraqi soldiers, when in fact she was in the United States during the whole crisis. The media, therefore, can be a catalyst for getting parties to the table or in facilitating dialogue.

Research, Training and Education

Research, training and education are a critical component of any peacebuilding system because these efforts attempt to influence perceptions and attitudes, and build a culture of peace.

For example, the Lester B. Pearson Canadian International Peacekeeping Training Center (PPC) was established by the Canadian Government in 1994 to assist national and international groups in examining specific peacekeeping issues and in updating their knowledge with the latest peacekeeping practices through workshops, training and educational courses. Similarly, the Nordic countries established their own Center in 1964 to train soldiers designated for United Nations peacekeeping duties in conflict resolution and peacemaking skills.[49]

An International Civil Society course and storytelling classes could also be a part of the common curriculum in high school education around the world, focusing on multicultural reality and eliminating the 'lonely people in a lonely world' idea.[50] Different cultural perspectives should be injected into adult continuing education programs to counter the nationalism and xenophobia that permeates the civil society.

The expanded growth of the integrated school sector and a visible war-weariness in Northern Ireland in the 1990s was one important early-warning indicator to suggest that the political bubble was about to burst, and a window of opportunity had emerged to suggest that a possible peace process was imminent. Integrated schools are unique cultural experiences. These institutions provide a haven so that children feel safe from the outside violence and can freely mingle and express themselves. Within the Northern Ireland context integrated schools have provided a critical space for Unionist and Nationalist schoolchildren to learn about each other's cultural experiences, history and religion. The contact has allowed these children to expand and widen the identity pie so that in the process they have developed a 'shared identity.'[51]

Also, the Carter Center in the U.S. monitors elections, mediates international and intra-nation negotiations, offers conflict resolution, training and education programs, talks to pariah states, and tries to understand how people speak in negotiations. The Carter Center also tries to find out what kind of language leads to positive and negative evaluations – for example, the Greek government and the Macedonian government negotiations over the name of the Republic.

Thus, research, training and education are a critical track in a cross-level intervention strategy. Developing a civic education and citizenship process can facilitate peaceful change in protracted ethno-political conflicts by demystifying legends, distortions of perceptions, stereotypes of the other, thus effecting reconciliation and the empowerment of all citizens.

Religion

Religion is an important track of the multilevel peacebuilding system because religious figures can work together to create a respectful, cooperative and tolerant human infrastructure by focusing on the humanity of all individuals.

From 1995 to 1997, Archbishop Desmond Tutu's Truth and Reconciliation Commission (TRC) facilitated the reconciliation and healing between the survivors and perpetrators of violence in South Africa. The TRC was based in the Ubuntu theology of Archbishop Tutu which recognized the need of people to understand and empathize with other human beings in order to heal from South Africa's traumatic apartheid past and to restore harmony.[52] The dialogue process allowed both sides to listen and take responsibility by describing the violence committed.

In Northern Ireland, religious leaders have played a key role in facilitating ceasefires between the British government and paramilitary organizations. The 1981 Hunger Strike in Northern Ireland in which ten

PIRA prisoners on remand in the Maze jail died 'may be seen as a watershed in the Anglo-Irish conflict' because of the role of external and internal religious actors.[53] External religious figures such as the Papal Nuncio Monsignor Alabrandi and Fr. Magee, the Pope's Secretary, could not initially break through the negotiation impasse between the hunger strikers and the Thatcher government. Also, the internal intervention of the late all Ireland Catholic Primate, Cardinal O'Fiaich, could not break the negotiation deadlock because the PIRA had already established Brendan McFarlane – the PIRA's commanding officer in the Maze prison – in an arbitrator's role between the prisoners and the British government. In the end, third-party external and internal religious interveners successfully facilitated an agreement between the families of the men on strike and the British government.

Funding and Business

What role has external economic assistance in nurturing inter-communal reconciliation and facilitating the resolution of protracted ethno-political conflict? One can take the view that conflict de-escalation, economic prosperity and inter-communal cooperation are inextricably interconnected in a complex way.[54] International economic assistance exerts important but under-examined influences upon both intra and inter-ethnic relations in divided societies. Since much ethno-political conflict is rooted in competition for scarce resources, international assistance – in terms of both funding and policy recommendations – can obviously influence both economic and social development. At present, however, empirical studies of the dynamic process of interactive formation or reformulation of ethnic identities resulting from economic changes driven by international forces remain scarce. For example, external economic aid through the International Fund for Ireland and the European Union Peace and Reconciliation Fund has influenced sustainable economic aid in Northern Ireland by attempting to transform the conflict and build a positive peace.[55] Recent peace initiatives in Bosnia, Northern Ireland, the Middle East and South Africa indicate the necessity of economic aid and political initiatives in facilitating conflict resolution in divided nations.

With respect to business, Multinational Corporations (MNCs) and banks can play a crucial role in institutionalizing and facilitating conflict reduction by promoting economic growth in societies ravaged by violence and economic decline. These external MNCs can provide an important role in the reconstruction of the economy, infrastructure and other objective conditions that have escalated inter-communal conflicts in the past.

Also, the role of grassroots organizations primarily concerned with issues related to inter-communal reconciliation and cooperation within a strife-ridden society could play a very important role in this process. For example, the Phoenix West Belfast Trust and the West Belfast Economic Forum in Northern Ireland are important mechanisms in the economic renewal of West Belfast, attracting MNCs and monopoly capital to Belfast. They also work with small local entrepreneurs to develop a local economic development strategy.

Professional Conflict Resolution

Third-party interveners in protracted ethno-political conflicts are typically power brokers, problem-solvers, dominators or re-builders of relationships.[56] Furthermore, interveners can be private individuals, practitioner-academics, regional, transnational and international organizations, and small and large states who use formal and informal conflict resolution approaches to terminate and/or resolve ethno-political strife.[57]

However, third-party interveners must be careful to respect the cultural wisdom and creative conflict resolution processes of local cultures if the parties in conflict are to become empowered agents of social change.

Lederach warns against using one universal approach to transferring conflict resolution skills and processes.[58] Instead, he describes an elicitive approach that draws on the skills and implicit knowledge of local people who wish to transform their conflict milieu. The elicitive approach concentrates on using dialogue groups, focus groups, and storytelling in multicultural settings to empower local groups in taking charge of their conflict and its resolution. Insider-partials, who live in the conflict environment, often play a critical role in de-escalating tensions, terminating conflict, and in restoring harmony in the relationship.

Private Citizens, Local Groups and Grassroots Activism

Lederach suggests that 'people and their everyday understandings are key resources'.[59] Conflict interveners need to tap into that well of knowledge and local experience if they are to psychologically and politically empower people and successfully transform the conflict. Similarly, Schwerin argues that transformational politics is the politics of non-violent participation whereby every person can influence and change socio-economic and political institutions that impact their lives.[60] These people can learn and use new political and psychological empowerment skills to help others and empower themselves.

Citizen diplomats are important activists who intervene to transform conflict and act as catalysts for social change. Dorothy Schneider of St. Louis, Missouri has worked tenaciously since the end of World War II to create United Nations Day so that the citizens of the world would be cognizant of the continued valuable existence of the UN and of international

NGOs such as the Red Cross and Amnesty International. Ms Schneider spent over 40 years writing scores of letters to world leaders and lobbying members of the U.S. Congress to get the UN to recognize UN Day. Her persistence paid off when the UN unanimously adopted 24 October as the official International Peace Day. Schneider, a retired nurse, is an important example of what Lederach calls middle-tier leadership and clearly demonstrates the power of individual activism and commitment to peaceful change.[61]

Local middle-range organizations such as trade unions, universities, religious organizations and social groups are also an important network of peacebuilding agents who understand the plight of, and are connected to, activists working at the grass-roots levels of different societies. Middle-range organizations are also connected to political leaders in the top levels and have relationships that cut across boundaries and conflict lines.[62] For example, the 'Love Your Neighbor' NGO was set up in 1996 by a retired director of human resources in Metro-Dade County, Miami, Florida, Jim Ward, who is connected to both grass-roots organizations and political decision-makers. Love Your Neighbor seeks to promote contact, reconciliation, healing, and cultural understanding among South Florida's diverse cultural groups. Florence Ross, a founding member of a local Ft. Lauderdale chapter of 'Grandmothers for Peace', is starting an Elder Peacemaking Sage Center at Nova Southeastern University in Fort Lauderdale, Florida. This will provide a place for young people to come and learn from elder spiritual peacemakers who have worked throughout their lives in the peacemaking trenches. These organizations are an effective and efficient mechanism of peacebuilding and transformational conflict resolution. Consequently, individuals and groups other than those whose formal roles are to make peace, can do something to facilitate the peace process, for example construction workers, storytellers, practitioner-academics, pastors, school teachers, and nurses among others. We are all involved in this process just as we are all involved in war. It is our perception that private citizens are looking for opportunities for how they can become involved and make a difference.

External Actors and Factors

We need to distinguish between external intervention and internal intervention, non-invited third parties, and when the timing is ripe to intervene in protracted conflict situations. For example, the relations between outside interested parties – guarantors – is crucial in explaining ethno-political conflict and its resolution. The importance of external actors and exogenous factors in conflict and conflict resolution is underplayed in the literature, which often stresses endogenous factors.

In Northern Ireland, for example, Anglo-Irish cooperation is the key factor behind the 1998 Good Friday peace agreement. 'External ethno-guarantors,' because of their cooperative stance, have helped to bring about a settlement there, albeit still shaky.[63] Political efforts by both external ethno-guarantors attempting to impose a 'coercive consociational' elite power-sharing model on internal co-nationals in Northern Ireland have also recently escalated intragroup conflict within both the Unionist and Nationalist communities.[64] 'High impact issues' – decommissioning of arms and Northern Ireland's constitutional position within the United Kingdom – can endanger ethnic group identity and impede internal cohesion and group structure, or conflict can be functional in creating ethnic group norms and sentiment.[65] However, the external ethno-guarantor framework can help us understand the relationship between exogenous and endogenous factors and actors in Bosnia, Rwanda, and more recently in Kosovo.

Short-term intervention by humanitarian aid agencies can alleviate the plight of refugees fleeing violence and ethnic cleansing. For example, ongoing efforts in Albania and Macedonia to feed, cloth and shelter over 800,000 Kosovar Albanian refugees proved to be a tremendous challenge to international relief agencies operating on the ground. Yet the issues of refugees and displaced persons are critical considerations in any coordinated peacebuilding effort.

Coordination of Approaches

As Fisher and Keashly have noted, the challenge in proposing a complementarity of interventions is to identify the means of facilitating the desired coordination of effort.[66] One possible mechanism is the development of an early warning system to forecast ethno-political conflict as well as establishing an NGO to coordinate internal and external approaches to conflict resolution.

A world-wide Internet system promoting cross-regional fertilization by broadening the scope of shared knowledge and experience, and by promoting participation in the gathering and analysis and rapid dissemination of early warning information from a variety of multiple sources, is part of an ongoing debate within the social science community.[67] Moreover, Duffy suggests that:

An Internet-based system would afford an immediate forum for UN bureaucrats, government officials, insurgents, journalists, NGOs, academics, business executives, and ordinary citizens to brainstorm and problem solve together. It has no filters or screens to silence voices, yet no one is deluged with information.[68]

However, the Internet-based system should demonstrate practical results for the policy-making community to be taken seriously. The key concern becomes what is done by decision makers with the information in situations of escalated ethno-political conflicts.

Alternatively, it could become the mission of the United Nations to develop an NGO called Ethno-Watch that would be an international alert system focusing on the protection of ethnic groups from ethnic violence and cleansing, and gather data for an early warning database.[69] Ethno-Watch could also centralize the functions of different groups within protagonists, provide an information network for parties by acting as a clearing house and as a forum for local NGOs.

In the past, NGOs have been mainly used in the capacity of humanitarian aid and development. However, Ethno-Watch could help to create strategic points of contact and coordination by creating better links between the levels of activities of local and external groups, access to sharing resources, and in developing a framework for reconciliation. The idea would be to not only study the epidemiology of conflict but also to analyze the historical time lines. For example, why in one instance does an ethno-political conflict escalate and in another it is successfully managed? We need data on the process and dynamics of conflicts that have been resolved. Part of this process could be to establish the Delphi Method so that groups around the world could communicate with each other via E-mail to alert and mobilize the world leaders within the United Nations to a potential conflict situation. The Delphi technique is a useful instrument to elicit a broad range of up-to-date technological information and ideas about a specific question not available in the current academic literature. The technique assists key technical experts who are separated by long distances yet motivated by personal interest to clarify and share crucial information on a particularly important issue.[70]

Also, a field survey of NGO workers such as the Red Cross, United Nations High Commission for Refugees (UNHCR) and Amnesty International would be useful as an early warning system to get important indicators of a possible outbreak of violence. However, caution must be taken not to compromise the mission of the humanitarian NGOs, which is to be neutral regarding the conflict itself. Similarly, video cameras could be used as an early warning device, every six months, to collect data on the ground to see possible changes in a society. In-depth interviews would also be beneficial to tap into the local mind-set because people at the grassroots are sensitive in detecting changes in the system. A survey of the national and local papers could also indicate a change in the political rhetoric and the threat of possible escalation or outbreak of violence. We can use this knowledge from the culture group to identify early warning systems. Having an early warning data set would be an important step to cut across counter information and stereotypes, to provide important information for activist/advocacy interveners and practitioner-academics on when to intervene.

This discussion of coordination would be incomplete without acknowledging the role of current organizations that explicitly bring together actors from the various tracks or intervention modes. Consistent with their mission of promoting a systems approach to peacebuilding, the Institute for Multi-Track Diplomacy in Washington, D.C. headed by Louise Diamond and Former Ambassador John McDonald, is explicitly engaged in identifying and facilitating the development of partnerships among and across members of the various tracks within a particular conflict region on a variety of peacebuilding projects. They have been active in projects in Cyprus, Liberia, India and Pakistan, to mention a few.

The Lester B. Pearson Canadian International Peacekeeping Training Institute in Cornwallis Park, Nova Scotia, Canada, under the direction of Alex Morrison, brings together members of the 'new peacekeeping partnership' in a variety of training sessions and conferences. The new peacekeeping partnership expands the definition of peacekeeping beyond the military to include 'civilian peacekeepers' such as the media, elections, humanitarian NGOs, civil police and diplomats, all of whom are often involved in some capacity in ameliorating various conflicts. The idea behind bringing together these diverse participants is to expose them to the various perspectives and goals they bring, to note their similarities and differences, and to explore points of complementarity. The Pearson Center is one of several peacekeeping training centres throughout the world who meet on a regular basis to share experiences and build alliances.

In addition to the specific projects and educational opportunities both these organizations organize and facilitate, a key outcome central to the notion of coordinated action across interveners is that the participants in their activities develop personal and professional relationships that will be useful in current and future situations far beyond the specific project or meeting.

Conclusions

Kriesberg argues that conflicts can be 'waged constructively,' and in a transforming world 'many of our old paradigms are no longer valid'.[71] Thus, a healthy eclecticism in both practical application and theory building must be encouraged to simultaneously address subjective and objective criteria that fuel protracted ethno-political conflicts and, consequently, must be addressed in any peacebuilding efforts.

Through an initial statement of the value of a multi-modal, multilevel contingency approach to conflict intervention in protracted ethno-political conflicts and our subsequent discussion of multiple modes of intervention activities and potential coordinating mechanisms, we hope we have begun what will prove to be a lively and productive conversation with everyone interested in conflict resolution. In particular, we believe that such a model and the subsequent conversations and activities it stimulates could help practitioners and theory builders to recognize that: (1) complex and dynamic conflict milieus demand a flexible and sensitive approach to building theoretical models based on practitioner and protagonist input; (2) conflict resolution and peacebuilding necessitate a multi-modal complementarity approach at multiple levels; (3) a variety of activities and actors can be usefully considered as intervention; and (4) local and external agencies are needed to select and coordinate a series of efforts to fit the specific conflict context. In addition, we hope we have highlighted the value that can be gained by combining emic and etic approaches to conflict analysis and resolution, and by examining the interrelationship of Western and indigenous approaches to conflict resolution.

To the extent that a multi-modal, multilevel approach has value, the contingency aspect, which was not explored in this study, needs to be examined. Thus, further work needs to focus on identifying the specific cues and places where particular sequencing and/or simultaneous involvement of different interventions would be warranted and most effective. Fisher and Keashly's contingency model and subsequent interpretations and expansions of it (such as Bloomfield) provide some initial ideas in terms of social psychological cues to stages of escalation.[72]

ACKNOWLEDGEMENTS

We would like to take this opportunity to thank Tom Boudreau, Gaylene Lee, Fred Pearson, Ruzica Rosandic, Jessica Senehi, Bill Warters and Honggang Yang for reading an earlier draft of the paper. Their comments and feedback are deeply appreciated.

NOTES

1. Sean Byrne and Neal Carter, 'Social Cubism: Six Social Forces of Ethnoterritorial Politics in Northern Ireland and Quebec', *Peace and Conflict Studies*, Vol.3, No.2, 1996, pp.52–72.
2. Ronald Fisher and Loraleigh Keashly, 'The Potential Complementarity of Mediation and Consultation Within a Contingency Model of Conflict Resolution', *Journal of Peace Research*, Vol.28, No.1, 1991, pp.29–42; Loraleigh Keashly and Ronald Fisher, 'A Contingency Approach on Conflict Interventions: Theoretical and Practical Considerations', in Jacob Bercovitch (ed.), *Resolving International Conflicts: The Theory and Practice of Mediation*, Boulder: Lynne Rienner, 1996, pp.235–63; and idem, 'Towards A Contingency Approach to Third Party Intervention in Regional Conflict: A Cyprus Illustration', *International Journal*, Vol.45, No.1, 1990, pp.424–53.
3. Louise Diamond and John McDonald, *Multi-Track Diplomacy: A Systems Approach to Peace*, West Hartford: Kumarian Press, 1996.

4. John Paul Lederach, *Building Peace: Sustainable Reconciliation in Divided Societies* Washington D.C.: United States Institute of Peace Press, 1997, hereafter USIP Press.
5. Michael Lund, *Preventing Violent Conflicts: A Strategy for Preventive Diplomacy*, Washington D.C.: USIP Press, 1996.
6. Ronald Fisher, *Interactive Conflict Resolution: Pioneers, Potential and Prospects*, Syracuse: Syracuse UP, 1996.
7. David Bloomfield, *Peacemaking Strategies in Northern Ireland: Building Complementarity in Conflict Management Theory*, Basingstoke: Macmillan, 1996; Paul Dixon, 'Paths to Peace in Northern Ireland: Civil Society and Consociational Approaches', *Democratization*, Vol.4, No.2, 1997, pp.1–27; Mervyn Love, *Peace-Building Through Reconciliation in Northern Ireland*, Aldershot: Avebury, 1995; and Joseph Ruane and Jennifer Todd, *The Dynamics of Conflict in Northern Ireland: Power, Conflict and Emancipation*, Cambridge: Cambridge University Press, 1995.
8. See Bloomfield (n.7); Thomas Boudreau, *Universitas*, NY: Praeger, 1998; Elise Boulding, *Building a Global Civic Culture*, Syracuse: Syracuse UP, 1990; John Burton, *Conflict: Resolution and Provention*, London: Macmillan, 1990; Sean Byrne, *Growing Up in a Divided Society: The Influence of Conflict on Belfast Schoolchildren*, Cranbury: Associated UPs, 1997; idem, 'Belfast Schoolchildren's Images of Conflict and Social Change: Signs of Hope in Integrated Education', *Mind and Human Interaction*, Vol.8, No.3, 1997, pp.172–86; Adam Curle, *Tools for Transformation: A Personal Study*, Wallbridge: Hawthorn Press; Sean Byrne and Michael Ayulo, 'External Economic Aid in Ethno-Political Conflict: A View From Northern Ireland', *Security Dialogue*, Vol.29, No.4, 1998, pp.421–34; Ronald Fisher, 'Third Party Consultation as a Method of Inter-Group Conflict Resolution: A Review of Studies', *Journal of Conflict Resolution*, Vol.27, No.2, 1983, pp.301–34; idem, (n.6); Johan Galtung, *Peace by Peaceful Means: Peace and Conflict, Development and Civilization*, London: Sage, 1996; Michael Henderson, *The Forgiveness Factor: Stories of Hope in a World of Conflict*, London: Grovesenor, 1996; John Hume, *A New Ireland: Politics, Peace and Reconciliation*, Boulder: Roberts Rineheart, 1996; Cynthia Irvin and Sean Byrne, *The Politics and Practice of External Economic Assistance in Resolving Protracted Ethnic Conflicts: Lessons From Northern Ireland*, Washington D.C.: USIP Press, forthcoming; Herb Kelman, 'Group Processes in the Resolution of International Conflicts: Experiences from the Israeli–Palestinian Case,' *The American Psychologist*, Vol.52, No.3, 1997, pp.212–20; idem, 'Interactive Problem Solving: The Uses and Limits of a Therapeutic Model for the Resolution of International Conflicts', in Vamik Volkan, Demetrious Julius and Joseph Montville (eds.), *The Psychodynamics of International Relationships: Unofficial Diplomacy at Work*, Lexington: Lexington Books, 1991, pp.145–60; Louis Kriesberg, *Constructive Conflicts: From Escalation to Resolution*, Boulder: Rowman and Littlefield, 1998; Lederach (n.4); Love (n.7); Martha Minow, *Between Vengeance and Forgiveness: Facing History After Genocide and Mass Violence*, Boston: Beacon Press,,1998; Ruzica Rosandic and Vesna Pesic, 'Warfare, Patriotism and Patriarchy: The Analysis of Elementary School Textbooks', Belgrade: Center for Anti-War Action and Association, 1994, pp.1–78; Jay Rothman, *Resolving Identity Based Conflicts*, San Francisco: Jossey Bass, 1997; Ruane and Todd (n.7); Edward Schwerin, *Mediation, Citizen Empowerment and Transformational Politics*, Westport: Greenwood, 1996; Jessica Senehi, 'Language, Culture and Conflict: Storytelling as a Matter of Life and Death', *Mind and Human Interaction*, Vol.7, No.3, 1996, pp.150–64; idem, 'Constructive Storytelling in Intercommunal Conflicts: Building Community, Building Peace', in Sean Byrne and Cynthia Irvin, *Reconcilable Differences: Turning Points in Ethnopolitical Conflicts*, West Hartford: Kumarian Press, 2000, pp.125–53; idem, 'Constructive Storytelling: Building Community, Building Peace', doctoral dissertation, Maxwell School, Syracuse: Syracuse University, 2000; Warren Strobel, *Late Breaking Foreign Policy: The News Media's Influence on Peace Operations*, Washington D.C.: USIP Press, 1997; Vamik Volkan, *Blood Lines: From Ethnic Pride to Ethnic Terrorism*, Boulder: Westview, 1998; Stephen Woolport, Christa Daryl Slaton and Edward Schwerin (eds.), *Transformational Politics: Theory, Study and Practice*, Albany: State University of New York Press, 1998; and Honggang Yang, 'The Concept of Trust and Trustbuilding', *A Leadership Journal: Women in Leadership-Sharing the Vision*, Vol.2, No.2, 1998, pp.19–29.

9. Marc Howard Ross, *The Management of Conflicts: Interpretations and Interests in Comparative Perspective*, New Haven: Yale UP, 1993; Senehi (n.8); Anthony D. Smith, *National Identity*, Reno: University of Nevada Press, 1991.
10. Tozun Bahcheli, *Greek–Turkish Relations Since 1955*, Boulder: Westview, 1990; and Keashly and Fisher (n.2).
11. Volkan (n.8); and, Rosandic and Pesic (n.8).
12. Byrne (n.8).
13. See Fisher (n.6) and Keashly and Fisher (n.2). Note that this process of reconciliation occurred within the buffer zone established and monitored by the United Nations in Cyprus and may not have been possible without that critical space.
14. John Whyte, *Interpreting Northern Ireland*, Oxford: Clarendon Press, 1990.
15. Byrne and Carter (n.1), p.57.
16. Cynthia Irvin, *Militant Nationalism: Between Movement and Party in Northern Ireland and the Basque Country*, Duluth: University of Minnesota Press, 1999; and, John McGarry and Brendan O'Leary, *Explaining Northern Ireland: Broken Images*, Cambridge: Blackwell, 1995.
17. Ian Liebenberg and Abebe Zegeye, 'Pathway to Democracy: The Case of the South African Truth and Reconciliation Process', *Social Identities*, Vol.4, No.3, 1998, pp.541–58; and, John McGarry, 'Political Settlements in Northern Ireland and South Africa', *Political Studies*, Vol.46, No.5, 1998, pp.1–17.
18. Christopher Bennett, *Yugoslavia's Bloody Collapse: Causes, Courses and Consequences*, London: Hurst and Co., 1995.
19. Keashly and Fisher (n.2); Admanata Pollis, 'The Social Construction of Ethnicity and Nationality: The Case of Cyprus', *Nationalism and Ethnic Politics*, Vol.2, No.1, 1996, pp.67–90; and, Volkan (n.8).
20. Frank Wright, *Northern Ireland: A Comparative Perspective*, Dublin: Gill and Macmillan, 1987.
21. Sean Byrne, 'Power Politics as Usual in Cyprus and Northern Ireland: Divided Islands and the Roles of External Ethno-Guarantors', *Nationalism and Ethnic Politics*, Vol.6, No.1, 2000, pp.24–52.
22. Bahcheli (n.10); and, Pollis (n.19).
23. Ross (n.9).
24. Fisher and Keashly (n.2).
25. Kriesberg (n.8); Rothman (n.8); and, Volkan (n.8).
26. Strobel (n.8).
27. For example, see the robber's cave experiment of Muzafer Sherif, *In Common Predicament: Social Psychology of Intergroup Conflict and Cooperation*, Boston: Houghton Mifflin Co., 1966. Also, see Fisher (n.6); Kelman (n.8); and, Rothman (n.8).
28. See Fisher (n.6).
29. Lederach (n.4); Senehi (n.8); and, William Ury, *Getting to Peace: Transforming Conflict at Home, at Work, and in the World*, NY: Viking, 1999.
30. Ed Cairns, *Children and Political Violence*, Cambridge: Blackwell, 1996.
31. Diamond and McDonald (n.3); and, Lederach (n.4).
32. Diamond and McDonald (n.3).
33. David Mitrany, 'The Functional Approach to World Organization', *International Affairs*, Vol.24, No.3, 1948, pp.350–63; and, idem, *A Working Peace System*, Chicago: Quadrangle Books, 1966.
34. Ibid.
35. Amiatal Etzioni, *A Comparative Analysis of Complex Organizations*, NY: The Free Press, 1961; and, idem, *Political Unification*, NY: Holt, Rinehart and Winston, 1965.
36. Karl Deutsch (ed.), *Political Community and the North Atlantic Area*, Princeton: Princeton UP, 1957.
37. Robert Keohane, *After Hegemony: Cooperation and Discord in the World Political Economy*, Princeton: Princeton UP, 1984; and Robert Keohane and Joseph Nye, *Power and Interdependence: World Politics in Transition*, Boston: Little Brown and Co., 1977.
38. Lederach (n.4).

39. Ernest Haas, *The Uniting of Europe*, Stanford: Stanford UP, 1958; and, idem, *Tangles of Hope: American Commitments and World Order*, Englewood Cliffs: Prentice Hall, 1969.
40. Ernest Haas, 'Turbulent Fields and the Theory of Regional Integration', *International Organization*, Vol.30, No.2, 1976, p.179.
41. Ernest Haas, 'The Study of Regional Integration: Reflections on the Joy and Anguish of Pretheorizing,' in Leon Lindberg and Stuart Scheingold (eds.), *Regional Integration: Theory and Research*, Cambridge: Harvard UP, 1971, pp.56–78.
42. Arend Lijphart, *The Politics of Accommodation: Pluralism and Democracy in the Netherlands*, Berkley: University of California Press, 1968.
43. Marshall McLuhan, *Understanding Media: The Extensions of Man*, NY: McGraw Hill Book Co., 1964.
44. Jacques Ellul, *The Political Illusion*, NY: Alfred A. Knopf, 1967; and, Herbert Schiller, *Mass Communication and American Empire*, NY: Augustus M. Kelly, 1969.
45. Elizabeth Noelle-Neuman, *The Spiral of Silence: Public Opinion–Our Social Skin*, Chicago: University of Chicago Press, 1984.
46. In an interview with Michael Goldfarb, political correspondent for National Public Radio for the former Yugoslavia and Northern Ireland at the University of Missouri-St. Louis, 26 November 1994.
47. Paul Bew, Peter Gibbon and Henry Patterson, *Northern Ireland, 1921–1994: Political Forces and Social Classes*, London: Serif, 1995; and, Sean Byrne, 'Conflict Regulation or Conflict Resolution: Third Party Intervention in the Northern Ireland Conflict – Prospects for Peace', *Terrorism and Political Violence*, Vol.7, No.2, 1995, pp.1–24.
48. Strobel, 1997.
49. Michael Renner, 'Critical Juncture: The Future of Peacekeeping', *Worldwatch Paper 114*, Washington D.C.: Worldwatch Institute, 1993, pp.1–74.
50. Boulding (n.8); and, Senehi (n.8).
51. Byrne (n.8).
52. Minow (n.8).
53. David Beresford, *Ten Men Dead: The Story of the 1981 Irish Hunger Strike*, London: Grafton Books, 1987, p.332.
54. Milton Esman, 'Economic Performance and Ethnic Conflict', in Joseph Montiville (ed.), *Conflict and Peacemaking in Multiethnic Societies*, NY: Lexington Books, 1991, p.487.
55. Byrne and Ayulo (n.8); and, Irvin and Byrne (n.8).
56. Marieke Kleiboer, *The Multiple Realities of International Mediation*, Boulder: Lynne Rienner, 1998.
57. Jacob Bercovitch and Jeffrey Rubin (eds.), *Mediation in International Relations: Multiple Approaches to Conflict Management*, NY: St. Martins Press, 1992; Chester Crocker, Fen Osler Hampson and Pamela Aall, *Managing Global Chaos: Sources and Responses to International Conflict*, Washington D.C.: USIP Press, 1996; Christopher Mitchell and Keith Webb (eds.), *New Approaches to International Mediation*, NY: Greenwood Press, 1988; Jay Rothman, *From Confrontation to Cooperation: Resolving Ethnic and Regional Conflict*, London: Sage, 1992; William Zartman (ed.), *Elusive Peace: Negotiating An End to Civil War*, Washington D.C.: The Brookings Institution, 1995.
58. John Paul Lederach, *Preparing for Peace: Conflict Transformation Across Cultures*, Syracuse: Syracuse UP, 1995.
59. Ibid., p.26.
60. Schwerin (n.8).
61. Lederach (n.4).
62. Ibid.
63. Byrne (n.21).
64. McGarry and O'Leary (n.16); and, Brendan O'Leary and John McGarry, *The Politics of Antagonism: Understanding Northern Ireland*, Atlantic Highlands: Athlone Press.
65. Sean Byrne and Aimee Delman, 'Group Identity Formation and Intragroup Conflict', *Journal of Intergroup Relations*, Vol.25, No.4, 1999; and, Sean Byrne, 'Israel, Northern Ireland and South Africa at a Cross-Roads: Understanding Inter-Group Conflict, Peacebuilding and Conflict Resolution', *International Journal of Group Tensions*, 2000,

forthcoming.

66. Fisher and Keashly (n.2).
67. Doug Bond, Craig Jenkins, Charles Taylor and Kurt Schock, 'Mapping Mass Political Conflict and Civil Society: Issues and Prospects for the Automated Development of Event Data', *Journal of Conflict Resolution*, Vol.41, No.4, 1997, pp.553–79; Peter Brecke, 'What Stirs Concerns Is What Might Need to Be Done', *Mershon International Studies Review* (hereafter *MISR*), Vol.39, No.2, 1995, pp.321–3; John Davies and Ted Robert Gurr, *Preventive Measures: Building Risk Assessment and Crisis Early Warning Systems*, Boulder: Rowman and Littlefield, 1998; Gavan Duffy, 'An Early Warning System for the United Nations: Internet or Not?' *MISR*, Vol.39, No.2, 1995, pp.315–18; Ted Robert Gurr, *Minorities at Risk: A Global View of Ethnopolitical Conflicts*, Washington D.C.:USIP Press, 1993; idem, 'A Conceptual Framework for Screening and Interpreting Information is Required,' *MISR*, Vol.39, No.2, 1995, pp.318–19; Ted Robert Gurr and Davies; Gottfried Mayer-Kress, 'An Internet Based System Could be Productive of Peace', *MISR*, Vol.39, No.2, 1995, p.321; Philip Schrodt, 'Implementation and Methodology Present More Constraints Than Does Theory', *MISR*, Vol.39, No.2, 1995, pp.18–19.
68. Gavan Duffy, 'An Internet Based System Could Provide a Forum Across Frameworks', *MISR*, Vol.39, No.2, 1995, p.324.
69. This point was made by Professor Fred Pearson, Director of the Center for Peace and Conflict Studies, Wayne State University at the International Conference on Culture and Technology: Toward the Prevention of Genocide, Ethnocide, and Politicide, held at Wayne State University, 17 January 1995. This was the first international meeting of scholars led by Professor John Darby, former Director of INCORE, University of Ulster, Professor David Singer of the University of Michigan, and Professors Ted Robert Gurr and Barbara Harff of the Minorities at Risk project, University of Maryland, to develop a global data-bank to assist practitioners and international institutions to anticipate and respond to crisis situations before they become violent.
70. See N. Dalkey, *Delphi*, Santa Monica: Rand Corporation, 1967; and, A. Delbecg, A. Van de Ven, and D.H. Gustafson, *Group Techniques for Program Planning*, Middleton: Greenbrier Publications, 1986. An example of this technique in use is the delphi study carried out by Bill Warters, Assistant Professor of conflict resolution at Wayne State University's Center for Conflict and Peace Studies between February and April 1996 among conflict resolution programs across the U.S. to illicit key issues and concerns for graduate study in the field of conflict resolution and peace studies. The results of this study are available from the Department of Dispute Resolution at Nova Southeastern University, where Dr. Warters was a faculty colleague at that time.
71. Kriesberg (n.8), p.370.
72. Fisher and Keashly (n.2); Bloomfield (n.7); David Bloomfield, 'Towards a Complementarity in Conflict Management: Resolution and Settlement in Northern Ireland', *Journal of Peace Research*, Vol.29, No.2, 1992, pp.23–36; Dean Pruitt and Paul Olczak, 'Beyond Hope: Approaches to Resolving Seemingly Intractable Conflict', in Barbara Benedict Bunker and Jeffrey Rubin (eds.), *Conflict, Cooperation and Justice*, San Francisco: Jossey Bass, pp.59–93.

NGOs, Conflict Management and Peacekeeping

PAMELA AALL

The Background: Changes in the Nature of Peacekeeping

The current international response to conflict is a study in complexity, involving many different types of institutions, mandates, rules of engagement, decision-making structures and capabilities. The complexity itself can become a factor determining the success or failure of a third-party intervention, as these institutions launch competing initiatives or fail to support efforts by other peacemakers.[1] In no situation is this cacophony and its potential to do harm more noticeable than in the peace operations or complex emergencies that bring together the military, diplomats, international organizations, and non-governmental organizations (NGOs) in a humanitarian effort to stop the fighting and protect the innocent.

Of particular concern is the relationship between the military and the NGOs, which play essential but very different roles in peace operations. The military is tasked, usually by individual states or an intergovernmental organization like the UN, with keeping or enforcing the peace, while NGOs respond to the political, societal, and at times economic consequences of the conflict, responsible to funders and their own management. That their funders are often the same governments that sponsor the military intervention is not in itself a guarantee of coordination, as communication among government agencies is often lacking. In these circumstances, the potential for misunderstanding and miscommunication between these two communities is high, with possible negative consequences for the environment and viability of the peacekeeping mission.

Over the past decade, changes in the nature of conflict and in the international response to inter-state and intra-state wars have changed views on how the military instrument can be used for political ends.[2] In the past, the political ends for which military force was deployed centred around such issues as national expansion, territorial security, competition for resources, and ideological clashes. Force was an important tool of state making and an essential component of state maintenance. While military strength is still a vital measure of a state's capabilities, the political purposes for which force is deployed have broadened in the past 50 years well beyond the boundaries of creating and maintaining sovereign states or serving the interests of specific alliances. The creation of the United Nations as a collective security organization and the recognition in the UN Charter that its member states could employ many tools – including peacekeeping – to prevent or stop fighting opened the door to a whole series of collective efforts to guarantee or impose peace.

Until the late 1980s, peacekeeping entailed the deployment of lightly armed troops, provided by a number of different states, who would separate combatants and monitor the military component of the ceasefire or peace agreement. The arrangement occurred infrequently and then only with the agreement of the parties to the conflict. Ventures of this type included the UN Emergency Force during the Suez crisis, the UN Peacekeeping Force in Cyprus, and Interim Force in Lebanon (1978). From 1945 to 1988, the UN established only 15 peacekeeping missions, all of them reflecting a consensus that these operations should play an impartial – a neutral – role via-à-vis the conflict and should avoid exposing the peacekeepers to risk.

The end of the Cold War challenged the UN's traditional caution about intervening in the name of peace. The sudden collapse of the Soviet Union removed a potential source of veto from the Security Council and made the United Nations an attractive vehicle for an international response to conflict. At the same time, the relative stability created by the superpower stand-off gave way to a series of bloody civil and inter-communal conflicts in Haiti, Somalia, Sudan, Rwanda, Zaire, Congo-Brazzaville, Liberia, Bosnia, Central Asia and Serbia. Seismic changes in the world system rattled regimes and borders all over the globe, putting demands on the UN's capabilities and stretching the principles and practice of peacekeeping.[3] Donald Daniel, Bradd Hayes and Chantal de Jonge Oudraat identify features of the peacekeeping missions launched between 1988 and 1994 which contributed to a change the nature of peacekeeping operations, including: an enormous increase in the number of authorized peace operations, a broadening of activities undertaken by the missions, an increased willingness to use force, a willingness to give UN approval for state-based interventions with a higher element of risk than previous UN missions, a willingness to intervene in some cases without the consent of the warring parties, and – as a consequence of this added activity – difficulty in coming up with sufficient resources to staff and pay for the missions.

The peacekeeping situations that the state-based militaries found themselves in were very different from the war-fighting scenarios for which they had been trained. Although 118 countries contributed to UN peacekeeping missions between 1948 and 1998, few of them devoted significant resources to the kinds of training and preparation that these missions required. Instead of acting as a wall between combatants, peacekeepers found themselves drawn into the action, providing security for civilian agencies, building roads and carrying out government functions in collapsed states. Peacekeeping, along with peacemaking and peacebuilding, became one part of a three-course menu, as articulated by UN Secretary General Boutros Boutros-Ghali in his *Agenda for Peace*, which the international community offered war-torn states.[4] The common understanding of this continuum was that peacekeeping was the province of the military forces while peacemaking engaged political actors with the capacity to reach or broker an agreement. Peacebuilding, on the other hand, was the province of a variety of civilian forces: the UN and its specialized agencies, state-based diplomatic and development corps, and aid organizations. As reasonable as the continuum seemed, however, the UN and the international community were learning by doing, and the experience with mission creep in Somalia showed that it was not always clear where peacekeeping stopped and peacebuilding began.[5]

This confusion of roles and responsibilities between civilian and military agencies became a significant factor for peacekeeping operations in the 1990s. Institutions that had had fairly distinct roles, identities, modes of behaviour, and expectations found that all of these changed during the 1990s. Representatives of governments struggled with changes in the meaning and practice of sovereignty as both global and subnational forces challenged the status quo. In the US and other countries, the State Department and foreign ministries still played a central part, but developments such as the appointment of dozens of special envoys and special representatives by heads of states and the UN Secretary General brought a whole series of new actors into the official diplomatic process. The military underwent changes as it took on the new roles in peacekeeping and humanitarian assistance while maintaining its ability to fight wars.

Finally, the peacemaking roles for non-official actors also opened up, bringing many more individuals and institutions into the process and allowing private people and groups to intervene as third parties to bring peace to a troubled society, as the Community of Saint Egidio did in Mozambique and attempted in Algeria and Kosovo. In fact, after many years of being ignored by powerful states and impenetrable international organizations, NGOs were now being hailed as magicians of sorts, capable of bringing peace and reconciliation at the grassroots level to societies split by civil war and ethnic and religious strife. In their desire to help the vulnerable and powerless, these organizations have responded to conflict all over the world, sometimes as a function of their mission for humanitarian relief or human rights, and sometimes as a deliberate attempt to intervene in the conflict.

As relatively new and very independent players in the array of third party institutions that respond to conflict, it is difficult to gauge with certainty how their actions affect the international response. This difficulty is intensified by an understandable tendency to group all NGOs together, as if a common set of mandates and institutional structures governed the lot. In order to capture some of the diversity of this sector, this study will examine three major types of NGOs – humanitarian, human rights, and conflict resolution – operating in conflict, and will explore their strengths and weaknesses in conflict management. Understanding the various missions, mandates, and institutional structures represented in this world is critical to assessing their net contribution to conflict management.

NGOs and their Capacity for Conflict Management

One of the many problems of examining NGOs' capacity for conflict management is defining what an NGO is. Some descriptions focus on the functions that NGOs perform. The World Bank defines NGOs as 'private organizations that pursue activities to relieve suffering, promote the interests of the poor, protect the environment, provide basic social services, or undertake community development'.[6] Others define NGOs by what they are not, especially in relation to government and private business and industry. Lester Salamon talks about 'a global third sector: a massive array of self-governing private organizations, not dedicated to distributing profits to shareholders or directors, pursuing public purposes outside the formal apparatus of the state'.[7] For the purposes of this study, NGOs are defined as private, self-governing, non-profit institutions dedicated to alleviating human suffering, promoting education, economic development, health, environmental protection, human rights, and conflict resolution, and encouraging the establishment of democratic institutions and civil society.

A distinct characteristic of the NGO world is its recent rapid growth. A majority of the 160 members of Inter*Action*, an umbrella organization for major American relief and development NGOs, were founded after 1975.[8] Some of these NGOs were established in response to specific upheavals – in Haiti, Bosnia, Ethiopia, Bangladesh – but most offer emergency assistance and/or long-term development aid throughout a region or the world. Local NGOs have proliferated at a fantastic rate: one estimate placed the number of indigenous NGOs in the Tamil-Nadu province of southern India at 25,000 in 1994.[9]

Management structures differ around the world. For instance, most British, Canadian, and American NGOs are governed by a board of trustees according to the institution's by-laws. Board members are legally accountable for the NGO's operations and responsible for the fulfillment of its mission and financial obligations. NGOs in other parts of the world have sprung up according to (or sometimes in opposition to) their own national laws and traditions. Some are similar to American NGOs; some are quasi-governmental structures, fully funded and essentially managed by the state; some are effectively opposition parties and highly political in nature; some are locally organized cooperatives which depend on the energy and influence of one or two individuals.

NGOs have budgets ranging from next to nothing to several hundred million dollars. As one of the largest international NGOs, CARE has an annual budget approaching $400 million.[10] Funding comes from both public and private sources, with many organizations relying purely on private philanthropy. For others, public funding has become a significant part of their budgets. Working in partnership with government organizations or as private contractors to deliver services, NGOs received $8 billion or 10 per cent of public development aid given globally in 1994.[11]

In terms of staffing, some international NGOs operate with a mix of nationalities, with top management provided by the nationals of the NGO's country of origin, and many operational staff positions filled by local employees. Some international NGOs consist almost entirely of teams of outside experts who work with indigenous groups in a capacity-building arrangement. Some international human rights groups employ individuals from around the world, but are careful about engaging local employment in human rights monitoring for fear of jeopardizing their safety. On the other hand, these international human rights organizations often work closely with local human rights groups and serve the vital function of publicizing broadly the findings of these small organizations which otherwise would not be able to command international attention.

This short review of the institutional structures of NGOs is insufficient to describe the great variation in staffing, organization, management, funding, mission, activities, and culture in the NGO community, and serves mainly to point out the institutional differences that exist in this world, not only between NGOs with different missions, such as the humanitarian and human rights NGOs, but also among NGOs that share the same mission.

Humanitarian NGOs

Within the international NGO community, humanitarian organizations are by far the most extensive group and comprise some of the largest agencies: the Red Cross, CARE, Oxfam, International Rescue Committee, World Vision, Medicins Sans Frontières, Catholic Relief Services. Some of these organizations specialize in responding to humanitarian crises and some divide their efforts and resources between relief and development efforts.

Development is characterized by long-term projects which help communities achieve sustainable social, economic, and political structures. Development assistance often reaches into a community long before a crisis develops and remains through the growing process until the local capacity is sufficient to build a secure and healthy society. The assistance focuses on the development of vital components of society: agriculture, education, infrastructure, employment, and is deemed a success when continued aid becomes unnecessary because a society has become self-sufficient. Development work, which can have a significant effect on conflict management within a society, usually ceases during a conflict. International development staff, with their deep knowledge of local conditions, depart and return only when the conflict is over. During a crisis, they are replaced by relief staff whose area of expertise is responding to emergency situations wherever they may occur.

Relief is characterized by short-term, emergency service in the face of a disaster, both natural and man-made. These operations include airlifting food, clean water, and sanitation equipment to distressed populations, establishing shelter for homeless victims, providing repairs for salvageable structures, and the prevention, containment, and treatment of life-threatening diseases. The focus in relief work is on saving lives, not managing the conflict. However, according to John Prendergast, a practitioner with long experience in conflict-related relief work, these life-saving measures can exacerbate conflict and fuel the misery that the humanitarian NGO is trying to relieve.[12]

The starkest contrast between the humanitarian NGO intention to do good and its inability to prevent the bad has occurred in refugee work in civil conflicts. Refugee NGOs provide many specialized services with strong conflict management components. Refugee assistance ranges from supplying basic human needs during mass migrations of displaced persons to protecting the rights of individual asylum seekers. In the initial phase of a migration, which is typically accompanied by starvation, disease, and death on a large scale, the urgent need is for relief, providing the basics of water, food, and shelter for a frightened and exhausted population. During the course of a refugee crisis, these relief organizations search out and assist pockets of refugees, often in hostile areas. On a more long-term basis, they provide education, health care training, and community building skills to displaced populations. They work to strengthen local relief and health services and seek to reunite families. They help guide a refugee population towards self-sufficiency through training in agriculture and job skills, income generation, and the production of relief supplies.

Protection of displaced populations, however, is an equally important part of refugee work, and has increasingly come under siege in recent civil conflicts.[13] These wars result in extraordinary violence and produce huge numbers of refugees. The refugees cannot be individually screened on a routine basis, yet they include people who may have committed atrocities and participated in human rights abuses and genocide. Helping the innocent may entail unintended support for the conflict and lead to serious problems, not the least of which is ensuring security for genuine refugees and foreign relief officials.

Repatriation in these circumstances has become an especially difficult area. The experiences of spontaneous Rwandan repatriation from the Zaire camps, of less-than-voluntary repatriation from Tanzania, of failure of repatriation in Bosnia, and of refugee returns in unsafe conditions in Kosovo illustrate some external factors affecting the decision-making of humanitarian agencies, including NGOs and the United Nations High Commissioner for Refugees (UNHCR) about the return of refugees. Besides the militia intimidation of refugee camps, humanitarian agencies must deal with refugee fatigue or outright hostility in receiving countries; deep-seated fears among refugees about their safety after repatriation or, contrarily, a disregard for personal safety in their eagerness to return home; and political matters over which they have no control, such as internationally mandated election schedules that drive the repatriation timetable.

These circumstances have driven wedges among humanitarian actors. Amnesty International, a major human rights NGO, criticizes UNHCR for failing to protect refugees' lives and human rights.[14] NGOs pull out of refugee camps in protest only to be replaced by other humanitarian organizations as soon as they leave. In addition, humanitarian agencies complain that they are being used by the major political powers, first as substitutes for political response and then as scapegoats for failures when humanitarian efforts go wrong.

This work also challenges the humanitarian field's deep tradition of taking a neutral stand in the conflict. As a result of these recent experiences in working with refugees, humanitarian agencies have had to grapple with the question of whether this policy of neutrality is still possible, or whether in the face of intimidation by a small group of militia who continue to fight from the refugee camps, humanitarian NGOs should take action to bring the warmongers to justice, or at least exclude them from refugee camps.

These factors weaken humanitarian agencies' capacity for conflict management in these situations, and undermine their capacity to carry out their humanitarian mission. The humanitarian community itself is quite aware of its dilemmas, and has attempted to address them, in part through establishing codes of conduct and in part by some intensive soul-searching about the nature and limitations of humanitarian action. Mary Anderson has set the stage for this self-examination by developing the notion that humanitarian NGOs should at least subscribe to a Hippocratic oath that they will 'first do no harm' in the course of their work.[15] Anderson and others have taken this concept of 'no harm' much further, suggesting ways in which humanitarian aid can help ameliorate conflict.[16] These suggestions range from protective measures to prevent theft by warring forces of humanitarian food supplies and other goods, to wholesale incorporation of conflict management and resolution techniques into the planning and implementation of humanitarian activities. The capacity of humanitarian NGOs to act on their understanding of how their activities can feed conflict and to adopt procedures to prevent or counteract the negative effects of their work will determine how effective these organizations will be, not only in conflict management and peace operations but in humanitarian action in general.

Human Rights NGOs

Human rights NGOs, like Amnesty International and Human Rights Watch, attempt to define and promote the basic rights of all people regardless of beliefs or background and to prevent political and economic repression. Protection of the rights of the individual is a recent and often contentious issue, not only in states with repressive regimes but also with governments whose religious or cultural values are at odds with the principles of individual rights.[17] Human rights NGOs have traditionally monitored conflicts, but with the massive violations that resulted from the civil wars in Cambodia, Bosnia, and Rwanda, these organizations have played a key role in bringing these atrocities to international attention.

Organizations active in human rights are distinct from other NGOs in their style and activities. Their goal is to seek out, research, and address specific and general situations where repression occurs. To avoid compromising their work, most human rights organizations do not accept funding from government sources, lest they be pressured to act on behalf of issues other than those their mission requires of them.

Information-gathering on human right issues may be difficult and dangerous, often putting the human rights monitor at physical risk. In this effort, NGO staff, volunteers, and members may visit vulnerable areas as observers, gather information from local NGOs, churches, community groups, activists, professionals, and other sources, and/or seek official documentation relating to the issue. With the resulting research, they mount systematic campaigns to alert the public and officials to the plight of selected victims, both individuals or entire populations. These campaigns consist of testifying before government committees, international organizations, church councils, and other influential policy and law-making bodies, and reporting abuses to the world press. This serves the dual purpose of educating officials and the public and of exerting pressure on institutions to condemn offending parties.[18]

The assessment of how effective human rights organizations are in conflict management depends in part on the position of the assessor. Among specialists in conflict management, there is a pronounced difference on the issue of human rights accountability as part of the conflict management process.[19] Some believe that peacemaking and peacebuilding must involve all important parties to the conflict despite their records of human rights abuses. Without the essential cooperation of these groups, the peace agreement is constantly under threat of being undermined by a disaffected or antagonized combatant. The early hesitation of the international community to pursue indicted war criminals in Bosnia reflected not only a deep caution about further military engagement but a reluctance to drive Serbian President Slobodan Milosevic away from the Dayton agreement.[20]

On the other side, supporters of human rights activism claim that enduring peace occurs only when some sort of recognition of suffering and reckoning for abuses has occurred. Pointing to the Truth and Reconciliation Commission in South Africa and the Commission on the Truth for El Salvador, they note the importance that these exercises have had in establishing the basis for national reconciliation after civil strife. Without a commitment to individual accountability, say the human rights activists, a peace process may collapse under the weight of resentments which target whole populations and cause permanent societal fractures.

Whatever the stand of the assessor, it is clear that the work of human rights NGOs is not always a stabilizing factor in a conflict situation and can run counter, at least in the short term, to peacekeeping efforts. In their direct condemnation of human rights abusers, they may further antagonize parties within a conflict, criticize participants in a peacekeeping effort, and jeopardize the work of development agencies. In carrying out their mission, therefore, they may both bolster and undermine the conflict management process. Their increasing sophistication and ability to carry out their primary mission, however, ensure that they will remain key players in conflict and post-conflict situations. Their contribution to conflict management will depend in part on their ability to influence and willingness to work with other peacemakers, including the military. The nature and extent of this cooperation may be one of the key factors in determining the future success of any international effort in conflict mediation.

Conflict Resolution NGOs

The Carter Center's International Guide of NGO Activities in Conflict Prevention and Resolution lists 83 organizations devoted to conflict management.[21] These organizations are specifically dedicated to averting crises through preventive measures or to acting as intermediaries in an active conflict. In so doing they work with opposing parties, facilitate negotiations, and help to uphold accepted solutions. In some cases they actually initiate and catalyse dialogue between parties; in others, they simply monitor and expedite it.

The field of conflict resolution has many sources, including the academic disciplines of political science, international relations, psychology, sociology, anthropology, biology, economics, mathematics, and law. Other seed beds include a long history of domestic labour-management disputes and negotiation, as well as the civil rights movement and other work on racial, community, and domestic ethnic conflict. The emergence of social activism in the 1960s and 1970s, including the anti-war, feminist, and environmental movements, has played an important part. Another influence has been the development of alternative dispute settlement mechanisms – such as arbitration and mediation – which take place outside of the domestic court system. Also influential has been the work of non-governmental organizations, including religiously-based organizations dedicated to non-violence, such as the Quakers and the Mennonites. And finally, there has been the contribution of foreign policymakers and official practitioners whose practice of negotiation, mediation, and conflict resolution on a national and multilateral basis has long provided insights for the field.[22]

The practice of conflict resolution reflects these varied sources. Most of these organizations represent a specific approach to conflict management and resolution, many of which involve the development of activities that are devised to make the participants aware of their own role in a conflict and to give them tools for resolving or at least ameliorating the situation. Beneath this broad canopy lie many different programs in conflict management, ranging from courses to improve negotiation skills to strategies to identify and resolve the underlying causes of conflict.[23]

Some examples illustrate the variety of approaches that organizations and conflict resolution experts take to conflict resolution. The first approach was developed by Roger Fisher and William Ury at Harvard University and focuses on negotiation and on developing skills and habits which will allow the user to emerge successfully from a negotiating experience.[24] A principal element is to develop the analytical and strategic abilities of the parties in conflict, allowing them to separate their attitudes towards the negotiation and the personalities involved from the objectives of the negotiation.

A second approach to conflict resolution has been mapped out by John Paul Lederach of Eastern Mennonite University.[25] Instead of concentrating on the immediate goals at hand, defining needs and interests tied to a specific circumstance, Lederach focuses on the transformation of a conflictual relationship into a non-conflictual or reconciled one. Lederach's goal is to encourage reconciliation in societies where trust and a sense of common goals have been destroyed by civil fighting. His approach to conflict resolution is multi-level and defines roles for many groups and organizations, including official third party interveners and non-official, local NGOs, to play in effecting reconciliation.

Harvard professor Herbert Kelman's problem-solving workshop approach brings together in a neutral setting influential – although not necessarily official – individuals who represent differing parties to a conflict. The objective of the workshop is to increase understanding of each party's position and circumstances and to identify acceptable solutions to the conflict. As the participants return to their own communities, they take their new insights and suggestions for action and feed these into the political process.[26]

Using these and other conflict resolution techniques, conflict resolution NGOs focus on different levels of society and different groups. Some work almost entirely at the grassroots level and others work with opinion leaders or potentially explosive elements in a society. For instance, the Washington-based Strategic Initiatives of Women works in Somalia to train women in conflict management skills and to develop peacebuilding networks and increase political participation among Somali women.[27] In Bosnia, the Center for Strategic and International Studies' Program on Preventive Diplomacy holds training sessions in which clergy and lay people come together from different communities: the Serbian Orthodox Church, the Roman Catholic Church, the Muslim and Jewish communities, and various Protestant churches.

The London organization, International Alert, operates in West Africa, the Great Lakes region, and the former Soviet Union and Sri Lanka to support peacemaking and peacebuilding efforts, working with official and non-official groups to increase institutional capacity and to offer parties to the conflict a chance to discuss issues and form relationships in an informal setting. For instance, in Sri Lanka, it has attempted to create a bipartisan approach to peace negotiations through informal meetings for Sri Lankan parliamentarians in Crete, Northern Ireland, and the Philippines.

In addition, some of the large relief and development NGOs have added a conflict resolution component to their work, recognizing that development itself can create new tensions and/or alter old relationships. As long-term and community-level participants in strife-ridden areas, these NGOs are well suited to partake in relationship-building and civil society-building paths to a lasting peace. For instance, the United Methodist Committee on Relief created a special conflict resolution program in Bosnia to set up a multicultural conflict resolution centre at Sarajevo University, establish forums and training programs for local police, create centres where conflict resolution can be institutionalized, and provide training and workshops.

The focus of many conflict resolution organizations on transforming how the individual approaches conflict makes this work time-consuming and labour-intensive. The institutions which engage in this work are often small and depend heavily on the skills and expertise of a few individuals.

These institutional characteristics can limit the effectiveness of these NGOs. One criticism of conflict resolution work is that it is sporadic, consisting of one-time programs that focus on developing conflict resolution skills or bringing contending parties of the conflict together for discussion or workshops. These programs, claim their detractors, lack long-term commitment which would allow conflict resolution activities to build on each other. In a simplistic characterization of this behaviour, these organizations have been accused of parachuting into a conflict, introducing some foreign problem-solving techniques based on Western principles and values, and leaving rapidly to do the same in someone else's conflict.[28]

This criticism can be quite unfair, as many institutions work closely with local groups to build on indigenous methods of conflict resolution and to build up capacity for peacebuilding within the society in conflict. In addition, many of these institutions are committed to long-term programs but have to scramble for resources to fund that work. This is not an easy task. The field of conflict resolution is not only young and just beginning to establish itself, but there is also some scepticism among funders and others about whether it is possible to promote reconciliation in enduring conflict, especially conflicts based on ethnic or religious schisms. Unlike humanitarian NGOs which can point to physical reconstruction as proof of their effectiveness, conflict resolution NGOs must resort to pointing to the dog that did not bark – or to the conflict that did not re-ignite – as proof of their success. Without quick and tangible results, it is difficult to develop a long-term relationship with a funder willing to take the risk that the slow, hard work of conflict resolution will bear fruit. Without long-term funding, conflict resolution NGOs are hobbled in the kinds of programs they can conduct.

In addition, conflict resolution institutions can also represent a threat to existing power structures and become subject to negative responses on the part of the host government and other authorities. Individuals working on conflict resolution in Bosnia tell stories of being thrown out of officials' offices simply for using the word 'reconciliation'.[29] Lacking the large resources of humanitarian NGOs or the major private foundations, or the protective cover of large UN institutions such as UNHCR, these NGOs can be easily intimidated or shut down by antipathetic political powers.

Intersection of Military Peacekeeping and NGOs: Problems of Coordination

As the previous section catalogues, NGOs can and do make significant contributions to conflict management.[30] Through their work at the grassroots level in aid, protection, and capacity-building, international NGOs often establish long-term relationships within societies. NGOs can provide early warning of impending conflict, provide good offices or act as mediator among groups in conflict, galvanize the international community into action, and mobilize vital resources for post-conflict societal reconstruction and reconciliation. At the same time, their dependence on the goodwill, or at least tolerance, of their host country and lack of political and military clout can leave them vulnerable and ineffective in a rapidly deteriorating situation, and can result in actions that lead to further conflict rather than conflict resolution. There is one more complicating factor in assessing NGOs' net contribution to conflict management: their ability to work with other third party institutions like the military, international organizations, and other international NGOs. It is to these challenges we now turn.

In the past, NGOs have acted in an independent manner, with little coordination either among themselves or with the international organizations and the military forces active in a peace operation. With the proliferation in the 1990s both of NGOs and of relief operations involving military personnel, coordination between NGOs and the military became one of the central concerns of international multilateral responses to conflict. Both sides of the equation recognize that a stronger relationship should develop between these two sectors, and the military has been particularly assiduous in including the NGO perspective into its training sessions. It has been so effective, in fact, that members of the humanitarian community have complained that they do not have the personnel to meet the military's demand for authentic NGO or UNHCR voices in their programs.[31] This observation brings out one of the issues that bedevils this relationship: the difference in size and resources between the military and the NGO community.

Traditionally, NGOs and the military have perceived their roles to be distinctly different. Many NGOs felt uneasy working with military forces, whether from their own countries or from the country receiving assistance. NGOs, conscious of the need to preserve their neutrality and the protection that vulnerability affords them, have sometimes felt themselves to be endangered by a close association with the military. In addition, some NGO staff and local people may see peacekeeping and peace enforcement missions as repressive rather than protective in nature. For their part, military leaders tended to regard NGOs as undisciplined and their operations as uncoordinated and disjointed.

Recently, attitudes on both sides have begun to change. Exposure to each other's strengths and capabilities has served to increase the military's respect for the innovation and dedication of NGOs, and to foster an appreciation among NGOs for the unsurpassed logistical capacity of the military. In recent years, militaries have sought to improve their coordination with NGOs by creating civil-military operations centres (CMOCs) or other coordinating mechanisms that allow military, NGO, and international organization personnel to meet and work together to advance mutual goals. These operations centres allow the three groups to share information and views as well as provide a venue for practical matters such as briefings by the military on landmines or security conditions. They do not, however, serve as coordinating mechanisms, and they have a mixed record in bringing the three communities together.

In operations in Iraq and Somalia, the establishment of closer working relationships between NGOs and the military contributed to the successful delivery of humanitarian assistance within an extremely volatile and dangerous environment. These same operations, however, also underlined the importance of establishing better and more rapid communications among the international actors responding to the conflict and a clear comprehension of the mission's overall objectives.

While they enjoyed a high level of cooperation in the Somalia operations, the military and NGOs had different interpretations of the mission's objectives. The military's concern to avoid 'mission creep' accentuated its desire to go in, fix the problem and get out quickly. Conversely, the NGO perspective during this crisis was long term, aimed as much at addressing the root causes of the crisis as at delivering relief.

An example from Somalia of this difference in definition of mission was the military's decision to send in engineers and soldiers to rebuild roads and other infrastructure. The military, conscious of the urgent need to repair the transportation system, and aware that the job would take longer than a few months if untrained locals or NGOs were given the task, did not hire Somalis to do the work. From the perspective of NGOs active in Somalia, however, this was a short-sighted policy that ignored the longer-term peacebuilding benefits of hiring unemployed Somalis. In this case, although the principal objective of rebuilding infrastructure was met, a potential side-benefit for internal development and indigenous employment was lost.

Because of their long-standing relationships with the local community, NGOs possess valuable information about such subjects as how best to set up a distribution system within a particular area, and the relative dependability of various local groups and individuals. However, NGOs are sensitive about sharing information. They see their long-term success as dependent on good and open relationships with the indigenous population, and are consequently wary of compromising the trust they have established by providing information to the military; they may even be reluctant to be seen with military personnel.

Difficulties in cooperation and mutual support are not caused solely by the differences in mandates, objectives and capabilities of the two institutions. The organizational culture is also a barrier to collaboration. In a number of areas – patterns of decision-making, attitudes towards authority, attitudes towards the population they are aiding, educational background, philosophical grounding – there are marked differences between the two communities.

For instance, most NGOs do not have an elaborate hierarchical structure but are quite decentralized and relatively flat in their authority structures. Employees work independently and arrive at decisions through consensus rather than by a chain of command. NGOs are heavily dependent on the individual commitment and initiative of their staff. In this situation, the managerial style is informal and works through personal engagement.

The military, on the other hand, has a strong hierarchical structure in which the lines of authority are clear and duties well defined. In this structure, missions are generally articulated before the exercise begins, and rules of engagement give guidance to all parts of the structure from senior decision-makers to the soldiers on the ground. Planning for flexibility plays a part in the decision-making operation, but here the key word is 'planning:' militaries spend a great deal of time in preparation for all sorts of conditions and contingencies, planning for worst-case scenarios and simulating real conditions in their training programs.

In a tumultuous situation, the decentralized, independent approach to management can be a great asset. The willingness of NGOs to act when speed is essential and detailed planning is impossible make these organizations among the best equipped to respond to sudden challenges. This ability, however, to turn on a dime – to change strategies, shift resources, quickly expand or shut down operations – can appear as chaotic to organizations such as the military whose operations involve large numbers of people and resources, and which value detailed planning and preparation.

The complexities of this challenge of cooperation are illustrated by looking at one natural area for close collaboration between the two groups: the issue of physical security. Providing security is usually a principal objective of a military peacekeeping mission. Security is an enormous concern of international NGOs, especially those engaged in relief, refugee, and human rights work in situations of conflict. As the total number of NGO workers grows and local employees – who face the greatest risk of being caught in the conflict – take over more roles, the problems raised by inadequate security and a lack of basic security training become critical.

NGO staff working in a conflict zone often experience significant hardship and real danger. This is especially the case when the government of an area has collapsed and no other force has exerted its authority; in such an anarchic environment, neither the government nor its adversaries is likely to be able to provide routine security. In Somalia in the early 1990s, belligerents frequently hijacked relief supplies meant for civilian populations. In Mogadishu, a bomb was planted in an NGO office in retaliation for interference by the international community in the conflict.

The often conspicuous disparity in the standards of living between NGO field staff and the population of the communities in which they work can make them a target for crime. In meeting their own needs, NGOs may absorb the best of what is available locally in terms of office and living space, as well as local staff. NGO transportation and communication facilities may be better even than those of the local government. This can cause tension in the best of circumstances; in the worst, NGOs can become caught in the belligerency.

NGOs have taken steps to increase their own ability to provide security. InterAction, the American umbrella organization for humanitarian NGOs, has developed materials and conducted training on security for staff working in conflict or unstable circumstances. A major recent study carried out under the auspices of the University of Toronto and CARE Canada has recommended that NGOs provide for their own security by hiring private security guards.[32] NGO reaction to this last proposal, however, has been mixed as a number have had negative experiences with this sort of arrangement. In Somalia, employing private guards at times drew NGOs into inter-clan fighting as their guards were also partisans in the conflict.

These situations argue for a close relationship between NGOs and the international military peacekeeping forces. The experience in Bosnia, however, shows that rules of engagement can dilute efforts even in this area. Official and public concern in the United States for the safety of their military personnel led to the requirement that US officials, including military staff, travel only in convoys of four vehicles, in order to provide protection for the group. On the other hand, the ability to move quickly around the country was important to the work of international NGO staff. American NGO workers, therefore, often traveled by themselves in private cars or hitched rides in armoured vehicles with officials of the OSCE (Organization for Security and Cooperation in Europe) or UNHCR. Waiting for a military convoy would have hampered their capacity to work, so most chose to take the risk of being unprotected over curtailment of their freedom of movement.

In the end, the question still remains: has there been any learning among the two communities about how to interact based on the experience that they shared in Somalia, Rwanda, and Cambodia? The sheer amount of attention devoted to this topic among both practitioners and scholars argues that there has been a good attempt to distill the lessons of the past engagements. Given the benefits that each community can bring to each other, the attempts to increase understanding among these civilian and military actors can only serve to improve peacekeeping capacity. This learning, however, has not been subjected to a rigorous test. Bosnia was not the same kind of laboratory that the earlier other complex emergencies were, as NGOs and the military peacekeeping forces had little to do with each other. Aside from weekly briefings on security and instruction on landmine identification, there was in the early days little reason for the military and NGOs to interact.[33] This situation may change as the military starts to think about and plan for disengagement.

Understanding coordination from the NGO perspective also requires a deeper analysis of the differences between headquarters and staff about coordination. Often problems with collaboration are the result of a disconnection between the decision-making centres of the third party institutions, rather than a reluctance to coordinate between staff on the ground. Another question revolves around the timing of the coordination. Are there periods in the response to conflict in which cooperation among institutions is much more important than at others: in, for instance, the first flush of peacekeeping or during periods of institutional hand-off or transition from one stage to the next?

Towards Collaboration in Peacekeeping: Issues on the Table

This study has argued that despite their different decision-making structures, sources of support, and missions, NGOs can undertake a great variety of conflict management roles: among them, providing early warning of impending conflict, acting as channels of communication between parties in conflict, working at the grassroots to effect reconciliation at the local level, and providing training for post conflict administrators in the intricacies of civil society.[34] Their ability to respond quickly to changing circumstances and extensive knowledge of the societies in which they operate help them to design appropriate programs and to make shifts in direction or priorities to meet the constantly changing challenges of working in conflict.

How effective they are in managing conflict depends in part upon how the term 'conflict management' is defined. If the definition includes an ability to mobilize international resources and political will, to impose a settlement, to offer incentives and threats to opposing parties to change their behaviour, then NGOs often operate at the margins. They can prompt the principals from behind the curtain and on occasion can briefly enter on to the stage, but they are dependent on the stars of the production – individual states or international organizations – to carry the action forward and bring the drama to some conclusion.

If, on the other hand, the definition of conflict management includes a broad array of actions to prevent, mitigate, and resolve conflict, NGOs are central to conflict management at every phase of the conflict cycle. Acting alone or in concert, they can affect behaviour at many levels of society and are especially potent in states struggling to rebuild a social, economic, and political infrastructure after a civil war.

There are, however, a number of issues that NGOs will have to face as they continue to be significant players in the response to conflict. Accountability is a key issue for NGOs, especially those active in conflict situations. As discussed above, NGOs can be dragged into conflicts by choosing to work with one group in need rather than another group; by bringing supplies and resources into the war zone; or by becoming a target of the war effort. In addition, in a number of crisis situations, NGOs have come to assume responsibilities that far exceed their original missions. For instance, in both Rwanda and Somalia, NGOs moved into the political vacuum caused by the collapse of central authority. They undertook many of the services usually provided by the local governments, and in the process effectively replaced the state. The NGOs' ability to swiftly initiate and improvise alternative services certainly benefited the local people, but it also raised a critical issue. To whom or to what is a NGO accountable: the local people, the international community, the government of the country in which it is headquartered, its board of trustees, its funders, or all of the above?

It is not the good intentions of the NGOs that are in question. Rather concern focuses on the unintended consequences of the international NGO's pursuit of its mission to help, protect or empower. Another set of concerns revolves around the traditional independence of these private voluntary organizations. Not obligated to enter into a situation, nor – once in – to stay committed, nor to pull out if other third parties disengage, NGOs can contribute to the unpredictability of the international community and to its seeming inability to coordinate an effective response to conflict.

Coordination among all third party institutions in conflict has been the subject of much attention on the part of the UN, individual governments, militaries, and non-governmental organizations since the Operation *Provide Comfort* in Iraq in 1991.[35] Although consultation between NGOs and official structures has increased a great deal over the past decade, the problems that still exist in areas such as information-sharing indicate that coordination with other types of organizations is still an elusive condition, especially in a fast-moving, chaotic, complex emergency or conflict situation.[36] Here, the challenge for NGOs is to define what, if any, institution would be acceptable to the non-governmental community as a coordinating body, and how much coordination would be tolerable for a traditionally independent group of institutions.

This raises a larger issue that underlies the preceding analysis. In complex emergencies and other peacekeeping situations, it is not the military or NGOs that are ultimately in charge of the decision-making process. While these communities can make efforts to collaborate on a local basis, they have neither the authority nor resources to mandate closer coordination. This authority rests in country capitals of the state powers behind the response to conflict and in their willingness to support, politically and financially over a long period, a peacekeeping/peacebuilding effort coordinated by the UN or other selected multilateral mechanism.

In the drama of conflict resolution, many communities – individual states, international organizations, the relevant militaries, and the private non-governmental organizations – play a role in quelling or preventing conflict and laying foundation for a lasting peace. For the moment, however, this drama lacks a full-time director who can bring the coordination of effort that would allow the unique properties of these different organizations to build a coherent peace. The UN has attempted to rectify this situation through the creation of the Office of the Coordinator for Humanitarian Affairs (OCHA), although the success of this office will depend on the willingness of the major powers to support the UN as lead agency in a peacekeeping effort, support that they have been often unwilling to give in the past.

As long as this is the case, the burden for making a cohesive whole of the action will depend on the background of individual actors, on their skill, persuasiveness, and personal ability to draw the operation together. Under these circumstances, the challenge for international community – for those responsible for making decisions on peacekeeping in governments, international organizations, and non-governmental organizations – over the coming years remains the same as it has over the last ten years: how to identify, mobilize and support individuals who can bring coherence to peacekeeping, peacemaking, and peacebuilding in messy and often devastating conflicts.

NOTES

1. Chester A. Crocker, Fen Osler Hampson, and Pamela Aall (eds.), *Herding Cats: Multiparty Mediation in a Complex World*, Washington, DC: U.S. Institute of Peace Press, 1999.
2. Alexander L. George, *Forceful Persuasion: Coercive Diplomacy As an Alternative to War*, Washington, DC: U.S. Institute of Peace Press, 1991; also Alexander L. George and William P. Simons (eds.), *The Limits of Coercive Diplomacy* Boulder, Colorado: Westview Press, 1994.
3. Donald C.F. Daniel and Bradd C. Hayes with Chantal de Jonge Oudraat, *Coercive Inducement and the Containment of International Crises*, Washington, DC: U.S. Institute of Peace Press, 1999, pp.10–15.
4. Boutros Boutros-Ghali, *An Agenda for Peace: Preventive Diplomacy, Peacemaking, Peacekeeping*, Report of the Secretary General, 17 June 1992.
5. William J. Durch, *UN Peacekeeping, American Politics and the Uncivil Wars of the 1990s*, New York: St. Martin's Press, 1996.

6. Carmen Malena, *Working with NGOs: A Practical Guide to Operational Collaboration between the World Bank and Non-governmental Organizations* Washington: Operations Policy Department, World Bank, March 1995, p.13.
7. Lester M. Salamon, 'The Rise of the Non-Profit Sector', *Foreign Affairs*, Vol.73, No.4, July/August, 1994, p.109.
8. Figures taken from Tracy Geoghegan and Kirsten Allen (eds.), *InterAction Members Profiles 1995–1996* Washington, Inter*Action*, 1995.
9. Julia Taft, President of Inter*Action*, at the U.S. Institute of Peace's conference on *Managing Chaos*, Washington, DC, November 30–1 December 1994.
10. *CARE Annual Report 1998* Atlanta: CARE, 1998. CARE's total support and revenue in 1998 totaled $379.6 million.
11. Leon Gordenker and Thomas Weiss, 'Pluralizing Global Governance: Analytical Approaches and Dimension,' in Thomas G. Weiss and Leon Gordenker (eds.), *NGOs, the UN, and Global Governance*, Boulder: Lynne Rienner, 1996, p.25.
12. See John Prendergast, *Frontline Diplomacy: Humanitarian Aid and Conflict in Africa*, Boulder: Lynne Reiner, 1996; and David Smock, *Humanitarian Assistance and Conflict in Africa*, Washington: U.S. Institute of Peace Press, 1996.
13. This topic was the focus of a meeting held at the U.S. Institute of Peace in March 1997 with UNHCR and NGO officials. I am particularly grateful to Iain Guest for his insights on the dilemmas of humanitarian response.
14. *Amnesty International–USA Press Release*, 18 June 1997, 'International Community Failing to Provide Solutions for Massive Human Rights Violations in 1996'; also *Amnesty International-USA Press Release*, 6 December 1996, 'Tanzania/Rwanda: International Cooperation in Forcing Refugees Back from Tanzania', www.amnestyusa.org.
15. Mary Anderson, *Do No Harm: Supporting Local Capacities for Peace through Aid*, Cambridge: The Collaborative for Development Action, 1996.
16. See also Prendergast (n.12 above); John Paul Lederach, *Building Peace: Sustained Reconciliation in Divided Societies*, Washington, DC: U.S. Institute of Peace, 1997; Lisa A. Mullins, *Disaster Response: When Good Intentions Aren't Enough*, Washington, DC: Inter*Action*, 1990.
17. Arie Bloed, *Monitoring Human Rights in Europe: Comparing International Procedures and Mechanisms*, Norwell, MA: M. Nijhoff in cooperation with the International Helsinki Foundation for Human Rights, 1993.
18. See for instance the regular reports of Human Rights Watch and the Annual Review of Amnesty International.
19. An excellent analysis of the two camps can be found in the chapter by Pauline H. Baker entitled 'Conflict Resolution Versus Democratic Governance: Divergent Paths to Peace?', in Chester A. Crocker and Fen Osler Hampson with Pamela Aall (eds.), *Managing Global Chaos: Sources of and Responses to International Conflict*, Washington, DC: U.S. Institute of Peace, 1996.
20. Milosevic was indicted by the International War Crimes Tribunal in the Hague on 27 May 1999 in the midst of the NATO campaign against Serbia. Whether this indictment represents a shift in great power thinking about this balance of accountability and peacemaking remains to be seen. That the indictment only occurred after he was in a state of war with the Western alliance seems to indicate that European and North American governments are still cautious about mixing the two activities.
21. The Carter Center, *International Guide to NGO Activities in Conflict Prevention*, Atlanta: The Carter Center, December 1995.
22. Excellent summaries of the field are: Hugh Miall, Oliver Ramsbotham and Tom Woodhouse, *Contemporary Conflict Resolution*, Cambridge, Polity Press, 1999; Martha Harty and John Modell, 'The First Conflict Resolution Movement, 1956–1971: An Attempt to Institutionalize Applied Interdisciplinary Social Science', in *Journal of Conflict Resolution*, Vol.35, No.4, December 1991, pp.720–58; Louis Kriesberg, 'The Development of the Conflict Resolution Field', in I. William Zartman and J. Lewis Rasmussen (eds.), *Peacemaking in International Conflict: Methods and Techniques*, Washington, DC: U.S. Institute of Peace Press, 1997; and James H. Laue, 'Contributions to the Emerging Field of

Conflict Resolution', in W. Scott Thompson and Kenneth M. Jensen with Richard N. Smith and Kimber M. Schraub, *Approaches to Peace: An Intellectual Map*, Washington, DC: U.S. Institute of Peace Press, 1992.

23. See Eileen F. Babbitt, 'The Contribution of Training to Conflict Resolution', in Zartman and Rasmussen (eds.), *Peacemaking in International Conflict*, Washington, DC: U.S. Institute of Peace, 1997.
24. Roger Fisher, William Ury and Bruce Patton, *Getting to YES: Negotiating Agreement without Giving In*, New York: Penguin, 1991.
25. John Paul Lederach, *Building Peace: Sustainable Reconciliation in Divided Societies*, Washington, DC: U.S. Institute of Peace Press, 1997.
26. Herbert C. Kelman, 'The Interactive Problem-Solving Approach,' in Crocker (n.19 above), pp.501–19.
27. See David Smock (ed.), 'Creative Approaches to Managing Conflict in Africa', *Peaceworks No.15*, Washington, DC: U.S. Institute of Peace, 1997 for a summary of this and other conflict management projects, some involving NGOs, in Africa; and David Smock (ed.), 'Private Peacemaking', *Peaceworks # 20*, Washington, DC: U.S. Institute of Peace Press, 1998.
28. See, for example, Irving Kristol, 'Conflicts That Can't Be Resolved', in the *Wall Street Journal*, 5 September 1997, or the thoughtful criticisms by Gunnar M. Sorbo, Joanna Macrae and Lennart Wohlegemuth in *NGOs in Conflict – An Evaluation of International Alert*, Bergen: Chr. Michelsen Institute, 1997.
29. Based on interviews with international NGO staff, Sarajevo, May, 1996.
30. Cultural and institutional differences between the military, NGOs, and intergovernmental organizations are the subject of a work in progress which is being developed by the Peacekeeping Institute at the U.S. Army War College and the U.S. Institute of Peace, entitled *A Guide to the Military, NGOs and IGOs: A Handbook for Practitioners* by Pamela Aall, Dan Miltenberger, and Thomas Weiss, Washington, DC: U.S. Institute of Peace Press, forthcoming.
31. U.S. military exploration of these issues occurs in such diverse settings as the Army peacekeeping simulations at Fort Polk, the Marines' annual Emerald Express exercises, and a recent two-day symposium at the National Defense University on 'Beyond Jointness', which examines civil–military relations in peace operations.
32. Michael Bryans, Bruce D. Jones and Janice Gross Stein, *Mean Times: Adapting the Humanitarian Imperative for the 21st Century*, Toronto: Program on Conflict Management and Negotiation, October, 1998, unpublished version.
33. 38 Interview with World Vision staff, Sarajevo, May 1996.
34. 38 For an in-depth review of NGO work in early warning and conflict resolution in Guatemala, Macedonia, Sir Lanka, Nigeria, Sudan, Rwanda, and Burundi, see Robert I. Rotberg (ed.), *Vigilence and Vengeance: NGOs Preventing Ethnic Conflict in Divided Societies*, Washington: Brookings Institution Press, 1996.
35. See, for instance, Andrew Natsios, 'NGOs and the UN System in Complex Humanitarian Emergencies: Conflict or Cooperation?' in *NGOs, the UN, and Global Governance.*, Boulder, Colorado: Lynne Rienner, 1996, pp.67–81.
36. See 'Managing Communications: Lessons from Interventions in Africa', a summary of the proceedings of a conference sponsored by the U.S. Institute of Peace and the National Defense University, 20 June 1996, Washington, DC: U.S. Institute of Peace, March 1997.

Cultural Issues in Contemporary Peacekeeping

TAMARA DUFFEY

Following the end of the Cold War, the nature of international conflict shifted from interstate conflicts (handled by traditional methods of coercive diplomacy and crisis management through the superpower rivalry) to predominantly intrastate conflicts that require different responses by the international community. In terms of peacekeeping, this demanded a more committed performance beyond that of unsubstantial conflict containment. 'Traditional' operations – involving the deployment of a small, unarmed or lightly armed military force to monitor a ceasefire agreement between two parties while a political solution to the conflict was sought – were exchanged for an increasing number of highly elaborate, multilateral and multifunctional operations. At this turn, peacekeeping – by a United Nations force or a coalition of forces – became the most widely employed means of managing violent conflict and contributing towards its ultimate resolution. (By the end of 1998, 35 UN operations had been established – compared with 13 during the period 1948–78 and none in the decade that followed, 1988–98 – with many deployed in regions previously off-limits to outside intervention). This dramatic expansion in number was further accompanied by a broadening of tasks and actors. The single function associated with traditional operations evolved into a multiplicity of tasks, including humanitarian assistance, electoral monitoring, human rights observation, peacemaking and peacebuilding. Such activities have involved a coordinated effort by a multicultural composition of military and civilian personnel who are nevertheless required to possess a diverse repertoire of skills. Subsequently, post-Cold War peacekeeping has been convincingly identified as a valuable agency of third party intervention and conflict resolution, not merely a token military presence in a fractured zone of the world.

However, following the international debacles in Bosnia, Rwanda and Somalia, peacekeeping encountered widespread criticism: extremists advocated abandoning the tool altogether; minimalists argued for limited deployment and a resumption of traditionally characterized missions; optimists defended peacekeeping, yet subjected it to lengthy discussions on how to strengthen it through serious reform measures. The latter has prevailed, but it has led to a continuously rigorous review of the endemic set of problems that has undermined the international community's effectiveness in responding to contemporary conflict. Some of the problems that have been identified are: financial constraints and lack of resources; the abandonment of the fundamental principles of peaceful third party intervention (that is, consent, impartiality, and the non-use of force); occasional violation of human rights; ambiguous mandates; inadequate logistical planning; command, control and communications difficulties; and the lack of coordination between the military and civilian components.

While attempts have been made to correct these commonly accepted shortcomings, the international peacekeeping community has failed to consider the saliency of culture. Yet, culture impresses upon many of the aforementioned problems, thereby partially re-framing them as cultural challenges; moreover, culture has a powerful influence on the peacekeeping environment, both positively or, in most cases due to lack of cultural understanding, negatively. Problems associated with culture have arisen, in part, from the expanded nature of contemporary peacekeeping operations (although cultural issues are evident to some degree in traditional missions): today's missions are multiculturally composed and transnationally executed across a diversity of cultural contexts. Everyone involved in a peacekeeping operation – from those planning the mission, to the military and civilian peacekeepers deployed to carry it out, to the local population in whose surroundings it is carried out – is part of a cultural framework. This framework provides the context within which the actors' beliefs and actions are constructed, expressed, interpreted and understood.[1] The challenge of culture and cultural differences merits systematic analysis insofar as the reform of peacekeeping focuses on developing a fuller understanding of how it interacts with and responds to the conflict environment. In recent years, peacekeeping has looked to the theory and practice of conflict resolution for answers to many of its challenges; once again, conflict resolution can offer insights through its increasing regard for culture. The next section will briefly outline the role of culture in conflict resolution theory and practice.

Conflict Resolution and Culture

Born from and nurtured by scholars working in institutions throughout Europe and North America, the field of Conflict Resolution has reflected Western intellectual traditions – the expectations, values and rationality that are embedded in Western culture.[2] The discipline has falsely assumed that its theories and methods have universal applicability. Yet, the means for managing and resolving conflict have always existed within social and cultural groups. Over the last decade discussions have emerged in the field of conflict resolution regarding the 'culture question', or the role that culture should assume in conflict intervention.[3] Two levels of analysis can be deduced from the culture question: interaction and process.

The former refers to the interpersonal interactions that third parties engage in with individuals from cultures other than their own. As communities become increasingly multicultural and individuals and organizations intervene in conflicts around the globe, it is unlikely that a conflict resolution environment will be culturally homogenous. Conflict resolution practitioners are beginning to acknowledge the powerful effects that cultural differences can have on the interactions between the actors (interveners and conflictants) involved in resolution processes. This intercultural perspective has arisen variously out of experiences working in multicultural conflict settings (particularly in community mediation), research from the field of communication on intercultural communication and negotiation, and from political science research on international negotiation and national styles.[4] The purpose of the interactional level of analysis is to understand the dynamics of cultural differences before they lead to misunderstandings and conflict at the micro-level, which, in conflict resolution terms, may obstruct the macro-level process. This includes awareness of cultural differences in perspectives towards conflict and conflict resolution, worldview, verbal and non-verbal language (such as space, touch, gestures, facial expressions, use of time), and cultural rituals and practices.

At the process level, conflict resolution has come under considerable attack for its insistence on developing universal models and techniques applicable across all social and cultural contexts.[5] The discipline has principally relegated cultural specificity to the background and diminished, even rejected, the importance of the diverse cultural milieus that conflict is embedded in. However, various scholar-practitioners have sought to expose the misleading generalizability of the distinctly 'Western' perspective on conflict resolution theory and practice and have sagaciously unveiled the remarkable cultural variation of the expression and resolution of conflict.[6] Through comparative cross-cultural studies and experiences, they have concluded that attention to culture is essential in shaping theories of conflict and developing methods for its resolution. Since the criticisms have been raised, two important methodological contributions to theory and practice have been advanced.

In the early 1990s, Avruch and Black proposed a substantially innovative theoretical perspective to conflict resolution in the form of a culture-specific methodology.[7] The methodology was inspired by ethnographic case studies in anthropology, particularly in the field of anthropology of law. Avruch and Black reason that cultural understandings of being and action are used by people in the production and interpretation of conflict behaviour. These local understandings are systematic enough to comprise reasonably coherent cultural theories of conflict and its resolution. Ethnoconflict theory – or, simply, the local common sense about conflict – is influenced by a set of complex, interdependent determinants that vary cross-culturally, including language, social, political and economic structures, religion and folk psychology (or ethnopsychology – the local assumptions about people and relationships). Ethnopraxes are the corresponding ethnoconflict resolution techniques and practices (for example, Hawaiian *ho'oponopono*, Kalahari *xotla*, Inuit song duels, Indian *panchayats*, Pakistani *jirga* system, Tongan *kava* drinking circles). In addition to prescribing the rules for conflict regulation within a given society, ethnoconflict theory may also inform outsiders of the most appropriate strategies for intervention.

From his early experiences conducting conflict management workshops in Central America, Lederach proposed an elicitive process of conflict resolution as an alternative to the prescriptive process.[8] The latter is based on transferring conflict resolution techniques from one setting to another, primarily referring to the transfer of Western methods to non-Western conflict environments. The elicitive approach, on the other hand, is based on building or creating appropriate models from the cultural resources and implicit knowledge available in a given setting. In other words, it aims to get at what Avruch and Black refer to as ethnoconflict theory and praxis. The elicitive approach has important implications for 'peacebuilding from below'[9] – a recent departure from conventional 'top-down' approaches to conflict based on the manipulation of peace agreements by international diplomats and elites in collaboration with unrecognized, often illegitimate leaders detached from local communities (warlords and military figures) and valuing peacemaking resources from outside the affected community. In the peacebuilding from below perspective, solutions are derived from cultural resources, relying on local actors and local knowledge, including the local understanding of conflict and its resolution. Convergence of bottom-up, elicitive processes with state-level political negotiations produces a more holistic approach to conflict intervention.

This discussion of the culture question in conflict resolution has considerable relevance for understanding many of the problems associated with contemporary peacekeeping. The next section reviews the cultural obstacles that influence mission performance and considers how the interactional and processual levels of cultural analysis are applicable to peacekeeping intervention.

The Culture Question in Contemporary Peacekeeping

Although issues around culture have been alluded to in the peacekeeping literature, attempts to formulate a framework for analysing the significance of the cultural dimensions in contemporary peacekeeping are largely absent.[10] Yet, the need for systematic investigation is obvious, as Rubinstein suggests:

> A peacekeeping mission may mean many different things to different people, because each may have a different political understanding of the situation. Peacekeeping operations take place in the context of the daily lives of multiple communities: diplomatic, military, [humanitarian] and local. Each of these communities embodies culturally constituted ways of behaving and understanding the objectives and practices of the operation. Sometimes the intersection of these cultural spheres is problematic.[11]

To understand the relevance of culture, first we must identify the distinctly different cultural communities who engage in varying degrees of intercultural interaction so as to prevent unnecessary conflict from arising and impeding the process. The most notable interactions occur, internally, between the mosaic of national troops that comprise the peacekeeping 'force' and between the military and civilian agencies and personnel involved in establishing and sustaining the mission; and, externally, between the peacekeepers (both military and civilian, governmental and non-governmental) and the local population. Second, we must consider the cultural applicability of the conflict resolution processes employed by the mission and its participants. Culturally sensitive approaches are more likely to support sustainable peace processes.

The Peacekeeping Force: A Fusion of Cultures

Peacekeeping operations employ the use of an international military force, composed of troops from a multitude of nations operating under the central command of the United Nations or a regional organization. Traditionally, peacekeeping relied only on a handful of states to provide the personnel and equipment required to execute a mission. In 1988, only 26 countries had participated in peacekeeping, compared to more than 80 who have now contributed troops. Clearly, today's peacekeeping force is not a homogenous group. Language issues aside, 'each national battalion brings with it its own particular cultural complex and set of assumptions, the distinctiveness of which is not erased by a UN uniform'.[12] Their cultural differences may give rise to barriers to interaction, misunderstandings, prejudices, and unkowningly offensive behaviour that may reduce the chances for constructive activity. Differing national interpretations of mission mandates and application of rules of engagement (including the use of 'protective force'), resulting from the contingents' diverse strategic cultures and national military experiences, encroach upon the effectiveness of the intervention. Command and control arrangements are often complicated by national differences in staff procedures, training, equipment and language. Problems may also arise when contingents are reluctant to be subordinated to another nation's command, occasionally creating 'fiefdoms' that are reinforced by deep-seated cultural differences.[13] A recurring problem has been the discontinuity between the logistics capabilities of national contingents due to the absence of any centralized logistic distribution. Lack of uniformity may strain relations between contingents as some troops are more reliant on the better-equipped troops. Although guidelines are provided by the UN, training of military personnel is the responsibility of the troop-contributing nation; thus, disparities in resources, experience, and cultural interpretations of objectives frequently result in uneven levels of training. Some nations' peacekeeping training is simply insufficient, particularly with respect to specific peacekeeping and conflict resolution skills, further impeding the military efficiency of the force. Such discontinuities within a peacekeeping force limit its ability to operate in a coordinated military manner and significantly influence local perceptions of the credibility and legitimacy of the intervention.

While these issues will be illustrated with reference to the experiences in Somalia, it is worth pointing out that in the most recently deployed operation, the International Force for East Timor (Interfet), differences are evident. It has been noted that there are some reservations over the robust style adopted by the Australians – who have taken the lead in the operation – which is more akin to the American doctrine of maximum force protection. This has been compared to the more cooperative approach adopted by the British, in particular the Gurkhas, who are currently waging a pro-active 'hearts and minds' campaign to build rapport with the East Timorese.[14]

Organizational Culture Clashes

With continuous and multiple points of interface between the political, humanitarian and military components, interagency coordination is essential in securing an effective response in post-Cold War peacekeeping. However, Fetherston and Nordstrom remind us that peacekeepers (and humanitarians) interpret the world through the lens of their own culture, i.e., their own habitus,[15] often leading to the components of the mission working in the same theatre of operation in isolation or in opposition to one another. Lack of familiarity with the differences embedded in the organizations' professional cultures is a breeding ground for misunderstanding and poor coordination.

An organizational culture is, broadly, the way a group is organized and how it functions. The culture is reflected in the values, methods, and symbols that serve as a macro-level climate within which members of the organization must operate.[16] Weiss and Minear refer to this cultural dimension as 'agency culture'. They describe the concept as 'an organization's way of approaching its tasks, its relationships with other agencies, its self-image and public image, and its standard operating procedures'.[17] Through enculturation processes – much like those experienced by individuals in ethnic-cultural communities – the individuals who comprise an organization learn and internalize the rules and patterns of behaviour that are prescribed by the organizational culture. Hence, organizations (and individuals) may act according to learned patterns of behaviour, rather than respond to the actual conditions of a particular situation (for example, when under threat in a peacekeeping environment, a soldier may respond using armed force rather than communication techniques).

The organizational dichotomy often referred to as military–civilian is, in fact, more complex. There are several very different organizational cultures operating in any peacekeeping operation. The most notable components are the diplomatic (including UN agencies and regional organizations); military (the land, naval and air forces – each with its own branch culture – comprised of both armed and unarmed soldiers); civilian police; and civilian (government and non-government organizations, including humanitarian aid, human rights, development, and conflict resolution agencies, which can be further categorized as international, multinational, national, and community-based or grassroots organizations). Each operates within its own cultural sphere, according to its own understanding of the situation and its own intervention policies and practices. Guided by experiences over time, each component has developed a unique organizational culture that helps to promulgate and reinforce the norms, values, attitudes, beliefs, and behaviours, which, in a reciprocal relationship, have created that particular culture.

Over the last few years, there has been widespread acknowledgement of this cultural dimension of peacekeeping. For example, Mackinlay's guide to peace support operations seeks to 'promote better understanding of each other's organization and functions'[18] by discussing the characteristics, values, and activities of each of the components. It also examines the cultural differences between the organizations and how these differences influence interagency coordination. Similarly, Slim examines the relationship between the international military force and civilian humanitarian organizations and the perceptions each has of the other. He provides an insightful comparison of the military and humanitarian organizational cultures and identifies areas of conflict and collaboration.[19]

On the ground, as personnel from civilian organizations interact more regularly with military personnel, culture clashes become apparent. Cedric Thornberry, former-Head of UNPROFOR's Civil Affairs, explains that the lack of agency cooperation can be largely blamed on a 'two-way lack of familiarity for the attitudinal abyss which separates aid workers from the military'.[20] Aid workers are often suspicious of the military, and the military is similarly incredulous of aid workers. Such unfamiliarity inevitably encourages the promulgation of ill-informed stereotypes (for example, the military is often characterized as an insensitive, ill-informed, controlling, and inflexible war-machine, while NGO personnel are seen as sandal-wearing, two-faced, undisciplined and uncoordinated liberals.) Military actors frequently clash with civilian actors over basic questions of the means and ends of their mission, based on differing conceptions of the mandate. The two cultures also differ in methods of decision-making, approaches to accountability, operational and management styles (command structures, hierarchy and procedure versus fast-moving flexibility and decentralization), use of force, approaches to time and success (short-term objectives versus long-term processes), media styles (theatrical versus secrecy and control), and relationship with the local populations.

Peacekeepers, Humanitarians and Local Cultures

In peacekeeping operations since the Cold War, retaining consent and legitimacy of the intervention has been seriously challenged. In several cases (for example, Bosnia, Somalia, Rwanda), these fundamental principles have been forfeited for the sake of humanitarian intervention. To preserve consent and legitimacy, better and fuller cultural understanding of the conflict and the conflictants is required: consent will be promoted if the parties feel understood and are made shareholders of the peace process; intervention will be viewed as legitimate if the international community invests time to understand and support the local resources and institutions.

Interaction between military and civilian peacekeepers – from a multiplicity of cultural groups – and the culturally complex local populations within which they are operating is a critical issue, yet, it has received relatively little attention. However, as early as 1976 Galtung and Hveem raised the issue in a study of Norwegian peacekeepers in UNEF (Gaza) and ONUC (Congo). They sought to explore the role of the UN forces as seen by some of these soldiers themselves and to locate that role on an axis from distance from the social reality in which they were embedded to closeness and involvement. Their premise was that although a UN soldier (at this point, involved in traditional peacekeeping) is characterized as having a minimum role with a certain amount of social distance from the situation, they are often faced with more active tasks of trying to bring the parties together (that is, third party responsibilities of peacemaking and peacebuilding – an increasingly likely role in contemporary peacekeeping). In the latter case, knowledge of the local culture is fundamental. With this in mind, Galtung and Hveem's findings are not surprising: they found that the participants wanted more closeness to the local inhabitants; they wanted a much higher level of insight into the conflict and the local culture; and they wanted better training in dealing with people from other countries. They also learned that the soldiers received what little information they had from briefings; most of the information about the conflict was obtained through talks with others in the UN force or reading books and newspapers beforehand, rather than through any formal cultural training.

In a comparable study on the relations between the multinational forces of UNIFIL and the local Lebanese, Heiberg and Holst confirmed that, 'the nature of the relationship such a peacekeeping force achieves with the population within its area of control is a decisive element determining the operation's success or failure'.[21] Their findings indicated that the relationship between the peacekeepers and the locals varied from contingent to contingent and was largely related to the peacekeepers' awareness of the local cultural context. For example,

> Only the Italian contingent of some 2,200 people operated as part of the local environment and became an active element in restoring normal living conditions. Its soldiers were provided with the training required to acquaint them with the cultural, political and social situation of the people among whom they worked. Operating in a sector that contained approximately 600,000 inhabitants, mostly Shi'ites, the Italians carefully nurtured contact with the ordinary citizens and the political leaders in their area.[22]

The peacekeepers who were the most ambitious peacemakers – the American and French contingents – were, unfortunately, those most removed from the individuals and groups between whom they wished to establish peace. Hammond's study of US involvement in Lebanon confirms Heiberg and Holst's observation.

> While the Americans thought they were becoming involved in Lebanese politics, they entered into Lebanese culture and history with little or no understanding of the way things worked – or didn't work...

> Most Americans did not understand the subtleties of short-term alliances, the length of memories and blood feuds, the strength of *aln* [kin] in Arab cultures nor the nuances of religious differences.[23]

Maintaining good relations with the local community, a prerequisite for successful operations, relies on peacekeepers' understanding of the local population's culture and respect for their cultural traditions. The reality is, however, that peacekeepers often lack cultural insight into the population they are attempting to develop positive community relations with Diplomatic and humanitarian personnel are not exempt from this argument. Faced with the immediate requirements to save lives, civilian personnel may sacrifice cultural sensitivity in their interactions with those affected by the conflict in order to provide the humanitarian assistance. (Although, humanitarian agencies are likely to have been in the field long before the military troops, thus, they tend to be more familiar with the cultural contexts within which the intervention is taking place.)

In process terms, the cultural challenge for peacekeeping is that the bottom-up perspective is often overlooked by the international community whose habitus focuses on a short-term, linear, top-down process of state-centric conflict containment.[24] Within this process there is an implicit assumption that the peacekeeping approach is right, without considering the reality of the conflict on the ground as viewed by the people directly involved. For example, top-down oriented systems attempt to manage conflict by focusing on establishing political order within a sovereign and internationally recognized state. The result is negotiated settlement packages that focus almost exclusively on democratic elections aimed at re-establishing political authority.[25] Yet, this type of settlement may not be traditionally appropriate, nor culturally accepted (for example, as seen in the Western political approach to the Paris Peace Agreements during the operation in Cambodia[26]). It also leaves the political authority responsible for attending to the social, cultural, economic, and political consequences of the conflict, which is even more problematic in collapsed states, like Somalia, where there is no centralized authority. Consequently, the top-down approach to peacekeeping is aimed at the leadership of the conflicting parties – predominantly men and, often, warlords and faction leaders without majority support of the community – and international officials who make decisions to be implemented throughout the conflict communities. Yet, when the intended beneficiaries of peace operations are divorced from the search for solutions, the process is less likely to have long-term positive impact. Women, for example, are largely excluded from processes aimed at ending conflicts and their gendered concerns are often ignored, despite women's participation in local peace movements and community networks.[27]

The delivery of humanitarian aid is, like other forms of international intervention, 'carried out in a high-speed, top down fashion.'[28] This approach assumes a prescriptive stance: 'we know what's best for them'. Although rapid delivery of relief is a priority, failure to consult the local population may result in future problems. For example, relief distribution procedures often undermine women's responsibility for household management, thus diminishing their spheres of influence in their communities. As described by a recipient of aid, 'It is precisely the norms, the values, and the management systems of the [aid recipients] that government programmes and NGOs often tend to destroy through their wrongly conceived interventions and programmes.'[29]

An important feature of peacebuilding from below is the need to understand the cultural conceptions of the conflict, the structures of the local society that may give rise to or influence the nature of the conflict or how it is expressed, and the cultural mechanisms for managing conflict – what was earlier described as ethnoconflict theory and ethnopraxis. Peacekeeping intervention that prescribes processes based on the outsider's own cultural assumptions about conflict and conflict resolution and which fail to consider the cultural framework within which the conflict is embedded, diminishes the chances of a culturally appropriate and effective intervention. For example, the issue of impartiality has been widely debated in both conflict resolution and peacekeeping circles. The prevalent view, rooted in a predominantly Western assumption of the role of third parties, is that impartiality is fundamental to effective conflict intervention. However, cultural perspectives suggest that it is not only unnecessary for third parties to be impartial, but may be undesirable and impossible. In many cultures, third parties who come from within the conflict gain acceptance and legitimacy from their connectedness and trusted relationships with the conflict parties. Wehr and Lederach have developed the concept of 'insider-partial', in contrast to 'outsider-neutral', to characterize the third party from within.[30] They conclude that the success of the Esquipulas II peace process in Central America can be credited largely to the *confianza* [trust]-inspired, insider-partial model of intervention employed which emphasized the continuing relationships of trust that the Conciliation Commission had with the Contras and the Sandinista government. The success of the Central American peacekeeping operations (ONUCA, ONUSAL) may have been influenced by the culturally sensitive approach taken early on.

The cultural contexts in Bosnia – and, more recently, in Kosovo – have been poorly understood. Historical and cultural experiences have provided each party with a framework for conceptualizing their conflict behaviours, attitudes towards group relationships and approaches to resolving differences. The notion of revenge, for example, has its roots in pre-modern times when groups in the former-Yugoslav republics practised the tradition of 'blood feuds'. Klein advises that sensitivity to such cultural values might have facilitated an understanding of the belligerents' behaviour and suggested appropriate means for intervention by outsiders. Such sensitivity might have suggested, for example, that measures like trade sanctions and arms embargoes by the UN in this cultural context were likely to have the opposite effect to the one that was intended.[31]

Rarely are the cultural elements of a society in conflict understood by the international community. Formal or informal channels of contact are not created, locals are not consulted, and sufficient information is not gathered to guide the formulation of intervention policy and practice. It is frequently only once peacekeepers, diplomats and humanitarians arrive in the conflict crisis do they realize the obvious: the society has different conceptions of the conflict, different ways of managing it, and different approaches to seemingly simple everyday tasks. The next section will consider the peacekeeping operations deployed in Somalia to illustrate how culture may influence the success or failure of intervention efforts at all levels of cultural analysis.

Somalia: Failed Peacekeeping or Cultural Misjudgement?

Characteristic of today's breed of conflict, Somalia was a laboratory for applying the new theories of peacekeeping and, thus, represented one of the UN's greatest challenges. Despite a number of auspicious efforts, the international community's intervention in Somalia has been widely and severely criticized. While the composite of operations in Somalia[32] exhibited most of the ongoing debates in the theory-building, policy-making and practice of peacekeeping, it is particularly significant in that it exemplifies the cultural challenges facing contemporary peacekeeping. Throughout the various phases of the intervention cultural issues are evident at both interaction and process levels. The international community's experience in Somalia clearly demonstrates the critical need for consideration of the cultural dimensions in contemporary peacekeeping.

Cultural Differences Within the Peacekeeping Force

To understand some of the problems that occurred as a result of national and cultural differences between troop-contributing countries, it is useful to define the size and diversity of the peacekeeping force in Somalia. UNOSOM was composed of a 50-member military observer unit and a 500-member security force; it was enlarged to include 3,500 additional military personnel. UNITAF consisted of 37,000 troops, including 29,000 US troops. The authorized strength of UNOSOM II was 28,800 troops. More than 30 nations contributed military personnel to the three multinational forces. Given this manifold force composition, cultural differences in peacekeeping approach and operational doctrine, command, logistics, language and pre-deployment preparation are assured.

One of the most observable problems in the military intervention in Somalia emanated from the divergent national military cultures' interpretation and execution of the rules of engagement. US troops sought to 'coerce cooperation – using force that was sometimes pro-active and far from discriminating in its effect', in contrast to other units who 'tended to adopt approaches that were not so confrontational, relying less on the explicit use of force and more on fostering local support for the UN's long-term peace objectives'.[33] In disarming the Somali militias, for example, the US chose to use force before exhausting conciliatory measures, while others (for example, the Australians) adopted a less obtrusive approach based on dialogue and mediation. National differences over the use of force gave rise to severe tensions between the European and Australian and the American contingents.

Command and control was another challenge that reduced the UN's effectiveness. Some contingents would not work with or for other contingents (for example, neither the French nor the Italians were willing to place their units under the operational control of a Pakistani commander). Some UN forces, dissatisfied with the highly American-influenced intervention, received orders from home and pursued their own political agendas. For example, Italy attempted to facilitate private negotiations with one of the warlords, General Mohammed Aideed's SNA (Somali National Alliance). The US declared their own war on Aideed and his supporters. Subsequently, the widely publicized dispute between the Commander of the Italian contingent to UNOSOM II and the UN Force Commander demonstrated the weakness of multinational peacekeeping functioning like 'some kind of feudal fiefdom'.[34] Differences in logistics capabilities and pre-deployment preparation also complicated the mission in Somalia: there were many ill-equipped contingents and several units had no common language or training.

Military and Civilian Components: Same Objectives, Different Perspectives

Although military–civilian cooperation was sufficient to improve security and provide humanitarian assistance (largely as a result of the establishment of Civil–Military Operation Centres (CMOC)), some problems emerged as a result of cultural differences. In his study on humanitarian aid in Somalia, Sommer cites 'the very different institutional cultures, languages, assumptions, approaches, and motivations of NGOs and the military, which often led to frustration and misunderstanding'.[35] The medley of civilian agencies was sizeably and characteristically as diverse as the military component: there were nine UN organizations at work in Somalia, more than 75 (although some estimates are in the hundreds) international and national NGOs, and many local NGOs.

From the very onset, the military and civilian components of UNOSOM/UNITAF had very different perceptions of the mission and their roles: the military believed that their primary responsibility was to secure the environment – a military role which would indirectly assist humanitarian agencies – and viewed the humanitarian agencies as having a supporting role. The UN agencies and NGOs, however, believed that their responsibilities were primary, and the military was there, in a supplemental role, to directly support their humanitarian efforts. As a result of their ill-defined roles, the respective organizational cultures of the military and civilian agencies commanded the disparate intervention strategies they adopted and the uncooperative attitudes they developed towards each other. This inevitably strained relations and had a detrimental effect on coordination. In several cases, the military and humanitarian agencies failed to involve each other in decisions that required cooperative military–civilian relations; neither side brought the other into their planning process until it was nearly complete.[36]

Through her work with CMOC, Visman reports a number of coordination problems between UNITAF and the humanitarian component. UNITAF command suspected humanitarian organizations of being sustained by an alliance with certain groups (hence, their reliance on Somali guards), while complaints were frequently made by humanitarian organizations about UNITAF's vague policies (the most contentious issue was the weapons policy). Moreover, UNITAF was often unwilling to respect UNOSOM humanitarian staff and, when staff was lacking, UNITAF was sometimes forced to take on humanitarian roles. She describes UNITAF as being 'disenchanted with the unstructured method in which humanitarian activities were being conducted and the slow pace of UN mechanisms'.[37] Yet, when UNITAF initiated long-term projects, it did so without consultation and, consequently, many of these activities were not sustainable.

Dworken, who was assigned to III Marine Expeditionary Force, also found that differences in organizational culture created a considerable degree of mutual suspicion and negative stereotyping.

> The military was frustrated by what they viewed as disorganization and waste growing out of a tendency not to conduct detailed planning. Individually, they saw relief workers as young, liberal, anti-military, academic, self-righteous, incompetent, expatriate cowboys who came

> to an area for a short time to 'do good' without fully considering the consequences. Officers simply did not see women in their late-twenties wearing Birkenstock sandals and 'Save the Whales' T-shirts as experts worthy of consultation. At the same time, many relief workers saw military officers as inflexible, conservative and bureaucratic. They found them insensitive to Somali suffering and viewed their concern over 'mission creep' as obsessive, an excuse to do the minimum and go home.[38]

Some soldiers' attitudes in Somalia were typified as 'only we understand the security situation', hence they adopted a dictatorial role towards the NGOs. This attitude was unwelcome and unproductive as the soldiers were less knowledgeable about the cultural, social and political realities of the situation.[39] On the other hand, the military found it difficult to work with humanitarian organizations because of their high turn-over rates.[40] Many aid workers arrived after the military intervention and knew little about what had gone on before. The efficiency of humanitarian coordination was also reduced because of the significant numbers of NGOs operating without proper experience or understanding of the country and, often, without the willingness to consult those with knowledge. Instead, they were inclined to 'do their own thing'. The tendency for aid agencies to compete, rather than collaborate, also exaggerated differences and made coordination difficult.

The operations in Somalia exposed serious organizational culture differences between the military and the diversity of civilian agencies. Charles Petrie, then-Deputy Humanitarian Coordinator at the United Nations, shrewdly concluded that: 'Somalia confirmed that you cannot have two distinct structures [military and humanitarian] and expect that to work. The two components must understand each other and how they can complement each other... Each must be coopted into the other's way of thinking.'[41]

(Mis)understanding Somali Culture

While the multiplicity of troop-contributing cultures and the disparate organizational cultures of the military and civilian components produced some obstruction to UN peacekeeping in Somalia, the most significant problems were those resulting from the failure to understand Somali culture.[42] Lack of cultural understanding started from the highest level of decision-making at the very beginning. After months of delay the UN finally recognized the impending crisis in Somalia, and its immediate response was to send in forces. Mohamed Sahnoun, Special Representative to the Secretary General, however, urged the UN *not* to send troops until the conditions had been negotiated: the warlords were against UN military intervention and the presence of troops would intensify the fighting. Sahnoun eventually persuaded the factions to accept 500 troops to secure the delivery of humanitarian aid, yet the UN's response was to continue to send in troops until, in the end, 30,000 troops were deployed in Somalia. Sahnoun has openly criticized this strategy as it was applied without any real understanding of the cultural conditions on the ground.[43] Furthermore, the UN Secretariat did not understand the unusual Somali political or cultural context well enough to realize that UNSCR 814 (authorizing the use of force in March 1993) *increased* the risk of a major confrontation with armed Somali.[44] With the exception of US Special Envoy Robert Oakley and SRSG Mohammad Sahnoun, 'UN officials generally could hardly have been more inadequately briefed about Somali society and culture.'[45] Director of UN Operations in Kismayo, Mark Walsh, candidly expressed the lack of cultural understanding of the environment he and the UN were operating in: 'If I could make a statement of bad experience in Somalia, the most dominant thing is how culturally unaware I was about everything.'[46]

Many contingents arrived in the mission area without knowledge of Somalia, its history and culture, or the conditions on the ground. As a result, there were significant, and consequential, differences in how the national troops dealt with the local population. Indiscriminate use of force and other human rights abuses by some troops (for example, Belgian, Canadian, Italian, Pakistani, American) have been well documented. There was also regular harassment of the civilian population, including unacceptable levels of racism. Aside from the fundamental propriety of observing and respecting a people and their culture, the importance of local civilian support in a peacekeeping operation cannot be underestimated. A close relationship between peacekeepers and humanitarians and their recipient counterparts is essential to the establishment of security, the distribution of aid and, ultimately, the resolution of conflict. Ignorance of or indifference towards the Somali people impaired that relationship. The unfortunate behaviour by a small number of troops damaged the credibility of the UN mission, leading to mistrust and estrangement by the local population.

It is worth noting, however, that some contingents took the time to enhance their understanding of Somali culture. For example, prior to their deployment, the Australian contingent consulted the NGO CARE Australia to assist with preparation (CARE was active in Somalia early on and had considerable experience and knowledge of the Somali situation). The Australians also adopted a conscientious 'marketing approach' in Baidoa during Operation *Restore Hope*: they were 'marketeers' who were interested in the 'customer'; they were 'consumer-oriented', visiting the NGOs and Somali communities and asking 'What can we do for you?'[47]

Understanding Somali Ethnoconflict Theory and Ethnopraxes

There are several cultural features in Somali society that required particular understanding to effectively engage in sustainable conflict resolution activities. Ignorance of these elements most certainly affected the outcome of UNOSOM/UNITAF. Analysis using the ethnoconflict theory/ethnopraxis framework may have better informed the processes employed by the international community in the Somali context.[48]

Politics and the Somali Clan

The importance of the clan system as a political institution and a source of pride and social security in Somali society was flagrantly misunderstood by the international community. The notion of collective responsibility (embedded in Somali customary law and *diya* [blood money] payments) requires the clan to protect and support its members. Despite this fundamental feature of Somali culture, the UN and the US held Aideed *individually* responsible for his failure to cooperate in finding a solution to the conflict. When the international community tried to marginalize Aideed, they failed to realize that they also took on his clan who would support and protect their leader from a 'hostile clan'. In their desperate attempt to nullify Aideed's power base – by offering US$25,000 for information leading to his capture – UNOSOM II put him in a stronger position than before. (This situation could have been further complicated by the traditional system of blood compensation, that is, if Aideed was killed and retribution was sought by his kinsmen).

Furthermore, the UN's misunderstanding of the clan system and the decentralized nature of traditional Somali political institutions led the UN to pursue basic political errors. This is most clearly illustrated by the UN's insistence that a clan should hold the presidency of the country. Amid this view, UNOSOM's efforts were concentrated on reconciling the leadership within the Hawiye (Aideed and Ali Mahdi's clan family) rather than promoting the maintenance of traditional clan equilibrium and power-sharing.[49] This approach also endowed the main Somali warlords with a degree of power and authority which they desired but which they did not legitimately possess. Negotiations and reconciliation conferences that focused largely on the leaders who the UN thought were the most powerful at the time upset the traditional balance of the Somali kinship system[50] and further illustrated the international community's lack of awareness of and respect for Somali culture.

Time and Talk

The Somali conception of time is considerably different to Western conceptions. In the West, time is highly scheduled and broken down into minutes, hours, days, and so forth. As nomads, Somali time was traditionally measured by the movements of herds and the availability of food; thus, time is slow and is neither compartmentalized nor scheduled. The nomads had nothing but time and 'talk'. Much of their time was spent assembled under the acacia tree, debating, discussing and reciting poetry. This has most probably influenced their dynamic circular negotiating and problem-solving style (in contrast to the linear style of, for example, Western negotiation): Somalis will take an initial agreement made today as a point of departure for further negotiations tomorrow. This key cultural difference explains much of the problem encountered by international diplomacy in Somalia throughout the crisis.[51] Sahnoun, Oakley and others adapted their diplomatic styles in accordance with Somali culture (that is, meeting frequently and patiently with traditional community leaders). For example, Oakley arranged meetings between Ali Mahdi and Aideed and simply let them 'talk'. He also organized the equivalent of town meetings where he and his staff agreed to talk to anyone who wished to talk (200–300 people – clan and religious leaders, teachers, women – would assemble).[52] Walsh took an analogous approach in his dealings with Somalis in Kismayo. Nearly two months of discussions and negotiations with a broad representation of Somalis led to the Jubaland Peace Agreement.[53] Progress was made in a slow, albeit Somali, fashion.

However, the Western desire for a 'quick fix' political solution was in sharp contrast to the policies promoted by Sahnoun and others and contradicted the Somali oral tradition of 'sitting carpet'. The UN made relentless demands and placed often unrealistic time constraints on the Somalis and the peace process. For example, when Sahnoun's replacement, Ismat Kittani, visited Somaliland, he showed little interest in nurturing the Somali practice of attentuated negotiations: 'Speaking to a committee of elders whose patient negotiation had brought to an end many months of bloody internecine strife, he arrogantly commanded them to produce a full agreement within two hours. The elders ordered Kittani out of their territory.'[54]

An Oral Society

Somali culture is rooted in oral traditions; poetry and oratory play crucial roles in politics, war and peace. Most nomadic Somalis have transistor radios on which they listen to a variety of national and international programmes broadcast in Somali, including the BBC World News, which they listen to every day with 'at least the same attention they give to their daily Muslim prayers'.[55] At the beginning, Lewis and others advised the UN of the importance of effective broadcasting in the presentation of UN aims and policies and the use of oratory in counselling for peace. They were ignored; instead, the UN chose to drop leaflets.

> Here the bizarre image of American helicopters dropping leaflets, couched in pigeon Somali over Mogadishu's primarily oral population fittingly encapsulates the style of an over-grandiose western intervention which is high on technology but low on culturally appropriate human understanding.[56]

Lewis notes how the first leaflets dropped at the beginning of Operation *Restore Hope* read 'slave nations have come to help you' (instead of 'United Nations') – possibly a simple translation oversight, but one which had serious repercussions. Eventually, UNITAF's Joint Psychological Operations Task Force (JPOTF) acknowledged Lewis' advice. In addition to leaflet drops, the JPOTF broadcast news on military activities, public service announcements and messages of peace in Somali.

National Reconciliation: Top-down versus Bottom-Up

Self-motivated peacemaking is highly valued in Somali society, and uninvited intervention by others rarely solves the problem.[57] The Somali are intolerant of a third party directing them, influencing them or making suggestions; the role of the third party is one of facilitator only. Yet, the lack of cultural understanding in Somalia is most exemplified by the UN's prescribed top-down process for national reconciliation that thwarted early initiatives by Sahnoun and Oakley to build on local resources and traditional institutions.[58] To assume that because the Somali society was engaged in a protracted, internecine conflict, mechanisms to mitigate and resolve conflict were non-existent is erroneous. Somalis' rich history of traditional mechanisms for dealing with inter-clan disputes makes them 'as experienced at peacemaking and conflict resolution as they are at making war'.[59] Traditional means for resolving conflict were available, including: Somali moral commonwealth, *umma*, comprised of customary social code of conduct or *xeer* and Islamic *qanoon* or religious moral code; assemblies of elders, *guurti*, responsible for arbitrating conflicts; use of elders as mediators (*Ergo*); *shirs*, or open councils, used for discussion and negotiation; *diya* payments or compensations for death and injury.[60] These were evident in isolated cases in the south (for example, the Kismayo reconciliation initiative) and, more prominently, in the flourishing grassroots peacemaking processes in the north (for example, the Boroma conference that led to a National Charter for the Republic of Somaliland).

However, the enormous potential for a bottom-up, grassroots approach to the Somali conflict was ignored by the UN in favour of hierarchical political structures and formal, highly publicized, and costly peace conferences. In March 1993, the UN sponsored a national reconciliation conference in Addis Ababa, with the intention of being a two-track approach. In response to widespread criticism preceding the conference, efforts were made to broaden the representation, enabling traditional and religious leaders, women, intellectuals, artists and local NGO representatives to attend. However, while the faction leaders were lavishly treated, community representatives were only to participate because of generous sponsorships given by international NGOs. Although they were able to make their voices heard, the signatories of the agreement produced were the 15 faction leaders. The agreement divorced the faction leaders from the larger clan groups and further empowered their illegitimate positions. Furthermore, the UN attempted to establish transitional mechanisms of governance at the district, regional and national levels. The Addis Ababa Agreement proposed that the Transitional National Council (TNC) would be the 'sole repository of Somali sovereignty' and the 'prime political authority, having legislative functions'. Imposition of the Western concept of government frustrated the Somalis because it was incompatible with Somali political culture rooted in decentralized, egalitarian, community-based systems of power. The agreement also angered the delegation of observers from Somaliland because it contradicted the wishes of those in the northwest (characteristic of UN policy throughout its intervention), who were simultaneously involved in their own national reconciliation conference in Boroma; hence, the delegation disassociated themselves from the agreement and any future initiatives.

The provisional government structure was essentially a top-down structure, with political emphasis on the TNC. The Regional Councils and District Councils – in which composition appeared to indicate a bottom-up approach through local delegations – were dependent structures.[61] Power and responsibility were delegated from the TNC down to the RCs and DCs. In the end, the desired two-track approach to peace (with peacemaking at the grassroots level paralleling a process of accommodating warlords at the top level) was dominated by the warlords. The process used to form the councils,

> suggests that UNOSOM have spent no time in trying to understand how localised political reconciliation can work in Somalia... UNOSOM are, in effect, supporting the formation of 'top-down' albeit localised, political structures in the hope that they will be a catalyst for a 'bottom-up', broad-based reconciliation process... In many ways there is little difference between this system of district and regional councils and the one set up by Siad Barre during his regime... A centralised government structure is the very thing many Somalis have been fighting against.[62]

In March 1994, the UN attempted to revive the process of political reconciliation by convening another meeting in Nairobi, only this time the UN's approach was clearly top-down. Aideed and Ali Mahdi were brought together for face-to-face negotiations, resulting in the signing of the Nairobi Declaration, a manifesto on national reconciliation. The Nairobi meeting brought widespread criticism as it was dominated by the same warlords who were responsible for the civil strife and the death and starvation of thousands of Somalis. Critics argue that the UN dealt with the warlords as if they were national leaders and, once again, ignored the critical role that elders, traditional leaders and women play in resolving conflict. Faction leaders used the UN-sponsored national reconciliation conferences to enhance their own prestige within their clans rather than to seek a genuine solution.[63]

The UN practice of 'holding lavish and formal peace conferences in regional capitals, which isolated members from their constituencies was in flagrant violation of Somali practices'.[64] It is part of Somali culture to care about the specific part of the country where one lives, therefore, taking the peace process away from Somali lands dishonoured their local identities and sense of community.[65] Moreover, Somali negotiators must be able to process the information, negotiate, and consider their progress regularly. These formal meetings did not allow the Somalis to meet in an atmosphere where they could speak openly and confidentially to one another. The UN also failed to acknowledge that traditional Somali reconciliation is an ongoing process of consultations, assemblies and negotiations and, therefore, takes a considerable amount of time. Conferences held as far away as in Addis Ababa or Nairobi are, therefore, incongruous with Somali processes. The UN clearly lacked understanding of the nature of Somali culture and, ultimately, worked against rather than with local practices of conflict management.

What proved more successful than the large national/factional conferences were the locally and regionally based clan reconciliation conferences which, for the most part, did not involve UNOSOM (for example, the Galkaiyo and Kismayo conferences in the south and the Boroma conference in the north). Serious attention to cultural factors enhanced these peace processes: they were always conducted in local areas, enabling the participation of elders and community members and ensuring that these representatives were not isolated from their constituencies; they allowed sufficient time for confidence-building and reconciliation (for example, in Kismayo a consensus was reached after 47 days of negotiating); and they employed traditional methods of resolving conflict, including the *shir* and *guurti* (for example, to signal the reconciliation of the community in Kismayo, Walsh provided an opportunity for the Somali practice of 'compensation for the dead').

Towards More Culturally Sensitive Peacekeeping

Two areas regarding the future role of culture in peacekeeping merit consideration. First, the bottom-up approach to resolving conflict and building peace – rooted in specific cultural contexts – must be a feature of the international community's intervention strategy. Current peacekeeping policy is culturally insensitive, focusing predominantly at the top level of diplomatic negotiations and the prescription of 'quick-fix' Western processes and institutions. International intervention would produce more sustainable outcomes if policy sought to combine top-down with bottom-up efforts, focusing largely on the cultural resources available. Anthropological analysis, for example, could inform peacekeeping policy[66] (for example, using ethnoconflict theory or elicitation, employing 'cultural informants' – advisors from anthropology, individuals who have lived or worked in the area, and, particularly, individuals from the culture in question).

The second concern regards the deficiency in constructive conflict resolution skills (or 'contact skills') among military and civilian peacekeepers, which has been noted elsewhere.[67] Since this was exposed as a significant shortcoming of contemporary peacekeeping, military and civilian organizations have undertaken the challenge to train personnel in some of the specific third party skills required for field-based peacekeeping activities, including communication, negotiation and mediation. However, while the number of peacekeeping training institutions has grown considerably and the content of their programmes has broadened to encompass conflict resolution training, the cultural content of peacekeeping training remains considerably underdeveloped.[68] Intercultural skills are essential tools in any third party's toolbox; cultural training needs to be strategically included in the preparation and training of anyone involved in a peacekeeping mission. As peacekeepers and humanitarian workers find themselves responding to the same crisis, it is imperative that these disparate components of the complex humanitarian network learn how to work effectively together in order to mutually reinforce each other's aims and objectives. This requires, first and foremost, an increased awareness and understanding of the cultures of the other. Moreover, those involved in peacekeeping operations are frequently unattuned to local customs and lack adequate understanding of the conflict situation, including the local conceptions of the conflict and cultural means for resolving it. As a result of lack of training, the potential for cultural misunderstanding in interactions is exacerbated and relations with local populations are undermined. The understanding of local cultures may, in turn, encourage peacekeepers to build upon and local resources or to employ more sensitive processes of intervention.

Cultural training should include two interdependent components: *culture-general* and *culture-specific* training. The function of culture-general training is to provide an understanding of cultural differences and their implications for interpersonal interactions. This includes exploring how the individual's own cultural framework influences their beliefs, values, assumptions and behaviours, and how personal cultural experiences have shaped their conceptions of conflict and approaches to managing and resolving conflict. Once trainees have acquired an increased level of cultural self-awareness – moving beyond their 'ethnocentric roots and primordial sentiments'[69] – training should focus on improving intercultural communication skills, both verbal and non-verbal. Culture-general training should also incorporate developing an awareness of military and civilian organizational cultures, including mutual 'socialization' (that is, joint training and activities that enhance and sustain cooperation).

Culture-specific training focuses on developing an understanding of a specific cultural context – in peacekeeping terms, the host culture in which intervention will be take place. This includes, more generally, orientation to the background, origins and parties to the conflict, the history, religion, local customs, and language of the local population; and, specifically, it involves an exploration of the cultural dynamics of conflict and peace and traditional methods for managing conflict. The latter may involve an ethnoconflict theory and ethnopraxis analysis.

Both forms of training should be conducted through a combination of lectures, participatory exercises, role-plays and real-time simulations. Ideally, the training should be facilitated *prior* to the arrival of troops or humanitarians in the conflict area. Culture-general training could be part of an early training programme for potential peacekeepers due to its rudimentary content. However, culture-specific training can only take place once participants are informed of their cultural destination. While pre-deployment training is, again, more favourable, specific training could be carried out in a regional location or in-theatre. The concern here, of course, is that the potential for cultural misunderstanding is conceivable the moment a diplomat, peacekeeper or humanitarian arrives in the field. Specific cultural training, however, is ongoing: so long as peacekeeping participants are working with individuals from another cultural group, they must be mindful of cultural differences and revere them not as obstacles but as starting points to develop unique and creative solutions.

Conclusion

The argument presented above does not imply that culture is the root of all problems besetting peacekeeping, nor does it assume that better training and preparation will prevent problems from arising. Although cultural understanding does not guarantee success, it does preclude the introduction of a strategy that is useless and unproductive. Culture is a largely unrecognized dynamic that has been found to play an important role in determining the success or failure of conflict resolution processes in peacekeeping intervention. If peacekeeping is to remain an effective instrument for managing contemporary conflict, improved efforts must be made towards understanding the cultural issues at all levels of interpersonal interaction and process implementation.

NOTES

1. Robert A. Rubinstein, 'Culture, International Affairs, and Multilateral Peacekeeping: Confusing Process and Pattern', *Cultural Dynamics*, Vol.2, No.1, 1989, pp.41–61.
2. Definition of the term 'culture' is a matter of extensive debate; consequently, it is not the intention here to enter into or resolve this convoluted discussion. In its simplest form, and for the purposes of this study, culture is a system of implicit and explicit beliefs, values and behaviours shared by the members of a community or group, through which experience is expressed and interpreted.
3. Misunderstandings arising from cultural differences often lead to conflict. Indeed, many of the intractable conflicts in the post-Cold War world are rooted in cultural differences. Struggles over ethnicity and religion, for example, involve deeply rooted beliefs and values that are often more consequential than (or intrinsically linked to) economic or political factors. While understanding the cultural bases of past and present conflicts is essential, our concern here is not so much with culture as a cause of conflict, but with the dynamic role that culture plays in the overall process of conflict *resolution*.
4. There exists a wide range of literature covering these areas; see, for example: Pierre Casse and Surinder Deol, *Managing Intercultural Negotiations*, Washington, DC: SIETAR International, 1985; Raymond Cohen, *Negotiating Across Cultures: Communication Obstacles in International Diplomacy*, Washington, DC: USIP, 1995; William B. Gudykunst, *Bridging Differences*, London: Sage, 3rd Edition, 1998.
5. See, for example, Kevin Avruch and Peter Black, 'A Generic Theory of Conflict Resolution: A Critique', *Negotiation Journal*, Vol.3, No.1, 1987, pp.87–96; Kevin Avruch and Peter Black, 'The Culture Question and Conflict Resolution', *Peace and Change*, Vol.16, No. 1, pp.22–45, 1991; and Paul Salem, 'A Critique of Western Conflict Resolution from a Non-Western Perspective', in Salem (ed.), *Conflict Resolution in the Arab World*, Beirut: American University of Beirut, 1997, pp.11–24.
6. See, for example, Kevin Avruch, Peter W. Black, and Joseph A. Scimecca (eds.), *Conflict Resolution: Cross-Cultural Perspectives*, London: Greenwood Press, 1991; Douglas P. Fry and Kaj Bjorkqvist (eds.), *Cultural Variation in Conflict Resolution*, Mahway , NJ: LEA; and Karen Watson-Gegeo and Geoffrey White (eds.), *Disentangling: Conflict Discourse in Pacific Societies*, Stanford: Stanford University Press, 1990. See also, Kevin Avruch , *Culture & Conflict Resolution*, Washington, DC: United States Institute of Peace, 1998.
7. See, Avruch and Black, 1991 (n.5 above), pp.31–2.
8. John Paul Lederach, *Preparing for Peace: Conflict Transformation Across Cultures*, Syracuse: Syracuse University Press, 1995.
9. See, John Paul Lederach, *Building Peace: Sustainable Reconciliation in Divided Societies*, Washington, DC: United States Institute of Peace, 1997.
10. Important contributions that have reflected on some aspect of culture in peacekeeping include: A.B. Fetherston and Carolyn Nordstrom, 'Overcoming *Habitus* in Conflict Management: UN Peacekeeping and War Zone Ethnography', *Peace and Change*, Vol.20,

No.1, pp.94–119, 1995; Amitav Ghosh, 'The Global Reservation: Notes Toward an Ethnography of International Peacekeeping', *Cultural Anthropology*, Vol.9, No.3, pp.412–22, 1994; Marianne Heiberg, 'Peacekeepers and Local Populations: Some Comments on UNIFIL', in Rikye and Skjelsbaek (eds.), *The United Nations and Peacekeeping*, Basingstoke: Macmillan, 1990, pp.147–69; Paul R. Kimmel, 'Cultural and Ethnic Issues of Conflict and Peacekeeping', in Langholtz (ed.), *The Psychology of Peacekeeping*, London: Praeger, 1998, pp.57–71; John Mackinlay (ed.), *A Guide to Peace Support Operations*, Providence, RI: The Thomas J. Watson, Jr. Institute for International Studies, Brown University, 1996; Robert A. Rubinstein, 1989 (n.1 above), pp.41–61; Robert A. Rubinstein, 'Cultural Aspects of Peacekeeping: Notes on the Substance of Symbols', *Millenium*, Vol.22, No.3, pp.547–62, 1993; and Hugo Slim, 'The Stretcher and the Drum: Civil–Military Relations in Peace Support Operations', *International Peacekeeping*, Vol.3, No.2, pp.123–40, 1996.

11. Rubinstein, 1993 (n.10 above), p.553.
12. Referring to the peacekeeping force in UNIFIL, Heiberg, 'Peacekeepers and Local Populations', in Rikye and Skjelsbaek, 1990, (n.10 above) p.157. Although, Rubinstein has proposed that, in culturally challenging situations, symbolic material and activities are useful tools for coordinating disparate perceptions. For example, the most obvious symbols – the blue beret and helmet, the UN flag, the white vehicles – serve to identify the national contingents with a collective UN force, thus bringing together diverse cultural communities to form 'the mission'. See, Rubinstein, 1993 (n.10 above), pp.547–62.
13. Mats Berdal, 'Wither UN Peacekeeping? An Analysis of the Changing Military Requirements of UN Peacekeeping with Proposals for its Enhancement', *Adelphi Papers 281*, International Institute of Strategic Studies, 1993, p.8.
14. See, Patrick Bishop, 'Caution is the byword for Australian peacekeepers', *The Daily Telegraph*, 23 September 1999, p.17; and Janine di Giovanni, 'Gurkhas tread softly in tense city', *The Times*, 25 September 1999, p.13.
15. Fetherston and Nordstrom, 1995 (n.10 above), p.106.
16. David Matsumoto, *Culture and Psychology*, Pacific Grove, California: Brooks/Cole, 1996, p.112.
17. Larry Minear and Thomas G. Weiss, *A Handbook for Practitioners: Humanitarian Action in Times of War*, London: Lynne Reinner, 1993, p.69.
18. Mackinlay (n.10 above), p.2.
19. Slim, 1996, (n.10 above) pp.123–40.
20. Cedric Thornberry, 'Peacekeepers, Humanitarian Aid, and Civil Conflict', *Journal of Humanitarian Assistance*, WWW, 1995.
21. Marianne Heiberg and Johan Jürgen Holst, 'Peacekeeping in Lebanon: Comparing UNIFIL and the MNF', *Survival*, Vol.28, No.5, 1986, pp.410–11.
22. Ibid., p.411.
23. Grant T. Hammond, 'The Perils of Peacekeeping for the US: Relearning Lessons from Beirut for Bosnia', in Moxon-Browne (ed.), *A Future for Peacekeeping?*, Basingstoke: Macmillan, 1998, p.76.
24. Fetherston and Nordstrom, 1995 (n.10 above).
25. A.B. Fetherston, 'UN Peacekeepers and Cultures of Violence', *Cultural Survival Quarterly*, Vol.10, No.1, 1995, pp.1–8.
26. For an insightful account of the culturally inappropriate conflict management approach that formed the basis of UNTAC, see Pierre Lizèe, 'Peacekeeping, Peacebuilding and the Challenge of Conflict Resolution in Cambodia', in Charters (ed.), *Peacekeeping and the Challenge of Civil Conflict Resolution*, New Brunswick: Centre for Conflict Studies, University of New Brunswick, 1994, pp.135–48.
27. For a fuller discussion of the role of women in conflict resolution, see Tsehai Berhane-Selassie, 'African Women in Conflict Resolution', *Centre Focus*, No.120, 1994, pp.1–3 and Bridget Byrne, 'Towards a Gendered Understanding of Conflict', *IDS Bulletin*, Vol.27, No.3, 1996, pp.31–40.
28. Byrne, ibid., p.36.
29. Karunawathie Menike, 'People's Empowerment from the People's Perspective',

Development in Practice, Vol.3, No.3, 1993, p.178.
30. Paul Wehr and John Paul Lederach, 'Mediating Conflict in Central America', in Bercovitch (ed.), *Resolving International Conflicts: The Theory and Practice of Mediation*, London: Lynne Reiner, 1996, pp.55–74.
31. Edith S. Klein, 'Obstacles to Conflict Resolution in the Territories of the Former-Yugoslavia', in Charters (ed.), *Peacekeeping and the Challenges of Civil Conflict Resolution*, New Brunswick: Centre for Conflict Studies, University of New Brunswick, 1994, pp.155–6.
32. The peacekeeping intervention in Somalia involved three phases: the United Nations Operation in Somalia (UNOSOM), conceived as a traditional observer mission (but with a capacious mandate), established in April 1992; the US-led Unified Task Force (UNITAF), code-named Operation *Restore Hope*, established in December 1992 with a Chapter VII mandate; and the United Nations Operation in Somalia (UNOSOM II), established in March 1993 with the same enforcement powers.
33. Charles Dobbie, 'A Concept for Post-Cold War Peacekeeping', *Survival*, Vol.36, No.3, 1994, p.127.
34. Clement E. Adibe, 'Learning from the Failure of Disarmament and Conflict Resolution in Somalia', in Moxon-Brown, 1997 (n.23 above), p.145.
35. John G. Sommer, *Hope Restored?: Humanitarian Aid in Somalia, 1990–1994*, Washington, DC: Refugee Policy Group, Centre for Policy Analysis and Research on Refugee Issues, 1994, p.36.
36. Jonathan T. Dworken, 'Restore Hope: Coordinating Relief Operations', *Joint Forces Quarterly*, Vol.8, 1995, p.19.
37. Emma Visman, *Military 'Humanitarian' Intervention in Somalia*, London: Save the Children, 1993, p.28.
38. Dworken, 1995 (n.36 above), pp.19–20.
39. Peter Kieseker, 'Relationships Between Non-Government Organisations and Multinational Forces in the Field', in Smith (ed.), *Peacekeeping: Challenges for the Future*, Canberra: Australian Defence Force Academy, 1993, p.68.
40. Dworken, 1995 (n.36 above), pp.19–20.
41. Janes, 1996, p.48.
42. Somali culture is fascinating and highly elaborate, yet, it is often misunderstood and oversimplified. The doyen of Somali scholars, I.M. Lewis, has written widely on Somali culture, including: *Blood and Bone: The Call of Kinship in Somalia Society*, Lawrenceville, NJ: The Red Sea Press, 1994, and *Understanding Somalia: Guide to Culture, History and Social Institutions*, London: HAAN, 1993, Second Edition.
43. See, Mohamed Sahnoun, *Somalia: The Missed Opportunities*, Washington, DC: USIP, 1994 and 'Flashlights Over Mogadishu', *New Internationalist*, December, 1994, pp.9–11.
44. Robert Oakley and David Bentley, *Peace Operations: A Comparison of Somalia and Haiti*, Strategic Forum, No.30, 1995, Ft. McNair: Institute for Strategic Studies, National Defense University, p.3.
45. Ioan Lewis and James Mayall, 'Somalia', in Mayall (ed.), *The New Interventionalism, 1991–1994*, Cambridge: Cambridge University Press, 1996, p.121.
46. Author's interview with Professor Mark Walsh, US Army Peacekeeping Institute, Carlisle, Pennsylvania, 12 December 1995.
47. See, Keiseker's article: 'Relationships Between Non-Government Organisations and Multinational Forces in the Field', in Smith, 1993 (n.39 above).
48. A comprehensive analysis of Somali ethnoconflict theory and ethnopraxis has been given elsewhere. See, Tamara Duffey, *Culture, Conflict Resolution and Peacekeeping*, Unpublished PhD Thesis, Department of Peace Studies, University of Bradford, 1998.
49. Abdisalam Issa-Salwe, *The Collapse of the Somali State: The Impact of the Colonial Legacy*, London: HAAN, 1996, p.143–4.
50. Ahmed-Khadar Hussen Egal-Aymo, 'Towards Reconciliation', in Salih and Wohlgemuth (eds.), *Crisis Management and The Politics of Reconciliation in Somalia*, Uppsala: Nordiska Afrikainstitutet, 1994, p.87.
51. Sommer, 1994 (n.35 above), p.26.
52. Author's interview with US Special Envoy to Somalia, Robert Oakley, Washington, DC, 14

December 1996.

53. Author's interview with Profesor Mark Walsh, US Army Peacekeeping Institute, Carlisle, Pennsylvania, 12 December 1996.
54. Rakiya Omaar and Alex de Waal, 'Saving Somalia Without the Somalis', *Africa News Service*, 21 December 1992 – 3 January 1993, p.2.
55. Ioan M. Lewis, *Making History in Somalia: Humanitarian Intervention in a Stateless Society*, Paper Presented to the Forum of the Centre for the Study of Global Governance, London School of Economics, 'Rethinking Global Institutions', 10–12 September 1993, Hampshire, p.16.
56. Ibid., p.17.
57. Anab M. Hassan, 'Self-Help for Somali Reconciliation, Peace and Reconstruction', in Salih and Wohlgemuth, 1994 (n.50 above), pp.69.
58. Sahnoun's position was articulated by the Ergada (a forum of Somali intellectuals for peace) and supported by the Uppsala Advisory Group at the Life & Peace Institute in Sweden. Throughout the intervention, the Advisory Group resolutely advised the UN to follow a bottom-up approach to peacemaking and peacebuilding in Somalia. For discussions on the Ergada and the Uppsala Advisory Group, see: Wolfgang Heinrich, *Building the Peace: Experiences of Collaborative Peacebuilding in Somalia, 1993–1996*, Uppsala: Life & Peace Institute, 1997 and Lederach, 1997 (n.9 above).
59. Mark Bradbury, *The Somali Conflict: Prospects for Peace*, Oxford: Oxfam, 1994, p.6.
60. For further discussion of the traditional practices available in Somalia/Somaliland, see: Bradbury, ibid.; Ahmed Yusuf Farah and Ioan M. Lewis, 'Making Peace in Somaliland', *Cahiers d'études africaines*, Vol.37, No.2, 1997, pp.349–77; and Ahmed Yusuf Farah and Ioan M. Lewis, *Somalia, The Roots of Reconciliation: Peacemaking Endeavours of Contemporary Lineage Leaders – A Survey of Grassroots Peace Conferences in 'Somaliland'*, London: ACTIONAID, 1993.
61. Heinrich, 1997 (n.58 above).
62. Bradbury, 1994 (n.59 above), pp.43–4.
63. Ameen Jan, *Peacebuilding in Somalia*, IPA Policy Briefing Series, New York: International Peace Academy, 1996.
64. Ken Menkhaus, 'International Peacebuilding and the Dynamics of Local and National Reconciliation in Somalia', *International Peacekeeping*, Vol.3, No.1, 1996, p.57.
65. Charles Geshekter, 'The Death of Somalia in Historical Perspective', in Adam and Ford (eds.), *Mending Rips in the Sky*, Lawrenceville, NJ: The Red Sea Press, 1997, p.66.
66. See, Rubinstein, 1993 (n.10 above), and Ghosh, 1994 (n.10 above).
67. See, for example: A.B. Fetherston, *Towards a Theory of United Nations Peacekeeping*, London: Macmillan, 1994; and A.B. Fetherston, O. Ramsbotham and T. Woodhouse, 'UNPROFOR: Some Observations from a Conflict Resolution Perspective', *International Peacekeeping*, Vol.1, No.2, 1994, pp.179–203; and David Last, *Theory, Doctrine and Practice of Conflict De-Escalation in Peacekeeping Operations*, Clementsport, Nova Scotia: The Canadian Peacekeeping Press, 1997.
68. This is not to suggest that the importance of cultural training has not been observed: many writing on peacekeeping training have acknowledged the need for more substantial training on the culture of the local population prior to deployment and on the skills necessary for effective intercultural ineraction. While 'culture' does feature in some military and civilian training programmes and manuals, its appearance is minimal.
69. Paul R. Kimmel, 'Cultural and Ethnic Issues of Conflict and Peacekeeping', in Langholtz (ed.), *The Psychology of Peacekeeping*, London: Praeger, 1998, p.63. Kimmel offers an insightful discussion on training in cultural awareness; in particular, he suggests improving cultural self-awareness and understanding through the 'culture contrast training exercise', using role plays and realistic scenarios to directly experience misperceptions and miscommunications and to become more aware of trainees' own cultural backgrounds and their impact on others.

Reflections on UN Post-Settlement Peacebuilding

OLIVER RAMSBOTHAM

> It is, of course, well known that the only source of war is politics – the intercourse of governments and peoples; but it is apt to be assumed that war supends that intercourse and replaces it with a wholly different condition, ruled by no law but its own.
> We maintain, on the contrary, that war is simply a continuation of political intercourse, with the addition of other means. We deliberately use the phrase 'with the addition of other means' because we also want to make it clear that war in itself does not suspend political intercourse or change it into something entirely different. In essentials, that intercourse continues, irrespective of the means it employs.
>
> K.M. von Clausewitz[1]

'Every war must end'[2] – but there are many ways in which this can happen. One side may win outright, the fighting may peter out sporadically, or there may be a military stalemate leading to a formal peace agreement. This study is concerned with the last of these. In particular it takes post-Cold War settlements in which the United Nations has played a major interventionary role as its subject domain, a somewhat restricted inventory, but one which has the merit of including conflicts in three continents: Asia (Cambodia), America (El Salvador) and Africa (Nambia, Angola, Mozambique). UN interventions in pre-Dayton Bosnia (UNPROFOR) and Somalia (UNOSOM) did much to discredit such enterprises, but these were interventions in active war zones where there had been no prior formal peace agreements. Interventions in Rwanda (UNAMIR) and in Liberia to the end of 1996 (UNOMIL) were also abortive, the former blamed by some for precipitating the 1994 genocide, the latter a relatively small operation in support of the regional ECOWAS states. To set against these is the contribution made by ONUCA to the peace process in Honduras and Nicaragua, not included here because it was originally deployed to verify an interstate non-intervention agreement, even though ONUCA's mandate was subsequently expanded to take on something of a peacebuilding role in those two countries. Intervention in Haiti (UNMIH) was not an intervention after a war. In contrast, there are several examples of attempts at post-settlement peacebuilding without a substantial UN presence, while IFOR/SFOR in Bosnia and KFOR in Kosovo offer an alternative model within the same generic family – peace enforcement operations under the aegis of the United Nations, but built around a non-UN core (and with attendant UN peacekeeping components). MINURCA in the Central African Republic (April 1998), and UNAMSIL in Sierra Leone (October 1999) may suggest that, after a period of severe doubt, the enterprise of UN post-settlement peacebuilding still commands some support among Western powers. From a different perspective, so also perhaps does UNTAET in East Timor (October 1999).

Large-scale UN peace support operations of the kind being considered here offer insight into a set of assumptions about conflict resolution in non-interstate wars which became current at the end of the Cold War as part of a new global agenda, set, as Christopher Clapham notes, by the dominant Western capitalist and liberal democratic states, the civil societies within them, Western non-governmental organizations, and the international institutions which those states largely controlled.[3] What Clapham calls 'a fairly standardised conflict resolution mechanism' derived from this was applied like a template to a wide range of disparate conflicts, rather like Wittgenstein's locomotive cabin in which a uniform-looking set of handles in fact fulfil a number of diverse functions. This might be called the UN's post-settlement peacebuilding 'standard operating procedure'.

Post-settlement Peacebuilding Defined

When the UN Secretary-General was asked by Security Council Heads of Government meeting on 31 January 1992 to draft general principles that would 'guide decisions on when a domestic situation warrants international action',[4] he based his response in part on distinctions that had long been current in the peace research and conflict resolution field, and in part on ideas drawn from the disaster relief and sustainable development literature.[5] So far as concerns the former, Johan Galtung had distinguished 'three approaches' to peace in the 1960s: peacekeeping which aimed 'to halt and reduce the manifest violence of the conflict through the intervention of military forces in an interpository role'; peacemaking which was 'directed at reconciling political and strategical attitudes through mediation, negotiation, arbitration and conciliation' mainly at elite level; and peacebuilding which addressed 'the practical implementation of peaceful social change through socio-economic reconstruction and development'.[6] Stephen Ryan, critical of the neglect of the relational dimension in Galtung's characterization of peacebuilding, put his emphasis on changing mutually negative conflict *attitudes* at grass-roots level.[7] With reference to the 'conflict triangle', he contrasted this with peacekeeping which aims for a reduction in violent conflict *behaviour*, and peacemaking which aims to resolve conflicting *interests*.[8] All of this has been brought together within the conflict resolution field in John Paul Lederach's characterizaton of peacebuilding as the attempt to address the underlying structural, relational and cultural roots of conflict: 'I am suggesting that "peacebuilding" be understood as a comprehensive term that encompasses the full array of stages and approaches needed to transform conflict towards sustainable, peaceful relations and outcomes.'[9]

Drawing on this tradition, but narrowing it so that it applied specifically to post-war reconstruction, the UN Secretary-General distinguished 'post-conflict peacebuilding' from pre-conflict 'preventive diplomacy' in his June 1992 *Agenda for Peace*, while retaining the original contrast between peacebuilding, peacekeeping and peacemaking. He defined post-conflict peacebuilding as 'actions to identify and support structures which will tend to strengthen and solidify peace in order to avoid a relapse into conflict'.[10] This was at first largely identified with military demobilization and the political transition to participatory electoral democracy, and this remains the core of the UN's post-settlement peacebuilding SOP. In the 1995 *Supplement to An Agenda for Peace* it was envisaged that post-conflict peacebuilding would initially be undertaken by multifunctional UN operations, then handed over to civilian agencies under a resident coordinator, and finally transferred entirely to local agents.[11] Since *Agenda for Peace* the concept was progressively expanded in subsequent versions[12] to include a broader agenda aimed at alleviating the worst effects of war on the population and promoting what Michael Pugh calls 'a sustainable development approach which tackles the root causes of emergencies'. He sums this up as follows:

> In the context of UN-authorized peace support measures, peacebuilding can be defined as a policy of external international help for developing countries designed to support indigenous social, cultural and economic development and self-reliance, by aiding recovery from war and reducing or eliminating resort to future violence.[13]

In order to clarify what is at issue here, it is helpful to note a distinction made in the peace research and conflict resolution literature between 'negative' and 'positive' peace, where the former is defined as the cessation of 'direct' violence and the latter as the removal of 'structural' and 'cultural' violence.[14] From this viewpoint, post-settlement peacebuilding can be said to be made up of: (A) the 'negative' task of preventing a relapse into overt violence, and (B) the 'positive' tasks of aiding national recovery and expediting the eventual removal of the underlying causes of internal war. The distinctive but close relationship between these two complementary sets of tasks is indicated (albeit in reverse order) in the UN Secretary-General's definition of 'post-conflict peacebuilding' as 'the various concurrent and integrated actions undertaken at the end of a conflict to consolidate peace and prevent a recurrence of armed confrontation'.[15] Peacebuilding is distinguished here from on-going *humanitarian* and *development* activities in 'countries emerging from crisis' insofar as it has the specific *political* aims of (1) reducing 'the risk of resumption of conflict' and (2) contributing to the creation of 'conditions most conducive to reconciliation, reconstruction and recovery'. We will call the first task 'preventing a relapse into war' and the second task 'constructing a self-sustaining peace'. Some of the most testing challenges in post-settlement peacebuilding concern the relationship between the two.

'Clausewitz in Reverse' and the Challenge of Post-Settlement Peacebuilding

A brief look at the situation in the five cases under scrutiny gives an idea of the scale of the challenge facing peacebuilders after long periods of war. In each instance the original causes of the war, themselves often deep-rooted and difficult to eradicate, had been overlaid by the traumatic experience of many years of intense fighting. Compared with the tasks facing those attempting pre-war conflict prevention, post-settlement peacebuilders may in some senses have an easier job, insofar as the main conflict parties have at least been induced to reach an agreement, outside governments may be exerting concerted pressure to sustain the settlement, and war-weariness if not war-revulsion may predominate within the population at large. In most other respects, however, the tasks confronting post-war peacebuilders are much more demanding. We look first at the challenge of preventing a relapse into war, then at the challenge of constructing a self-sustaining peace, then at the relationship between the two.

Preventing a relapse into war (Task A) – means confronting the challenge of 'Clausewitz in reverse', the most immediate and urgent political task facing post-settlement peacebuilders. Clausewitz's insight that war is the 'continuation of political intercourse with the addition of other means' also implies the reverse – that post-war politics is a continuation of the conflict albeit transmuted into non-military mode. In fact, Clausewitz himself, prescient as ever, anticipated this observation in a continuation of the passage cited at the head of this contribution: 'The main lines along which military events progress, and to which they are restricted, are political lines that continue throughout the war *into the subsequent peace*' (italics added). The 'additional means' which characterize war will also have left their mark on the post-settlement process in the form of broken lives and shattered communities, as well as new actors, interests and political agendas spawned by what has usually been a prolonged period of fighting.[16] The term 'post-conflict peacebuilding', therefore, despite its UN *imprimatur*, is a misnomer (hence the use of the term 'post-settlement peacebuilding' in this study). 'Post-conflict' is precisely what it is not. On the contrary, the peace agreement is not the end of the conflict, but 'the means through which the parties hope to resolve the unfinished business of war'.[17] Nor is this an accidental feature of the post-war political situation. It is its very essence, as is made plain in recent analyses of internal war endings, where it is shown that the most difficult task facing those trying to bring about a lasting peace agreement is to persuade the conflict parties that their continuing interests will now be better served by entering the peace process than by continuing to fight.[18] For Roy Licklider, for example, this is seen to underlie all three of the 'intrinsic' features regarded as critical to the ending of violent internal conflict: (1) a shift in the way conflict issues are perceived by conflict parties so that interests seem better served by settlement than by fighting; (2) the internal politics of the conflict parties themselves so that 'peace constituencies' come to predominate over 'war constituencies'; and (3) the military power balance in the field so that a 'mutually hurting stalemate' precipitates accommodation. Two 'extrinsic' factors are also closely related to it: (4) the 'terms of the settlement' which need both to mirror and to reinforce those factors, and (5) the 'activities of third parties' which need to help sustain them through the uncertain vicissitudes of the post-war period.[19] In other words, it is exactly because they are persuaded that the continuing interests for which they have been waging intense and prolonged war are now more likely to be served by transmuting the struggle into non-forcible politics that undefeated belligerents are induced to go along with the peace process in the first place. This feature subsequently constitutes the core of the settlement itself, which thereby, as it were, *projects* the politics of war forward, albeit transmuted, into the politics of peace.

Two additional points can be made about the nature of post-settlement politics in the light of this. First, that most of these instances involve 'qualitatively asymmetric conflicts' in which a government is fighting a rebel force: the South African government against SWAPO in Namibia, the SOC regime against the allied CGDK forces in Cambodia, the MPLA government against UNITA in Angola, the ARENA government against the FMNL in El Salvador, the FRELIMO government against RENAMO in Mozambique. Anatol Rapoport describes the crux of the problem:

> In [qualitatively] asymmetric conflict, the systems may be widely disparate or may perceive each other in different ways. A revolt or a revolution is an example of an asymmetric conflict. The system

> revolted against 'perceives' itself as defending order and legitimacy; the insurgents 'perceive' themselves as an instrument of social change or of bringing new systems into being… Asymmetric conflicts [are those] whose genesis is not 'issues' to be 'settled' but the very structure of a situation that cannot be eliminated or modified without conflict. Indeed, the suspension of conflict or making conflict impossible is in these instances entirely in the interests of one of the parties – the dominant one.[20]

Second, that the general context for post-settlement peacebuilding is what Grenier and Daudelin call the 'peacebuilding market-place' in which 'peace' (the cessation of violence) is traded for other commodities such as political opportunity (elections) and economic advantage (land): 'Exchanging resources of violence against other resources is arguably the pivotal type of 'trade' in peacebuilding'.[21] The key bargain in qualitatively asymmetric conflicts, therefore, is between governments asked to surrender their claim to a permanent monopoly of political power (they are asked to accept a democratic process in which they may lose), and opposition groups asked to give up the threat or use of violence (they are asked to submit to a process of disarmament which may be irreversible). Each is required voluntarily to cede its main power asset and risks having to accept an outcome equivalent to military defeat. Needless to say, these are highly precarious processes to deliver when there is an atmosphere of intense mistrust and leaders are not only negotiating with opponents but also struggling to satisfy disparate demands from factions within their own ranks or even beyond their control. It is difficult to ensure that the cards remain stacked against a resumption of hostilities in the eyes of erstwhile belligerents during the inevitably unstable, precarious and unpredictable jockeying for power which constitutes post-settlement politics.

The second cluster of tasks which make up the composite process of post-settlement peacebuilding is 'constructing a self-sustaining peace' (Task B). This is the positive aspect of the enterprise. The aim is to underpin Task A with a view to long-term sustainability by constitutional and institutional reform, social reconstruction and reconciliation, and the rebuilding of shattered polities, economies and communities. It is a colossal undertaking which is difficult to summarize briefly, merging as it does into longer-term processes that at a certain point can no longer be clearly related to the post-settlement scenario. Perhaps it is best described as an attempt to make up three interlinked deficits which characteristically afflict countries after prolonged internal war and hamper the consolidation of peace: political/constitutional incapacity, economic/social debilitation, and psycho/social trauma. In addition, there is an initial critical deficit in the military/security sphere. All these deficits must be made up if peace is to be permanently sustained. The immediate challenge here is the sheer destructiveness of modern warfare. Two examples make the point. In Cambodia, in addition to the unimaginable human cost of more than 20 years of fighting and political extremism, pre-existing political structures had been largely obliterated, the per capita GDP which in 1969 had been higher than neighbouring Thailand was by 1991 only one sixth, over two thirds of the population were women, while the psycho-social effects of protracted violence on this scale meant that the war zone was not just the battlefield but extended into the most intimate lives of what Martin has termed a 'shattered society'.[22] By the end of the 1980s the *International Index of Human Suffering* rated Mozambique 'the most unhappy nation on earth', nearly one million having died in the fighting and associated deprivation, a quarter of the population having been displaced, and one and a half million having fled abroad. In the eyes of some analysts to attempt to tackle all of this comprehensively and simultaneously at the break-neck speed envisaged in a succession of UN Security Council mandates was not only daunting, but, as in the case of the Cambodian peace plan according to one of its chief architects 'overly ambitious and clearly not achievable'.[23]

In addition to the difficulties inherent in these two sets of complementary challenges taken separately, there are also unavoidable tensions between them when they are taken together. The challenge of managing 'Clausewitz in reverse' (Task A) predominates in the immediate aftermath of a peace settlement. Without it, almost nothing else can subsequently be achieved. The more ambitious challenge of building capacities for a 'self-sustaining peace' (Task B), is more significant over the longer term. Without it, the cessation of overt violence is likely to prove little more than temporary. Each presupposes the other, yet, as a number of commentators have observed, the logic inherent in Task A is at odds with important elements in Task B, while key assumptions behind Task B are often at cross purposes with the more pressing short-term priorities involved in Task A. For example, the negative task of preventing a relapse into war demands uncomfortable trade-offs and compromises which may jeopardize the longer-term goal of sustainable peace. Conversely, measures adopted on the assumption that it is market democracy that best sustains peace long-term, may *en route* increase the risk of a reversion to war. On the political/constitutional front it is pointed out how conflictual electoral processes may exacerbate political differences and increase conflict in certain circumstances.[24] On the economic/social front the competitive nature of free-market capitalism is also seen to engender instability and conflict.[25] On the psycho-social front there are well-known tensions between the priorities of peace, reconciliation and justice.[26]

The UN's Post-Settlement Peacebuilding 'Standard Operating Procedure' (SOP)

The UN's continuous involvement in post-settlement peacebuilding of this kind goes back at least as far as the 1978 Settlement Proposal in Namibia, devised by the Contact Group of Western states, where UNTAG's mandate under SCR 435 was to assist a Special Representative appointed by the UN Secretary-General 'to ensure the early independence of Namibia through free and fair elections under the supervision and control of the United Nations'. The transition phase was to last a year. This unexceptionable formula for expediting the withdrawal of a former colonial master and its replacement by a fledgling independent state, put into practice in the interim in Southern Rhodesia/ Zimbabwe, was revived ten years later in very different circumstances and immediately, and surprisingly, became the main model for the UN's new post-settlement peacebuilding efforts in a number of long-standing internal wars. In a sharp break with earlier international practice, rebel forces were now to be accorded equal status with governments and both were to be regarded as proto-political parties deserving of equal access to a new UN-sanctioned reformed political process. The ending of the Cold War drew a line under what had been an almost automatic backing of rival sides by the superpowers, opened up the possibility of concerted action through the Security Council, and ushered in the apparent global triumph of what Roland Paris terms 'liberal internationalism' in its twin manifestations as liberal parliamentary democracy and liberal market capitalism. With reference to post-settlement peacebuilding, in Paris' words, 'The central tenet of this paradigm is the assumption that the surest foundation for peace...is market democracy, that is, a liberal democratic polity and a market-oriented economy.'

> Peacebuilding is in effect an enormous experiment in social engineering – an experiment that involves transplanting western models of social, political, and economic organization into war-shattered states in order to control civil conflict: in other words, pacification through political and economic liberalization.[27]

The individual elements in the UN's post-settlement peacebuilding SOP have varied in detail from case to case, but within a recognizable overall pattern. In 1992 the UN Secretary-General described the main tasks as:

> disarming the previously warring parties and the restoration of order, the custody and possible destruction of weapons, repatriating refugees, advisory and training support for security personnel, monitoring elections, advancing efforts to protect human rights, reforming or strengthening governmental institutions and promoting formal and informal processes of political participation.[28]

Three years later, in *Supplement to An Agenda for Peace*, the key elements of peacebuilding were described in similar if expanded terms as 'demilitarization, the control of small arms, institutional reform, improved police and judicial systems, the monitoring of human rights, electoral reform, and social and economic development' (paragraph 47), while in 1997 post-conflict peacebuilding was seen to involve 'the creation or strengthening of national institutions, the monitoring of elections, the promotion of human rights, the provision of reintegration and rehabilitation programmes and the creation of conditions for resumed development'.[29] So far as concerns specific missions, UNTAG's five main tasks were: the separation of military forces and demobilization of those not needed in the new national army; the demilitarization of the South West Africa Police (SWAPOL); supervision of the interim Administrator-General's government and repeal of discriminatory laws; return of refugees; electoral registration and monitoring. UNTAC was made up of seven main components: military, civilian police, human rights, civil administration, electoral, repatriation, rehabilitation. ONUSAL's original human rights division was subsequently supplemented by a military division, a police division, and an electoral division. UNAVEM III's five main mission components were: political, military, police, humanitarian, electoral. ONUMOZ's original mandate included four 'interrelated' components: political, military, electoral and humanitarian. A civilian police component was later added. In the 1997 formulation this was seen to be an integrated programme, with the Department of Political Affairs (DPA), in its then capacity as convenor of the Executive Committee on Peace and Security (ECPS), as coordinator of a joint enterprise involving the Office of the High Commissioner for Human Rights, the Department of Peacekeeping Operations (DPKO), the United Nations High Commissioner for Refugees (UNHCR), the United Nations Development Programme (UNDP) and the World Bank. As the 'focal point' of this vast enterprise, the convenor of ECPS would also support and reinforce the individual task forces established 'to ensure integrated action by the entire United Nations system' in each case. In all this the planners were to bear in mind in particular 'the point at which the emphasis on the peacebuilding role will give way to full-fledged reconstruction and development activities'.

Reflections on the UN's Post-settlement Peacebuilding SOP: The end of a Ten-year Experiment?

Ten years after this ambitious experiment in post-settlement 'social engineering' was initiated with the reanimation of UNTAG in the wake of the December 1988 Namibia Accords, all of the original large-scale missions have now formally ended with the withdrawal of MONUA from Angola in February 1999. It seems a fitting moment, therefore, to look back on the undertaking and to offer some reflections. What is the overall verdict on the venture? Is the experiment one which should be repeated and built upon? Or have shortcomings in individual missions, or the lack of effectiveness of UN-run peacebuilding in general, or wholesale rejection of the liberal universalist assumptions upon which the whole enterprise has been based now discredited it?

Much has been written about the cases under review,[30] and about peacebuilding in general.[31] Opinions have ranged from what are in effect official UN apologiae,[32] through accounts which accept the overall enterprise but are critical of aspects of particular missions,[33] to those which criticize the means by which the UN's liberal internationalist agenda has been promoted but nevertheless accept it as a long-term aspiration,[34] and on to those which reject the whole attempt to universalize what are seen as inappropriate Western models in this way.[35] Others again are critical of what purport to be impartial non-forcible interventions in conflict zones.[36] Setting aside for the moment criticisms from those who favour more forcible interventions as in post-Dayton Bosnia and Kosovo, six main criticisms seem to be made from a conflict resolution perspective:

- First, an emphasis on the importance of distinguishing different levels of application and of agency in peacebuilding. For example, John Paul Lederach differentiates between: the level of national leadership (including leaders of rebel factions); the level of middle range ethnic, religious and regional leadership; and the level of local leadership and grassroots groups and communities.[37] This relates to what is seen as the importance of 'peacebuilding from below' and criticism of the tendency of major actors, including the UN, to adopt a state-centric top-down approach to post-settlement peacebuilding which neglects smaller NGOs, local agents and indigenous resources.[38] From this perspective much more emphasis should be placed on the lower end of the triangle, more resources should be concentrated here, and interveners should make sure that their activities serve to support indigenous practices and initiatives, rather than ignoring or overwhelming them.

- Second, so far as concerns the different types of deficit to be made up, there are arguments for more emphasis to be put on aspects of the economic/social dimension and the relatively neglected psycho/social dimension.[39] On the former, the logic of 'local empowerment' is often a radical one and may imply deep involvement in indigenous struggles for social justice.[40]

- Third, there is criticism of the foreshortened time-frame within which most missions have been put together and propelled into the conflict arena, to be as abruptly removed a few months later after a frenetic period of activity largely dictated by the interests of powerful donor governments and the blueprints of planners in national capitals or the UN. Conflict parties are seen to have been frogmarched towards elections and then abandoned. Some have contrasted the 2 to 5 years needed to stabilize the military and political situation, the 5 to 10 years needed to rebuild infrastructures and start to regenerate the economy, and the generation or so needed to reconcile formerly warring parties and communities.[41]

- Fourth, an argument that the nature of the third party intervention should be more consciously questioned, both because of the disproportionate power/interest relations of intervening states and because of the need to embed the peacebuilding process in the larger context of regional and global politics. External peacebuilders should see themselves as one further element in the situation, not some *deus ex machina* immune to criticism, accountability or control.[42]

- Fifth, related to this, is the so-called culture question which challenges the applicability of what are seen as essentially Western approaches in peacebuilding to the non-Western countries which are their usual targets. Criticism ranges here from sharp exception taken to particular examples of cultural insensitivity in individual UN missions to a more radical wholesale rejection of what is seen as the Westernized liberal internationalist model. This is part of a long-standing internal debate between those who advocate universal or 'generic' approaches to conflict intervention and those who argue for radical cultural pluralism and difference.[43]

- Finally, sixth, there is the question of the use of force, and, more broadly, the suitability of what are seen as predominantly military operations in terms of numbers of personnel deployed for what are mainly non-military tasks in post-settlement peacebuilding.[44]

So far as concerns the more restricted theme of this study, however, what strikes me is, first, how critics of the UN record as often as not end up recommending more, not less, international intervention, and, second, that there has as yet been little systematic discussion of the liberal universalist assumptions behind the whole undertaking nor debate about what the alternatives might be. In short, if the experiment were to be abandoned at this point – as seemed likely until recently, and may still turn out to be the case – then this would not be because it has been conclusively shown to have failed. A few further comments may elaborate this.

Task A: Preventing a Relapse into War

Can it be said in the five cases under consideration here that the international community has succeeded in Task A, that is to say in helping to 'make the settlement stick' and preventing a relapse into war? And could this have been achieved without such outside intervention? Clearly these are counter-factual questions which cannot be finally determined one way or the other. Nevertheless, a number of commentators who are prepared to pronounce relative 'success' in some cases see the UN intervention as essential to it. For example in El Salvador Hampson concludes that 'without ONUSAL's active and constructive involvement in the implementation, the peace process would surely have come unstuck',[45] while Grenier and Daudelin agree that 'left alone, El Salvador could not have generated the necessary political guarantees and economic compensations to make peace and democratization possible'.[46] Similarly in Namibia UNTAG is seen to have played a critical role in monitoring and pressuring the South African Administrator-General, who, in contrast to 1978 intentions, remained in charge of the government during the transition phase, thus keeping SWAPO on board the peace process. In Mozambique RENAMO leader, Afonso Dhlakama, announced his decision to withdraw from the election on 26 October 1994, the day before polling was due to begin. It took concerted pressure from the international community, and an extension of the voting period being run by ONUMOZ to persuade him to change his mind. In Cambodia, where the Khmer Rouge defected and Phase II of the cantonment and demobilization plan was abandoned in November 1992, UNTAC nevertheless succeeded against the odds in sustaining the peace process with the remaining parties through to the May 1993 elections. Only in Angola has UN-run post-settlement peacebuilding in the end failed. For UN Special Representative Margaret Anstee a key reason for the failure of UNAVEM II in preventing the defection of UNITA leader, Jonas Savimbi, after the September 1992 elections followed by a resumption of war, was the fact that the UN had not played a lead role in the May 1991 Bicesse Accords and was not properly resourced to oversee implementation.[47] Discouragingly, although many of these shortcomings appeared to have been remedied in UNAVEM III's much larger role in the implementation of the November 1994 Lusaka Protocol, this, too, subsequently unravelled, giving credence to those who argue that forcible intervention is essential to underpin such operations.

More broadly, Task A can only be said to have been finally secured when an incumbent government voluntarily and peacefully relinquishes power after losing an election. In Namibia, although an incumbent government (Pretoria) did peacefully handed over power, this had already been agreed in the peace settlement as part of the independence process, unlike the other four cases which were civil wars. At the time of writing the second general election since independence is taking place amid accusations of fraud and intimidation by opposition parties, and the expectation is that President Nujoma's SWAPO party will again win easily. In El Salvador, Mozambique and Angola the governing party has retained power after subsequent elections, while in Cambodia the evergreen Hun Sen managed to survive yet again by joining a coalition government despite losing the 1993 election, subsequently ousted his FUNCINPEC coalition partner, and is still in power after the 1998 election.

In conclusion, therefore, so far as concerns Task A, the jury is still out, but there is a strong body of informed opinion which agrees with Hampson in relation to UN operations in Namibia, Cambodia and El Salvador that:

> In general, our findings lend support to the proposition that external third-party involvement in all phases of the peace process does indeed matter to political outcomes, and that success and failure are indeed linked to the quality and level of support given by third parties to the peace process, especially during implementation of an agreement.[48]

Task B: Creating a Self-Sustaining Peace

Turning to the broader aims embodied in Task B, the positive task of creating a self-sustaining peace, we may note that the tough bargaining process at the heart of Task A involves securing the key interests of elites on both sides. The rank and file, as well as the dispossessed in whose name rebel factions have often purportedly been fighting, tend to lose out. The euphoria which accompanies the early stages of the post-settlement period, therefore, easily turns to disillusionment as what are often unrealistic hopes subsequently evaporate. The crime rate soars as the peacetime economy is unable to absorb large numbers of unemployed ex-soldiers and their families as well as hundreds of thousands of returning refugees, while a continuing wartime black economy, a ready availability of weaponry, and the destabilizing effects of what has usually been abrupt introduction of free market conditionalities further destabilize the situation. Erstwhile heroes of the revolution lose touch with their followers and join the establishment. This clearly provides fuel for future conflict unless the basic needs of individuals and groups are satisfied. The making up of the three major deficits in war-shattered countries, political/constitutional incapacity, economic/social debilitation, psycho/social trauma, noted above as the key components of Task B, is an enormous undertaking. It is also a long-term project upon which it is difficult to pronounce with any confidence so soon after the ending of the war. Some idea of the vastness of the project implicit in the UN's post-settlement peacebuilding SOP may be conveyed by the conceptual framework below.

TABLE 1
A CONCEPTUAL FRAMEWORK FOR UN POST-SETTLEMENT PEACEBUILDING

(i) Interim/short-term measures (up to the first election);
(ii) Medium-term measures (through to the second election or to the next election where there is a peaceful change of government);
(iii) = Long-term measures (beyond (ii)).

The military/security dimension[49]
(i) Disarmament/demobilization of factions, separation of army/police.
(ii) Consolidation of new national army under civilian control.
Steps towards creation of integrated non-politicized national police.
Progress in protecting civilians from organized crime.
(iii) Demilitarized politics, societal security, transformation of cultures of violence.

The political/constitutional dimension[50]
(i) Manage problems of transitional government/constitutional reform.
(ii) Overcome the challenge of the second election/peaceful transfer of power.
(iii) Establish tradition of good governance including respect for democracy, human rights and rule of law.
Development of civil society within genuine political community.

The economic/social dimension[51]
(i) Humanitarian relief, essential services/communications.
(ii) Rehabilitation of resettled population/demobilized soldiers.
Progress in rebuilding infrastructure, reviving agriculture, and demining.
(iii) Stable long-term macroeconomic policies and economic management.
Locally sustainable community development/distributional justice.

The psycho/social dimension[52]
(i) Overcoming initial distrust.
(ii) Managing conflicting priorities of peace and justice.
(iii) Healing psychological wounds/long-term reconciliation.

The international dimension
(i) Direct, culturally sensitive, support for the peace process.
(ii) Transference to local control avoiding undue interference/neglect.
(iii) Integration into cooperative and equitable regional and global structures.

In making up the political/constitutional deficit the UN template prescribes power sharing arrangements and a new constitution underpinned by regular 'free and fair' national and local elections – in short, liberal democracy. A surprising number of commentators, not only in the West but also elsewhere, seem to accept this principle. Roland Paris, mindful of what he describes as the 'tumultuous' effect of the raw democratic process on vulnerable war-shattered countries, while accepting the principle, advocates a longer period of adjustment in which the international community would be more active, among other things, in excluding extremists and controlling the media.[53] This implies deeper involvement and more intimate embroilment in local politics than was attempted in five of our six cases. For example, it implies a considerable use of military force where 'extremists' are major players like Pol Pot in Cambodia, Savimbi in Angola or Karadzic in Bosnia. Only in the latter case has the international community intervened along the lines advocated by Paris. Control of the media also implies a use of force, as shown, for example, in Somalia in the '5 June 1993 incident', when General Aidid's USC/SNA forces ambushed UN Pakistani troops in southern Mogadishu purportedly in retaliation for UN attempts to close down 'Radio Mogadishu'. Those who reject the liberal democratic principle behind the UN's SOP are seldom clear about what the alternative would be. Some form of traditional hierarchical authoritarianism seems to be in mind.[54] In any case, it seems likely that, no matter what UN framework is applied, local politics will evolve idiosyncratically in different parts of the world as can be seen to be already the case by those who look beneath the 'democratic' surface elsewhere. Elections or no elections, Mozambique and Angola may evolve along the lines of neighbouring Zimbabwe, where President Mugabe has presided continuously since independence. Cambodia may evolve into what is effectively a one-party democracy like fellow-ASEAN Malaysia.

In making up the economic/social deficit the UN has applied a liberal market economy template, underpinned by conditionalities determined by International Financial Institutions (IFIs). Here there is some agreement that IMF stringency was at first damaging in cases such as Mozambique in 1995, where an already struggling government was initially required to make further cutbacks likely to undermine the peace process. Similar consequences were seen in Cambodia and El Salvador, where initial increased growth rates subsequently slowed and widening economic inequalities threatened stability. Paris recommends a shift of priorities within the UN's SOP towards 'peace-oriented adjustment policies' which recognize the priority of stimulating rapid economic growth even at the risk of higher inflation, and target resources at supporting those hardest hit during the transition period.[55] Others place their emphasis on enabling indigenous economic systems to flourish protected from the harsh climate of international capital, controlled and manipulated as it is seen to be by the economic interests of the developed world. Despite all this, at the time of writing, in Namibia, Cambodia, El Salvador and Mozambique, there now seem to be hopeful signs of economic recovery.

Making up the psycho-social deficit involves difficult trade-offs between 'peace', 'justice' and 'reconciliation'. Pauline Baker, for example, somewhat starkly contrasts 'conflict managers' for whom the priority is peace and 'democratizers' whose priority is justice.[56] She concludes that the 'conflict managers' approach prevailed in Cambodia, Mozambique and Angola because the Khmer Rouge, RENAMO and UNITA were not brought to book for atrocities (a rather one-sided assumption?), whereas the 'democratizers' prevailed in Namibia and El Salvador – and I imagine she would add Bosnia. The UN's remarkable 1993 'Commission on the Truth' report in El Salvador, which confirmed more than 7,000 complaints of human rights abuses, 97 per cent perpetrated by rightist military and security death squads, was aptly titled *From Madness to Hope*.[57] Those guilty of particularly heinous crimes were named by the commission against the advice of the President, but were subsequently granted an amnesty. In fact, the relations between peace, justice and reconciliation seem rather more complex than Baker suggests, inasmuch as the 'negative peace' of order may at times be in tension with justice, but the 'positive peace' of reconciliation in large part presupposes it. And 'justice' contains a spectrum of possibilities, which runs from acknowledgement of the fact of abuse by perpetrators (truth), through publicly expressed regret (contrition), to judicial trial for war crimes or 'crimes against humanity' (punishment).[58] Within this spectrum there seems to be room for various measures of forgiveness and reconciliation along the way. Behind all of this lie as yet barely explored understandings of widely divergent resources for reconciliation and psycho-social healing within different cultures.[59]

Clearly, Task B of the UN's post-settlement peacebuilding programme in its various manifestations raises deep questions which are beyond the scope of this study to deal with adequately. The central points to be made here are, first, that it is much too early to be able to judge the efficacy of the 'positive peace' dimensions of the UN's SOP, and, second, that commentators once again seem to be divided about it, as often as not advocating deeper not lighter international intervention. Proper debate about the appropriateness and international legitimacy of the liberal universalist assumptions which lie behind the UN's peacebuilding SOP has hardly begun, with full and equal participation by a representative cross-section of commentators from developing countries an essential precondition. In short, as in the case of the assessment of Task A, the efforts of the international community to help create a self-sustaining peace in the countries under consideration have not been conclusively shown to have been misguided, counter-productive or flawed.

Conclusion

The conclusion which follows from these reflections is that the UN's post-Namibia peacebuilding SOP – exemplifying what Lizèe calls the 'end of history syndrome' as the collapse of world communism left liberal universalism without a rival – is still in its early stages in the five cases where it has been tried out systematically, with Angola the only example where apparently hopeful beginnings have so far come to nothing. In the other four cases, neither Task A, the negative task of preventing a relapse into war, nor Task B, the positive task of creating a self-sustaining peace, is complete in any one country, but neither has been conclusively shown to have failed. Both tasks have, unsurprisingly, turned out to be problematic, for linked but differing reasons. Interveners have had to face hard choices and difficult dilemmas. Strong criticisms have been made of individual missions and of individual elements within missions. The choice of target countries has been seen to have been arbitrary. But no concerted attempt has yet been made to draw up an overall balance sheet, nor to answer two simple questions: Are these countries better off than they would have been had the UN's post-settlement peacebuilding experiment not been attempted? And have overall benefits outweighed overall costs compared with alternatives? The gruelling experiences of UNPROFOR and UNOSOM II have no doubt discredited what were wrongly bracketed together as 'UN peacekeeping operations'. But these were not post-settlement peacebuilding missions. They were risky interventions in active war zones. Nor have alternatives, such as non-intervention on the one hand, or large-scale non-UN-run peace enforcement on the other, been demonstrated to have more universal applicability or likely success in the long run.

Until recently it looked as if the UN's ten year experiment in post-settlement peacebuilding might be effectively coming to an end with the withdrawal of MONUA from Angola. For example, it was unclear as late as August 1999 whether political backing for a UN peacekeeping force to support a discouraged ECOMOG in consolidating the 7 July 1999 Lome Peace Agreement in Sierra Leone would be forthcoming from the West. In the event, a 6,000-strong UN Mission in Sierra Leone has since been approved, although at the time of writing, given a vulnerable internal settlement and lukewarm international backing, the omens do not look particularly good. Either way, the conclusion to this study is that, if the UN's post-settlement peacebuilding experiment is now abandoned, this will have little to do with the demonstrated success or failure of the experiment itself. Other explanations will have to be found for the ending, as for the inception, of what may turn out to have been a remarkable, if transient, phenomenon – an unexpected and unplanned episode in world history in which the sudden manifestation of a possible solidarist future in the event proved premature.

NOTES

1. Karl Maria von Clausewitz, *On War*, Michael Howard and Peter Paret (ed. and trans.), Princeton: Princeton University Press, 1976, p.75.
2. Fred Ikle, *Every War Must End*, New York: University of Columbia Press, 1971.
3. Christopher Clapham, 'Rwanda: the perils of peace-making', paper presented at the African Studies Conference of the United Kingdom, University of Bristol, 9–11 September 1996.
4. UN Doc. S/PV. 3046, 131.
5. Michael Pugh, 'Peacebuilding as Developmentalism: Concepts from Disaster Research', *Contemporary Security Policy*, Vol.16, No.3, 1995, pp.320–46.
6. Johan Galtung, 'Three Approaches to Peace: Peacekeeping, Peacemaking and Peacebuilding', in *Peace, War and Defence – Essays in Peace Research Vol.2*, Copenhagen: Christian Ejlers, 1975, pp.282–304.
7. Stephan Ryan, *Ethnic Conflict and International Relations*, Aldershot: Dartmouth, 1990, p.50.
8. The 'conflict triangle' model of conflict, long popular in the conflict resolution literature, distinguishes the underlying structure of a 'conflict situation' from 'conflict behaviour' and 'conflict attitude', and sees these three as intimately related in the dynamics of conflict escalation and de-escalation: see Chris Mitchell, *The Structure of International Conflict*, Basingstoke: Macmillan, 1981, pp.15–68.
9. John Paul Lederach, *Building Peace-Sustainable Reconciliation in Divided Societies*, Tokyo: United Nations University Press, 1994. p.14.
10. Boutros Boutros-Ghali, *An Agenda for Peace*, New York: United Nations, 1992, p.11.
11. Boutros Boutros-Ghali, *General Assembly/Security Council Supplement to An Agenda for Peace: Position Paper of the Secretary-General on the Occasion of the Fiftieth Anniversary of the United Nations*, 1995, UN Doc. A/50/60.
12. Boutros Boutros-Ghali, 'An Agenda for Peace: One Year Later', *Orbis*, 1993, 323–32; Boutros Boutros-Ghali, *General Assembly Report of the Secretary-General on the Work of the Organization*, UN Doc. A/49/1, 2 September; 1994; Boutros Boutros-Ghali, *An Agenda for Development: Report of the Secretary-General*, UN S/1995/1, 3 January 1995.
13. Pugh (n.5 above), p.328.
14. Johan Galtung, 'Cultural Violence', *Journal of Peace Research*, Vol.27, No.3, 1981, pp.291–305.
15. UN Secretary-General's Reform Announcement, 16 July 1997, Part II: Measures and Proposals: Peace, Security and Disarmament.
16. Ted Gurr estimates an average length of between 17 and 25 years for ethnonationalist wars, depending upon category, 'Transforming Ethnopolitical Conflicts: Exit, Autonomy or Access?' in Kumar Rupesinghe (ed.), *Conflict Transformation*, New York: St. Martin's Press, 1995, pp.1–30 at p.6.
17. Nicole Ball, 'The Challenge of Rebuilding War-torn Societies' in Chester A. Crocker and Fen Osler Hampson, *Managing Global Chaos: Sources of and Reponses to International Conflict*, Washington DC: United States Institute of Peace, 1996, p.608. In fact, the parties do not so much hope to 'resolve the unfinished business of war' as to win.
18. See Roy Licklider, *Stopping the Killing: How Civil Wars End*, New York: New York University Press, 1993; Richard Haass, *Conflicts Unending: The United States and Regional Disputes*, New Haven: Yale University Press, 1990; William Zartman (ed.), *Elusive Peace: Negotiating an End to Civil Wars*, Washington DC: The Brookings Institution, 1996; see also

Fen Osler Hampson, *Nurturing Peace: Why Peace Settlements Succeed or Fail*, Washington DC: United States Institute of Peace Press, 1996, pp.13–16.

19. Licklider (n.18 above), pp. 14–17.
20. Anatol Rapoport, 'Various Conceptions of Peace Research', *Peace Research Society (International) Papers*, XIX, 1971, pp.91–106. See also Chris Mitchell, 'Classifying Conflicts: Asymmetry and Resolution', *The Annals of the American Academy of Political and Social Science*, 518, 1991, pp.23–38.
21. Yvon Grenier and Jean Daudelin, 'Foreign Assistance and the Market-place of Peacemaking: Lessons from El Salvador', *International* Peacekeeping, Vol.2, No.3, 1995, p.350.
22. M. Martin, *Cambodia: A Shattered Society*, Los Angeles: University of California Press, 1994.
23. Gareth Evans, 'Peacekeeping in Cambodia: Lessons Learned', *NATO Review*, Vol.42, No.4, 1994, pp.24–7 at p.27.
24. Renee de Nevers, 'Democratization and Ethnic Conflict' in Michael Smith (ed.), *Ethnic Conflict and International Security*, Princeton: Princeton University Press, 1993, pp.61–78; E. Mansfield and J. Snyder, 'Democratization and the Danger of War', *International Security*, Vol.20, No.1, 1995, pp.5–38.
25. 'The simultaneous occurrence of contradictory forms of *Vergesellschaftung* [roughly, socialization] is thus the basic fact that characterizes developing countries at war, for whereas the traditional patterns are dissolved by the advancement of the market economy, new 'modern' forms cannot yet be developed sufficiently to resolve emerging social conflicts': Dietrich Jung, Klaus Schlichte and Jens Siegelberg, 'Ongoing Wars and their Explanation', in Luc van de Goor, Kumar Rupesinghe and Paul Sciarone (eds.), *Between Development and Destruction: An Enquiry into the Causes of Conflict in Post-Colonial States*, New York: St.Martin's Press, 1996, pp.50–63 at p.55.
26. Pauline H. Baker, 'Conflict Resolution versus Democratic Governance: Divergent Paths to Peace?' in Crocker and Hampson (n.17 above), pp.563–72.
27. Roland Paris, 'Peacebuilding and the Limits of Liberal Internationalism', *International Security*, Vol.22, No.2, 1997, pp.54–89 at p.56.
28. Boutros-Ghali (n.10 above), p.32.
29. Kofi Annan, *Reform Announcement*, 16 July 1997, Part II.
30. See, for example, references given in footnote 7 in Hugh Miall, Oliver Ramsbotham and Tom Woodhouse, *Contemporary Conflict Resolution*, Cambridge: Polity Press, 1999, p. 237.
31. For example, K. Kumar (ed.), *Rebuilding Societies After Civil War: Critical Roles for International Assistance*, Boulder, CO: Lynne Rienner, 1997; Jeremy Ginifer (ed.), *Beyond the Emergency: Development Within UN Peace Missions*, London: Frank Cass, 1997; E. Bertram, 'Reinventing Governments: The Promise and Perils of United Nations Peacebuilding', *Journal of Conflict Resolution*, Vol.39, No.3, pp.387–418.
32. For example, *The Blue Helmets: A Review of United Nations Peacekeeping*, 1996, and the UN Blue Books Series.
33. For example, Fen Osler Hampson, *Nurturing Peace: Why Peace Settlements Succeed or Fail*, Washington D.C.: United States Institute of peace, 1996, pp.171–204. Hampson, based on a study of peace settlements in Cyprus, Namibia, Angola, El Salvador and Cambodia, concludes that there were successes (El Salvador, Namibia), partial successes (Cambodia) and failures (Cyprus, Angola) and assesses reasons for this. He is more concerned with Task A (preventing a relapse into war) than with the wider ambitions of Task B (constructing a self-sustaining peace).
34. For example, Paris (n.27 above).
35. For example, P. Lizée, 'Peacekeeping, Peacebuilding and the Challenge of Conflict Resolution in Cambodia' in D. Charters (ed.), *Peacekeeping and the Challenge of Civil Conflict Resolution*, New Brunswick: Centre for Conflict Studies, University of New Brunswick, pp.135–48.
36. Richard Betts, 'The Delusion of Impartial Intervention', *Foreign Affairs*, Vol.73, No.6, pp.20–33.
37. John Paul Lederach (n.9 above), p.16.
38. John Paul Lederach, *Preparing for Peace: Conflict Transformation Across Cultures*,

Syracuse, NY: Syracuse University Press, 1995; Adam Curle, 'New Challenges for Citizen Peacemaking' *Medicine and War*, Vol.10, No.2, 1994, pp.96–105; Tom Woodhouse, 'Peacebuilding from below', *World Encyclopaedia of Peace*, Pergamon, 2000.

39. For the psychological aspects of conflict see Karl Larsen (ed.), *Conflict and Social Psychology*, London: Sage, 1993. On its application to peacebuilding see D. Charters (ed.), *Peacekeeping and the Challenge of Civil Conflict Resolution*, New Brunswick: Centre for Conflict Studies, University of New Brunswick, 1994.
40. Where structural inequalities are seen to lie at the root of the conflict, as for example in El Salvador, the only long-term remedy may be 'an agrarian reform carried out within a broad process of radical social transformation', Jenny Pearce, *Promised Land: Peasant Rebellion in Chalatenango El Salvador*, London: Latin American Bureau, 1988, p.303.
41. John Paul Lederach (n.9 above), pp.73–85.
42. On the role of third parties in conflict intervention, see James Laue, 'The Emergence and Institutionalisation of Third-party Roles in Conflict' in J. Burton and F. Dukes (eds.) *Conflict: Readings in Management and Resolution*, London: Macmillan, 1990, pp.256–72; T. Encarnacion, C. McCartney and C. Rosas, 'The Impact of Concerned Parties on the Resolution of Disputes' in G. Lindgren, G. Wallensteen and K. Nordquist (eds.), *Issues in Third World Conflict Resolution*, Uppsala: Department of Peace and Conflict Research, 1990, pp.42–96.
43. On the culture question in general see K. Avruch and P. Black, 'The Culture Question and Conflict Resolution', *Peace and Change*, Vol.16, No.1, 1991, pp.22–45; K. Avruch, P. Black and J. Scimecca (eds.), *Conflict Resolution: Cross-Cultural Perspectives*, Westport, CT: Greenwood Press, 1991; D, Augsburger, *Intercultural Mediation*, Philadelphia: Westminster Press, 1991; R. Cohen, *Negotiation Across Cultures*, Washington: United States Institute of Peace, 1991; Paul Salem, 'In Theory: A Critique of Western Conflict Resolution from a Non-western Perspective', *Negotiation Journal*, Vol.9, No.4, 1993, pp.361–9.
44. Betts Fetherston, 'UN Peacekeepers and Cultures of Violence', *Cultural Survival Quarterly*, Spring, pp.19–23. Behind this lies sociological, anthropological and feminist critiques of militarized 'cultures' and 'discourses' of violence seen to be as much a part of the UN's SOP as of the conflicts it is intended to address.
45. Hampson (n.33 above), p.169.
46. Grenier and Daudelin (n.21 above), p. 360.
47. Margaret Anstee *Orphan of the Cold War: The Iside Story of the Collapse of the Angolan Peace Process, 1992–93*, Basingstoke: Macmillan, 1996.
48. Hampson (n.33 above), p.210. Hampson also considers the case of Cyprus.
49. Ball lists ten ways in which donors can help to meet post-war social and economic needs: assessing damage; planning reconstruction; rehabilitating basic infrastructure; resettling displaced groups; revitalizing communities; reactivating the smallholder agricultural sector; rehabilitating export agriculture, key industries and housing; generating employment; settling disputes over land and other assets; demining; and implementing environmental awareness and protection programmes, (n.17 above), p.616.
50. Kumar lists five tasks in Political Rehabilitation in peacebuilding: (1) improving the institutional capacity for governance; (2) providing support for elections; (3) human rights monitoring and promotion; (4) disarmament and demobilization; (5) reforming the security sector (n.31 above), pp.4–14.
51. Ball (n.17 above).
52. Maynard gives five phases in Psychosocial Recovery: (1) establishing safety; (2) communalization and bereavement; (3) rebuilding trust and the capacity to trust; (4) re-establishing personal and social morality; (5) reintegrating and restoring democratic discourse, K. Maynard, 'Rebuilding Community: Psychosocial Healing, Reintegration and Reconciliation at the Grassroots Level' in Kumar (n.31 above), p.210.
53. Paris (n.27 above), pp.82–3.
54. For example, Lizée concludes that the Western democratic model just does not fit some non-Western cultures, such as the pyramidal Brahmanic and fatalistic Buddhist social system in Cambodia sustained by traditional patronage structures not popular consent: (n.35 above), p.143.

55. Paris (n.27 above), pp.85–6.
56. Baker (n.26 above),.
57. *Report of the Commission on the Truth for El Salvador: From Madness to Hope*, UN Doc. S/25500.
58. On reconciliation see J. Montville, 'The Healing Function in Political Conflict Resolution' in Dennis Sandole and Hugo van der Merwe (eds.), *Conflict Resolution: Theory and Practice*, Manchester: Manchester University Press, 1993, pp.112–28; K. Asmal, L. Asmal and R. Roberts, *Reconciliation Through Truth: A Reckoning of Apartheid's Criminal Governance*, Capetown: Mayibuye Books, 1996; A. Boraine, J. Levy and R. Scheffer (eds.), *Dealing with the Past: Truth and Reconciliation in South Africa*, IDASA, 1997 (second edition). On justice see N. Kritz (ed.), *Transitional Justice: How Emerging Democracies Reckon with Former Regimes*, Washington DC: United States Institute of Peace, 1995 – three volumes, although none of our five cases included in the case studies of 'transitional justice' in Vol.2.
59. On the cultural dimension of psycho-social healing, including a questioning of the relevance of Western 'post-traumatic stress disorder' approaches for non-Western societies, see M. Parker, 'The Mental Health of War-damaged Populations', *War and Rural Development in Africa*, Vol.27, No.3, 1996, pp.77–85; C. Petty and S. Campbell, *Re-thinking the Trauma of War*, Save the Children Conference Report, 23–24 May 1996, Church House, Westminster; P. Reynolds, 'Children of Tribulation: The Need to Heal and the Means to Heal War Trauma', *Africa*, Vol.60, No.1, 1990, pp.1–38. See I. Agger, *Theory and Practice of Psycho-Social Projects Under War Conditions in Bosnia-Herzegovina and Croatia*, Zagreb: ECHO/ECTF, 1995, for an assessment of current enterprises in one war zone, and D. Summerfield, *The Impact of War and Atrocity on Civilian Populations: Basic Principles for NGO Interventions and a Critique of Psychosocial Trauma Projects*, ODI Relief and Rehabilitation Network, April 1996, for a critique.

Peacekeeping, Conflict Resolution and Peacebuilding: A Reconsideration of Theoretical Frameworks

A.B. FETHERSTON

The approach taken to peacekeeping, conflict resolution and peacebuilding in this analysis is unusual, and because of this, some explanation is an appropriate beginning point. The study makes use of social theory especially ideas of discourse, modernity and post-modernity, problematization, power, hegemony and counter-hegemony with an overriding theme of critical questioning of taken-for-granted assumptions which underlie much of the work in the fields being considered. Such a critical approach has emerged over the last two decades in the field of International Relations and has made important contributions to re-thinking the theoretical bases of that field. Some of this important work is cited later in this study. Although care is taken to provide signposts for technical terms throughout the text, it will be useful to 'set the scene', with a brief examination of the term discourse, since this idea is fundamental to the arguments set out below.

The power of discourse is to render 'right', 'legitimate', 'taken-for-granted', 'natural' specific ways of knowing, acting and organizing social life. More precisely, 'it makes "real" that which it prescribes as meaningful.'[1] Crucially, this rendering of 'right' silences other possibilities (they are unknowable since they are not possible). A discourse also sets the limits of critique especially in the sense that it 'constructs narratives that tell us unambiguously, what the varied and changing events of history must be taken to mean'.[2] Critical analysis within discursive knowing can only rearrange certain practices, and perhaps make them more efficient – it cannot transform. The unproblematized discourse of modernity which is at the heart of both International Relations and Conflict Resolution theory and practice demands that this objective knowing be uncontaminated by subjectivities, the contingencies of social life – although ironically the main purpose of modernity is to itself 'contaminate' social life. The knowledge this discourse produces is rational, universal and permanent. The end project of modernity is total knowledge, total power, total enlightenment, the end of history, and simultaneously, the end of difference. Thus we have such work as Fukiyama's *The End of History*, proclaiming, among other things, the triumph of liberalism/democracy/capitalism as *the* way to organize social life. The point, for our present discussion, is to reflect on the discourse within which theories and practices of peacekeeping, conflict resolution and peacebuilding are formed and reformed. Out of this reflection space can be opened to think differently, to ask different questions, and, perhaps, to generate different practices than the field has thus far been able produce. The scale of current problems and continuing inability of interventions to initiate long-term sustainable solutions to them is the impetus for such a critical analysis.

Theories of Peacekeeping

Peacekeeping is not a highly theorized topic. Much of the writing on the subject has been done by diplomats and military people with experience in the field. This has tended to limit the accumulation of knowledge on peacekeeping as an intervention to case histories – interesting, often, in themselves, but with little generalizable value beyond a tentative list of do's and don'ts. One notable exception came from a British Brigadier, Michael Harbottle, who very early on saw the value of linking peacekeeping with peacebuilding.[3] As recently as last year Diehl *et al.* wrote:

> Changes in peacekeeping operations have not been matched by alterations in the way that scholars analyze them. The standard study of peacekeeping remains one of a single case study, in which description is the primary goal... An approach based on the uniqueness of peacekeeping missions does not assist us in building a theory of peacekeeping, nor does it provide much guidance in making policy.[4]

Their attempt to correct this shortcoming is considered at greater length below, but their general point is an important one. In essence, we are still largely in the dark in terms of improving analysis, effectiveness and success of peacekeeping. This can be attributed directly to the lack of theoretical underpinnings for the field. The rest of this section will consider attempts, within the last decade to develop a theoretical framework for peacekeeping. This short list is mainly characterized by the application of theoretical work from the fields of conflict management and resolution to peacekeeping.

Towards a Theory of United Nations Peacekeeping, 1994

In my 1994 contribution to these debates,[5] I argued that for such complex practices and demands peacekeeping's primary shortcoming was insufficient theoretical work that would allow researchers, policy analysts, and practitioners to address the still highly troublesome issues of increasing effectiveness and success, both in the short and long terms. The main thrust of my theoretical argument was that UN peacekeeping as a third-party activity based on consent is a type of conflict resolution and as such could make use of the theoretical developments in that field. This meant, in practice, making use both of John Burton's human needs approach[6] and Ronald Fisher and Loraleigh Keashly's ideas of contingency and complementarity.[7] Set within such a framework, peacekeeping is understood as an intervention utilized only after a conflict has become violent and protracted. Its functions, therefore, must be at least two-fold: first, to act as a means of separation, a breathing space where both sides can step back from confrontation; second, and crucially, peacekeeping functions as peacebuilding – working on improving communication and on social, political and economic regeneration.

Peacekeeping as peacebuilding – a function crucial to peacekeeping if understood within a conflict resolution framework – was, I argued at the time, vastly under-utilized, with predictable results in effectiveness and success especially in the long term. Even since the expansion of peacekeeping practice, the rise of multidimensional missions, and more concerted involvement, particularly in elections, peacekeeping has not for the most part facilitated the establishment of long-term sustainable peace – it has not created, in other words, space for conflict resolution. It may even be argued that in some cases peacekeeping missions have had a negative impact on the situation.

My point about this expansion of activity and its relationship to conflict resolution and peacebuilding was based on two key points. First, I suggested that any such expansion in practice needed to be accompanied by much more systematic theoretical thinking so that, at the very least, we could develop appropriate short and long-term goals, improve the means of analysing mission effectiveness and establish benchmarks for good practice. Methodologically, conflict resolution would also provide the basis for generating and analysing both quantitative and qualitative data. Fisher and Keashly's contingency model would, I argued, be especially useful here. Second, I pointed out that using military peacekeepers on missions which required skills of conflict resolution and peacebuilding (I called these 'contact skills') without any significant preparation was highly problematic. In this context, developing a theoretical framework for peacekeeping using conflict resolution seemed to offer a positive way forward.

International Peacekeeping and Conflict Resolution, 1998

Paul Diehl, Daniel Druckman and James Wall provide a quantitative analysis of peacekeeping missions using statistical techniques.[8] Their efforts are situated within a framework which can be described as a mix of the theory and quantitative methodology of organizational/industrial and social psychology and the quantitative methodology used in certain areas of international relations. Theirs is not a Burtonian approach and not one much related to Fisher and Keashly's work. It might, therefore, best be thought of as conflict management, rather than conflict resolution.[9] In any case, it is a brand of conflict resolution – or management which is more prevalent in the United States than in Europe and which makes greater use of laboratory studies of mediation, negotiation, game theory and quantitative analysis than is used by, for example, peace researchers who work in the conflict resolution area. They are also careful to distinguish their work from historical case-study accounts of peacekeeping, arguing that the analysis they offer is 'superior' to other types because, among other things, it allows analysts to focus on 'two or more different functions performed by peacekeeping missions' (especially useful given the increased complexity of missions), and provides the potential for a multi-factoral account of success both within one mission and between missions.[10]

They begin in much the same way as Fisher and Keashly did in their seminal article on contingency theory,[11] with a useful review of the literature, a discussion of the lack of theory in peacekeeping, and then the development of a typology and a categorization of the key characteristics of peacekeeping missions. For example, the role of a peacekeeper could be categorized as primary, mixed or third party, while the conflict management process could be distributive, mixed or integrative.[12] There then follows a statistical analysis 'designed to discover a pattern of relationships among the missions'.[13] Their analysis shows in the case of UNPROFOR in Bosnia, for example, 'that the Bosnian mission does not require some middle ground of different conflict management roles and orientations but a *simultaneous* adoption of divergent and sometimes contradictory roles, skills and behaviors.'[14] This, they argue, 'helps an analyst understand why these missions had such difficulty in achieving their goals'.[15] This may sound like a quite limited version of success, defined as the goals set by the mission designers themselves, and it is. However, Diehl *et al.* at the end of their analysis suggest going further, in fact suggest exactly what *Towards a Theory* concluded four years before. They argue that, 'by placing peacekeeping in a conflict resolution framework, we expand our conceptualization of missions from instruments of conflict control to approaches that contribute to more enduring resolutions of conflicts.'[16]

The problem for Diehl *et al.* is that they are operating in a conflict management framework, not a conflict resolution one. In doing this they lose the potential strength of a much broader sociological understanding of peacebuilding which was, in the case of conflict resolution, placed on the conceptual map by John Burton. I say 'potential' because, as I will argue below, conflict resolution suffers from theoretical shortcomings which make the adoption of a conflict resolution framework for peacekeeping, as *Towards A Theory* attempts, problematic. The analysis of Diehl *et al.* runs into the same dead end *Towards a Theory* did in 1994, and, incidentally, Burton does through his generic theory of conflict. They do not reflect the complexity and diversity or the cultures of violence of the social spaces within which these operations take place. Indeed, the trend towards increasingly complex statistical analyses tends to leave people out altogether. After all how can social space, cultures of violence and militarization, and discourses be statistically analysed – requiring as it does such a reductive process, with any hope of encompassing such huge categories of theory and practice? Even the increased complexity of peacekeeping missions, which could be seen as an *ad hoc* attempt to 'do something' about this deficiency, cannot begin to do so until theorizing takes on board the full implications of the war zone.[17] In this sense, interventions will continue to be successful or unsuccessful only in the vastly limited sense of the prescribed goals of the missions formulated within the confining boundaries of the discourse of international relations and to a lesser extent, conflict management.[18] It is this inadequacy that will be addressed in the remainder of this study.

Using Conflict Resolution as a Basis for a Theory of Peacekeeping: A Reconsideration

Any of the preceding arguments made about peacekeeping can be carried only so far as the theoretical foundations of conflict resolution can provide ways forward which promise greater understanding, clarity and perspective. It can be argued from one perspective, at least, that conflict resolution has been a critical force in the theories and practices of conflict management. It has also brought an alternative voice to taken-for-granted practices in international relations. Burton, especially, through the concept of 'provention', stretches conflict resolution towards transformation. Even Burton, though, seems to get stuck within the problematic discourses of international relations (and psychology).[19] These problems of conflict resolution, and, even more so, of conflict management, envelope peacekeeping when used as its theoretical base. What literature there is on theorizing peacekeeping within conflict resolution relies too heavily on the presumed virtues of its theory, unquestioningly taking on its value/culture/discourse laden assumptions without examining their consequences.

This is not to say that criticism is absent, but as Robert Cox has noted, it is perfectly possible to be critical and never step outside the bounds of your own discourse.[20] What the work presented above, and by implication in all work on peacekeeping, lacks is a self-reflexivity which casts a critical gaze on the assumptions which – mostly – confine both the theory and practice of conflict resolution to the problematic discourse of modernity. Research which seeks to understand the basis of social meaning and practice is distinct from research which empirically seeks to render that practice more efficient and controllable. To be critical, Cox points out, is more than mere problem-solving which functions from within the dominant framework of social relations and institutions. A critical approach begins by problematizing those dominant frameworks and seeks to find alternatives which would transform those institutions and social meanings – that is seeks to shift the basis on which everyday life and meaning are constituted and practised.[21]

It is crucial, therefore, to distinguish between what is transformative from the view of critical theory, and what is transformative from the point of view of conflict resolution, even in the best cases offered where social change is the goal. Critical theory offers the *possibility* of transformation, as Foucault put it, 'in the sense that it will not deduce from the form of what we are what it is impossible for us to do and to know; but it will separate out, from the contingency that has made us what we are, the possibility of no longer, being, doing, or thinking what we are, do, or think.'[22]

The rest of this section will consider three points which make reliance on unproblematized conflict resolution (or management) problematic, and in this specific case, problematic for peacekeeping: the irrationality of war zones, conflict resolution as a project of modernity, and conflict resolution/peacekeeping as discursive practices. Following this necessarily brief discussion, some thought will be given to the possibilities offered by peacebuilding situated in social theory as a more suitable theoretical framework for peacekeeping and, more widely, intervention.

The Rational and Irrational in War Zones

The understandings of war implied in the definitions, researches and methodologies of conflict resolution lack connection to the everydayness of the war zone. These are points that I and others have made elsewhere.[23] These kinds of descriptions of war and its aftermath fail to catch its complexity and deep effects on social space and meaning. Carolyn Nordstrom has written extensively on the ways in which violence fractures communities and lives and becomes fixed into social meanings.[24] The irrationality of violence and the psycho-social effects it inflicts, do not just come and then go. They become part of the everyday or what Pierre Bourdieu has called 'habitus'.[25] The fear, insecurity, and violence of death, torture, disappearances, rape become 'normal' and 'natural'. As Bourdieu puts it, 'every established order tends to produce (to very different degrees and with very different means) the naturalization of its own arbitrariness ... out of which arises the sense of limits, commonly called the sense of reality.'[26] We understand little of the ways in which such extensive social damage plays out over lifetimes, much less how processes aimed at resolution (or management or transformation) effect people's lives at this level. In a wider context, we need to understand not just the particulars of any single case, but the networks of institutions, structures, social meanings that are global and that have specific effects through various levels of activity.

From this global perspective, then, it is possible to situate and then analyse specific cases of war and intervention in the context of globalized discourses of violence. A specific culture of violence, in Bosnia for example, needs not only to be understood in all its local complexities but as also enveloped in wider discourses of violence and militarism that pervade the state system. What this perspective provides is a means of seeing the 'everydayness' of a war zone as not a 'special' case outside of the norm, although it may generate some unique practices, as 'rape camps' in Bosnia appear to have been.[27] Rather, it is one outcome of international and domestic structures, institutions, ways of life that are fundamentally based on repression.[28] Vivienne Jabri has argued that we need to seek critical understandings 'by situating war and violent conflict in the constitution of the human self and human society.'[29] She assumes 'that specific instances of war are a manifestation of the longer-term processes which have established war as a form of institution linked to discursive and institutional practices which define social continuities.'[30] Moreover, our understandings of war are both constituted and constituting of the social institution and practices of war – we participate in the continuity. It is also probable that our management and resolution efforts, if unproblematized, work to continue, rather than challenge, these same institutions.

Studying war, Jabri proposes, must, 'incorporate both understanding and the practical intent of promoting emancipatory social transformation' not only at the most visible site of war – the war zone – but in our own localities as well.[31] The extent to which conflict resolution in theory and practice does not wrestle with these deep complexities suggests the limits of its usefulness for creating opportunities for emancipatory social transformation. The emphasis on emancipatory in this case is to suggest something beyond reinstitution of a status quo or RE-solution of a problem (which will only have to be RE-solved again later).[32] If, as is argued here, conflict is caused, enabled, reproduced by particular social structures and institutions which favour a dominant group, 'we cannot hope to remove or alleviate those causes without altering those structures.'[33] In this sense, then, peacekeeping becomes another aspect of a system which only seeks stability within the confines of that system, a system which already made the war possible. The unstated job of peacekeeping and other interventions, is to manage a RE-solution of the war rather than transformation of the system itself, since such a transformation would necessitate a self-critical moment leading, potentially, to wider transformation.

Conflict Resolution and the Project of Modernity

Theories and practices of conflict and conflict resolution are constituted within problematic discourses of violence. These discourses of violence are central to the functioning of an unproblematized discourse of modernity.[34] How much is conflict resolution part of these discourses? This section addresses three aspects of this large and complicated question. First, some attention is given to the unproblematized project of modernity within conflict resolution. Following on, the extent to which conflict resolution constitutes sets of problematic discursive practices is considered. Finally, the issue of power in conflict resolution is discussed as illustrative of the implications of critical analysis for reconsidering theories and practices of conflict resolution and, therefore, peacekeeping.

Conflict resolution as part of the modern project comes with baggage that is made invisible because of its seeming 'rightness'. Set within an unproblematized version of a discourse of modernity, conflict resolution assumes that we can 'know' – objectify, make rational, understand – violent conflict to such an extent that we can have *power over* it – solve the problem of it. Eventually, à la enlightenment, violent conflict will cease to exist, the implication being that we will all 'come to understand' both the cause and solution of violent conflict and re-arrange practices, institutions, social meaning accordingly. Parties in conflict become aware and are enlightened by the prescribed knowing and rational processes of conflict resolution. They then join, are socialized into, the enlightened and rational system of being, called, among other things, capitalism. As Alejandro Bendaña has pointed out,

> conflict resolution and management are, in effect, social accords which constitute the containment of societal contraditions within a framework upholding neoliberal dogmas with regard to the role of the state, the central place of the market, fiscal responsibility, and the primacy of the private sector.[35]

The modern project privileges the rational knowing subject and in doing so a world of the 'other' is both generated and silenced. 'Rational' is legitimized at the same time that everything else – labelled 'irrational' – is othered, delegitimized and set outside the bounds of the discourse. The unknown and uncontrollable are made separate from our own lives. Jabri, as previously described, has argued that this 'othering' of violence, makes its practice separate from ourselves, thus silencing ways in which we are part of a discourse of violence that supports, legitimizes and normalizes war. War and other forms of violence, e.g. systems of oppression, from Jabri's perspective are rational, are part of our everyday lives, of social activity, institutions, structures, and are constituted and constituting of social meaning. Her point brings home the extent to which conflict resolution forecloses discussion of its own participation in discourses of violence and tends to normalize particular ways of thinking about violent conflict and exclude others. And because of this, unproblematized practices of conflict resolution also tend to lead, naturally, to particular ways of 'solving' violent conflict. As Bendaña notes, 'techniques are not separable from politics. That is to say, we cannot separate the field from the political framework in which it appears.'[36] The extent to which conflict resolution and peacekeeping in both theory and practice are fundamentally mis-directed is the extent to which they are unable to make visible the political framework within which they are formed as well as to understand the ways in which this political framework creates barriers to emancipatory transformation.

The answer, though, is not to throw out conflict resolution altogether. 'We cannot afford to dismiss conflict resolution,' Bendaña argues, 'and deprive working people of valuable rational civic instruments – a situation which would only serve the powerful, all too ready to monopolize such tools for their own use, deploying them to control the unruly masses.'[37] The point to make here is that reformism in resolution is not necessarily incompatible with emancipatory transformation. It may be that the two need to work together in some ways. The question is, which will be the ultimate goal of intervention. If it is RE-solution and not transformation, then our tools have led us down the wrong road and we have not asked the important questions about what kind of world it is we want to live in and in whose interests we want social institutions and structures to work. Is this a radical agenda? Yes, but only from the point of view of those who hold and wish to keep power. For the disempowered, and particularly those who have suffered the consequences of war and violence, this is simply common sense.

Conflict Resolution/Peacekeeping as Discursive Practice: Power

The prescriptive rationality that underlies conflict resolution sets up several difficulties. Rationality within a modern project prescribes a singular 'objectively' reasoned truth. Ultimately, the application of unproblematized mediation, consultation or problem-solving methods leads to resolution because the participants have been 'corrected' (however subtly) and, armed with this new perspective, can together seek resolution.

This discursive practice has its limitations. What is considered right (and therefore 'rational') is really merely 'point of view', but is rendered as discursive truth. And although most conflict resolution scholars would not pretend to have all the answers, they operate from within modernity where they are on the 'right' track and where further research and application will refine what is now known. This progressive linearity of knowledge pervades modernity. Perhaps more interesting than what is considered 'rational' is the unstated but implied consideration of what is 'irrational' and therefore in need of enlightenment. The whole of the Balkans is looked at through this lens of irrationality, cut off from normal rational living and in need of instruction. Participants in mediation, consultation or problem-solving processes have to re-perceive the totality of their war as irrational, simultaneously rendering their experiences and practices illegitimate and irrelevant – and cutting off, at least, an understanding of the power of war as a social construct which creates social meaning while simultaneously legitimizing and delegitimizing particular practices of survival and resistance.

Power, here, is a significant issue. Although power is evident in conflict management processes where it is power that decides, it is not so clearly present in conflict resolution with its insistence on 'neutral third parties' and 'facilitative non-coercive processes'. This need to de-power the conflict resolution process, though, still brings with it an understanding of power as 'power *over*', as negative power . Conflict resolution scholars, of course, are not unaware of this 'problem of power', and suggest that it may be important to 'empower' certain groups in conflict before resolution processes become possible.[38] By denying this kind of power within the analytic process of problem solving, it does not disappear and participants have to re-enter the social context where negative power is apparent and problematic. Problem-solving offers no way out of this dilemma, and its analysis of power is quite weak. One of the results of seeing only this totalizing power to which individuals have little access, is *dis*empowerment. The potential for the transformation of structures and institutions which exercise this power (like the state) seems a remote – if not impossible – prospect. To work, problem-solving depends on convincing power-holders to change their ways, to become enlightened, through the analytic process which shows them the path. This is an unlikely scenario.

The analysis of power by Michel Foucault, though, transverses the boundaries of modern power and suggests a way out of the power-bind of problem-solving, conflict resolution, and by implication, peacekeeping. The State, according to Foucault, exercises a form of negative meta-power, conceived as a series of prohibitionary powers. Foucault argues that 'this meta-power...can only take hold and secure its footing where it is rooted in a whole series of multiple and indefinite power relations that supply the necessary basis for the great negative forms of power.'[39] State power is impossible, Foucault theorizes, in the absence of a pervasive network of disciplinary and normalizing 'positive power'. These indefinite networks of positive power are knowledge-producing and function throughout the social body through all forms of institutions and social organizations to 'normalize' – to make visible, measurable and compliant – the entire social body. More fundamental than repressive power, Foucault's conception posits an array of disciplines, discourses, specialized knowledges, techniques, and institutions which together function not to prohibit or repress, but to exhort and to normalize modes of thought and action. Scholarly 'knowledge', empirically tested, objectively signified, is part of the normalizing process. The *productive* conjunction of power/knowledge generates, through the use of technologies of power, 'discourses of truth' where truth 'isn't outside power' rather, 'it induces regular effects of power.'[40]

Using this Foucauldian analysis of productive power it becomes possible to consider conflict resolution as part of an apparatus of power which attempts to discipline and normalize. Mediation, consultation, and problem-solving are productive processes constituted from within a regime of truth, part of an apparatus which produces docile social bodies and seeks to establish the disciplinary power of the regime of truth. Delivering 'rational' understandings and practices through conflict resolution methodologies – including peacekeeping – is part of rendering a social body ready to accept, for example, neo-liberal forms of social/economic/political organization. These strategies can be seen as a means of re-establishing juridical power, part of the mechanism of repressive power of the State and of the international system, but also might be understood as an apparatus of positive forms of power, which normalize and induce particular practices.

It is here that Foucault's analysis of micro-power opens spaces for transformative activity and suggests the means by which the power-bind of conflict resolution practices could be addressed. He argues that 'there are no relations of power without resistances; the latter are all the more real and effective because they are formed right at the point where relations of power are exercised.'[41] Resistance is not formulated, in Foucault's mind, as an inconceivable process of organizing against – and overthrowing, all at once – state power. It is rather understood as diverse, dispersed multiple forms of activity which can change relations of power at their locality. Moreover, Foucault suggests that even as it is possible for micro-procedures of power to be 'adapted, reinforced and transformed' by global strategies of domination, the opposite is also possible, that 'resistance is multiple and can be integrated into global strategies.'[42]

Two points are particularly important: first, that resistance – to cultures of violence for example – occurs within localities and has the possibility to transform those localities; and second, that these micro-resistances can be connected to a broader global change of power relations. Finally, in relation to taking a critical theoretical approach to conflict and the problem of transformation, Foucault notes, 'The role of theory today seems to me to be just this: not to formulate the global systemic theory which holds everything in place, but to analyse the specificity of mechanisms of power, to locate the connections and extensions, to build little by little a strategic knowledge.'[43] What this indicates about theory-building in conflict resolution and management is that these approaches are fundamentally missing the point as transformative theory. As discursive practices situated within the project of modernity they are exactly on track.

These reconsiderations suggest the need to direct our gaze to the constituted and constituting conditions of our existence. In this direction lies the possibility of the transformation of power relations and therefore the networks, apparatus, institutions, structures, and techniques which empower meaning. To hold that conflict resolution or any other action, structure or thought can stand outside this discursive mess (i.e. stands in a privileged position) consigns us 'to deduce from the form of what we are what it is impossible for us to do and to know.'[44] The next section will consider a different theoretical framework for conflict resolution and peacekeeping as offering potential fruitful ways out of Foucault's dead end.

Using Peacebuilding as a Basis for a Theory of Peacekeeping

If conflict resolution presents us with a number of shortcomings as a theoretical (and, therefore, practical) framework for peacekeeping, where might we look for a more effective alternative? Peacebuilding may offer a broader, more inclusive, and less discursively tied means of rethinking interventions. This is not, though, the peacebuilding of Boutros Boutros-Ghali's *Agenda for Peace* which offers the limited kind of reform discussed above. In *An Agenda for Peace* peacebuilding is 'action to identify and support structures which tend to strengthen and solidify peace in order to avoid a relapse into conflict.'[45] This action was to be undertaken through the following mechanisms: *restoring* order, advice and training of security personnel, promoting human rights, and *reforming and strengthening* government institutions.[46] Perhaps such measures are necessary, but not as unproblematized actions, and not in the absence of a long-term transformative agenda. In practice, it is clear that the international community (including inter-governmental organizations – most visibly, the UN – as well as international aid agencies) practise reform or RE-solution, not transformation, with predictable ineffectiveness.

In turning our focus to peacebuilding it is, consequently, important that we avoid falling back on those old 'truths'; 'we should not imitate some capitalist propagators of the field by adopting an instrumentalist approach, divorcing the field from the ideal of the pursuit of peace with justice by reducing it to a narrowly defined notion of politics and alliances.'[47] To do as Bendaña exhorts it will be useful to look at where the concept of peacebuilding has come from. As an idea that has emerged out of peace research it has claims to radicalism that are similar to John Burton's form of conflict resolution. Peacebuilding has a long history which will not be explored here. The point of departure for this analysis is the emergent field of peace research and one of its important thinkers, Johan Galtung, who introduced the idea of structural violence.[48]

Galtung's analysis of violence as being not only direct, but also present within structures which denied people access to physical and social well-being, was seminal.[49] His emphasis on the structural causes of violence then led him to prescribe peacebuilding as opposed to peacemaking and peacekeeping, as the only possible means of dealing with these structural causes.[50] Peace research has also introduced the concepts of negative and positive peace. Negative peace refers to a situation that is 'not war' but where structural violence exists. Whereas positive peace is a situation where human beings are not impeded from fully developing and living out their life-span – a situation sometimes referred to as peace with justice.[51] This distinction is crucial for the idea of peacebuilding, which is tied to positive peace rather than negative peace. It is in the concept of positive peace that there is potential for a critical, problematized form of theory and practice of conflict resolution or what will be called here, conflict transformation.[52] More will be said on this in the next section.

Conflict Resolution and Provention: The Work of John Burton

These early works in peace research form part of the base from which the field of conflict resolution developed. This is especially apparent in the work of John Burton who, through his sociologically-rooted conflict resolution, developed the idea of 'provention'. This concept, he seems to argue, should be the larger framework within which conflict resolution is understood and practiced.[53] Burton's work is based on his human needs theory, later called a generic theory of conflict.[54] Much has been written on this both in support and in critique.[55] Briefly, Burton argues that deep-rooted conflict is caused by the denial of basic human needs. Three needs are particularly important (although he originally posited nine): identity, security, and distributive justice. Crucially, these needs are not subject to the economics of resource scarcity, in other words, more for one side does not necessarily mean less for another. Here is the origin of the idea of win–win, rather than win–lose senarios, and it is on this idea that Burton's problem-solving methodology is based.[56]

Returning to Burton's theoretical framework, based on a generic theory of conflict (i.e. human needs theory), he produced what amounts to a two-part model of peacebuilding. First, conflict resolution offers short-term methodologies which focus on the processes and procedures of facilitated problem solving. These processes, Burton argues, have been tried, tested, improved, and importantly, conceptually developed. Provention, on the other hand, provides a long-term, societal focus, dealing with issues of the common good, political interests and ideologies. He defines provention as

> [the] means of deducing from an adequate explanation of the phenomenon of conflict, including its human dimensions, not merely the conditions that create an environment of conflict, and the structural changes required to remove it, but more importantly, the promotion of conditions that create cooperative relationships.[57]

It is through the idea of provention, with as yet underdeveloped theory and no developed methodologies, *not* through conflict resolution, that Burton seeks the transformation of discourses, social institutions and structures. This is made more clear in Burton's definition of resolution as 'the transformation of relationships *in a particular* case by the solution of the problems which led to the conflictual behaviour in the first place' [emphasis added].[58] According to Burton, the two – provention and resolution – might work most effectively with resolution to achieve success in particular cases which could pave the way for the application of provention measures to those particular situations. This success could then be built upon. This is as far as Burton's mapping of a theoretical framework goes.

In all, Burton's is an interesting effort, and a pioneering one, especially in the context of conflict resolution. And although Burton calls for a kind of social action/social education, based on analytic problem-solving processes which emphasizes re-framing and re-defining the problems with the goal of opening space for creative solutions, the work relies too heavily on a problematic conflict resolution methodology and on human needs theory. Both need to be subjected to deeper analysis and criticism of the kind which would seek to uncover and problematize their discursive foundations. In addition, although sociological, Burton's work is disconnected from the social spaces inhabited by people, including war zones. A critical appraisal making use of a 'war zone' focus would, no doubt, raise further problems and limitations for this approach. Nevertheless, Burton's two-part framework of peacebuilding does suggest the importance of an emphasis on long-term, emancipatory transformation, and in this sense especially his work, often overlooked in recent times, has real value for the field of conflict resolution.

An Integrated Model for Peacebuilding: The Work of John Paul Lederach

The work most often cited in any discussion of peacebuilding – at least in the field of peace research – is that of John Paul Lederach. His framework of reconcilation and elicitive approach provides an important advance in thinking about intervention. Although Lederach's earlier work was more clearly dependent on conflict resolution theory,[59] he has since developed his thinking on peacebuilding as situated in the context of reconciliation.[60] Based on his casework in different parts of the world, he has formulated an elicitive methodology founded on the idea that techniques of peacebuilding should be developed and thereby embedded in the localities in which they are employed. Taken together he calls this an integrated framework for peacebuilding.

Lederach is careful to distinguish this framework from conflict management. He suggests the need for a shift away from a 'concern with the resolution of issues and towards a frame of reference that focuses on the restoration and rebuilding of relationships,' while at the same time engaging 'the relational aspects of reconciliation as the central component of peacebuilding'.[61] The long-term goal of this work is the sustainable transformation of societies. Here Lederach makes use of Azar's notion of protracted social conflict,[62] arguing, in the tradition of Burton[63] and others, that such conflict requires action beyond the international relations methodology of conflict management. Lederach sees protracted social conflict as a system and focuses his elicitive approach on the relationships within that system. Reconciliation is, then, work on relationships and is specifically understood as situated in a specific place or locus – indeed the creation of such a social space, for encounter facilitating acknowledgement of the past, envisioning the future and, therefore, enabling a re-framing of the present.[64] Why does Lederach focus on reconciliation? He argues that

> the immediacy of hatred and prejudice, of racism and xenophobia, as primary factors and motivators of the conflict means that its transformation must be rooted in social-psychological and spiritual dimensions that traditionally have been seen as either irrelevant or outside the competency of international diplomacy.[65]

Lederach's understanding of reconciliation is then supposed to provide the theoretical backbone of the integrated framework of peacebuilding that he develops. This framework is based on, first, an analysis of the types of actors at different leadership levels matched with particular methodologies of conflict resolution and peacebuilding (a format which strongly suggests some influence of a contingency approach). What is most interesting and different about this analysis is its representation as a pyramid where the grassroots represent the largest constituency at the pyramid's base. This inclusion of the grassroots, coupled with an argument for a bottom-up approach to peacebuilding, is significantly different from other approaches and represents an important departure and development of the idea of peacebuilding. However, Lederach still argues that it is 'the middle range [of leadership, which] holds the potential for helping to establish a relationship – and skill-based infrastructure for sustaining the peacebuilding process.'[66] While he acknowledges that 'important ideas and practical efforts do emerge' from the grassroots, he points out that for many people conflict resolution is 'an unaffordable luxury'.[67]

Having set the immediate scene, Ledearch moves his focus from issues, actors and specific methodologies to systems. He makes use of Maire Dugan's concept of a nested paradigm[68] which allows for an analysis of a local problem within the context of subsystem and system causes. In other words, the local problem is *nested* (visually encircled) within the subsystem, which is nested within the system. The level of subsystem is important here because it enables a peacebuilding strategy to be developed for a local or specific situation while taking into account the systemic problems (one might say discursive problems) which are present as well.[69] For an integrated framework of peacebuilding Lederach envisions a nested paradigm beginning with the issue, moving into relationship, subsystem and final system levels. He then makes the interesting link to the levels of actors (top, middle and grassroots) in his pyramid – that is, that the middle level, equated with a subsystem level, could provide 'the strategic link to the other levels.'[70] This systemic analysis is only one half, or one axis of the integrated framework. Along the other axis is the time dimension of peacebuilding. This is comprised again as a nested paradigm first of crisis intervention (immediate action, 2–6 months), preparation and training (short-range planning, 1–2 years), design of social change (decade thinking, 5–10 years), and finally, desired future (generational vision 20+ years).[71] The point of the nested paradigm approach is significant because it points out the importance of long-term thinking, planning and envisioning, and suggests, for example, the dependence of crisis intervention (or in our case peacekeeping) on systemic understanding, analysis, and action over a generational time frame.

Transformation in Lederach's Model

Transformation, in the context of Lederach's integrated framework, is situated at the subsystem level as, first, an analytic tool or what he refers to as a *descriptive* understanding of the transformative impact of conflict. Second, transformation can be understood as practices or what he refers to as *prescriptive* intervention to bring about transformation to more peaceful societies. Taken together, descriptive and prescriptive levels are the means by which we can shift from focus on immediate issues and crisis to long-term change of relationships and social structures. These two levels then can be applied across four interdependent dimensions – personal, relational, structural, and cultural, initially for understanding the impact of violence and then for creating practices aimed at social change.[72]

Lederach's approach 'begins with a recognition that the middle range holds special potential for transformation...'[73] Again this refers to the middle level leadership operating at the subsystem and acting as a link between top leadership and grassroots activity. He summarizes his integrated framework as providing 'a platform for understanding and responding to conflict and developing peacebuilding initiatives'.[74] While reconciliation more or less disappears after its initial introduction, Lederach ends by suggesting that reconciliation permeates the structures and processes of the integrated framework and is fundamental to transformation: 'The overall process of conflict transformation is related to our broader theme of reconciliation inasmuch as it is oriented towards changing the nature of relationships at every level of human interaction and experience.'[75]

The development of the concept of peacebuilding, especially in Lederach's model, seems to encompass conflict resolution, and provides it with some useful re-direction, especially towards grassroots activity and bottom-up approaches. It also suggests the importance of going beyond the resolution of issues to transforming relationships (something which other approaches within conflict resolution had already focused on) but, importantly, of also transforming social space, structures and institutions over the long term.

Peacebuilding and Emancipatory Transformation: Critical Reflections on Lederach's Integrated Model of Peacebuilding

As with conflict resolution, Lederach's peacebuilding remains a largely unproblematized set of theories and practices. Again, as with conflict resolution, this is not to say that the integrated model is useless, rather that it lacks a self-critical gaze which addresses discursive issues not just in the context of specific intervention but also in the broader global context of actions. In addition, his idea of reconcilation seems to be only minimally reflected in the integrated model and is based on what could be viewed as an overreliance on elicitive production of peacebuilding and reconciliation. On this latter point, Bendaña has argued that although 'the teaching and practice of conflict resolution cannot be a project originating from outside a society...neither is it a purely indigenous or what scholars such as John Paul Lederach term an 'elicited' approach.'[76] Bendaña goes on to point out that using this kind of 'anthroplogical' formula

> could lead to yet other versions of ethnocentrism, ignoring in the name of cultural purity what is positive and constructive in the conflict resolution field, independent of its geographical origin. Worse yet, pure elicitation could lead to the glorification of the culture of poverty: that is, interpreting conflict resolution, or participative community development, simply as the means of localistic, day-to-day survival and economic revindication.[77]

An awareness of the confines of discourses of violence and militarization must be a first step towards emancipatory transformation. As was argued above, this is as much about understanding our own participation in these discourses as it is about understanding how they are being played out in the context of a specific conflict. This again leads us back to Foucault's analysis of power, and the lack of an analysis of power in Lederach's framework. Understanding power is linked tightly to a critical discursive analysis and, therefore, to greater understanding of how the institutions, structures and relationships of different social spaces are infused with particular normative practices. How can we avoid, through Lederach's reconcilation, Burton's problem-solving, or the specific practices of peacekeeping, falling into old habits of discourse? It is a fundamental problem, and one that a truly transformative intervention needs to address.

More specifically, the question might be posed, what is emancipatory transformation, as something distinct in aims and effects from conflict resolution or peacebuilding which merely RE-solve? How can we develop a continually self-reflective stance, which can go at the same time, goes on working in the often overwhelming immediacy of war zones? In most work on peacekeeping, conflict resolution and peacebuilding these kinds of questions are not noticed, much less addressed. The next section seeks to begin to develop some theoretical ground through which local/global discourses of war, militarism and violence and the sets of practices they constitute can be uncovered, understood and changed in relation to peacebuilding.

From Critical Reflection to Emancipatory Transformation in Peacebuilding

Critical Reflection: Anti-Hegemonic Projects

An analysis which challenges given frameworks for understanding is an important point of departure for transformative peacebuilding. How can we critically view 'normal', taken-for-granted discourses, understand the mechanisms through which such discourses are maintained and consider how we ourselves shape and are shaped by discursive practices? And how can we deconstruct this 'normal'? Michel Foucault's analyses of power and of 'regimes of truth' expose the mechanisms through which certain discourses come to inscribe, describe, and normalize social meaning and action.

As discussed earlier, Foucault's analysis revises the limits of conventional understandings of the nature of power as repression or domination, by uncovering a diffuse positive power. In order to analyse the operations of 'regimes of truth', Foucault employs what he calls a genealogical method which sees history not as a singularity or as a progression but as a 'profusion of entangled events'.[78] Its aim is to chart the emergence of a single interpretation of events through history in the context of a multiplicity of interpretations and possibilities, thereby separating power and truth and affirming 'knowledge as perspective'.[79]

What are the benefits of Foucault's analysis of power/knowledge and his genealogical method for transformative peacebuilding? Foucault offers a means of uncovering and disabling the power of truth on the one hand (recognizing the limits of truth or questioning what is true but also what is untrue, invalid, illegitimate), and the possibility of multiplying 'truths' through an alternative power of perspective, on the other. How, for example, are the 'truths' of nationalism produced and reproduced in the Balkans? What is the process through which complex identities are progressively narrowed and confined? Foucault provides a basis for constructing critical accounts of the various Balkan nationalisms which do not reproduce the unifying tendencies of the 'regime of truth'.

Moreover, Foucault opens space to consider the extent to which State 'power' is dependent on the normalizing and disciplining practices of, for example, educational and religious institutions. More crucially, perhaps, a Foucauldian perspective also examines how everyday practices produce and reinforce 'habits' of normalized behaviour. Foucault's rejection of power as merely domination, and his contention that power is diffuse and, in some sense, *within our grasp*, opens space for transformations. Foucault himself points to the space created for, but ultimately, the limitations of transformation, when he suggests that the micro-physics of power

> are not univocal; they define innumerable points of confrontation, focuses of instability, each of which has its own risks of conflict, of struggles, and of an at least temporary inversion of the power relations. The overthrow of these 'micro-powers' does not, then, obey the law of all or nothing... on the other hand, none of its localized episodes may be inscribed in history except by the effects that it induces on the entire network in which it is caught up.[80]

Building on this Foucauldian analysis, Davina Cooper uses the concept of anti-hegemony to operationalize the (small) space Foucault's analysis leaves for progressive social change. Cooper contends that anti-hegemonic projects are 'localized episodes' of confrontation and change which do not privilege any particular social force and are, therefore, not 'univocal'. A defining feature of anti-hegemony is to avoid 'the tendency to establish norms and standards, which then become rules to be policed'.[81] Anti-hegemonic projects aim to 'contest and deconstruct the status quo from diverse positionings without putting any single project in its place',[82] thereby opening space for critical social movements. While Cooper suggests the possibility of forming solidarities between such movements, like Foucault, she does not 'address the strategic question of the cumulative connections between the elements of micro-politics that are essential if a counter-hegemony is to succeed in displacing an existing hegemonic bloc.'[83]

While anti-hegemonic practices seek to open space for 'knowledge as perspective', thereby contesting the status quo and facilitating the emergence of a multiplicity of diverse critical (localized) social movements, the possibility for broader social change is only minimally conceived. This potential for change is implied in Cooper's assertion that 'forging solidarities' across different projects or movements is a possibility, but any more concerted effort to harness or direct the accumulating effects of localized anti-hegemonic practices runs into the problem of establishing more than minimal boundaries for meaning and practice. This, in Cooper's view, only builds an alternative 'regime of truth' creating, among other things, alternative marginalizations.

Practices that are anti-hegemonic offer a *minimal reach* of transformative peacebuilding (and the minimum that peacebuilding should set out to do). It is minimal because the potential for a widespread transformation of regimes of truth (or hegemonies, or discourses) is viewed with a large dose of deconstructionist skepticism. However, the strength of this 'minimal' peacebuilding lies in avoiding the potential for homogenization present in consensus-building. Because of this, anti-hegemony offers perhaps the greatest potential space for difference. The question remains, though: if enough diverse practices emerge that challenge dominant discourses in localized spaces, does this, in the end, enable change in State power or globalized discourses? Can transformation be extended beyond contestation and deconstruction to a more concerted engagement with hegemonic power?

Emancipatory Transformation: Counter-(local) Hegemonic Projects

An analysis using the work of Antonio Gramsci might offer the possibility for finding a *maximal reach* for transformative peacebuilding. Gramsci argues that dominance in society is not maintained primarily through state intervention by force. It is maintained, rather, through a civil society in which a range of institutions (educational, religious and associational), imbued with social meaning constructed by the bourgeoisie, function to manufacture the consent of non-dominant groups. Hegemony, Gramsci contends, is based on 'the spontaneous consent given by the great masses of the population to the general direction imposed on social life by the dominant fundamental group'.[84] Although practiced through the institutions of civil society which 'operate to shape, directly or indirectly, the cognitive and affective structure whereby men [sic] perceive and evaluate problematic social reality', hegemony must be rooted in the control that dominant groups maintain over the economy.[85] The economic base therefore determines, to a large degree, social practices and meanings. Gramsci tried to avoid the trap of total economic determinism by leaving space for the determining power of human creativity (and the possibility of active, rather than passive revolution). Ideas, Gramsci argued, have material force.[86]

In societies where civil space can be characterized as complex networks of social relations and institutions which support a prevailing hegemonic view of the meaning and direction of social life, and which are resistant to direct, immediate influence, successful social transformation must take the form described by Gramsci as a 'war of position'.[87] Such a *counter-hegemonic project* aims to build a consensus among non-dominant groups which articulates an alternative direction for social life. If consensus can be reached and maintained among enough groups, a new hegemony can emerge. This process develops over a long period of time as more groups are drawn into articulating and practising alternative social meanings. Gramsci concludes, it 'is not a question of introducing from scratch a scientific form of thought into everyone's individual life, but of renovating and making "critical" an already existing activity.'[88] He describes this as constructing 'good sense from common sense'.[89]

Reaching some counter-hegemonic consensus, even at the state level, is challenged by a number of aspects of modern life. These include the expanding number of social movements and organizations, the increasing intensity of global–local interactions and effects, the rising fragmentation as challenges to state power continue, the growing power of global economic systems and so on. In this context, Alan Hunt considers a more localized application of the idea of counter-hegemony. He argues that it is possible that the action of particular groups working for change around their own core agendas, can 'both necessitate and occasion wider structural changes'.[90] Pivotal to his argument is the ability to identify movements which have 'hegemonic capacity', in that achieving their aims requires wider-scale transformation of social practice and meaning. This concept of 'local hegemony' does not necessitate the 'unitary agency' suggested in a more generalized Gramscian counter-hegemony, but opens the conceptual space to consider the potential of a more fragmentary means of change and a more *maximal form* of transformative peacebuilding.

Local hegemony is based on particular fundamental values which are favoured or privileged over other alternatives and this can be problematic. Counter-hegemonic projects are not necessarily progressive (neo-fascism and religious fundamentalism are just two examples). This raises the issue, indicated by Cooper, of the establishment of new norms which are then policed within the counter-hegemony. Even more problematically, this raises the Foucauldian problem of the substitution of a new 'regime of truth', whether or not it is a 'progressive' one. Fundamental to any project attempting transformation is its normative base (in progressive projects this is likely to be tolerance, respect for diversity and human rights, equality and so on). But even if we can subscribe to the legitimacy of these values, there remains the hugely complex problem of living them – an arena of intense contestation. In an increasingly diverse 'differentiated' modern world, how can some consensus be reached on these fundamentals which would avoid 'manufacturing and policing consent' and reclaim the potential for arriving at mutually satisfactory understandings based on some minimal normative framework? Constructing a framework of transformative peacebuilding that can go beyond the *minimal scope* outlined above requires 'steering between the Scylla of absolutism and the Charybdis of relativism'[91] to find mutually satisfactory normative ground.

Reconstructing a Normative Consensus: Making Space for Continuous Transformation

In other words, even if we come to better understand how hegemonic control is maintained through multiple forms of constraint and normalization processes, we are still faced with the question of how to construct some foundation from which radical agendas for change could emerge. Jürgen Habermas, in his theory of communicative action, attempts to rehabilitate the normative content of modernity – to find some means through which to 'generate some sort of objective and theoretical knowledge'.[92] Habermas claims that 'minimal criteria of justice are derivable from [his central conceptions of]...communicative action and communicative rationality.'[93]

According to Habermas, communicative action is a means of intersubjective dialogue between a community of actors which enables them to reconstruct common understandings of their lifeworld and, therefore, renew the shared basis for culture, social integration, and socialization that underlie a mutual existence.[94] In such a way communicative action makes possible the reproduction of the lifeworld. This normative content of the lifeworld 'has to be acquired and justified from the rational potential inherent in everyday practice, if it is not to remain arbitrary.'[95] The use of force or manipulation are distortions of the lifeworld which subvert communicative action and erode the basis for renewal of the lifeworld and, therefore, the basis of a stable, healthy community.

How can communicative action be related to transformative peacebuilding? Creating spaces where intersubjectively produced mutual understandings become possible enables the reconstruction of communication networks (which are free of manipulation, coercion etc) and a renewal of the threefold basis for the reproduction of the lifeworld – cultural traditions, social solidarity and personality (the maintenance of 'identity in the shifting contexts of interaction'[96]). Through the 'unforced force of a better insight',[97] the knowledge encompassed in the lifeworld through which the ability for mutual understanding arises, is 'submitted to an ongoing test across its entire breadth'.[98] It is clear that an 'ideal' space for communicative action cannot exist, but that does not lessen the validity of opening space for the necessarily incomplete and imperfect possibility of reconstructing the basis for meaningful and peaceful social existence. Communicative action does provide a means of renegotiating the bases of mutual existence distorted by war, distortions apparent in cultures of violence.

These are brief reflections on the potential uses of social theory applied to the problem of unproblematized peacekeeping, conflict resolution and peacebuilding. More thought needs to be given to this level of theory and analysis of practices.[99] In addition, an analysis of how different understandings of intervention from peacekeeping to peacebuilding could be usefully analysed against the above understandings of the minimal and maximal forms of peacebuilding is needed. Lederach's integrated model, in particular, holds some interesting parallels with, for example, Habermas's idea of communicative action. Two things need to be reiterated regarding existing theoretical formulations of peacekeeping, conflict resolution, and peacebuilding. First, theory and practice developed outside of thinking which is discursively critical is potentially problematic particularly in its formulation of success (the aims of intervention). Second, the practices developed from these theories are potentially more destructive than constructive, especially in the long term. This is especially the case, as Bendaña has argued, to the extent that in reproducing the existing system, methodologies of conflict management, resolution, peacekeeping, and so on, are 'ever careful to sustain the minimal levels of redistribution and representation which make the system viable and the ideology more appealing.'[100]

Towards Post-Hegemonic Societies

One implication of Habermas's analysis is the possibility of building post-hegemonic societies. From this perspective transformative peacebuilding as sets of counter-hegemonic practices may be best aimed (if aimed at all) not at producing a new hegemonic order, but at creating the outlines for the co-existence and legitimation of a multiplicity of social meanings and realities. In this respect, transformative peacebuilding suggests the possibility of a post-hegemonic world that, as Cox proposes, 'will no longer be the global reach of one particular form of civilization but rather consist of a plurality of visions of world order with the challenge of achieving some common ground as the basis for dynamic coexistence among them.'[101] It is at the point of this basis for 'dynamic coexistence' that Habermasian communicative action could be most visibly deployed.

But what can be said for transformative peacebuilding? A *minimal requirement* appears to be opening critical space, where the very foundations of social meaning and practice are examined and where a diversity of critical social movements contest the 'regime of truth' without reproducing it. A *maximal potential*, encompassing some minimal shared normative base (produced through communicative action) would *attempt* to reconstruct a consensual basis for local hegemony, repairing and reforging distorted communication networks at localized 'everyday' sites of social structures and action.

Such a 'framework' suggests at least two uses: first, it offers a means of understanding and evaluating the discursive reproduction of social meaning of war zones, as well as practices of existing local peacebuilding. Second, it offers a challenge and a means of fundamentally re-thinking theories and practices of interventions including issues of success and ethics, use of military/diplomatic personnel, short and long-term commitments and goals, specific methodologies, training and so on. The framework can go further by supporting, developing, facilitating shifts in theory and practice of interventions and existing local peacebuilding initiatives which open the possibility of a more maximal transformation. Not to engage the theory and practice of peacekeeping, conflict resolution or peacebuilding with this level of problematization will mean the continuation of practices which literally cannot build sustainable peace with justice. These are not impossibilities, as my own research work in Croatia attests,[102] but to tackle them requires that we begin by following Foucault's lead and think beyond the limits of our own experience.

NOTES

1. J. George, *Discourses of Global Politics: A Critical (Re)Introduction to International Relations*, Boulder, CO: Lynne Rienner, 1994, pp.29–30.
2. R.K. Ashley, 'Living on Border Lines: Man, Poststructuralism, and War', in J. Der Derian and M. Shapiro (eds.), *International/Intertextual Relations: Postmodern Readings of World Politics*, New York: Lexington, 1989, pp.274–5.
3. See for example, M. Harbottle, *The Blue Berets: The Story of the United Nations Peacekeeping Forces*. London: Leo Cooper, 1971; M. Harbottle, 'The Strategy of Third Party Interventions in Conflict Resolution', *International Journal*, Vol.35, No.1, 1980, pp.118–31; M. Harbottle, *What is Proper Soldiering? A Study on New Perspectives for the Future Uses of the Armed Forces in the 1990s*, Oxen, UK: Centre for International Peacebuilding, 1991.
4. P.F. Diehl, D. Druckman and J. Wall, 'International Peacekeeping and Conflict Resolution', *Journal of Conflict Resolution*, Vol.42, No.1, 1998, p.34.
5. A.B. Fetherston, *Towards a Theory of United Nations Peacekeeping*, Basingstoke/New York: Macmillan/St. Martin's, 1994.
6. J.W. Burton, *Conflict: Resolution and Provention, Vol.1*, Basingstoke: Macmillan, 1990.
7. R.J. Fisher and L. Keashly, 'The Potential Complementarity of Mediation and Consultation Within a Contingency Model of Third Party Intervention', *Journal of Peace Research*, Vol.28, No.1, 1991, pp.29–42.
8. Diehl, *et al.* (n.4 above). See also, D. Druckman, J.A. Wall and P.F. Diehl, 'Conflict Resolution Roles in International Peacekeeping Missions', in Ho-Won Jeong (ed.). *The New Agenda for Peace Research*, Aldershot, UK: Ashgate, 1999, pp.105–34.
9. In fact it is more related to the work of Jacob Bercovitch which is more firmly situated in a conflict management approach if conflict management is described as encompassing all potential methods that could be used to deal with conflict, as Bercovitch *et al.* , do in the 1991 study listed below. Conflict resolution, on the other hand, is based entirely on non-coercive means (there are other distinctions, especially theoretical, too complex to discuss further here). See for example, J. Bercovitch and J.W. Lamare, 'The Process of International Mediation: An Analysis of the Determinants of Successful and Unsuccessful Outcomes', *Australian Journal of Political Science*, Vol.28, 1993, pp.290–305; J. Bercovitch, J.T. Anagnoson, and D.L. Willie, 'Some Conceptual Issues and Empirical Trends in the Study of Successful Mediation in International Relations', *Journal of Peace Research*, Vol.28, No.1, 1991, pp.7–17; J. Bercovitch (ed.), *Resolving International Conflicts: The Theory and Practice of Mediation*, Boulder, CO: Lynne Rienner, 1996.
10. Diehl *et al.* (n.4 above), p.50.
11. Fisher and Keashly (n.7 above); see also, R.J. Fisher and L. Keashly, 'Third Party Interventions in Intergroup Conflict: Consultation Is Not Mediation', *Negotiation Journal*, Vol.4, No.4, 1988, pp.381–93; and, R.J. Fisher, *The Social Psychology of Intergroup and International Conflict Resolution*, New York: Springer-Verlag, 1990.
12. Diehl, *et al.* (n.4 above), p.41.
13. Ibid., p.42.
14. Ibid., p.49.
15. Ibid., p.49.

16. Ibid., pp.50–1.
17. See for example, A.B. Fetherston and C. Nordstrom, 'Overcoming *habitus* in Conflict Management: UN Peacekeeping and Warzone Ethnography', *Peace and Change*, Vol.20, No.1, 1995, pp.94–119; A.B. Fetherston, 'Voices from Warzones: Implications for Training UN Peacekeepers', in E. Moxon-Browne (ed.), *A Future for UN Peacekeeping?* Basingstoke: Macmillan, 1998, pp.158–75; and, A.B. Fetherston, 'Peacekeeping as Peacebuilding: Towards a Transformative Agenda', in L-A. Broadhead (ed.). *Issues in Peace Research, 1995–6*, Bradford: Bradford University Press, 1996, pp.95–115.
18. A discussion of the relevance of social theory for conflict resolution and the limits of the discursive reality of international relations is provided in, A.B. Fetherston and A.C. Parkin, 'Transforming Violent Conflict: Contributions from Social Theory', in L.-A. Broadhead (ed.). *Issues in Peace Research, 1997–98: Theory and Practice*, Bradford: Bradford University Press, 1997, pp.19–57.
19. This is discussed at greater length in, A.B. Fetherston, 'The Limits of Conflict Resolution', paper presented at the International Studies Association Annual Convention, 16–20 February 1999, Washington DC, USA.
20. R.W. Cox, 'Social Forces, States and World Orders: Beyond International Relations Theory', *Millennium*, Vol.10, No.2, 1981, pp.129–30. See also, R.W. Cox, 'Gramsci, Hegemony and International Relations: An Essay on Method', *Millennium*, Vol.12, No.2, 1983, pp.162–75; R.W. Cox, *Production, Power, and World Order: Social Forces in the Making of History*, New York: Columbia University Press, 1987.
21. Ibid., 129–30.
22. Michel Foucault, 'What is Enlightenment?' in P. Rabinow (ed.). *The Foucault Reader*, London: Penguin, 1984, p.46.
23. See L. Green, 'Fear as a Way of Life', *Cultural Anthropology*,Vol.9, No.2, 1994, pp.227–56; C. Nordstrom and J. Martin (eds.), *The Paths to Domination, Resistance, and Terror*, Berkeley CA.: University of California Press, 1992.
24. C. Nordstrom, 'Warzones: Cultures of Violence, Militarisation and Peace', *Working Paper, No.145*. Canberra: Peace Research Centre, Australian National University, 1994; see also Nordstrom and Martin (n. 23 above).
25. P. Bourdieu, *Outline of a Theory of Practice* (trans. Richard Nice), Cambridge: Cambridge University Press, 1977. See also, P. Bourdieu, *Language and Symbolic Power* (ed. J.B. Thompson, trans. G. Raymond and M. Adamson), Cambridge: Polity Press, 1991.
26. Ibid., p.164.
27. A. Stiglmayer (ed.), *Mass Rape: The War Against Women in Bosnia-Herzegovina*, Lincoln: University of Nebraska Press, 1994.
28. See Der Derian and Shapiro (n.2 above); R.B.J. Walker, *Inside/Outside: International Relations as Political Theory*, Cambridge: Cambridge University Press, 1993.
29. V. Jabri, *Discourses on Violence: Conflict Analysis Reconsidered*, Manchester, U.K.: Manchester University Press, 1996, p.22.
30. Ibid., p.22–3.
31. Ibid., p.23
32. C. Nordstrom, 'Contested Identities/Essentially Contested Powers', in K. Rupesinghe (ed.), *Conflict Transformation*, New York: St. Martin's, 1995, p.106.
33. J.A. Sluka, 'The Anthropology of Conflict', in Nordstrom and Martin (n. 23 above), p.31.
34. Jabri (n.29 above).
35. A. Bendaña, 'Conflict Resolution: Empowerment and Disempowerment', *Peace & Change*, Vol.21, No.1, 1996, pp.69–70.
36. Ibid., p.72.
37. Ibid., p.73.
38. J.A. Scimecca, 'Theory and Alternative Dispute Resolution: A Contradiction in Terms?' in D.J.D. Sandole and H. van der Merwe (eds). *Conflict Resolution Theory and Practice: Integration and Application*, Manchester: Manchester University Press, 1993, pp.211–21.
39. M. Foucault, *Power and Knowledge, Selected Interviews and Other Writings, 1972–1977*

(trans. C. Gordon *et al.*), New York: Harvester Wheatsheaf, 1980, p.122. See also, M. Foucault, *Discipline and Punish: The Birth of the Prison* (trans. A. Sheridan), London: Penguin, 1977; M. Foucault, *The History of Sexuality, Vol.1* (trans. R. Hurley), London: Penguin, 1990.

40. Ibid., p.131.
41. Ibid., p.142.
42. Ibid., p.142.
43. Ibid., p.145.
44. Foucault (n.22 above), p.46.
45. B. Boutros-Ghali, *An Agenda for Peace: Preventive Diplomacy, Peacemaking and Peacekeeping*, New York: UN Department of Public Information, 1992, para. 21.
46. Ibid., para. 55.
47. Bendaña (n.35 above), p.76.
48. J. Galtung, 'A Structural Theory of Imperialism', *Journal of Peace Research*, Vol.8, No.2, 1971, pp.81–117.
49. Later work attempted to give structural violence a statistical base, suggesting, for example, that structural violence was responsible for 86 million deaths a year, whereas direct violence, 19 million. W. Eckhardt, 'Civilizations, Empires, and Wars', *Journal of Peace Research*, Vol.27, No.1, 1990, pp.9–24. In addition, the publication, *World Military and Social Expenditures*, edited by Ruth Sivard, and published by World Priorities appeared every few years and has provided interesting, if usually horrific, support for the idea of structural violence. For an interesting analysis of Galtung's work and his influence on the field of peace research see, P. Lawler, *A Question of Values: Johan Galtung's Peace Research*, Boulder, CO: Lynne Rienner, 1995.
50. J. Galtung, *Peace, War and Defense: Essays in Peace Research, Vol.II*. Copenhagen: Christian Ejlers, see Chapter 2.2, 'Three Approaches to Peace: Peacekeeping, Peacemaking, and Peacebuilding', 1976, pp.282–304.
51. Although these are terms used frequently especially in early work in peace research, they are defined in Adam Curle's work in the context of mediation, see A. Curle, *Making Peace*, London: Tavistock, 1971, and A. Curle, *Tools for Transformation: A Personal Study*, Stroud, UK: Hawthorne Press, 1990.
52. The idea of conflict transformation in peace research owes much to the work of Raimo Väyrynen, see for example, R. Väyrynen (ed.), *New Directions in Conflict Theory: Conflict Resolution and Conflict Transformation*, London: Sage, 1991; further development of this earlier work is offered in, R. Väyrynen, 'From Conflict Resolution to Conflict Transformation: A Critical Review', in Ho-Wong Jeong (ed.), *The New Agenda for Peace Research*, Aldershot, UK: Ashgate, 1999, pp.135–60. See also, Rupesinghe (n. 32 above).
53. Burton (n.6 above).
54. See especially, J.W. Burton, *Deviance, Terrorism and War*, Oxford: Martin Robertson, 1979; J.W. Burton and D.J.D. Sandole, 'Generic Theory: The Basis of Conflict Resolution', *Negotiation Journal*, Vol.2, No.2, 1986, pp.333–44; J.W. Burton and D.J.D. Sandole, 'Expanding the Debate on Generic Theory of Conflict Resolution: A Response to Critique', *Negotiation Journal*, Vol.3, No.1, 1987, pp.97–100.
55. K. Avruch and P.W. Black, 'A Generic Theory of Conflict Resolution: A Critique', *Negotiation Journal*, Vol.3, No.1, 1987, pp.87–96; K. Avruch and P.W. Black, 'Ideas of Human Nature in Contemporary Conflict Resolution Theory', *Negotiation Journal*, Vol.6, No.3, 1990, pp.221–8; K. Avruch and P.W. Black, 'The Culture Question and Conflict Resolution', *Peace & Change*, Vol.16, No.1, 1991, pp.22–45; and, J.W. Burton (ed.), *Conflict: Human Needs Theory, Vol.2*, Basingstoke, UK: Macmillan, 1990.
56. The initial testing of this methodology was written up in, J.W. Burton, *Conflict and Communication*, London: Macmillan, 1969.
57. Burton (n.6 above), p.3.
58. Ibid., p.3.
59. P. Wehr and J.P. Lederach, 'Mediating Conflict in Central America', *Journal of Peace*

Research, Vol.28, No.1, 1991, pp.85–98.

60. The most sustained account of his reconciliation approach is offered in, J.P. Lederach, *Building Peace: Sustainable Reconciliation in Divided Societies*, Washington, DC: United States Institute of Peace Press, 1997. But see also, J.P. Lederach, *Preparing for Peace: Conflict Transformation Across Cultures*, Syracuse, NY: Syracuse University Press, 1995, and; J.P. Lederach, 'Conflict Transformation in Protracted Internal Conflicts: The Case for a Comprehensive Framework', in K. Rupesinghe (ed.), *Conflict Transformation*, New York: St. Martin's, 1995, pp.201–22.
61. J. P. Lederach, *Building Peace: Sustainable Reconciliation in Divided Societies*, Washington D.C.: United States Institute of Peace Press, 1997, p. 24.
62. E.E. Azar, *The Management of Protracted Social Conflict: Theory and Cases*, Aldershot: Dartmouth, 1990.
63. Burton uses the term 'deep-rooted conflict', see Burton, 1990, Vol.1.
64. Lederach (n.61 above), p.27.
65. Ibid., p.29.
66. Ibid., p.51.
67. Ibid., p.52.
68. As cited in ibid., p.56, Maire Dugan, 'A Nested Theory of Conflict', *Women in Leadership*, Vol.1, No.1, 1996, pp.9–20.
69. Ibid., p.55–7.
70. Ibid., p.58.
71. Ibid., p.77.
72. Ibid., p.82–3.
73. Ibid., p.81.
74. Ibid., p.83–4.
75. Ibid., p.84.
76. Bendaña (n.35 above), p.75.
77. Ibid., pp.75–6.
78. Foucault (n.22 above), p.89.
79. Ibid., p.90.
80. Ibid., p.174.
81. D. Cooper, *Power in Struggle: Feminism, Sexuality and the State*, New York: New York University Press, 1995, p.138.
82. Ibid., p.137.
83. A. Hunt, 'Rights and Social Movements: Counter-Hegemonic Strategies', *Journal of Law and Society*, Vol.17, No.3, 1990, p.315.
84. A. Gramsci, *Selections from the Prison Notebooks* (ed. and trans. by Q. Hoare and G.N. Smith), London: Lawrence and Wishart, 1971, p.12; see also p.263.
85. J.V. Femia (). *Gramsci's Political Thought: Hegemony, Consciousness, and the Revolutionary Process*, Oxford: Clarendon, 1981, p.24.
86. Gramsci (n.84 above), p.165.
87. Ibid., pp.229–39.
88. Ibid., pp.330–1
89. Hunt (n.83 above), p.314.
90. Ibid., p.319.
91. J. Habermas, *The Philosophical Discourse of Modernity* (trans. F. Lawrence), Cambridge: Polity, 1987, p.300.
92. As quoted in, L. Kohlberg, C. Levine, and A. Hewer, *Moral Stages: A Current Formulation and a Response to Critics*, Basel: Karger, 1983, p.14.
93. S.K. White, *The Recent Work of Jurgen Habermas: Reason, Justice and Modernity*, Cambridge: Cambridge University Press, 1988, p.23.
94. Habermas (n.91 above), pp.343–4.
95. Ibid., p.341.
96. Ibid., p.343.

97. Ibid., p.305.
98. Ibid., p.321.
99. I have undertaken research in Croatia which attempts to address this issue; a preliminary report of the findings can be found in, A.B. Fetherston, 'Transformative Peacebuilding: Peace Studies in Croatia', paper presented at the International Studies Association Annual Convention, Minneapolis, Minnesota, 17–21 March 1998, pp.1–32.
100. Bendaña (n.35 above), p.71.
101. R.W. Cox, 'An Alternative Approach to Multi-lateralism for the Twenty-first Century', *Global Governance*, Vol.3, pp.111, 1997.
102. See, Fetherston (n.19 and 99 above).

Conflict Prevention: Options for Rapid Deployment and UN Standing Forces

H. PETER LANGILLE

> The planning of peacekeeping operations is the ultimate challenge because you never know where you have to operate; you never know what they want you to do; you don't have the mandate in advance; you don't have forces; you don't have transport; and you don't have money... We always have to start from zero. Each and every operation that we start, we start with nothing.
>
> *Major-General Frank van Kappen,*
> Military Advisor to the UN DPKO, March 1997[1]

Fifty-five years after the United Nations was formed, we continue to explore ways to empower the Organization. On balance, its record in preventing and resolving violent conflict is characterized by modest progress; not what it could or should be. Recent efforts to enhance a UN rapid deployment capability parallel that assessment. One defining moment and opportunity has already passed in the past decade, but in exposing our collective limitations, another arises. Finally, there is agreement that preventive action, through a combination of conflict resolution, diplomacy and even prompt deployments, is far more cost-effective than later, larger efforts. Similarly, many recognize that one essential mechanism for conflict prevention is a reliable and effective UN rapid deployment capability. Whether these will be lessons learned and institutionalized or lessons spurned may depend on the extent to which 'we the people' organize, inform and democratize further efforts. It is time to consider a more inclusive approach, one that draws on new partnerships to encourage the ideas and approaches essential for effective political, military and humanitarian responses to complex emergencies.

The rationale underlying recent initiatives to enhance UN rapid deployment capabilities was very compelling. Frequent delays, vast human suffering and death, diminished credibility, opportunities lost, escalating costs – these were just some of the tragic consequences of slow and inappropriate responses. Unprecedented demand for prompt UN assistance highlighted the deficiencies of existing arrangements, challenging the Organization, as well as member states. Most recognize the UN was denied sufficient resources, as well as appropriate mechanisms with which to respond. Fortunately, an array of complementary reforms have combined to expand the options. As expected, there are limitations and competing alternatives, but few easy or immediate remedies.

International efforts in this endeavour focused primarily on improving peacekeeping. The larger process involves measures to organize the contributions of member states, as well as the establishment of basic mechanisms within the UN's Department of Peacekeeping Operations (DPKO). Several initiatives are quite promising.

Approximately 27 member states, designated 'Friends of Rapid Deployment', cooperated with the DPKO to secure support for developing a rapidly deployable mission headquarters (RDMHQ). As well, since 1994 a DPKO team has organized the UN Standby Arrangement System (UNSAS) to expand the quality and quantity of resources that member states might provide. To complement this arrangement, the Danish government, in cooperation with 13 regular troop contributors, has organized a multinational Standby High Readiness brigade (SHIRBRIG).

SHIRBRIG is improving the tactical foundation by promoting further cooperation in multilateral planning, establishing training and readiness standards, and furthering the pursuit of inter-operability. By the end of the year 2000, the void at the operational level within the Secretariat may be partially filled by a permanent, albeit skeletal, UN rapid deployment mission headquarters. Once funded and staffed, it will simply enable the prompt coordination and control of diverse missions authorized by the Security Council. At the strategic level, the Security Council has agreed to provide further consultation with troop contributors.[2]

Thus, as the tactical, operational, and strategic foundation is strengthened, participants look for a corresponding response at the political level. Hopefully, these arrangements will combine to inspire a higher degree of confidence and commitment among member states. In short, these various 'building blocks' are gradually forming the institutional foundation for future peacekeeping. Initially, they are likely to circumscribe activity to Chapter VI, albeit within a flexible interpretation of peace support operations for complex political emergencies.[3]

The efforts of the UN Secretariat, the 'Friends' and member states such as Denmark, Canada, and the Netherlands were laudable and deserve support. There remain a number of issues, however, that warrant further effort and scrutiny. This study explores several initiatives to enhance a UN rapid deployment capability. It provides an overview of recent proposals, considers the progress within DPKO and the related efforts of Friends of Rapid Deployment, and it identifies the potential limitations of the new arrangements. To activate and revitalize support for further measures, it points to the need for a new 'soft power' approach. Finally, a vision-oriented, cumulative development process is proposed as a means to expand on this foundation.

How are we to assess such initiatives? Within the Secretariat, one focus is on reducing response times.[4] Other considerations must address whether these measures, when combined, contribute to:

- Providing a widely-valued service;
- Increasing confidence in the UN's capacity to plan, deploy, manage, and support at short notice;
- Alleviating the primary worries of potential troop contributors and other member states;
- Generating wider political will and adequate financing;
- Encouraging broad participation;
- Ensuring sufficient multidimensional and multifunctional elements for modern conflict prevention and management;
- Enhancing the training, preparation, and overall competence of potential participants; and
- Instilling a unity of purpose and effort among the various participants.[5]

We must also ask whether the measures under way are sufficient to build an effective and reliable UN capability. Are these initial efforts likely to build a solid foundation with the capacity for modernization and expansion? Alternatively, is there a risk of being locked into another *ad hoc*, conditional system requiring last-minute political approval and improvisation prior to each mission? Can we identify national defence reforms that would complement UN rapid deployment and conflict prevention? The question also arises as to what additional measures will be necessary to institutionalize and consolidate a dedicated UN standing capability?

Background

Since the release in 1992 of former Secretary-General Boutros-Ghali's *An Agenda for Peace*, there has been a wide-ranging discussion of the UN's options for responding to violent conflict.[6] Among the various catalysts for the debate were the Secretary-General's call for peace enforcement units and Article 43-type arrangements, as well as Sir Brian Urquhart's efforts to revive Trygvie Lie's proposal for a UN Legion.[7] As these ideas began to attract a constituency, they also generated apprehension and a search for less ambitious options in many national capitals.

Opinion on the subject of any UN capability is always mixed. The debate here tended to follow two perspectives: the 'practitioners' who favoured strengthening current arrangements, and the 'visionaries' who desired a dedicated UN standing force or standing emergency capability.[8] With notable exceptions, the official preference focused on pragmatic, incremental reform within the structure of the UN Secretariat and available resources.[9] The latter was also assumed to entail fewer risks, fewer obligations and more control.

In the early years of the past decade, there were promising indications of support for some form of UN rapid reaction force.[10] The need for a new instrument was widely recognized in the aftermath of Bosnia, Somalia and the failure to avert the Rwandan genocide. Regrettably, few governments were willing to back their rhetoric with meaningful reform. Prior commitments tended to be followed by carefully nuanced retractions.[11] There were exceptions, notably among middle-power, regular UN troop contributors. Yet, even supportive governments were worried about moving ahead of public opinion, fellow member states, the international defence community and their own capacity to secure more ambitious reforms.

National Studies

Prior to the fiftieth anniversary of the United Nations, the Netherlands, Canada, and Denmark commenced studies and consultative processes to develop options for a UN rapid reaction capability. These studies were followed by concerted diplomatic efforts to organize a wider coalition of member states and secure the cooperation of the UN Secretariat. These initiatives were instrumental, first, in narrowing the range of short-term options – allaying official fears of a potentially large and expensive supranational intervention force – and second, in informing others as to how they might best contribute to the process.

The Netherlands Study

In 1994, the Netherlands began to explore the possibility of creating a permanent, rapidly deployable brigade at the service of the United Nations Security Council. A team of experts conducted the study, and an international conference was convened to review their initial report. They then released the Netherlands Non-Paper, 'A UN Rapid Deployment Brigade: A Preliminary Study,' which identified a critical void in the UN peacekeeping system. If a crisis were not to escalate into widespread violence, they argued it could only be met by dedicated units that were instantly deployable: 'The sooner an international "fire brigade" can turn out, the better the chance that the situation can be contained.'[12]

The focus, the Dutch stressed, should not be on the further development of the UN Standby Arrangements System[13] so much as a military force along the lines advocated by Robert Johansen[14] and Brian Urquhart[15] – a permanent, rapidly deployable brigade that would guarantee the immediate availability of troops when they were urgently needed. The brigade would complement existing components in the field of peacekeeping and crisis management. Its chief value would be as a 'stop-gap' measure when a crisis was imminent,[16] and its deployments would be of strictly limited duration.

The brigade's tasks would include preventive action, peacekeeping during the interval between a Security Council decision and the arrival of an international peacekeeping force, and deployment in emergency humanitarian situations. The annual cost of a 5,000-person brigade was projected at approximately US$300 million, the initial procurement of its equipment at $500-550 million. 'Adoption' of the brigade by one or more member states or by an existing organization such as NATO was recommended as a means of reducing the expenses of basing, transportation, and equipment acquisition.

The non-paper succeeded in stimulating an international exchange of views. It was clear, however, that only a less binding, less ambitious arrangement would be acceptable, at least for the immediate future. A few member states were supportive of the Dutch initiative, but the majority were opposed to any standing UN force, and even the modest expenditures outlined.

The Canadian Study

In September 1995, the Government of Canada presented the UN with a study entitled, *Towards a Rapid Reaction Capability for the United Nations*,[17] with twenty-one recommendations to close the UN's capability gap in the short to mid term. The report also offered five recommendations to stimulate further research and development over the long term.

After establishing the need for a rapid reaction capability, the report examined a number of principles such as reliability, quality, and cost-effectiveness before identifying the primary components of such forces in France, the United States, and NATO. Among the elements deemed necessary were an early warning mechanism, an effective decision-making process, reliable transportation and infrastructure, logistical support, sufficient finances, and well-trained and equipped personnel. The UN system was then evaluated with respect to these requirements.

A range of problems spanning the political,[18] strategic, operational, and tactical levels were identified and addressed. The intent was to 'create an integrated model for rapid reaction from decision-making at the highest level to the deployment of tactical levels in the field.' The report made a case for building on existing arrangements to improve the broader range of peacekeeping activities.

At the operational level, however, the UN suffered a dearth of related capabilities. Several new mechanisms were imperative, including a permanent operational-level rapid reaction headquarters. This multinational group of thirty to fifty personnel, augmented in times of crisis, would conduct contingency planning and rapid deployment as authorized by the Security Council. The headquarters would have a civil affairs branch and links to related agencies, non-governmental and regional organizations.[19] Aside from liaison and planning, it was to be tasked to an array of training objectives.

The vanguard concept was highlighted as 'the most crucial innovation in the UN's peace support operations over the next few years.'[20] It would 'link the operational level headquarters with tactical elements provided by member states to the Secretary-General through the Standby arrangements system.' It entailed identifying national 'vanguard component groups' that might be called upon as needed by the operational-level headquarters.[21] These forces would remain in their home countries under the command of national authorities until they were notified by the Secretary-General and authorized to deploy by their own national government.

The Canadian study reaffirmed 'broad support for the general directions of the Secretary-General and the UN Secretariat in building its peace operations capability for the future.'[22] Recommendations were refined to appeal to a broad range of supportive member states. This would be an inclusive, cooperative building process with the objective of developing a unity of both purpose and effort. Charter reform would be unnecessary, nor would there be additional expenses for the organization. In many respects, it was a compelling case for pragmatic, realisable change within the short to medium term. 'Clearly, ' the report cautioned, 'the first step is to implement these ideas before embarking upon more far-reaching schemes which may in the end prove unnecessary.'[23]

The Danish-led Multinational Study

In January 1995, the Danish government announced that it would be approaching a number of nations for support in establishing a working group to develop a UN Standby Forces High Readiness Brigade (SHIRBRIG).[24] Thirteen member states with extensive experience in peacekeeping agreed to explore the option of a rapid deployment force within the framework of the UN's Standby Arrangement System.[25]

The guiding assumption of the study was that a number of countries could, 'by forming an affiliation between appropriate contributions to the [UNSAS], make a pre-established, multinational UN Standby Forces High Readiness Brigade available to the United Nations, thus providing a rapid deployment capability for deployments of a limited duration.'[26] It noted that the brigade should be reserved solely for providing an effective presence at short notice, and solely for peacekeeping operations, including humanitarian tasks.[27] National units would be required on fifteen to thirty days notice and be sustainable for 180 days.

Standardized training and operating procedures, familiar equipment, and joint exercises, it was felt, would speed up national decision-making processes in times of crisis, as would the fact that the operating conditions for troop contributors would be understood in advance. Moreover, with an agreed focus on being 'first in' and 'first out', participants would have some assurance of the limited duration of their deployment.

Agreement would still be required from individual participating nations. To address the concerns of countries that might have reservations over a particular operation, a relatively broad pool of participants would provide sufficient redundancy among units.[28] States could, therefore, abstain from an operation without jeopardizing the brigade's deployment.

As proposed, SHIRBRIG was to provide the United Nations with prompt access to a versatile force comprising a balance of peacekeeping capabilities, thus overcoming a primary impediment to rapid reaction. The proposal soon attracted a supportive constituency within the UN Secretariat and among regular troop contributors, including Canada and the Netherlands. The Canadian study, similarly, generated considerable enthusiasm among member states.[29] Owing to its comprehensive approach, the UN MILAD, Major-General Frank van Kappen, referred to the Canadian study as the 'red wine that linked the other studies together.'[30]

These three national studies were not viewed as mutually exclusive but as compatible by their respective Foreign Ministers.31 In 1995, UN Under Secretary-General for Peacekeeping, Ismail Kittani, categorized them under '(a) what the UN can do now, (b) what member states can do, and (c) what is still in the future.'[32]

Corresponding Developments

The Friends of Rapid Deployment (FORD)

On the occasion of the United Nations' fiftieth anniversary, Canadian Foreign Minister, André Ouellet and his counterpart from the Netherlands, Hans Van Mierlo, organized a Ministerial meeting to generate political support for enhancing UN rapid deployment capabilities.[33] To promote the initiative, especially among the major powers; Canada and the Netherlands announced the creation of an informal group called the 'Friends of Rapid Reaction', co-chaired by the Canadian and Dutch Permanent representatives in New York. Although they used the Canadian study as a baseline for their discussions, they agreed that this would henceforth be a multinational effort.[34] As a Canadian briefing paper on the status of the initiative acknowledges, 'the recommendations that are being implemented are, therefore, no longer just Canadian, but part of discussions and input from many different nations world-wide.' Indeed, by the autumn of 1996, the group had expanded to include Argentina, Australia, Bangladesh, Brazil, Canada, Chile, Denmark, Egypt, Finland, Germany, Indonesia, Ireland, Jamaica, Japan, Jordan, Malaysia, the Netherlands, New Zealand, Nicaragua, Norway, Poland, Senegal, South Korea, Sweden, Ukraine, and

Zambia. The Friends also succeeded in attracting the cooperation of the UN Secretariat, particularly officials in DPKO.

Initially, they concentrated on building the base of support for an operational-level headquarters, expanding Standby arrangements and explaining the vanguard concept. As it became apparent that the Danish proposal included many of the objectives of the vanguard concept, and the technical details had already been researched and agreed upon through an extensive multinational study, interest in the vanguard concept was superseded by a wider interest in the SHIRBRIG model.[35]

The Friend's efforts in 1996 continued to focus on improving the Standby Arrangements System, but they also began to assist DPKO in implementing the Rapidly Deployable Mission Headquarters. A number of technical working groups were established to refine plans and proposals to improve logistics, administration, financing, sustainability and strategic lift.[36]

Despite having secured a relatively broad base of international support, it is apparent that the consultative process of the 'Friends' could have been more thorough. Several representatives of the non-aligned movement, including a few of the larger troop-contributing member states, were annoyed at having been excluded. In October 1996, for example, Pakistani ambassador Ahmad Kamal said that he 'supported the concept of a rapid deployment headquarters team but was concerned at the action of a self-appointed group of 'Friends of Rapid Reaction' operating without legitimacy, and having half-baked ideas developed without broad consultations with the countries most concerned'.[37] In turn, the Friends' agenda would be delayed as some members of the non-aligned movement (NAM) challenged specific arrangements. As the NAM included 132 member states, they had the potential to block further progress.

However, efforts to develop a UN rapid deployment capability were not confined solely to the 'Friends'. Britain, France and the United States were working on improving the peacekeeping capabilities of numerous African member states. Italy and Argentina were promoting the creation of a rapid response capability for humanitarian purposes.

The United Nations Special Committee on Peacekeeping Operations, otherwise known as the Committee of 34, also continued to meet each spring to consider new requirements and forward related recommendations to the wider membership through the General Assembly. In 1996, the Committee was composed of 36 member states with 57 additional member states attending in observer status. It would continue to attract wider participation over the next four years. Although the Committee hardly represents a vanguard of new thinking on peacekeeping, it provides an important consultative forum for discussing proposals and generating the base of consensus necessary to implement changes.[38] Rapid deployment featured prominently in their reports with strong endorsements of both Standby arrangements and the Rapidly Deployable Mission Headquarters.[39] Concerns would subsequently arise over equitable representation in the RDMHQ and the wider use of gratis personnel within DPKO. Some member states were also initially reluctant to support the SHIRBRIG on the grounds that it appeared to be an exclusive coalition that had no authority to present their arrangement as a 'UN' brigade.[40]

Senior officials from within the Secretariat participate in the discussions of the Special Committee on Peacekeeping, as well as in the former meetings of the Friends of Rapid Deployment. These were cooperative endeavours. After the first meeting of Foreign Ministers to establish the 'Friends', it was reported that 'what was most important to Kofi Annan was an implementation plan, where the proposals of various countries could be structured into achievable pieces and pushed to a useful conclusion.'[41] The UN Secretariat, particularly the DPKO, were already committed to the process of implementing related measures and they needed help.

DPKO and the UN Secretariat

Despite a persistent shortage of personnel and funds, there have been numerous heartening changes within the UN Secretariat over the past eight years.[42] In 1992, for example, the office responsible for peacekeeping was reorganized as the Department for Peace-keeping Operations (DPKO) in order to improve the capacity to plan, conduct and manage operations. Within a relatively short period, this restructuring served to co-locate, and coordinate, within one department, the political, operational, logistics, civil police, de-mining, training, personnel and administrative aspects of peace-keeping operations. A Situation Centre was established within DPKO in May 1993, to maintain round-the-clock communications with the field and provide information necessary to missions and troop contributors. At the same time, a Civilian Police Unit was developed in DPKO's Office of Planning and Support, assuming responsibility for all matters affecting civilian police in peacekeeping operations.

A Training Unit was established in DPKO in June 1993 to increase the availability of trained military and civilian personnel for timely deployment.[43] In 1994, the DPKO established the Mission Planning Service (MPS) for the detailed planning and coordination of complex operations.[44] To enhance analysis, evaluation and institutional memory, the Lessons Learned Unit was instituted in early 1995. To improve logistics, especially in the start-up phase of an operation, the Field Administrative and Logistics Division was incorporated into DPKO. Approval was given to utilize the

Logistics Base at Brindisi, Italy as a centre for the management of peacekeeping assets. Aside from maintaining an inventory of UN material, it is overseeing the stockpiling and delivery of supplies and equipment for missions. Mission Start-up Kits are now assembled at the Logistics Base. Despite limited financial and personnel resources, DPKO achieved a professional level of planning and coordination across a challenging spectrum of tasks.

The development of a Rapidly Deployable Mission Headquarters and the expansion of the UN Standby Arrangement System are themselves part of a larger process to improve the UN's capacity to promptly manage increasingly complex operations. Rapid reaction was a prominent theme within the former UN Secretary-General's 1995 *Supplement to An Agenda for Peace.*[45] He cautioned that problems had become steadily more serious with respect to the availability of troops and equipment.[46] Although the then Secretary-General Boutros-Ghali repeated his support for a UN rapid reaction force, he did not endorse the development of a permanent UN standing force. On several occasions he stipulated that the answer was not to create a UN standing force, which he described as being 'impractical and inappropriate'.[47] This hesitancy should, however, be understood within the context of his having received little support for his earlier attempt to generate peace enforcement units and even less enthusiasm for negotiating Article 43-type agreements. In response to the 1995 *Supplement*, the President of the Security Council indicated that, 'all interested member states were invited by the Council to present further reflections on United Nations peace-keeping operations, and in particular on ways and means to improve the capacity of the United Nations for rapid deployment.'[48] The Security Council also narrowed the range of options, expressing its concern that the first priority in improving the capacity for rapid deployment should be the further enhancement of the existing Standby arrangements. Nothing was explicitly rejected, but the short-term priority was clearly standby rather than a standing force.[49] In December, UN Secretary-General Elect, Kofi Annan, reflected these concerns, stating:

> I don't think we can have a standing United Nations army. The membership is not ready for that. There are financial questions and great legal issues as to which laws would apply and where it would be stationed. But short of having a standing United Nations army, we have taken initiatives that will perhaps help us achieve what we were hoping to get out of a standing army. The real problem has been rapidity of deployment. We are now encouraging governments to set up rapidly deployable brigades and battalions that could be moved into a theater very quickly, should the governments decide to participate in peacekeeping operations.[50]

In the short term, it appeared the UN Standby Arrangement System was to be the foundation, upon which much of the potential for rapid deployment would depend.

United Nations Standby Arrangement System (UNSAS)

In 1993, Boutros-Ghali identified the need for a system of Standby Arrangements to secure the personnel and material resources required for peacekeeping.[51] This system was specifically intended to improve the capability for rapid deployment. The Standby Arrangements system (UNSAS) is based on conditional commitments from member states of specified resources that could be made available within agreed response times. The resources range from military units, individual civilian, military and police personnel to specialized services, equipment and other capabilities.[52]

UNSAS serves several objectives. First, it provides the UN with a precise understanding of the forces and other capabilities a member state will have available at an agreed state of readiness. Second, it facilitates planning, training and preparation for both participating member states and the UN. Third, it provides the UN not only with foreknowledge of a range of national assets, but also a list of potential options if a member or members refrain from participating in an operation. Finally, although the arrangements are only conditional, it is hoped that those members who have confirmed their willingness to provide standby resources will be more forthcoming and committed than might otherwise be the case. In short, UNSAS provides an initial commitment to service, and a better advance understanding of the requirements, but is in no way a binding obligation.

In 1994, a Standby Arrangements Management Team was established within DPKO to identify the UN requirements in peacekeeping operations, establish readiness standards, negotiate with potential participants, establish a data base of resources, and assist in mission planning. They also reformed procedures for determining reimbursement of member's contingent-owned equipment. Progress to date is encouraging.

By March of 2000, 88 member states had confirmed their willingness to provide standby resources, representing a total of 147,500 personnel that could, in principle, be called on.[53] The majority of states also provided detailed information on their specific capabilities. Response times were registered according to the declared national capabilities. Resources were divided into four groups on the basis of their potential. Earlier reports suggested the majority (58 per cent) of the overall pool fall into the first two categories of (1) up to 30 days, and (2) 30–60 days.[54] In other words, the UN has a conditional commitment of over 50,000 personnel on standby assumed to be capable of rapid deployment. While UNSAS cannot guarantee a reliable response, UN planners now have the option of developing contingency and 'fall-back' strategies when they anticipate delays. Member states are also more familiar with the system and with what they are expected to contribute. This has increased confidence and, as the numbers infer, a willingness to participate. In the words of one senior DPKO official, 'this is now the maximum feasible option.'

Some mission success has been partially attributed to UNSAS.[55] The former Secretary-General wisely cautioned, however, that while national readiness is a necessary pre-requisite, it does not in itself give the UN a capacity for rapid deployment.[56] Several limitations remain. For example, many participants lack a capacity to provide their own support functions. The Organization is still confronted with shortages in a number of critical areas, including headquarters support, communications, and both sea and air transport.

United Nations Rapidly Deployable Mission Headquarters (RDMHQ)

As a complement to the UN Standby Arrangement System, the Secretary-General decided to pursue the Canadian proposal to create a rapidly deployable mission headquarters (RDMHQ).[57] This is a multidimensional core headquarters unit of military and civilian personnel tasked to assist rapid deployment and manage the initial phases of a peacekeeping operation.[58] The RDMHQ is designed as an operational unit with a tactical planning function.

On account of budgetary constraints, the RDMHQ is officially described as the 'skeleton' of a mission headquarters. Once financing is approved, eight individuals are to be assigned to the RDMHQ on a full-time basis including its Chief of Staff and specialists in fields such as operations, logistics, engineering and civilian police. They are to be based in New York. The UN has received approval for their deployment into a mission area without further authorization at the national level.

Aside from the eight full-time staff, an additional 24 personnel are to remain earmarked in their home countries until required for training or deployment. Twenty-nine personnel in the Secretariat are also to be double-tasked and assigned to the RDMHQ, but will continue with their regular assignments until needed.[59] This initial team of 61 personnel is to coordinate rapid deployment and manage an operational-level headquarters, even in missions with the broadest, multidisciplinary mandates. Once deployed this headquarters is to be in a mission area for 3–6 months pending the arrival of and transition to a normal headquarters. Major-General Frank Van Kappen has detailed the five primary tasks of the RDMHQ:

- Translating the concept of operations prepared by the mission planning service into tactical sub-plans;
- Developing and implementing RDMHQ preparedness and training activities; providing advice to the Head of Mission for decision-making and coordination purposes;
- Establishing an administrative infrastructure for the mission;
- Providing, during the early stages of the operation, essential liaison with the parties;
- Working with incoming mission headquarters personnel to ensure that, as the operation grows to its full size and complexity, unity of effort to implement the Security Council mandate is maintained.

The Friends Group has stipulated that the RDMHQ will require the following capabilities:

- It must be deployable at very short notice.
- It should be able to deploy for up to six months.
- It should provide initially the nucleus of a headquarters for a new PKO.
- It must be integrated into DPKO as a core function in order to retain its interoperability with the UN headquarters in New York.
- It must be capable of undertaking technical reconnaissance missions prior to deployment.
- It must have undertaken operational deployment preparations prior to its commitment. This must include such things as the production of Standard Operating Procedures and the completion of pre-deployment training.[60]

When the RDMHQ was initially proposed, it attracted broad support in the UN Secretariat. In welcoming the proposal, Boutros-Ghali stated that the idea fostered a 'culture of prevention' and that, 'even if it will not be used it is a kind of dissuasion.'[61]

However, recruitment and staffing of this headquarters was far more controversial than initially anticipated. Only two posts have been established to date.[62] The remaining six positions were approved in the autumn of 1999, but without the additional funding required.

Valid concerns also arose over the initial plans for the RDMHQ – whether it might be a 'silver bullet' – a single-mission mechanism that once deployed could leave DPKO with insufficient personnel to manage ongoing departmental and mission requirements. Many recognized the need for a surge and a steady-state capability if the new mission headquarters was to succeed in meeting wider expectations. Some of the earlier plans would have to be adapted. As a first step, in March 2000 the Special Committee on Peacekeeping reiterated its 1995 request for the RDMHQ and demanded that the remaining six positions be established and filled as quickly as possible.[63]

Yet, in response to persistant fears of extending already over-tasked personnel, officials within DPKO released a compromise plan in the same month for a smaller Rapid Deployment Management Unit (RDMU). As proposed, this would entail a static planning element of four civilians to identify required skills and develop a roster of individual expertise who might be called on short notice to fill diverse headquarter functions.[64]

The optimum compromise in the short term would be to pursue both the RDMHQ and the RDMU as complementary mechanism that would provide both the operational and planning capacity, as well as the surge and steady-state requirement, with only an additional ten personnel. This could represent a 'win–win' solution, addressing the NAM's insistance on broader representation and the 'Friends' desire for an effective operational headquarters. The importance of satisfying both these requirements and objectives is evident. The issue, nevertheless, remains unresolved. The RDMHQ is still not operational, but it is also clear that numerous member states expect that it will be within the year.

Multinational Standby Forces High Readiness Brigade (SHIRBRIG)

The Danish-led initiative to develop a Multinational United Nations Standby Forces High Readiness Brigade (SHIRBRIG) will complement the UNSAS with a complete, integrated unit that has a projected response time of 15–30 days. As proposed, the SHIRBRIG is to consist of 4,000–5,000 troops, comprising a headquarters unit, infantry battalions, and reconnaissance units, as well as engineering and logistical support. The brigade is to be self-sustaining in deployments of up to six months' duration and capable of self-defence.[65]

On 15 December 1996, seven countries signed a letter of intent to cooperate in establishing and maintaining this high readiness brigade.[66] This initial group has expanded, as have the number of members providing a commitment to the actual brigade pool.[67] A steering committee and a permanent planning element are in place, as are arrangements for its operational headquarters and logistics. SHIRBRIG is now expected to be fully operational. The objective, and the basis for cooperation, is to provide the UN with a 'well-trained, cohesive multinational force to be deployed in Chapter VI operations mandated by the Security Council and with the consent of the parties'.[68] Participants would thus have a mutual understanding of their combined capabilities, as well as their specific roles and requirements:

> This would enhance the efficiency of a possible deployment and would enhance the safety of the troops when deployed. Common

> procedures and interoperability would be developed to allow for better operational planning, to insure common assessment of the operational requirements, optimise movement planning and reduce costs.[69]

Cooperation is clearly more cost-effective as participants have the option to pursue functional role specialization in a coherent division of labour and resources. For example, rather than carrying a long independent national logistics train, such a task can be either shared or selected by one participant as their contribution.

Current Status: Modest Success in the Short Term

In five years, efforts to develop a UN rapid deployment capability have initiated changes at the political, strategic, operational and tactical levels. More countries are participating in the UNSAS, a significant proportion at a high level of readiness. The SHIRBRIG attracted additional participants and a sufficient brigade pool. As noted, it is now declared to be available to the UN. It has also attracted wider interest and a variation on the model is being considered in several other regions.[70] With relatively modest funding, the UNRDMHQ could provide the nucleus of an operational-level headquarters to assist in the planning and establishment of operations world-wide. Contingency planning is under way. Plans have reflected the need for diverse multidimensional participation in both the headquarters and among field-deployable elements. Training is gradually improving with the support of DPKO and national peacekeeping training centres. Participants have developed a better understanding of the various requirements, and many are increasingly confident of their ability to contribute. Partnership agreements are being encouraged to help ensure wider regional representation and competence. Improving the wider unity of effort and purpose is on the agenda of national civilian and military elements, NGOs, and the UN. Some member states and their defence establishments acknowledge marked progress in DPKO's planning and management of recent operations. This new level of professionalism may gradually inspire wider hopes and confidence.

In hindsight, one could argue there were good reasons for developing this UN capability in the context of prevailing practices, resources and structures. Considering the impediments of limited political will, insufficient funding, and overworked personnel answerable to 188 bosses with divergent interests, the progress to date should not be underestimated. Moreover, it was attained in the absence of powerful national champions, and most observers recognize that the larger UN system is not altogether amenable to rapid modernization. Some officials assume that the task is well under way, with 73 per cent of the recommendations either accomplished or in the process of being implemented. As early as 1996 a Canadian briefing paper noted that, 'between the Group of Friends and the initiative of the Secretariat, 19 of the 26 recommendations have been acted upon in the past nine months.'[71] In the same year, Kofi Annan claimed that the lead-time of the UN's rapid deployment capabilities would be reduced by 50 per cent during the next two years.[72]

Nevertheless, one might argue that these arrangements reflect the pursuit of agreement only slightly above the level of the lowest common denominator. The context placed a priority on modest short-to-mid term changes that could be promoted among diverse states without major controversy, major funding or major national contributions. Few can be heralded as visionary, courageous gestures that correspond to the wider human and global security challenges of the future. It remains to be seen whether these arrangements will attract a broad constituency of support. Few efforts were made, moreover, to build a coalition among NGOs, related agencies and the interested public, effectively limiting the leverage and political pressure that would be needed to launch further reforms.

Hans van Merlo, co-chair of the Friends of Rapid Deployment, acknowledged that progress has been modest; that 'given the complexities, this is going to be an incremental process, but one where we cannot afford to let up.'[73] Regrettably, some initiatives were deliberately stymied. For example, despite the Secretary-General's authorization to establish the RDMHQ, Pakistan succeeded in mobilizing wider resistance to this development.[74] In 1998, Cuba denied approval of the necessary funding for RDMHQ staff in the Advisory Committee on Adminstrative and Budgetary Questions (ACABQ). Unfortunately, controversy and political opposition have also diminished the momentum of the 'Friends' and, to a lesser extent, the Secretariat. The 'Friends' have yet to decide whether they will re-convene. They did not meet in 1998 or 1999. There are concerns that ideas emanating from this group will be actively opposed. In response, some diplomats believe that the only remaining option is to leave rapid deployment to the UN Secretariat – that a restructuring from within may gradually occur on the basis of pragmatic evaluations and lessons learned. However, due to budgetary constraints and the elimination of all gratis personnel, DPKO suffered the loss of nearly 100 professionals and numerous key positions due to the end of secondment. With fewer staff and fewer resources, DPKO claims it has retained a critical mass, but it may now be incapable of managing additional responsibilities. Moreover, given the recent intransigence of the Security Council, Secretary-General Kofi Annan has had insufficient support to encourage the process. Clearly, the wider initiative has reached a political impasse. There is little indication that further initiatives, or even incremental steps, are being actively pursued. Yet the larger task is far from finished.

Potential Limitations

If rapid reaction is a demanding concept, it is an even more difficult reality to achieve. The Organization must be sure of each critical element in the process. Missing components and conditional agreements can only lead to delays. It may be wise, therefore, to temper our expectations by acknowledging some inherent problems.

Standby arrangements for nationally-based units do not provide an assurance of their immediate availability. As the former Secretary-General acknowledged in 1995, 'a considerable effort has been made to expand and refine standby arrangements, but these provide no guarantee that troops will be provided for a specific operation.'[75] He noted further that 'the value of the arrangement would of course depend on how far the Security Council could be sure that the force would actually be available in an emergency.' With respect to UNSAS, there are few, if any, certainties. The promptness with which national contingents are provided will depend on the discretion of participating member states, the risks perceived, and the level of interests at stake.[76]

Reliability will be a key determinant of rapid deployment. In the case of UNSAS, there is no assurance that the political will exists. Critics frequently point to the refusal of member states to provide adequate forces to avert the 1994 catastrophe in Rwanda. Not one of the 19 governments that had undertaken to have troops on standby for UN peacekeeping agreed to contribute to the UNAMIR mission under these arrangements.[77] Proponents of UNSAS now have grounds to argue that the system has been expanded and improved, but commitment to the system will have to be far more comprehensive and binding if it is to succeed. The onus is now clearly on member states to demonstrate the viability of this system.

Once approved for deployment, standby units will have to stage independently and assemble in-theatre. For some, this will be their first experience working together, and it will likely occur under conditions of extreme stress. Some military establishments are reluctant to acknowledge the need for prior training of their personnel beyond a general combat capability. Thus, high standards of cohesiveness and interoperability will be difficult to assure in advance. Moreover, the UN will continue to confront the complex task of coordinating lift capabilities for participating elements across the world. This, too, can only slow deployment. Logistics and sustainment arrangements are gradually improving, but the UN is still coming to grips with the challenge of supplying different national contingents with a wide range of equipment.

A UN RDMHQ of some 61 personnel could provide the necessary impetus for developing and coordinating headquarters arrangements, but there are legitimate doubts about its ability to fulfil its five primary tasks in any period of intense activity where it may face multiple operations. Even in its full composition, it is still only the shell of an operational mission headquarters. As presently constituted, it is best seen as a necessary improvisation, an arrangement that may need to be rapidly augmented. As noted, one promising compromise that might begin to address the requirement for both a surge and steady-state capacity would be to staff the RDMHQ, as well as DPKO's recent initiative for a four-person Rapid Deployment Management Unit (RDMU).

Current plans entail a multidimensional RDMHQ of both civilian and military personnel. This is to be encouraged, as it has grown out of the requirement to address the diverse needs of people in desperate circumstances. SHIRBRIG, however, is a purely military force. While this facilitated the brigade's organization, planners would be wise to expand its composition with civilians in both planning and deployable elements. For there are limitations to what military force alone can achieve. To secure respect, legitimacy and consent (that is, host nation approval) it is increasingly important, even in rapid deployment, to provide a broader range of incentives and services in the initial stages of a UN operation.

In sum, while current efforts are definitely helpful, additional arrangements will be necessary to provide reliable and effective responses to increasingly complex conflicts.

Possible Roles

There are numerous potential tasks for a UN rapid deployment capability. Roles and responsibilities for specific missions will vary with Security Council mandates, of course, and much will depend on what is provided and on what terms. Expectations vary considerably over the tasks that should be incorporated into planning.

Many officials propose that any rapid deployment capability should assume responsibility for the initial stages of a peacekeeping mission. Deployable elements will be the first in to establish security, headquarters, and services, and then the first out, to be replaced by regular peacekeeping contingents within four to six months. Such a capability is also seen as the preferred instrument for preventive deployment.[78] Moreover, as the effectiveness of any UN rapid deployment capability will diminish once a conflict has escalated to open warfare, there is a case to be made for restricting its early use to proactive and preventive measures. If it is to succeed in stemming imminent crises, an enduring emphasis will have to be accorded to flexibility and mobility. In 1995, Sir Brian Urquhart outlined the following range of potential roles:

- To provide a UN presence in the crisis area immediately after the Security Council has decided it should be involved;
- To prevent violence from escalating;
- To assist, monitor, and otherwise facilitate a cease-fire;
- To provide the emergency framework for UN efforts to resolve the conflict and commence negotiations;
- To secure a base, communications, and airfield for a subsequent UN force;
- To provide safe areas for persons and groups whose lives are threatened by the conflict;
- To secure humanitarian relief operations; and
- To assess the situation and provide first-hand information for the Security Council so that an informed decision can be made on the utility and feasibility of further UN involvement.[79]

Urquhart expressed support for a new standing UN capability in which the 'rules of engagement and for the use of force will be different from either peacekeeping or enforcement actions'. Flexibility was a prerequisite: the force 'will be trained in peacekeeping and problem-solving techniques but will also have the training, expertise and esprit de corps to pursue those tasks in difficult, and even violent circumstances.'[80] Indeed, such a mechanism can be more easily justified if it can provide a cost-effective and timely response to an array of challenges.

The confusion emanating from discussions of what a rapid deployment capability is intended for stems partly from two distinct but complementary objectives.[81] Initial interest in developing a rapid-deployment capability was premised on the need to improve peacekeeping. But expectations were also raised at the prospect of a mechanism which would be capable of prompt, decisive responses to desperate situations; even those which necessitated humanitarian intervention and limited enforcement. In the near term, these latter hopes may not be fulfilled. It should be acknowledged that there are also far more ambitious objectives similar to those outlined in the UN Charter, including the gradual development of a collective security system that facilitates a wider process of disarmament.

However, as we begin to understand the need for increasingly flexible options and a wider array of instruments, the range of choice appears to have narrowed. UNSAS stipulates that the resources are to be used exclusively for peacekeeping.[82] Similarly, the RDMHQ and SHIRBRIG are also strictly for Chapter VI operations. While this may attract initial support, it may entail political and operational constraints. In cases involving extreme violations of human rights, including genocide, the UN may be unable to intervene rapidly if the situation demands a mandate beyond peacekeeping. Strict adherence to Chapter VI could diminish the wider deterrent effect, as well as its capacity for dissuasion.

The prospects for preventive deployment in the critical early stages of a conflict may be impeded by delays in arranging the consent of various factions or agreement among contributors. The experience of the past decade suggests that even supportive member states are inclined to 'wait and watch' as they assess the risks, the costs, and the conditions for participation. Incipient distant crises seldom present the images or the political pressure necessary to mobilize governments into preventive action.

This dilemma may be partially resolved with the 'wider' interpretation accorded to peace support operations. Over the past five years, this has become an increasingly sophisticated exercise combining positive incentives with coercive inducement strategies. Kofi Annan suggests that UN operations will continue to evolve and expand with two main tasks: first, suppressing violence with a credible coercive capacity, the purpose of which is to intimidate recalcitrants into cooperating; and second, assisting the parties towards reconciliation with the provision of rewards in the mission area, including what the military refers to as 'civic action', as well as broader peace incentives.[83] Expanded multidimensional operations entailed some of the more robust tools associated with limited enforcement, as well as broader peacebuilding services. Recent Security Council mandates for peace support operations began to acknowledge these wider requirements, and DPKO has demonstrated its capacity to provide sound guidance and planning. Notably, all four missions authorized in the past year (UNMIK, UNTAET, UNAMSIL and MONUC) included Chapter VII mandates. An array of expanded tasks may be accommodated within Chapters VI and VII, but these and others that require immediate preventive action will continue to challenge both the UN and its member states. Neither will be able to escape the need for more substantive resources, new mechanisms and innovative practices.[84]

Further Requirements: A Proposal to Expand the Foundation

The development of a reliable and effective UN capability will take time, vision and a coherent, goal-oriented plan – one that is guided by a long-term sense of purpose and the prospect of contributing to a critical mechanism for conflict prevention and humanitarian assistance.[85] As we look to the long term, it is evident that there will be a need for further measures that complement and build on the existing foundation. The prospect of immediately initiating some form of UN standing capability is remote, but an ongoing cumulative development process appears feasible. Several stages are envisaged in this development. As capabilities are consolidated at each stage, one can anticipate a parallel expansion in the scope and scale of potential activities. One assumes the UN will require a capability commensurate with the tasks it is likely to be assigned.

There are several cost-effective options that merit consideration by the United Nations, its member states and interested parties. The following sequential proposals are intended to stimulate further discussion and analysis.

Stage One

Revitalize and expand the consultative process of all supportive parties with the following objectives:

SHIRBRIG:

- Launch a concerted effort to promote establishment of similar arrangements in other regions;
- After an initial trial in peacekeeping, negotiate new MOU facilitating deployment to operations necessitating a mandate within Chapter VII.
- Integrate civilian elements to ensure provision of necessary services; and,
- Initiate research into the financing, administration, basing, equipment, and lift arrangements necessary to ensure immediate responses from co-located, standing national SHIRBRIG units.

UNSAS:

- Given the promising foundation established, promote standby political commitments whether through expanded Memoranda of Understanding or Article 43.

UN Standing Emergency Capability:

- Initiate a parallel inquiry into the option of dedicated UN volunteer elements with particular emphasis on administration, financing, recruitment, terms of service, remuneration, training, basing and command.

Stage Two

- Establish a UN rapid deployment base, with consideration accorded to the use of redundant military bases to provide existing infrastructure for training and equipment stock-piling, as well as nearby access to air and sea lift for prompt staging;
- Develop a permanent, operational-level headquarters at the UN base. Experienced officers, civilian experts, and qualified planners can be

seconded to the base and co-assigned responsibility to expand the operational and tactical foundation for future efforts.

- In order to manage a variety of complex tasks effectively, it is in the interests of all parties to shift from a skeletal RDMHQ within UNHQ, New York to an expanded operational-level headquarters at a UN base. It would also be prudent for cost-effectiveness, as well as for the obvious benefits from a military, doctrinal, and administrative perspective, to co-locate two field-deployable tactical (mission) headquarters at this base.

Stage Three

- Assign the national elements of a SHIRBRIG type group to the UN base for a one to two-year period of duty. The general reluctance to move quickly can be partially overcome by stationing these multinational elements in a sound operational and tactical structure. The response times of standing multinational elements should be considerably quicker than the projected fifteen- to thirty-day response from home-based national SHIRBRIG elements. Tactical units and civilians would still remain under national political control and operational command. Locating these elements under the operational control of the permanent headquarters would improve multinational training, exercises, lift, and logistics coordination. Standing co-located national units would enhance overall effectiveness, increase the prospect of timely national approval and lead to faster responses. Several multinational SHIRBRIGs might also fill a large void in the current system of conflict prevention and management.
- Launch an ongoing process of doctrine development for the range of diverse elements likely to be required in future multidimensional operations. Emphasize the unity of purpose and effort necessary to coordinate and integrate the various elements into a cohesive team;
- Identify five appropriately-dispersed regional facilities to serve as UN bases for the preparation and deployment of other SHIRBRIG groups;

Stage Four: A Composite Standing Emergency Capability

- Recruit and co-locate professional UN volunteers into distinct capability component groups of both the headquarters and field-deployable elements at the initial UN base. Integrate volunteers into a dedicated UN Standing Emergency Capability of 5,000 personnel under one of the two field-deployable mission headquarters. Provide personnel with advance training and two complete, modern equipment kits (one for training and one pre-packed for immediate staging). Ensure UN elements have a credible stand-alone strength for emergency deployments of approximately 4,000 civilian and military personnel.

The integration of UN volunteers into this group should be viewed as a complementary and mutually reinforcing stage in the development of an increasingly effective UN rapid deployment capability. Its relatively small size would alleviate fears of a new supranational force. Moreover, the use of this relatively discrete UN emergency capability could only be authorized by the UN Security Council and directed by the UN Secretary-General or his special representative.

A standing emergency capability with dedicated UN volunteers might begin to respond to a crisis within 24 hours of a decision by the Security Council. Expanding the operational and tactical structure of this capability to include dedicated UN personnel would also expand the range of options at the political and strategic levels. As the Commission on Global Governance reported in 1995, 'the very existence of an immediately available and effective UN Volunteer Force could be a deterrent in itself. It could also give important support for negotiation and the peaceful settlement of disputes.'[86] The Report of the Independent Working Group on the Future of the United Nations expressed its preference for a standing UN Volunteer Force to enhance the UN's performance in both time and function.[87] The Carnegie Commission report acknowledged that 'a standing force may well be necessary for effective prevention'.[88] A Canadian discussion paper on the issue acknowledges that:

> It would provide the UN with a small but totally reliable, well-trained and cohesive group for deployment by the Security Council in urgent situations. It would break one of the key log-jams in the current UN system, namely the insistence by troop-contributing nations that they authorise the use of their national forces prior to each deployment. It would also simplify command and control arrangements in UN peace support operations, and put an end to conflicts between UN commanders and contingent commanders reporting to national authorities.[89]

The case for such a capability is premised on the need not only to avert human suffering, but also to reduce the high costs of major peacekeeping and enforcement operations, not to mention the reconstruction of war-torn societies.[90] As Urquhart writes, it 'should be seen as a vital investment for the future, and one which by its very nature, is designed to act at the point where action can be most effective, thus eliminating or reducing the necessity for later, larger, less effective, more costly options.'[91]

Recurring costs for a standing UN brigade have been estimated at US$253 million per annum. Acquiring a redundant military base capable of hosting 10,000 personnel might reduce the start-up costs. Ultimately, the UN will also require its own equipment if the deployable elements of a standing capability are to be interoperable. Standardization of equipment and vehicles would greatly reduce overall costs in terms of manpower and overhead. To acquire equipment for a UN brigade would likely entail an expenditure of approximately US$500-600 million. Clearly, this new UN capability would not entail a significant financial burden if shared proportionally among 185 member states.[92]

A host of related issues will have to be addressed before any standing capability becomes a reality. Financing is one major concern. Developing the organizational and operational capacity of the United Nations to the point where it has the confidence of member states is another. But these issues hardly preclude the need to design a compelling sequence of steps that will facilitate the transition to a viable, permanent UN capability. Making the case for a more robust force, Carl Kaysen and George Rathjens write:

> There could be great benefit in getting on with dealing with these other problems – regardless of the creation of a standing military force – but we do not believe that progress in the analysis of the case for a standing force, and possibly its recruitment and training should be delayed pending its resolution. We do concede the case for such a force will be much stronger to the extent one can assume substantial progress in these other areas.[93]

The Netherlands study demonstrated that many of the technical obstacles are surmountable. The Danish study did not rule out permanently assigning military units to the UN, but acknowledged that it was a long-term option.[94] And the Canadian study noted that, 'no matter how difficult this goal now seems, it deserves continued study with a clear process for assessing its feasibility over the long term.'[95]

One of the initial statements of the Canadian study cautiously advised that, 'any plan to operate a standing force presupposes adjustments at the political, strategic and tactical levels, which in many cases must be put in place on an incremental basis, starting as soon as possible.'[96] Many of these adjustments are now in place. Although no time frames were established, it would appear we are now at the mid-term of a process that needs to be revitalized. Both the Security Council and other member states are likely to need powerful encouragement to resume and expand this process. In this respect, there are several preliminary yet, critical requirements.

First, the need for a wider educational process is now evident, as is the need for a broad-based coalition and constituency of support. A new 'soft power' approach could help to advance both objectives.[97] Aside from the benefits of informing member states and citizens, it might rejuvenate the 'Friends', prompt further partnerships, and activate numerous supportive NGOs and related parties. Of equal importance is the need to draw the initiative back from the exclusive domain of 'high politics' between states and what has become a relatively dysfunctional Security Council. This would effectively entail a campaign to democratize, politicize and publicize further discussions. By encouraging a clearer appreciation of the issues and current arrangements, there is the prospect of increasing confidence and commitment. This might also be a useful step towards acquiring wider political influence and leverage, as well as attracting powerful political champions. The latter can only lead as far as their constituents are prepared to provide support.

Second, if rapid deployment is to succeed as a legitimate and widely-valued mechanism for conflict prevention, there will be a need to ensure a far more comprehensive and sophisticated approach. Whereas much attention has been devoted to ensuring sufficient 'hard power' (military forces) capable of restoring security, greater efforts will have to be devoted to ensuring they are accompanied by civilian elements that can restore hope and address human needs. Complex political emergencies will demand prompt attention from both.

Third, it is time to restore the vision that inspired these and former efforts to empower the United Nations. Regrettably, the earlier sense of opportunity and hope has faded, replaced by heightened cynicism and despair. Few recognize the potential to transform the wider security environment through an expansion of these capabilities. If we hope to inspire a broader base of support, there will be a need to demonstrate the potential benefits.[98] In the short term, this capability should help to prevent and resolve some violent conflicts, though not all. That is progress, as well as an indication of potential. Although there are risks in being too ambitious at the outset, there are reasons why opponents of a UN rapid deployment capability view it as a subversive process and a 'slippery slope'. Any demonstration of success might encourage further cooperation towards the far more ambitious objective of a cooperative security system – a likely pre-requisite for moving on to an era of global human security.

Progress in addressing the three preliminary requirements of revitalizing wider efforts, ensuring the inclusion of appropriate elements and restoring the necessary vision, will likely depend on the extent to which officials begin to recognize the potential contribution of conflict resolution and peace studies. These are common objectives that cannot be managed in isolation. It is time for a far more inclusive and cooperative approach that draws on the respective strengths of all supportive parties.

Conclusion

In 2000 the UN will have a preliminary rapid deployment capability for peace support operations. Three middle powers – Canada, the Netherlands and Denmark – were instrumental in coordinating related studies and broad cooperation through national and international consultative processes, as well as the development of a supportive organizational framework. In turn the UN Secretariat and the Friends of Rapid Deployment played a pivotal role in both prompting and implementing supportive changes. The majority of their short-term objectives were either achieved or are being implemented. There are substantive increases in the quantity and quality of resources listed in the UN Standby Arrangement System. A UN Rapidly Deployable Mission Headquarters may soon be available to assist in the critical start-up phase of new operations. A multinational Standby High-Readiness brigade is available to the UN. As previously noted, over the past five years there has been supportive innovation at the political, strategic, operational and tactical levels.

As Kofi Annan wrote, 'The initiatives taken by these countries have been valuable both for what they have achieved in themselves and for the way in which they have refocused the debate among peace-keeping contributors at large.' He went on to note: 'In the context of that wider group, however, a number of further actions will need to be taken if we are to intervene more effectively in either a preventive or curative capacity.'[99] Fortunately, both the UN and member states now have a base foundation on which to take further action.

The potential for wider systemic change is evident. There are cost-effective and more reliable options that merit serious consideration and action. In the last several years, there have been noteworthy attempts to model the composition of viable UN standing forces.[100] Several of these studies have demonstrated that there are few, if any, insurmountable operational or tactical impediments. One shortcoming, that is also frequently evident in the numerous studies cited since 1945, is the inability to address how such a dedicated UN mechanism might be established. What approach or transition strategy might mobilize political will, attract wider support, increase confidence and restore the necessary momentum?

Both pragmatists and visionaries are aware that the recent political environment was not conducive to the immediate establishment of a UN standing force. Nor, in the earlier period of unprecedented activity, was the Organization prepared to manage additional, controversial capabilities. In addition, by 1997 the former political and diplomatic enthusiasm dissipated quickly when it encountered concerns related to sovereignty, risks, representation, limited support and insufficient financing. Yet rapid changes, ongoing conflicts, and the wider challenges of interdependence, are now altering the former context. We can anticipate a review of contemporary approaches and mechanisms for preventing and resolving violent conflict, including the option of a UN standing capability or force. In the earlier words of Stephen Kinloch, 'driven back, the idea will, as in the past, ineluctably re-emerge, Phoenix-like, at the most favourable opportunity.'[101]

Rather than await the next catastrophe, it is time to consider how additional SHIRBRIGs and dedicated UN standing elements might be introduced as a complementary expansion on current arrangements.[102] In this respect, independent analysis may still be necessary to generate the ideas that can move events.[103] Further progress will likely depend on far wider educational efforts directed not only at the governments of UN member states but also at global civil society. Among the challenges that warrant consideration are:

- Generating a broader public and professional understanding of current UN rapid deployment initiatives and the various options available for enhancing these efforts;
- Coordinating a 'soft power' approach not only to refocus the Security Council and revitalize the 'Friends', but also to organize a transnational coalition and constituency of support among citizens, non-governmental organizations, related agencies and academic communities;
- Planning a coherent, sequence of stages or 'building blocks' to facilitate the further development of UN and multilateral efforts; and
- Building the unity of effort and purpose necessary to coordinate national military and civilian units, as well as the conditions for integrating volunteers into a composite standing UN emergency capability.

Modest progress has been made since William R. Frye made the case for a planned evolution in his seminal 1957 study, *A United Nations Peace Force*. We have yet to achieve Frye's objective, but it is worth recalling his words:

> Establishment of a small, permanent peace force, or the machinery for one, could be the first step on the long road toward order and stability. Progress cannot be forced, but it can be helped to evolve. That which is radical one year can become conservative and accepted the next.[104]

The failure to avert organized mass murder in Rwanda prompted a reappraisal, as well as a multinational process that must now be revitalized and accelerated in the aftermath of Kosovo and East Timor. The phenomenon of 'too little', 'too late', 'too lame' or 'too lethal' has simply gone on for far too long.

ACKNOWLEDGEMENTS

This study expands on several themes presented in 1998 to the Eleventh Annual Meeting of the Academic Council on the United Nations System. It also includes research undertaken while the author was a member of the Core Working Group of the Canadian Study to Enhance a United Nations Rapid Reaction Capability. I am indebted to this group, particularly to Major James Hammond (CF) and Carlton Hughes. A number of individuals in the UN Secretariat provided additional insight and information. Special thanks are extended to: Chris Coleman, First Officer,

Policy and Analysis, DPKO; Andrew Greene, Policy and Analysis; Col. Cees van Egmond, Chief Mission Planning Service; Col. Kulikov, Deputy Director, Mission Planning; Col. Peter Leentjes, Chief Training Unit; Peter Dew, Office of Operations; Comm. Marik Jamke, Head Standby Arrangements Management Unit; Col. Carlos Daniel Ravazzola, Standby Arrangements Management Unit; LTC Bernard Saunders, RDMHQ Implementation Team; Frederick Schottler, Information Officer, DPI; Ambassador David Karsgaard, Permanent Representative of Canada to the United Nations; Ambassador Michel Duval, Permanent Representative of Canada to the United Nations; Gabriel Dueschner, First Officer, Mission of Canada to the United Nations; Paul Meyer, Director, IDC, DFAIT, Canada; Col. Ernie Reumiller, Head Peacekeeping Section, IDC, DFAIT, Canada; Line Poulin, Desk Officer, IDC, DFAIT, Canada; LTC. Ib Sorenson, Military Advisor, Danish Mission to the United Nations; Major Lollesgaard, Asst. MILAD, Danish Mission to the United Nations; LTC. Steve Moffat, Director Peacekeeping Policy, DND, Canada; and Sir Brian Urquhart, former UN Under-Secretary-General. For a very thoughtful review of an earlier draft, my sincere appreciation is extended to Col. (ret.) Douglas Frazer, Director of the Canadian Council for International Peace and Security. Unless otherwise indicated, the views expressed in this article, as well as any errors or omissions, are the author's.

NOTES

1. Major General Franklin van Kappen, Military Advisor to the UN DPKO quoted in 'Standby Arrangement System: Enhancing Rapid Deployment', *UN Chronicle*, No.1, 1997, p.2. (http://www.un.org/Pubs/chroncile/1997/pl3ily97.htm)
2. As noted in a Canadian briefing paper, 'the Security Council adopted a Presidential Statement which strengthens the consultations between the Council and troop contributor nations. The two key changes which enhance this process are: that consultations will be chaired by the Security Council Presidency alone rather than jointly with the UN Secretariat. This advance should allow for future meetings to focus on policy issues and political aspects of new or existing Security Council mandates. The UN Secretariat will continue to chair separate troop contributor meetings to discuss operational issues. The second change is that the Security Council, when considering peacekeeping operations, will now hold meetings with prospective troop contributors that have already been approached by the Secretariat.' See Canada, DFAIT, 'An Update on the Canadian Study, *Towards a Rapid Reaction Capability for the United Nations*', prepared by Daniel Livermore, Director of Regional Security and Peacekeeping, Summer 1996, p.5.
3. The term 'peace support operations' is an elaboration on the former concept of 'wider peacekeeping' involving tasks beyond those associated with traditional peacekeeping to 'cover a wide range of potential operations from conflict prevention to peacemaking, and to provide a doctrine which is relevant to the post-Cold War geostrategic environment'. See, British Ministry of Defence, Joint Warfare Publication 3.01, *Peace Support Operations*, Sept. 1997, thereafter issued as Joint Warfare Publication 3.50. For a thoughtful review see, Tom Woodhouse, 'The Gentle Hand of Peace? British Peacekeeping and Conflict Resolution in Complex Political Emergencies', *International Peacekeeping*, Vol.6, No.2, Summer 1999, pp.24–37.
4. United Nations Security Council, 'Progress Report of the Secretary-General on Standby Arrangements for Peacekeeping', S/1996/1067, 24 Dec. 1996, p.3.
5. A number of these criteria are drawn from the Government of Canada's report, *Towards a Rapid Reaction Capability*, Ottawa, Sept. 1995. See, for example, chapter 2, 'Principles of the Study', pp.8–16.
6. Boutros Boutros-Ghali, *An Agenda for Peace: Preventive Diplomacy, Peacemaking and Peace-keeping*, Report of the Secretary-General Pursuant to the Statement Adopted by the Summit Meeting of the Security Council on 31 Jan. 1992, New York, 17 Jun. 1992 (A/47/277-S/2411), paras. 42–4.
7. See, Brian Urquhart, 'For A U. N. Volunteer Military Force', *The New York Review of Books.*, Vol.XL, No.11, 10 June 1993, pp.3–4. For an early response to the Urquhart proposal, see Lord Richard Carver, 'A UN Volunteer Military Force: Four Views', *The New*

York Review of Books, Vol.XL, No.12, 24 June 1993, p.59.

8. For a more thorough overview of these diverse perspectives see, Stephen P. Kinloch, 'Utopian or Pragmatic? A UN Permanent Military Volunteer Force', *International Peacekeeping*, Vol.3, No.4, Winter 1996, pp.166–90.
9. Canada, Department of National Defence, 'Report on Consultations UN Rapid Reaction Capability Study', May 1995, Prepared by LTC Joe Culligan, DIPOL 3.
10. This was evident as early as August 1992, when US presidential candidate Bill Clinton expressed support for a voluntary UN rapid deployment force. In February 1993, US Secretary of State Warren Christopher informed the UN Secretary-General that the US would back proposals for a UN rapid deployment force. On various occasions, Russian statesmen endorsed UN standby forces, negotiation of Article 43 agreements, and even their readiness to commit forces to a UN army. In 1992 French President François Mitterand called for revitalizing the UN Military Staff Committee and offered to commit 1,000 French soldiers at its disposal on 48 hours' notice with another 1,000 ready for UN service within a week. See the section on 'Presidential Support' and 'International Support' in Capt. Edward I. Dennehy, LTC William J. Droll, Capt. Gregory P. Harker, LTC Stephen M. Speakes, and LTC Fred A. Treyz, III, *A Blue Helmet Combat Force* (Policy Analysis Paper 93–01, National Security Program, Harvard University, 1993, pp.9–10.
11. A number of the early commitments of member states such as the United States and France were overlooked in their subsequent responses to the UN General Assembly and to the Secretary-General's *An Agenda for Peace*. See 'Statement of France', 28 July 1993 in response to *An Agenda for Peace*, in 'Improving the Capacity of the United Nations for Peacekeeping: Report of the Secretary-General–Addendum, UN doe. A/48/403/Add. l/Corr. l, 2 November 1993; and US Presidential Decision Directive 25, or *The Clinton Administration's Policy on Reforming Multilateral Peace Operations*, Washington, DC, US Department of State Publication 10161, May 1994; cited in Adam Roberts, 'Proposals for UN Standing Forces: History, Tasks and Obstacles', in David Cox and Albert Legault (eds.), *UN Rapid Reaction Capabilities: Requirements and Prospects* (Cornwallis: The Canadian Peacekeeping Press, 1995, pp.l–15.
12. Government of The Netherlands, The Netherlands Non-Paper, 'A UN Rapid Deployment Brigade: A preliminary study' (revised version), April 1995, p.3.
13. Ibid., p.4.
14. See Robert C. Johansen, 'UN Peacekeeping: The Changing Utility of Military Force', *Third World Quarterly*, 12 Apr. 1990, pp.53–70.
15. Brian Urquhart, 'For A UN Volunteer Military Force'.
16. The Netherlands (n.12 above), p.5, 8, 14–15, 18.
17. *Towards a Rapid Reaction Capability for the United Nations*, Sep.1995. The report was formally tabled on Sep.26, during the UN's fiftieth anniversary. The rationale for the study was outlined by Canada's Minister of Foreign Affairs, André Ouellet: 'the experience of the last few years leads us to believe that we need to explore even more innovative options than those considered to date. Recent peacekeeping missions have shown that the traditional approach no longer applies. As we have seen in Rwanda, rapid deployment of intervention forces is essential. In light of the situation, the Government of Canada has decided to conduct an in-depth review of the short-, medium- and long-term options available to us to strengthen the UN's rapid response capability in times of crisis. Among these options, we feel the time has come to study the possibility, over the long term of creating a permanent UN military force. We will ask the world's leading experts for their input and will inform all member states of the results of the study.' Notes for An Address by André Ouellet, Minister of Foreign Affairs, to the 49th General Assembly of the United Nations, New York, Sep.29, 1994, p.7.
18. Among the proposals for reform at the political level were the establishment of a troop contributors' committee for each operation; a troop contributors' forum to consider general issues of an operational nature, and; convening informal groups of 'friends' to deal with related issues. Five recommendations pertained to improving various financial procedures. Ibid., pp.37–42. At the strategic level, there were calls for refining the early-warning capabilities of the Secretariat and advancing cooperation with member states toward the

development of an 'early-warning alert' system. The report advised strengthening the Department of Peacekeeping Operations with additional staff, enhancing the office of the Military Advisor, initiating rosters of senior military commanders, developing standing contractual arrangements with suppliers, particularly with respect to the provision of strategic movement, and producing packages of equipment for generic missions. Both the Secretary-General and member states were urged to continue refining and strengthening the Standby Arrangements System established in 1993. The Secretary-General was encouraged to use new techniques such as the 'peacekeeping services agreement' to facilitate more rapid deployment and efficient support services. Member states were asked to explore the advance identification of personnel with expertise in relevant areas to assist the UN in responding to urgent situations. pp.43–46.

19. As indicated in the report's title, a concern arose that the approach should be on enhancing a UN capability rather than simply a force. The increasing complexity of UN operations, as well as the requirement for a coordinated unity of effort also pointed to the need for both a multidimensional and a multifunctional capability.
20. The report noted that the vanguard concept 'is based on the principle of linking all of the levels of the UN system, especially an operational headquarters and mission groups provided by member states at the tactical level, for the purpose of deploying a force as rapidly as possible for a brief period, either to meet an immediate crisis or to anticipate the arrival of follow-on forces or a more traditionally-organised peacekeeping operation.' p.52.
21. Ibid., p.52. 'Both member states and the Secretary-General were encouraged to organise UN standby units into multinational-capability components', corresponding to function, with appropriate training and exercising to enhance readiness. 'These capability components might include some of the newer tasks of multidimensional operations (natural disaster relief, humanitarian emergencies), working in close conjunction with other sectors of the UN and other non-governmental organisations.'
22. Ibid.
23. Ibid., p.55.
24. Denmark, Chief of Defence, 'United Nations Standby Arrangements for Peacekeeping: A Multinational UN Standby Forces High Readiness Brigade', 25 Jan. 1995. Denmark conducted four international seminars between May and August 1995. Participating nations were Argentina, Belgium, Canada, Czech Republic, Denmark, Finland, Ireland, Netherlands, New Zealand, Norway, Poland and Sweden. The DPKO was also represented.
25. See Denmark, Chief of Defence, 'Report by the Working Group on a Multinational UN Standby Forces High Readiness Brigade', 15 Aug. 1995.
26. Ibid., p.9. It was noted that Allied nations with a tradition of peacekeeping were a natural choice when forming the core and setting the standards for a future brigade. Others would have to be encouraged to participate to secure impartiality.
27. 'Report by the Working Group' (n.25 above), pp.10–11.
28. A nation's right to decide whether or not to participate on a case-by-case basis would thus be protected. It was assumed 'this would be accomplished through the maintenance of a brigade pool of "extra" units which would "back up" those units which might not be made available due to national decision.'
29. Canada, DND, 'Report on Consultations UN Rapid Reaction Capability Study', May 1995, prepared by LTC. Joe Culligan, DIPOL 3.
30. Cited in the briefing summary of WKGR8708 – Friends of Rapid Reaction Meeting, 4 December 1995 prepared by Canadian MILAD, Col. Michael Snell.
31. Lloyd Axworthy, Hans van Mierlo, and Niels Helveg Petersen, 'Let's Team Up to Make UN Peacekeeping Work', *International Herald Tribune*, 22 Oct. 1996. (http://www. undp.org/ missions/denmarktpolicy/article. htm)
32. Briefing summary of WKGR8708 (n.30 above), 4 Dec. 1995.
33. Among the other participants attending this meeting were Ministers of Australia, Denmark, New Zealand, Senegal, Nicaragua, Ukraine and Jamaica.
34. See, Canada, DFAIT, 'An Update on the Canadian Study, Towards a Rapid Reaction Capability for the United Nations', Prepared by Daniel Livermore, Director of Regional Security and Peacekeeping, Summer, 1996, p.4.

35. Opinion on the future of the vanguard concept varies with some suggesting it has been replaced and others arguing that it is still being pursued through related arrangements such as the SHIRBRIG.
36. The emphasis for 1997 was initially to be on developing a mechanism to coordinate the activities of peacekeepers, UN police forces, NGOs, and other UN agencies, but the need to arrange clear guidelines for logistics emerged as a more urgent priority.
37. Cited in 'Daily Highlights', 25 October 1996, Central News Section, Department of Public Information, United Nations.
38. Many acknowledge that the Committee of 34 is an exceptionally slow vehicle that does not lend itself to quick action. This was a determining factor in the establishment of the 'Friends' as some member states wanted an informal body to act as a catalyst for change and to stimulate the work of the Committee of 34.
39. See, United Nations, General Assembly, Report of the Special Committee on Peacekeeping Operations, 'Comprehensive Review Of The Whole Question Of Peace-keeping Operations In All Their Aspects', A/50/230, 22 June 1995, Section 3, p.12. Also see, A/51/130, 7 May 1996, Section 5, p.13.
40. See, for example, 'Concerns Over High Readiness Brigade Expressed At Special Committee On Peacekeeping Operations', United Nations, GA/PK/152, 31 March 1998.
41. Cited in Canada, DFAIT, IDC1286, 'Report of the meeting of Foreign Ministers on a Rapid Reaction Capability for the UN', 27 September 1995.
42. For a brief review of the related changes in DPKO see Kofi Annan, 'The Peace-keeping Prescription', in Kevin M. Cahill (ed.), *Preventive Diplomacv: Stopping Wars Before They Start*, New York: Basic Books, 1996, pp.185–6. For a more critical perspective, also see Trevor Findley, 'Armed Conflict Prevention, Management and Resolution', *SIPRI Yearbook 1996: Armaments. Disarmament and International Securitv*, London: Oxford University Press, 1996, pp.53–60.
43. DPKO's Training Unit has written training guidelines, manuals and other materials to assist member states in preparing military, civilian and police personnel for UN assignments. Aside from its numerous publications, the Training Unit has also helped to improve and standardise peacekeeping training through seminars, workshops and training assistance teams.
44. The Mission Planning Service is the focal point for all peacekeeping planning. Its activities include: generic guidelines and procedures to streamline the process of mission planning; generic guidelines for troop-contributing countries, from which mission-specific guidelines are formulated; the preparation of standard operating procedures for essential functions; and in-house studies pertaining to important issues such as command and control, rules of engagement, structure of mission headquarters, etc. See 'General Framework', United Nations Peacekeeping' (http:/hvww.un.org:80/Depts/dpko/MP.HTM)
45. Boutros Boutros-Ghali, *Supplement to An Agenda for Peace*: Position Paper of the Secretary-General on the Occasion of the Fiftieth Anniversary of the United Nations, A/50/60, S/1995/1, January 3, 1995.
46. 'In these circumstances', the Secretary-General wrote, 'I have come to the conclusion that the United Nations does need to give serious thought to the idea of a rapid reaction force. Such a force would be the Security Council's strategic reserve for deployment when there was an emergency need for peacekeeping troops. It might comprise battalion-sized units from a number of member countries.' As he noted, 'these units would be trained to the same standards, use the same operating procedures, be equipped with integrated communications equipment and take part in joint exercises at regular intervals. They would be stationed in their home countries but maintained at a high state of readiness.' Ibid., p.11, para. 44.
47. See for example, Boutros Boutros-Ghali, 'Empowering the United Nations', *Foreign Affairs*, 1992, p.93. At the time, the UN Secretary-General suggested the solution was 'to extend and make more systematic standby arrangements by which governments commit themselves to hold ready, at an agreed period of notice, specially trained units for peacekeeping service'.
48. See, Statement by the President of the Security Council on 22 February 1995 (S/PRST/1995/9).
49. For a response to this statement and the impression that the Security Council had voiced its opposition to a rapid reaction force see, N.H. Biegman, Dutch Ambassador to the UN in New

York, 'The Netherlands gain honour with the idea for a UN brigade', *De Volksrant*, 1 March 1995. However, for some within military institutions opposed to a standing force, the message was interpreted as a decisive 'no' to the option. For example see, Canada, DND Facsimilie, 'Rapid Reaction Capability Study Communications Plan', from Col. M.W. Appelton, SPP 3, 3450-1 to Lt. Col. Bentley, 28 July 1995.

50. United Nations Press Release, GA/9212, 18 December 1996, p.9. It is noteworthy that the Secretary-General went on to state that 'a Government like Denmark's has set up a 5,000 man and woman brigade that could be deployed fairly quickly. It has indicated that the headquarters elements can be deployed within 48 hours and the bulk of the force within a month. If we can encourage 12 or 20 member states to do this, 12 or 20 member states who will have the will to respond if the Council makes an appeal, we should be able to reduce considerably the time it takes us to deploy troops in the field.'
51. It should be noted that the UN began to construct a system of stand by forces in 1964, but only a small number of member states demonstrated a willingness to enter into any related arrangement with the UN.
52. See United Nations, DPKO, 'United Nations Standby Arrangements System Description'. Also see United Nations, Security Council, 'Progress Report Of The Secretary-General On Standby Arrangements For Peacekeeping' (S/1996/1067) 24 December 1996.
53. See, United Nations Department of Peacekeeping Operations, 'Monthly Status Report: United Nations Standby Arrangements', Status Report as of 1 March 2000 (http://www.un.org/Depts/dpko/rapid/str.htm)
54. See United Nations DPKO, 'Annual Update Briefing to Member States on Standby Arrangements', 29 May 1997, p.2.
55. As reported, the information available under the standby arrangements proved most helpful in the planning for and subsequent deployment of peacekeeping operations in Haiti, Angola, and the former Yugoslavia, in particular the successful United Nations Transitional Administration in Eastern Slavonia, Baranja, and Western Sirmium (UNTAES). More recently, the UNSAS helped officials coordinate the preventive deployment operation (MINURCA) for the Central African Republic. Favourable circumstances in this instance also facilitated a rapid deployment.
56. Among the other determining factors noted are 'political approval and support at the national level, availability of airlift/sea-lift, a capacity for mission management and logistic sustainment in the field, as well as the conclusion of the necessary administrative procedures'.
57. Notably, the Special Committee on Peacekeeping Operations also urged the Secretary-General to develop a rapidly deployable headquarters team in their spring 1995 report. This request was subsequently endorsed by the General Assembly in Resolution 50/30(1995). The proposal for such a headquarters was also at the forefront of the priorities of the Friends of Rapid Deployment. It was reported that the Friends Group also submitted a similar proposal to the Secretary-General. See 'Rapid-reaction headquarters possible by fall: Canadian led proposal calls for small group to assess world crises', *Ottawa Citizen*, 23 July 1996.
58. See Major-General Frank Van Kappen, Military Advisor to the Secretary-General, 'Presentation on the Rapidly Deployable Mission Headquarters (RDMHQ)', to the Special Committee on Peacekeeping Operations, 24 October 1996. Also cited in Peacekeeping Operations Committee - 5 - Press Release PK/144 140th Meeting, 24 October 1996. Once operational, the UNRDMHQ should begin to fill the gap in DPKO's initial management of UN operations. In the past, there was a risk of serious operational difficulties and complications arising when military contingents and other components arrived in the mission area to operate over extended periods without a proper mission headquarters.
59. Major-General Frank Van Kappen, 'Presentation on the RDMHQ', 24 October 1996, pp.4–7.
60. Friends of Rapid Deployment, Technical Working Group Paper, 'A Rapidly Deployable Headquarters: Roles, Functions and Implementation', 26 March 1996. As this paper noted, 'this headquarters would be multinational, drawing its personnel widely from contributing member states of all regions. It would also be multidimensional, reflecting the requirements of the more complex operations of the 1990s, with a substantive civilian staff of diverse experience in the areas of civilian police, humanitarian assistance, human rights and legal

affairs. This headquarters would be a 'first-in, first-out' operation, moving into an area rapidly but capable of being removed equally quickly. It should be capable of directing at least 5,000 personnel, possibly more if it is augmented at the time of deployment. This staff, seconded or loaned by member states to the UN Secretariat, could be deployed into a theatre of operations under the authority of the Security Council and at the direction of the Secretary-General but without further authorisation at the national level.'

61. 'At the UN, A proposal to speed aid during crises', *New York Times*, 21 July 1996. Cited in, Patrick A. McCarthy, 'Towards an Independent United Nations Peacekeeping Capability', paper presented at the eleventh annual meeting of the Academic Council on the United Nations System (ACUNS), The Pearson Peacekeeping Training Centre, Cornwallis, Nova Scotia, 18 June 1998.
62. The two RDMHQ positions that received approval for funding in 1998 were in civilian police and humanitarian affairs.
63. United Nations Special Committee on Peacekeeping, Draft of 'Proposals, Recommendations and Conclusions', March 2000.
64. United Nations Department of Peacekeeping Operations, 'Review of the Rapidly Deployable Mission Headquaters Concept' (Excerpt from the Report of the Secretary-General on the Support Account for Peacekeeping Operations, 9 March 2000).
65. Ministry of Foreign Affairs, Denmark, 'Background Paper about establishing a Multinational UN Standby Forces Brigade at High Readiness (SHIRBRIG), Meeting of Foreign Affairs Ministers in the 'Friends of Rapid Deployment' Group, New York, 26 September 1996. (http://www.undp.org/missions/denmark/policy/shirbrig.htm)
66. Austria, Canada, the Netherlands, Norway, Poland, Sweden and Denmark. The Czech Republic, Finland and Ireland participated in the signing ceremony as observers. See 'Status in the establishment of the Multinational UN Standby Forces High Readiness Brigade', Danish Ministry of Defence, December 19, 1996. (http://www.undp.org/missions/denmark/policy/standby.htm)
67. Among the new members are: Argentina, Italy, Jordan, Romania and Spain. Belgium, the Czech Republic, Hungary, Ireland, Portugal and Slovenia are also participating as observers but have yet to sign a Memorandum of Understanding indicating their specific commitment.
68. Moreover, Danish officials write that when SHIRBRIG is deployed it will be 'subject to UN command and control arrangements and operate exclusively under the direction of the Secretary-General or his Special Representative and under the operational control of the Force Commander for the operation.' Ministry of Foreign Affairs, Denmark, 'Background Paper about establishing a Multinational UN Standby Forces Brigade at High Readiness (SHIRBRIG), pp.1–2.
69. Ibid., p.2.
70. For example, the Southern African Development Community (SADC) is pursuing a cooperative arrangement similar to that of the SHIRBRIG, albeit without sufficient funding to effectively organise their brigade. There are also indications that a coalition of states in South Eastern Europe are engaged in related plans.
71. Canada, DFAIT, 'An Update on the Canadian Study: Towards A Rapid Reaction Capability for the United Nations', Briefing Paper prepared by Daniel Livermore, Director, IDC, Summer 1996, p.4.
72. Cited in 'Daily Highlights', 25 October 1996, Central News Section, Department of Public Information, United Nations.
73. Statement by Hans van Merlo, Deputy Prime Minister and Minister of Foreign Affairs of The Kingdom of the Netherlands, 'The United Nations: Joining Forces', 23 September 1997, p.3. (http://www.undp.org/missions/netherlands/speeches/52ndga.htm#rapid)
74. Attempts to secure funding and wider political support for the RDMHQ's eight core positions were insufficient and repeatedly stymied. Several nations agreed to supply personnel, as well as a percentage of start-up costs in a specific trust fund. However, gratis personnel raised concerns over equitable opportunity for personnel of developing nations and the trust funds did not attract sufficient money. Some officials remain confident the required resources will eventually clear the committee approval process.
75. Boutros Boutros-Ghali (n.45 above), p.11, para 43–4.

76. The former Secretary-General previously cautioned, 'the system of standby arrangements does not so far ensure the reliability and speed of response which is required in such emergencies. It is essential that the necessary capabilities are reliably available when they are needed and can be deployed with the speed dictated by the situations. It is evident that member states possess such capabilities; what is needed is the will to make them available for the execution of Security Council mandates.' Cited in, 'Peace-keeping in a Changing Context'. (http://www.un.org)
77. Boutros-Ghali, *Supplement to An Agenda for Peace*, p.18, para. 43.
78. As Kofi Annan wrote, 'rapid response is vital particularly from a preventive perspective, because in cases like Rwanda, the conflict's worst effects are often felt in its earliest stages. A rapid response is thus essential if we are effectively to limit the range, extent and momentum of a conflict.' Kofi Annan, 'The Peacekeeping Prescription', in Cahill (n.42 above), p.184.
79. Sir Brian Urquhart, 'Prospects for a UN Rapid Response Capability', Address to the Twenty Fifth Vienna Seminar on Peacemaking and Peace-keeping for the Next Century, Government of Austria and the International Peace Academy, Vienna, 3 March 1995, p.6.
80. Ibid., p.7.
81. Confusion was partially compounded by the announcement that the Government of Canada would be conducting an in-depth study into the option of a UN Standing Force.
82. See 'United Nations Standby Arrangements: System Description', p.2.
83. Kofi A. Annan, 'P.K. and Crisis Management: Where are we going?' Tokyo, 23 Sept.1996, pp.3–8.
84. Fortunately, the arrangements now being implemented are not a 'done deal'. They represent a promising start, yet they need not, and should not, be viewed as having achieved sufficient reliability or a sophisticated capability.
85. This section draws on the previous work of Peter Langille, Maxime Faille, Carlton Hughes, and Major James Hammond, 'A Preliminary Blueprint of Long-Term Options for Enhancing a UN Rapid Reaction Capability', in Cox and Legault (n.11 above), pp.179–200.
86. Report of the Commission on Global Governance, *Our Global Neighbourhood*, New York: Oxford University Press, 1995, p.112.
87. The Report of the Independent Working Group on the Future of the United Nations, *The United Nations In Its Second Half-Century* (a project supported by Yale University and the Ford Foundation) 1995, pp.21–23.
88. Carnegie Commission on Preventing Deadly Conflict, *Preventing Deadly Conflict: Final Report*, Washington, DC: Carnegie Commission on Preventing Deadly Conflict, 1997, p.66. It should be noted that this report did not endorse UN volunteers but proposed the establishment of rapid reaction force of 5,000 to 10,000 troops to be drawn from sitting members of the Security Council.
89. Canada, DFAIT, 'Improving the 'UN's Rapid Reaction Capability: Discussion Paper', 29 April 1995, p.3.
90. For a recent variation of this argument see, Lionell Rosenblatt and Larry Thompson, 'The Door of Opportunity: Creating a Permanent Peacekeeping Force', *World Policy Journal*, Spring 1998, pp.36–42.
91. Brian Urquhart elaborates on this point: 'Experience of recent UN operations shows that even a small, highly-trained group, with high morale and dedication, arriving at the scene of action immediately after a Security Council decision, would in most cases have far greater effect than a larger and less well prepared force arriving weeks or even months later. The failure to come to grips with a situation before it gets completely out of hand usually necessitates a far larger, more expensive and less effective operation later on.' See Urquhart, 'Prospects for a UN Rapid Response Capability', in Cox and Legault (n.11 above), pp.3–35.
92. Ibid. p.196. For further detailed analysis of similar projected expenses see, Jean Krasno, 'A United Nation's Rapid-Deployment Permanent Force: Cost Analysis' (paper prepared for the Yale University United Nations Study Program, 1994).
93. Carl Kaysen and George Rathjens, *Peace Operation by the United Nations: The Need for a Volunteer Military Force*, Cambridge, MA: Committee on International Security Studies, 1996, p.13.

94. 'Report by the Working Group on a Multinational UN Standby Forces High Readiness Brigade', p.7.
95. *Towards a Rapid Reaction Capability* (n.17 above), p.62.
96. Canada, DFAIT, 'Canada Announces a Study to Improve the UN's Rapid Reaction Capability', Press Release No.l, 4 July 1995, p.4.
97. The term 'soft power' has been interpreted as entailing the ability to communicate, negotiate, mobilise opinion, work within multilateral bodies and promote international initiatives. It is essentially about increasing political leverage to advance peaceful change by building new partnerships and coalitions not only between governments, but also with other elements of civil society such as NGOs, related agencies, the media and interested parties. The term was coined by Joseph S. Nye, Jr. in, *Bound to Lead: The Changing Nature of American Power*, New York: Basic Books, 1990. It has since become a foreign policy strategy for a growing number of small and middle powers. For a Canadian perspective see, Lloyd Axworthy, 'Why 'soft power' is the right policy for Canada', *Ottawa Citizen*, 25 April 1998.
98. Even prior to the League of Nations, it was understood that an effective collective security system would provide states with more than simply a security guarantor. For one, it would reduce tensions, thereby, allowing all to reduce their national defence expenditures and devote those resources to other pressing challenges. It would also restore the conditions necessary for wider, if not universal, disarmament. In short, an empowered UN holds considerable promise to introduce further cooperation in a mutually-reinforcing and progressively positive manner. For a more contemporary assessment of the potential of UN rapid deployment capabilities see, The Centre for Defense Information, 'The United Nations at Fifty: A Force for the Future', *The Defense Monitor*, Vol.XXV, No.1, 1 January 1996.
99. Kofi Annan, 'The Peacekeeping Prescription', in Cahill (n.42 above), p.l86.
100. Aside from the Netherlands 'Non-Paper' and a section of the Canadian study, see Kaysen and Rathjens, *Peace Operations by the United Nations: The Case for a Volunteer UN Military Force*; Carl Conetta and Charles Knight, *Vital Force: A Proposal for the Overhaul of the UN Peace Operations System and for the Creation of a UN Legion*, Cambridge, MA, Commonwealth Institute, 1995; and Sir Brian Urquhart, 'Prospects for a UN Rapid Response Capability', in Cox and Legault (n.11 above), pp.30–35. Also see, Joseph E. Schwartzberg, 'A New Perspective on Peacekeeping: Lessons from Bosnia and Elsewhere', *Global Governance*, Vol.3, No.1, Jan.–April 1997, pp.1–15.
101. Stephen P. Kinloch, 'Utopian or Pragmatic? A UN Permanent Military Volunteer Force', *International Peacekeeping*, Vol.3, No.4, Winter 1996, p.185.
102. For a thoughtful example of recent work that encourages building on current UNSAS arrangements with Article 43 agreements, leading to a UN Volunteer Force see, Patrick A. McCarthy, 'Towards an Independent United Nations Peacekeeping Capability'. For an earlier attempt at outlining this stage-by-stage process, see Langille, Faille, Hughes and Hammond (n.83 above).
103. Unfortunately, at least in the near term, there is unlikely to be further research of this evolution within government. Major-General Frank van Kappen suggested that a study of a UN Standing Emergency Group would have to be conducted in cooperation with other UN Departments. Yet, one should not be overly optimistic about the prospects of these departments engaging in a cooperative inquiry that many member states do not support. Van Kappen acknowledged, however, that 'further studies could be done by establishing working groups to present their reports to DPKO. Working Groups could either be established within UNHQ and/or member states could sponsor a working group. Studies could be conducted in a sponsor country with participants from member states, as well as from UNHQ.' See, Major-General Frank van Kappen, MILAD, DPKO, 'Implementation of the Canadian Recommendation on Rapid Reaction Capability', Summary of Presentation on 4 Dec. 1995, pp.1–4.
104. William R. Frye, *A United Nations Peace Force,* New York: Oceana Publications, 1957, pp.106–7.

Select Bibliography

Adibe, Clement E., 'Learning from the Failure of Disarmament and Conflict Resolution in Somalia', in Edward Moxon-Browne (ed.). *A Future for Peacekeeping?* Basingstoke: Macmillan, 1997.

Alden, C., 'Swords into Ploughshares? The United Nations and Demilitarization in Mozambique', *International Peacekeeping*, Vol.2, No.2, 1995, pp.175–93.

Alger, Chadwick F. (ed.), *The Future of the United Nations System: Potential for the Twenty-First Century*, Tokyo: United Nations University Press, 1998.

Anderson, Mary, *Do No Harm: Supporting Local Capacities for Peace through Aid*, Cambridge MA: The Collaborative Project for Development Action, 1996.

Kofi, Annan, 'The Peace-keeping Prescription', Kevin M. Cahill (ed.), *Preventive Diplomacv: Stopping Wars Before They Start*, New York: Basic Books, 1996.

Anstee, Margaret, *Orphan of the Cold War: The Inside Story of the Collapse of the Angolan Peace Process 1992–93*, Basingstoke: Macmillan, 1996.

Avruch, Kevin, *Culture & Conflict Resolution*, Washington, DC: United States Institute of Peace, 1998.

Avruch, Kevin and Peter Black, 'A Generic Theory of Conflict Resolution: A Critique', *Negotiation Journal*, Vol.3, No.1, 1987, pp.87–96.

Avruch, Kevin and Peter Black, 'The Culture Question and Conflict Resolution', *Peace and Change*, Vol.16, No.1, 1991, pp.22 45.

Avruch, Kevin, Peter W. Black, and Joseph A. Scimecca (eds.), *Conflict Resolution: Cross-Cultural Perspectives*, London: Greenwood Press, 1991.

Axelrod, Robert, *The Evolution of Cooperation*, New York: Basic Books, 1984.

Azar, Edward E., *The Management of Protracted Social Conflict: Theory and Cases*, Aldershot: Dartmouth, 1990.

Babbitt, Eileen F., 'The Contribution of Training to Conflict Resolution', in Zartman and Rasmussen (eds.), *Peacemaking in International Conflict*, Washington, DC: U.S. Institute of Peace, 1997.

Bendaña, A. 'Conflict Resolution: Empowerment and Disempowerment,' *Peace & Change*, Vol.21, No.1, 1996, pp.69–70.

Bercovitch, Jacob (ed.), *Resolving International Conflicts: The Theory and Practice of Mediation*, London and Boulder: Lynne Reiner, 1996.

Bercovitch, Jacob and Jeffrey Rubin (eds.), *Mediation in International Relations: Multiple Approaches to Conflict Management*, New York: St. Martin's Press, 1992.

Berdal, Mats R., 'Fateful Encounter: The United States and UN Peacekeeping', *Survival*, Vol.36, No.1, 1994.

Bertram, E., 'Reinventing governments: the promise and perils of United Nations Peacebuilding', *Journal of Conflict Resolution*, Vol.39, No.3, 1995, pp.387–418.

Betts, Richard, 'The Delusion of Impartial Intervention', *Foreign Affairs*, Vol.73, No.6, 1994, pp.20–33.

Bloomfield, David, *Peacemaking Strategies in Northern Ireland: Building Complementarity in Conflict Management Theory*, Basingstoke: Macmillan, 1996.

Bradbury, Mark, *The Somali Conflict: Prospects for Peace*, Oxford:Oxfam, 1994.

Boraine, A., J. Levy and R. Scheffer (eds.), *Dealing with the Past: Truth and Reconciliation in South Africa*, IDASA, 1997.

Boulding, Elise, *Building A Global Civic Culture*, Syracuse, NY: Syracuse University Press, 1990.

Boulding, Elise and Jan Oberg, 'United Nations Peacekeeping and NGO Peace-building: Towards Partnership', in Alger (ed.), 1998, pp.127–54.

Boutros-Ghali, Boutros, *An Agenda for Peace* New York: United Nations, 1992.

Burton, John W., *Conflict: Resolution and Provention*, London: Macmillan, 1990.

Burton, John W., *Violence Explained* Manchester: Manchester University, 1997.

Burton, John W. and Frank Dukes (eds.), *Conflict: Readings in Management and Resolution*, London: Macmillan, 1990.

John .W. Burton and Dennis J.D. Sandole, 'Generic Theory: The Basis of Conflict Resolution', *Negotiation Journal*, Vol.2, No.2, 1986 pp.333–44.

Burton, John W. and Dennis J.D. Sandole, 'Expanding the Debate on Generic Theory of Conflict Resolution: A Response to Critique', *Negotiation Journal*, Vol.3, No.1, 1987, pp.97–100.

Byrne, Sean, and Michael Ayulo, 'External Economic Aid in Ethno-Political Conflict: A View From Northern Ireland', *Security Dialogue*, Vol.29, No.4, 1998, pp.421–34.

Byrne, Sean and Neal Carter, 'Social Cubism: Six Social Forces of Ethnoterritorial Politics in Northern Ireland and Quebec', *Peace and Conflict Studies*, Vol.3, No.2, 1996, pp.52–72.

Cahill, Kevin M. (ed.), *Preventive Diplomacy: Stopping Wars Before Thev Start*, New York: Basic Books, 1996.

Carment, David and Patrick James (eds.), *Peace in the Midst of Wars: Preventing and Managing International Ethnic Conflicts* Columbia: University of South Carolina Press, 1998.

Chopra, Jarat (ed.), *The Politics of Peace Maintenance* Boulder: Lynne Rienner, 1998.

Clapham, Christopher, 'Rwanda: The Perils of Peacemaking', *Journal of Peace Research*, Vol.35, No.2, 1998, pp.193–210.

Cox, David and Albert Legault (eds.), *UN Rapid Reaction Capabilities: Requirements and Prospects*, Cornwallis: The Canadian Peacekeeping Press, 1995.

Cox, Robert, 'An Alternative Approach to Multi-lateralism for the Twenty-first Century', *Global Governance*, Vol.3, No.111, 1997.

Conetta, Carl, and Charles Knight, *Vital Force: A Proposal for the Overhaul of the UN Peace Operations System and for the Creation of a UN Legion*, Cambridge, MA, Commonwealth Institute, 1995.

Crocker, Chester, Fen Osler Hampson and Pamela Aall, *Managing Global Chaos: Sources and Responses to International Conflict*, Washington D.C.: USIP Press, 1996.

Curle, Adam, *Making Peace*, London: Tavistock, 1971.

Curle, Adam, *Tools for Transformation: A Personal Study*, Wallbridge: Hawthorn Press, 1990.

Curle, Adam, 'New challenges for citizen peacemaking' *Medicine and War*, Vol.10, No.2, 1994, pp.96–105.

Daniel, Donald C.F. and Bradd C. Hayes with Chantal de Jonge Oudraat, *Coercive Inducement and the Containment of International Crises*, Washington, DC: U.S. Institute of Peace Press, 1999.

Diehl, Paul F., Daniel Druckman and J. Wall, 'International Peacekeeping and Conflict Resolution,' *Journal of Conflict Resolution*, 42(1), 1998, p.34.

Dixon, Paul, 'Paths to Peace in Northern Ireland: Civil Society and Consociational Approaches' *Democratization*, Vol.4, No.2, 1997, pp.1–27.

Dobbie, Charles, 'A Concept for Post-Cold War Peacekeeping', *Survival*, Vol.36, No.3, 1994.

Doyle, Michael W., *UN Peacekeeping in Cambodia: UNTAC's Civil Mandate* Boulder: Lynne Rienner for International Peace Academy, 1995.

Duffield, Mark, 'Evaluating conflict resolution-contexts, models and methodology', In: Gunnar M. Sorbo, Joanna Macrae, and Lennart Wohlegemuth (eds.), 1997, pp.79–112.

Durch, William J. *UN Peacekeeping, American Politics and the Uncivil Wars of the 1990s*, New York: St. Martin's Press, 1996.

Eriksson, John (ed.), *The International Response to Conflict and Genocide: Lessons from the Rwanda Experience*, Copenhagen: DANIDA/Steering Committee of Joint Evaluation of Emergency Assistance to Rwanda, 1996 (Three volumes).

Fetherston, A.B., *Towards a Theory of United Nations Peacekeeping*, London: Macmillan, 1994.

Fetherston, A.B. and Carolyn Nordstrom, 'Overcoming *Habitus* in Conflict Management: UN Peacekeeping and War Zone Ethnography', *Peace and Change*, Vol.20, No.1, 1995, pp.94–119.

Fetherston, A.B., Oliver Ramsbotham and Tom Woodhouse, 'UNPROFOR: Some Observations from a Conflict Resolution Perspective', *International Peacekeeping*, Vol.1, No.2, 1994, pp.179–203.

Findlay, Trevor, *Cambodia: The Legacy and Lessons of UNTAC*, Oxford: OUP for SIPRI, 1995.

Fishel, John T. (ed.), *The Savage Wars of Peace: Toward a New Paradigm of Peace Operations*, Boulder CO: Westview Press, 1998.

Fisher, Ronald, 'Third Party Consultation as a Method of Inter-Group Conflict Resolution: A Review of Studies', *Journal of Conflict Resolution*, Vol.27, No.2, 1983, pp.301–34.

Fisher, Ronald, *Interactive Conflict Resolution: Pioneers, Potential and Prospects* Syracuse: Syracuse UP, 1996.

Fisher, Ronald and Loraleigh Keashly, 'The Potential Complementarity of Mediation and Consultation Within a Contingency Model of Conflict Resolution', *Journal of Peace Research*, Vol.28, No.1, 1991, pp.29–42.

Galtung, Johan, 'A Structural Theory of Imperialism', *Journal of Peace Research*, Vol.8, No.2, 1971, pp.81–117.

Galtung, Johan, 'Three Approaches to Peace: Peacekeeping, Peacemaking, and Peacebuilding' in *Peace, War and Defence: Essays in Peace Research Volume II*, Copenhagen: Christian Eljers, 1976, pp.282–304.

Galtung, Johan, 'Cultural violence', *Journal of Peace Research*, Vol.27, No.3, 1981, pp.291–305.

Galtung, Johan, *Peace by Peaceful Means: Peace and Conflict, Development and Civilization*, London: Sage, 1996.

Ghosh, Amitav, 'The Global Reservation: Notes Toward an Ethnography of International Peacekeeping', *Cultural Anthropology*, Vol.9, No.3, 1994, pp.412–422.

Ginifer, Jeremy (ed.), *Beyond the Emergency: Development Within UN Peace Missions*, London: Frank Cass, 1997.

van de Goor, Luc, Kumar Rupesinghe and Paul Sciarone (eds.), *Between Development and Destruction: An Enquiry into the Causes of Conflict in Post-Colonial States*, New York: St. Martin's Press, 1996.

Gordenker, Leon and Thomas G. Weiss (eds.), *Soldiers, Peacekeepers and Disasters*, Basingstoke: Macmillan, 1991.

Gordenker, Leon and Thomas G. Weiss, 'Pluralizing Global Governance: Analytical

Approaches and Dimensions', in Thomas G. Weiss and Leon Gordenker (eds.), *NGOs, the UN, and Global Governance*, Boulder: Lynne Rienner, 1996.

Gurr, Ted Robert, *Minorities at Risk: A Global View of Ethnopolitical Conflicts*, Washington D.C.:USIP Press, 1993.

Gurr, Ted Robert and Barbara Harff, 'Systematic Early Warning of Humanitarian Emergencies', *Journal of Peace Research*, Vol.3, No.5, 1998, pp.557–80.

Habermas, Jurgen, *The Philosophical Discourse of Modernity* (trans. F. Lawrence, 1987), Cambridge: Polity Press, 1985.

Hampson, Fen Osler, *Nurturing Peace: Why Peace Settlements Succeed or Fail*, Washington DC: United States Institute of Peace Press, 1996.

Harbottle, M., *The Blue Berets: The Story of the United Nations Peacekeeping Forces*, London: Leo Cooper, 1971.

Hare, Paul, *Angola's Last Best Chance for Peace, An Insider's Account of the Peace Process* Washington D.C: United States Institute of Peace, 1998.

Harty, Martha and John Modell, 'The First Conflict Resolution Movement, 1956–1971: An Attempt to Institutionalize Applied Interdisciplinary Social Science', *Journal of Conflict Resolution*, Vol.35, No.4, December 1991, pp.720–58.

Heiberg, Marianne, 'Peacekeepers and Local Populations: Some Comments on UNIFIL', in Rikye and Skjelsbaek (eds.), *The United Nations and Peacekeeping*, Basingstoke: Macmillan, 1990, pp.147–69.

Heinrich, Wolfgang, *Building the Peace: Experiences of Collaborative Peacebuilding in Somalia, 1993–1996*, Uppsala: Life & Peace Institute, 1997.

Irvin, Cynthia and Sean Byrne, *The Politics and Practice of External Economic Assistance in Resolving Protracted Ethnic Conflicts: Lessons From Northern Ireland*, Washington DC: United States Institute of Peace Press, Forthcoming.

Jabri, Vivian, *Discourses on Violence: Conflict Analysis Reconsidered*, Manchester: Manchester University Press, 1996.

Johansen, Robert C., 'UN Peacekeeping: The Changing Utility of Military Force', *Third World Quarterly*, 12 April 1990.

Kaldor, Mary, *New and Old Wars*, Polity Press, Cambridge, 1999.

Kaysen, Carl and George Rathjens, *Peace Operation by the United Nations: The Need for a Volunteer Military Force*, Cambridge, MA: Committee on International Security Studies, 1996.

Keashly, Loraleigh and Ronald Fisher, 'A Contingency Approach on Conflict Interventions: Theoretical and Practical Considerations', in Jacob Bercovitch (ed.), *Resolving International Conflicts: the Theory and Practice of Mediation* (Boulder: Lynne Rienner, 1996, pp.235–63.

Keashly, Loraleigh and Ronald Fisher, 'Towards A Contingency Approach to Third Party Intervention in Regional Conflict: A Cyprus Illustration', *International Journal* Vol.45, No.1, 1990, pp.424–53.

Kelman, Herbert, 'Group Processes in the Resolution of International Conflicts: Experiences From the Israeli–Palestinian Case', *The American Psychologist*, Vol.52, No.3, 1997, pp.212–20.

Kelman, Herbert, 'Interactive Problem Solving: The Uses and Limits of a Therapeutic Model for the Resolution of International Conflicts', in Vamik Volkan, Demetrious Julius and Joseph Montville (eds.), *The Psychodynamics of International Relationships: Unofficial Diplomacy At Work*, Lexington, MA: Lexington Books, 1991, pp.145–60.

Kieseker, Peter, 'Relationships Between Non-Government Organisations and

Multinational Forces in the Field', in Hugh Smith (ed.), *Peacekeeping: Challenges for the Future*, Canberra: Australian Defence Force Academy, 1993.

Kimmel, Paul R., 'Cultural and Ethnic Issues of Conflict and Peacekeeping', in Harvey Langholtz (ed.), *The Psychology of Peacekeeping*, London: Praeger, 1998, pp.57–71.

Kinloch, Stephen P., 'Utopian or Pragmatic? A UN Permanent Military Volunteer Force', *International Peacekeeping*, Vol.3, No.4, Winter 1996, pp.166–90.

Kleiboer, Marieke, *The Multiple Realities of International Mediation*, Boulder, CO: Lynne Rienner, 1998.

Kriesberg, Louis, 'The Development of the Conflict Resolution Field', in I. William Zartman and J. Lewis Rasmussen (eds.), *Peacemaking in International Conflict: Methods and Techniques*, Washington, DC: U.S. Institute of Peace Press, 1997.

Kriesberg, Louis, *Constructive Conflicts: From Escalation to Resolution*, Boulder: Rowman and Littlefield, 1998.

Krska, V., 'Peacekeeping in Angola', *International Peacekeeping*, Vol.4, No.1, 1997, pp.75–92.

Kumar, Krishna (ed.), *Rebuilding Societies After Civil War*, Boulder: Lynne Rienner, 1997.

Langille, H. Peter *et al.*, 'A Preliminary Blueprint of Long-Term Options for Enhancing a UN Rapid Reaction Capability', in David Cox and Albert Legault (eds.), *UN Rapid Reaction Capabilities: Requirements and Prospects*, Cornwallis: The Lester B. Pearson Canadian International Peacekeeping Training Centre, 1995.

Lary, Diana, *Warlord Soldiers*, Cambridge University Press, 1985.

Last, David, *Theory, Doctrine and Practice of Conflict De-Escalation in Peacekeeping Operations*, Clementsport, Nova Scotia: The Canadian Peacekeeping Press, 1997.

Laue, James H., 'Contributions to the Emerging Field of Conflict Resolution', in W. Scott Thompson and Kenneth M. Jensen with Richard N. Smith and K.M. Schraub, *Approaches to Peace: An Intellectual Map*, Washington, DC: U.S. Institute of Peace Press, 1992.

Lederach, John Paul, *Preparing for Peace: Conflict Transformation Across Cultures*, Syracuse: Syracuse University Press, 1995.

Lederach, John Paul, *Building Peace: Sustainable Reconciliation in Divided Societies*, Washington, DC: United States Institute of Peace, 1997.

Lewer, Nick, 'International NGOs and Peacebuilding: Perspectives from Peace Studies and Conflict Resolution', *Centre for Conflict Resolution, Working Paper No.3*, University of Bradford, October 1999.

Lewis, Ioan M., *Somalia, The Roots of Reconciliation: Peacemaking Endeavours of Contemporary Lineage Leaders – A Survey of Grassroots Peace Conferences in 'Somaliland'*, London: ACTIONAID, 1993.

Lizée, Pierre, 'Peacekeeping, Peacebuilding and the Challenge of Conflict Resolution in Cambodia', in Charters (ed.), *Peacekeeping and the Challenge of Civil Conflict Resolution*, New Brunswick: Centre for Conflict Studies, University of New Brunswick, 1994, pp.135–48.

Lund, Michael, *Preventing Violent Conflicts: A Strategy for Preventive Diplomacy* Washington D.C.: USIP Press, 1996.

Luttwak, Edward, 'Give War a Chance', *Foreign Affairs*, Vol.78, No.4, 1999.

Mackinlay, John (ed.), *A Guide to Peace Support Operations*, Providence, Rhode Island: The Thomas J. Watson, Jr. Institute for International Studies, Brown University, 1996.

Malaquias, A., 'The UN in Mozambique and Angola: Lessons Learned, *International Peacekeeping*, Vol.3, No.2, 1996, pp.87–103.

Mccord, Edward, *The Power of the Gun*, Berkeley: University of California Press, 1993.

Menkhaus, Ken, 'International Peacebuilding and the Dynamics of Local and National Reconciliation in Somalia', *International Peacekeeping*, Vol.3, No.1, 1996.

Moxon-Browne, Edward (ed.), *A Future for Peacekeeping?* Basingstoke: Macmillan, 1998.

Miall, Hugh, Oliver Ramsbotham and Tom Woodhouse, *Contemporary Conflict Resolution*, Cambridge: Polity Press, 1999.

Mitchell, Christopher R., *The Structure of International Conflict*, Basingstoke: Macmillan, 1981.

Nordstrom, Carolyn and J. Martin (eds.), *The Paths to Domination, Resistance, and Terror*, Berkeley: University of California Press, 1992.

Oakley, Robert and David Bentley, *Peace Operations: A Comparison of Somalia and Haiti*, Strategic Forum, No.30, Ft. McNair: Institute for Strategic Studies, National Defense University, 1995.

Paris, Roland, 'Peacebuilding and the Limits of Liberal Internationalism', *International Security*, Vol.22, No.2, 1997, pp.54–89.

Pugh, Michael, 'Peacebuilding as Developmentalism: Concepts from Disaster Research', *Contemporary Security Policy*, Vol.16, No.3, 1995, pp.320–46.

Pugh, Michael (ed.), *International Peacekeeping*, Special Issue: The UN, Peace and Force, Vol.3, No.4, Winter 1996.

Pugh, Michael, 'From Mission Creep to Mission Cringe: Implications of New Peace Support Doctrine', *Forsvarstudier*, Vol.2, IFS, Norway, 1997.

Ramsbotham, Oliver and Tom Woodhouse, *Humanitarian Intervention in Contemporary Conflict*, Cambridge: Polity Press, 1996a.

Ramsbotham, Oliver and Tom Woodhouse, 'Terra Incognita: Here be Dragons; Peacekeeping and Conflict Resolution in Contemporary Conflict', University of Ulster/INCORE/United Nations University, Derry, 1996b.

Ramsbotham, Oliver and Tom Woodhouse, *Encyclopedia of International Peacekeeping Operations*, Denver and Oxford: BC/CLIO, 1999.

Ridley, Matt, *The Origins of Virtue: Human Instincts and the Evolution of Cooperation*, New York: Penguin, 1996.

Rieff, David, 'The Illusions of Peacekeeping', *World Policy Journal*, Vol.11, No.3, 1994, pp.1–18.

Ropers, Norbert, 'Towards a Hippocratic Oath of Conflict Management?', in *Prevention and Management of Violent Conflict: An International Directory*, European Platform for Conflict Prevention and Transformation: Utrecht, 1998, pp.27–33.

Rose, Michael, *Fighting for Peace: Bosnia 1994*, London: The Harvill Press, 1998.

Rosenblatt, Lionell and Larry Thompson, 'The Door of Opportunity: Creating a Permanent Peacekeeping Force', *World Policy Journal*, Spring 1998.

Rothman, Jay, *Resolving Identity Based Conflicts*, San Francisco, CA: Jossey Bass, 1997.

Ruane, Joseph and Jennifer Todd, *The Dynamics of Conflict in Northern Ireland: Power, Conflict and Emancipation*, Cambridge: Cambridge University Press, 1996.

Rotberg, Robert I. (ed.), *Vigilence and Vengeance: NGOs Preventing Ethnic Conflict in Divided Societies*, Washington: Brookings Institution Press, 1996.

Rubinstein, Robert A., 'Culture, International Affairs, and Multilateral Peacekeeping: Confusing Process and Pattern', *Cultural Dynamics*, Vol.2, No.1, 1989, pp.41–61.

Rubinstein, Robert A., 'Cultural Aspects of Peacekeeping: Notes on the Substance of Symbols', *Millennium*, Vol.22, No.3, 1993, pp.547–62.

Rupesinghe, Kumar (ed.) *Conflict Transformation*, New York: St. Martin's Press, 1995.

Rupesinghe, Kumar, 'Coping with Internal Conflicts: Teaching the Elephant to Dance', in Alger (ed.), 1998, pp.155–82.

Ryan, Stephen, 'The Theory of Conflict Resolution and the Practice of Peacekeeping', Moxon-Browne (ed.), 1998, pp.26–39.

Sahnoun, Mohamed, *Somalia: The Missed Opportunities*, Washington, DC: USIP, 1994.

Salem, Paul, 'A Critique of Western Conflict Resolution from a Non-Western Perspective', in Salem (ed.), *Conflict Resolution in the Arab World*, Beirut: American University of Beirut, 1997.

Sandole, Dennis and Hugo van der Merwe (eds.), *Conflict Resolution: Theory and Practice*, Manchester: Manchester University Press, 1993.

Schwartzberg, Joseph E., 'A New Perspective on Peacekeeping: Lessons from Bosnia and Elsewhere', *Global Governance*, Vol.3, No.1, January–April 1997.

Schwerin, Edward, *Mediation, Citizen Empowerment and Transformational Politics* Westport: Greenwood, 1996.

Senehi, Jessica, 'Getting A Handle on the Intangibles: Storytelling and Reconciliation In Inter-Communal Conflict', in Sean Byrne and Cynthia Irvin (eds.), *Reconcilable Differences: Turning Points in Ethnopolitics Conflicts*, Westport, CT: Kumarian Press, 2000, pp.165–96.

Senehi, Jessica, 'Language, Culture and Conflict: Storytelling as a Matter of Life and Death', *Mind and Human Interaction*, Vol.7, No.3, 1996, pp.150–64.

Shearer, David, 'Exploring the Limits of Consent: Conflict resolution in Sierra Leonne', *Millennium: Journal of International Studies*, Vol.26, No.3, 1997, pp.845–60.

Slim, Hugo, 'The Stretcher and the Drum: Civil–Military Relations in Peace Support Operations', *International Peacekeeping*, Vol.3, No.2, 1996, pp.123–40.

Smock, David, *Humanitarian Assistance and Conflict in Africa*, Washington: U.S. Institute of Peace Press, 1996.

Sorbo, Gunnar M., Joanna Macrae and Lennart Wohlegemuth, *NGOs in Conflict – An Evaluation of International Alert*, Bergen: Chr. Michelsen Institute, 1997.

Suliman, Mohamed, *Ecology, Politics and Violent Conflict*, London: Zed Press, 1999.

Tharoor, Shashi, 'Should United Nations Peacekeeping go "Back to Basics"?', *Survival*, Vol.37, No.2, 1995.

United Nations, 'Report on the Fall of Srebrenica', United Nations, New York, A54/549, November 1999.

United Nations, 'Report of the Independent Inquiry into the Actions of the United Nations during the 1994 Genocide in Rwanda', United Nations, New York, December 1999.

United Nations, Special Committee on Peacekeeping Operations, 'Comprehensive Review of the Whole Question of Peace-Keeping Operations in All Their Aspects', A/46/254, 1991 to A/54/87, 1999.

United Nations, 'Progress Report of the Secretary-General On Standby Arrangements for Peacekeeping', Security Council, New York, S/1999/361, 30 March 1999.

Urquhart, Brian, 'Beyond the Sheriff's Posse', *Survival*, Vol.XXII, No.3, May/June 1990.

Urquhart, Brian, 'Prospects for a UN Rapid Response Capability', in David Cox and Albert Legault (eds.) *UN Rapid Reaction Capabilities: Requirements and Prospects*, Cornwallis: The Lester B. Pearson Canadian International Peacekeeping Training Centre, 1995.

Vassall-Adams, Guy, *Rwanda: An Agenda for International Action*, Oxford: Oxfam, 1994.

Vayrynen, Raimo (ed.) *New Directions in Conflict Theory: Conflict Resolution and Conflict Transformation*, London: Sage, 1991.

Visman, Emma, *Military 'Humanitarian' Intervention in Somalia*, London: Save the Children, 1993.

Volkan, Vamik, *Blood Lines: From Ethnic Pride to Ethnic Terrorism*, Boulder, CO: Westview, 1998.

Wehr, Paul and John Paul Lederach, 'Mediating Conflict in Central America', in Jacob Bercovitch (ed.), *Resolving International Conflicts: The Theory and Practice of Mediation*, London: Lynne Reiner, 1996, pp.55–74.

Weiss, Thomas G., *Military–Civilian Interactions: Intervening in Humanitarian Crises*, Lanham: Rowman and Littlefield, 1999.

Whitman, Jim and David Pocock (eds.), *After Rwanda: The Coordination of United Nations Humanitarian Assistance*, London: Macmillan, 1996.

Wiseman, Henry, 'Peacekeeping in the International Political Context: Historical Analysis and Future Directions', in I.J. Rikhye and Kjell Skjelsbaek (eds.), *The United Nations and Peacekeeping: Results, Limitations and Prospects*, Basingstoke: Macmillan, 1990.

Woodhouse, Tom, 'The Gentle Hand of Peace? British Peacekeeping and Conflict Resolution in Complex Political Emergencies', *International Peacekeeping*, Vol.6, No.2, Summer 1999, pp.24–37.

Woodhouse, Tom, 'International Conflict Resolution: Some Critiques and a Response', *Centre for Conflict Resolution Working Paper 1*, University of Bradford, June 1999.

Woodhouse, Tom, Robert Bruce and Malcolm Dando (eds.), *Peacekeeping and Peacemaking: Towards Effective Intervention in Post-Cold War Conflicts*, Basingstoke: Macmillan, 1998.

Yang, Honggang, 'The Concept of Trust and Trust Building', *A Leadership Journal: Women in Leadership – Sharing the Vision*, Vol.2, No.2, 1998, pp.19–29.

Zartman, William (ed.), *Elusive Peace: Negotiating an End to Civil Wars*, Washington DC: The Brookings Institution, 1996.

Notes on Contributors

Pamela Aall is the Director of the Education Program for the U.S. Institute of Peace. Portions of her article appear in *Managing Global Chaos: Sources of and Responses to International Conflict* edited by Chester A. Crocker, Fen Osler Hampson with Pamela Aall (Washington, DC: U.S. Institute of Peace Press, 2nd edition, forthcoming).

Sean Byrne is Director of Doctoral Studies at the Department of Dispute Resolution, Nova Southeastern University, Fort Lauderdale. His current research interests include grassroots ethnopolitical conflict resolution, young people in conflict zones, and third party intervention in ethnic and international conflicts. With Cynthia Irvin, he is completing a book for the United States Institute for Peace that explores the role of external economic aid as a possible peace dividend in the Northern Ireland conflict.

Tamara Duffey is Research Fellow at the Centre for Conflict Resolution, Department of Peace Studies at the University of Bradford. She researches and lectures on conflict resolution, culture and peacekeeping issues. As the Centre's Training Officer, she is currently developing and facilitating conflict resolution and cultural awareness training for military and civilian peacekeepers. Her contribution to this collection has been developed from the author's doctoral thesis completed for the Department of Peace Studies, University of Bradford in July 1998.

A.B. Fetherston is a lecturer at the Department of Peace Studies, University of Bradford. She has published one of the leading studies on the relationship between peacekeeping and conflict resolution (*Towards a Theory of United Nations Peacekeeping*). She has recently completed a two-year training and research fellowship from the Social Science Research Foundation/MacArthur Foundation Program on Peace and Security in a Changing World and has as part of this work lived in Croatia for one year, researching her project on transformative peacebuilding. Her work contributed to the development of the course in peace studies offered by the Centre for Peace Studies in Zagreb.

H. Peter Langille teaches foreign policy and international conflict prevention and management at the University of Western Ontario. In 1995, he was on the Core Working Group of the Canadian Government's Study, to enhance a United Nations rapid reaction capability. As a partner in Common Security Consultants, he co-authored the initial proposals for a dedicated Canadian International Peacekeeping Training Centre at Cornwallis, Nova Scotia. He was a former member of the Canadian Government's Consultative Group on Arms Control and Disarmament. He is currently a co-director of the Canadian Peace Research and Education Association.

Loraleigh Keashly is Associate Professor, Urban and Labor Studies and the Academic Director, Master of Arts in Dispute Resolution at Wayne State University, (Center for Conflict & Peace Studies) in Detroit. Her current research interests include contingency approaches to conflict intervention, the role of identity in conflict, and psychological aggression in the workplace. She also conducts training sessions and gives presentations on various aspects of conflict resolution to organizations and community groups.

David Last is a Major in the Canadian Armed Forces with peacekeeping experience in Cyprus, Croatia and Bosnia. He developed courses at the Pearson Peacekeeping Centre for two years, and has served on arms control, policy, and special operations staffs. His book *Theory, Doctrine and Practice of Conflict De-escalation in Peacekeeping Operations* was published by the Canadian Peacekeeping Press (1997). Recent articles appear in *Canadian Foreign Policy, Low Intensity Conflict and Law Enforcement*, and other journals. He teaches political science at the Royal Military College of Canada.

John Mackinlay has extensive experience in the British Army; he was commissioned from the Royal Military College Sandhurst to the Sixth Gurkas and has served in Malaya, Brunei, Nepal, Hong Kong, Borneo and Northern Ireland. He has been a leading exponent of ideas concerning the nature of post-Cold War peacekeeping. He began his academic career in 1985 as a Defence Research Fellow at Churchill College Cambridge and completed a PhD at War Studies, Kings College, London. In 1991 he directed the Second-generation Multinational Operations Project at the Watson Institute, Brown University. He is currently Senior Research Fellow at the Centre for Defence Studies, Kings College, London.

Oliver Ramsbotham is Professor of Peace and Conflict Studies and Head of the Department of Peace Studies, University of Bradford. He has published, with Tom Woodhouse, *Humanitarian Intervention in Contemporary Conflict* (1996). He has also published, with Hugh Miall and Tom Woodhouse, *Contemporary Conflict Resolution: The Prevention, Management and Transformation of Deadly Conflict* (1999). He has published widely in the areas of peacekeeping, conflict resolution and humanitarian intervention, and on conflicts of belief systems including Muslim and Christian relations.

Stephen Ryan is a Senior Lecturer in Peace and Conflict Studies at Magee College, University of Ulster. He is the author of *Ethnic Conflict and International Politics* (1995), and *The United Nations and International Politics* (2000). He has written numerous articles on ethnic conflict, conflict resolution and UN peacekeeping. His research interests at present are the dynamics and transformation of ethnic conflict.

Philip Wilkinson OBE served with the Commando and Parachute Brigades and Special Forces prior to commanding the Artillery regiment in the UK's Airmobile Brigade. In 1993 he was given the task of writing peacekeeping doctrine for the more volatile circumstances the military increasingly found itself operating. This new doctrine subsequently became known as Peace Support Operations doctrine. Col. Wilkinson is the author of UK and NATO PSO doctrine and has written extensively on civil-military operations and the challenges of coordination. In January 2000 he left the Army and joined the Centre for Defence Studies at Kings College, London as a senior Fellow on the Security Sector Reform programme.

Tom Woodhouse joined the Department of Peace Studies at the University of Bradford when it was formed in 1974. He founded its Centre for Conflict Resolution in 1990. He is currently co-director of the Centre and Professor of Conflict Resolution (the Adam Curle Chair). Together with Hugh Miall and Oliver Ramsbotham, he published in 1999 *Contemporary Conflict Resolution: The Prevention, Management and Transformation of Deadly Conflict*. He has also published with Oliver Ramsbotham the *Encyclopedia of International Peacekeeping Operations*. His research interests are in the fields of conflict resolution theory and its relevance for international peacekeeping operations.

Index